MORTAL SPLENDOR

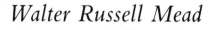

Walter Russell Mead

MORTAL SPLENDOR

THE
AMERICAN
EMPIRE
IN
TRANSITION

BOSTON

1 9 Houghton Mifflin Company *8 7*

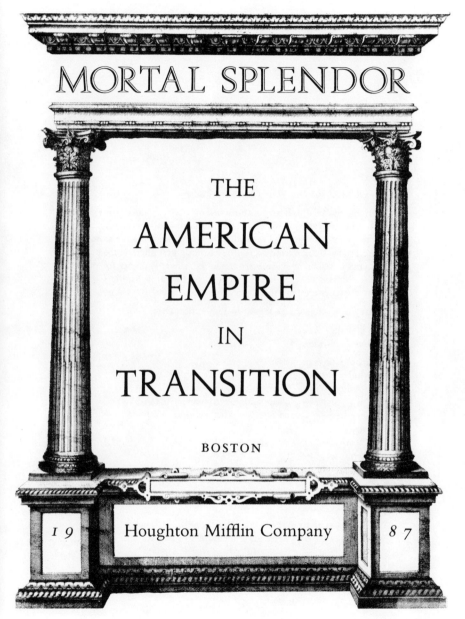

Library of Congress Cataloging-in-Publication Data

Mead, Walter Russell.
  Mortal splendor.

  Bibliography: p.
  Includes index.
  1. United States — Foreign relations — 1945–
  2. United States — Politics and government — 1945–
  3. Liberalism — United States — History — 20th century.
  I. Title.
E744.M418   1987   973.9   86-27303
ISBN 0-395-42954-4

Printed in the United States of America

P 10 9 8 7 6 5 4 3 2 1

To my parents,
Polly and Loren Mead,
with gratitude and my deepest love

You making haste haste on decay: not blameworthy;
life is good, be it stubbornly long or suddenly
A mortal splendor: meteors are not needed less than
mountains: shine, perishing republic.

ROBINSON JEFFERS
"Shine, Perishing Republic"
(1924)

ACKNOWLEDGMENTS

Thanks to the following who read and reviewed all or part of the manuscript: Meg Cox, Nancy Folbre, Robert Heilbroner, Jonathan Kwitney, John Loose, Marika Loose, Loren Mead, Polly Mead, Scott O'Brien, Jonathan Schell, Thomas Vietorisz, and Hunt Williams. Their comments encouraged me to go on with this work, and their criticism helped me improve it. I am of course responsible for any errors of fact or interpretation which remain.

Thanks also to Larry Kessenich, Elaine Markson, and my agent, Geri Thoma.

CONTENTS

Part Five
Rake's Progress: Politics in an Age of Decline

Part Six
Beyond the Liberal Empire

PART ONE

The Liberal Empire

✑ I ✑

THE IDEA OF EMPIRE

WE AMERICANS have always believed that we inhabit a special
universe, or at least a special part of the ordinary one. The
Puritans believed that God had called them across the sea to
build a new and purified state with a special relationship to the Deity.
The Indians and slaves no doubt had other words for the Puritan commonwealth, but the Pilgrims, like their successors, never cared much for
the opinions of heathens and savages.

The religion of Cotton Mather lost its hold on the minds of the American people, but not his idea that the nation was special. There was little
resemblance between seventeenth-century New England and the United
States after 1945. Religion, culture, government, even the ethnic composition of the people, had undergone a profound transformation on a
scale unmatched, perhaps, in the history of any land. Unchanged, though,
was the image of America, set like a city on a hill, a light unto the
Gentiles as they sit in immemorial darkness.

"I lift my lamp beside the golden door," says the Lady in the Harbor.

The fish, we are told, are the last to know they are living in water;
the late twentieth century finds Americans unaware that they live in the
midst of the greatest empire in history. The word *empire* is an awkward
one; it conjures up images of conquest, exploitation, and days gone by —
hardly the values associated with the Statue of Liberty, and hardly the
appropriate attributes of a great and progressive republic.

We could turn to euphemism and say, instead, that since the Second
World War the Pax Americana has provided the world with what peace
it has known. But, this statement only rephrases what we have said —
that after the war the United States of America became the center of the
largest empire in history. Americans, of course, are hardly the first to
make an empire and call it a peace; there was the Pax Britannica and the
Pax Romana, and for all we know the councilors of Sennacherib spoke
gravely of their responsibilities to the Assyrian peace.

Because the idea of empire has become unfashionable, a misplaced sense of patriotism leads some to deny that America has one. Since the United States is the last best hope of man, and since having an empire is a terrible sin, America therefore has no empire. From the other end of the political spectrum comes the equally futile observation that because the United States has the largest empire, it must be the worst country. Prince of Peace or Chief of Sinners — much of what passes for political debate in the United States assumes that the country personifies one or the other, and that the question is which. In the real world, however, nations are like what Catholic theologians tell us of most human souls: they either scrape ingloriously into Purgatory or slip by degrees into the outer circles of Hell. And when countries, or souls, escape mediocrity, they usually run not to one extreme, but to both. Great nations remind us of the characterization of a political rival by Senator John Randolph of Virginia, in the nineteenth century: they "shine and stink, like rotten mackerel by moonlight."

In fact, great nations have been shining and stinking since the start of recorded history, often shining brightest when they stink the worst. The Athenian republic, cradle of democracy and of philosophy, never showed itself in a more characteristic light than when, by a democratic vote, it ordered the execution of Socrates.

When we Americans refer to empires, we tend to think in simple terms. We speak of the Roman Empire, conquering everything within its reach, or the British Empire, raising the Union Jack around the globe. Because the United States has not annexed new territories in recent years, Americans assume that, in James Reston's words, "we are not an imperial nation."

But the empires of the past were much more complex, and more nearly resembled our own, than many believe. For example, the Athenian Empire grew up in the years after the Persian Wars. Athens, the state that originated the written democratic constitution, helped lead Greek resistance to the Persian invaders. After the Persian retreat from Europe, Athens organized continuing resistance and helped the Greek city-states of Asia Minor to throw off the Persian yoke. Simultaneously, the Athenians organized the Delian League for joint self-defense. The member cities contributed money to a common fund, which Athens used for the maintenance of their common freedom. At first. Later, as the navy grew, Athens usurped the right to spend league money on any project it wanted — including the erection of the Parthenon, which, for all its architectural magnificence, contributed relatively little to the security of Greek Asia.

The members of the league never lost their formal independence. They were independent city-states and exchanged ambassadors with cities other than Athens. They governed themselves under their own laws and fielded their own teams in the Olympics. Of course, the Athenians were always "consulted" on important matters.

The Roman Empire lasted for roughly two thousand years; during that time it underwent many changes, expanding from a single city into a world empire, then slowly contracting into another, and different, single city. Through much of its existence, the empire included both Roman territory proper and the land of "allies of Rome," who retained varying degrees of independence. Cleopatra of Egypt was once such an ally; Herod the Great was another. These rulers enjoyed unlimited power in their own countries, and some committed "human rights abuses" that embarrassed their Roman patrons. "I would rather be Herod's pig than his son," commented Augustus after learning that the ruler had done away with some of his offspring.

The allies of Rome held different ranks. Ancient and prestigious cities like Athens enjoyed rights and privileges denied to less illustrious places. The inhabitants of important or exceptionally loyal cities received Roman citizenship. Thus, St. Paul, a Turkish Jew, was able to declare proudly, *"Civis Romanus sum"* (I am a Roman citizen). As a citizen, he was entitled to certain privileges, including the right to a legal appeal of any sentence and an exemption from cruel or degrading punishment. Christ, the obscure inhabitant of a backward and rebellious province, could make no such claim. He was flogged and crucified after a brief hearing before a magistrate.

Empires serve, or ought to serve, two purposes for the imperial state. First, by ensuring friendly control of strategic points and by extending the state's military frontiers, the empire promotes self-defense. Athens depended on its control of the sea to defend it from the superior land forces arrayed against it; Rome, eventually protected by its vast territories, escaped occupation by foreign armies from 390 B.C. to A.D. 410. Second, the empire can yield substantial financial benefits. "Whose image do you see on this coin?" Jesus asked the Palestinian crowd.

"Caesar's," came the reply.

The benefits of empire require cultivation. Piracy and rapine, immediately gratifying though they may be, cannot provide a stable foundation for imperial prosperity. Roman military doctrine recognized two types of war: wars of conquest and punitive expeditions. In a punitive campaign, the Romans systematically caused as much damage as possible. They burned the towns, they massacred the men, and, if convenient, they sold the women and children into slavery. They conducted psychological warfare against their opponents, deliberately desecrating religious sites in the hope of demoralizing the enemy. In wars of conquest, by contrast, private property was respected as far as possible, the temples of the natives were scrupulously guarded, and no effort was spared to win the allegiance of the newly conquered people. In the long run, the most successful conquerors have been those who disguised their rule, employing local figures as functionaries and allowing the conquered to continue their daily lives. This farsighted policy reduced the cost of policing an empire and created the basis for economic prosperity.

One of the great benefits of empire results from the expansion of trade that accompanies its spread. The extension of Roman control around the Mediterranean gave the populist consul Gaius Gracchus the means to establish the world's first welfare state. With the reliance on a single currency and a single system of taxes, the reduction or elimination of internal tariffs, and establishment of physical security on sea and land, trade exploded in the Roman world, bringing with it a long period of prosperity and freedom from serious famine. As late as the nineteenth century, historians could argue that the Roman Empire had been both the most populous and prosperous human society ever known.

The empire with which we are most familiar today, and the largest one before our own, was the British. At its peak, it included about 25 percent of the world's land surface and a similar proportion of its inhabitants. It was not only the largest of the great European empires; it was the most complex. Among Britain's dominions, colonies, bases, protectorates, and allies could be found virtually every form of imperial domination ever conceived.

For Americans, the British Empire has more significance than any other. Not only did this country begin as a collection of British colonies, but the American Empire of today rests in large part on the ruins of Britain's. To understand the forces that created, and have lately begun to destroy, our empire, we do well to examine Britain's experience.

The countries closest to England — Scotland, Wales, Ireland, and France — all suffered from centuries of incursion and occupation. God helped St. Joan drive the British out of France but did no such favor for the Irish; perhaps St. Patrick had used up Ireland's assets when he drove out the snakes. Scotland and Wales saw their indigenous cultures almost wiped out. Ireland endured relentless and savage religious persecution, lost much of its native heritage, and saw many of its people displaced by foreign settlers.

In another group of colonies, including what later became the American South and the British Caribbean, the British exterminated the native population and introduced the large-scale cultivation of cash crops (tobacco, sugar cane, rice, and indigo) with imported slave labor.

In other colonies, among them the lands that became the American North, British Canada, Australia, and New Zealand, British misfits, paupers, and dissidents replaced the natives. The policy toward the indigenous peoples ranged from encouraging the deliberate extermination of the Tasmanians (British immigrants organized hunting parties that literally beat the bush from one end of the island to the other in the attempt to round up and kill every last native) to allowing for the uneasy coexistence between Maori and whites in New Zealand. In all these colonies, a white European society made room for itself at the expense of the natives. New European-type societies were established, and those few natives who survived found themselves exiles in their ancestral homes.

Where the British were too few or the natives too many, there were other forms of colonization. In the Indian subcontinent the British spread their language and their law, but they aspired only to rule rather than to replace the natives. In Africa, British aspirations did not reach even this level; in much of the continent the British were as interested in thwarting the ambitions of rivals as in exterminating or regulating the Africans themselves.

Other colonies were acquired for commercial or strategic reasons. Trading stations were established in West Africa during the heyday of the slave trade; Hong Kong was acquired to facilitate commerce with China. Gibraltar, Malta, and Singapore were great naval assets; with the introduction of steamships, coaling stations were set up on the previously uninteresting atolls of Polynesia.

This miscellaneous aggregation of territory, vast as it was, was only the outward and visible sign of the British Empire. The "invisible empire" was even more extensive. It included nominally independent states, like the Indian princedoms where British influence was decisive and British support the most important qualification for prospective rulers. It included the Latin American countries whose trade and industry were in British hands through much of the nineteenth century. It included the wealth that flowed to Britain from its visible empire; the institutions and banks that rose to administer and invest that wealth; the enterprises around the world built, bought, and run by British bankers; and the markets and marketing systems controlled by the British.

Additionally, British influence extended to territories that were nominally controlled by other European empires. Portugal and Britain maintained a strict alliance from the eighteenth century onward, so in practice Britain defended Portugal's overseas empire and shared in its wealth.

Through the nineteenth century British influence steadily advanced in the Ottoman Empire, and when that state was dismantled after the First World War, Britain ended up with Egypt, Jordan, Israel, Cyprus, and a controlling interest in much of the rest.

The nineteenth century marks a boundary between the old world and the new; during that time the world witnessed the unprecedented developments in technology that ushered in the world we know today. Those developments affected the nature of empire as well as everything else, and the century witnessed an explosion of empire building. The financial, invisible empires of the nineteenth century were as advanced beyond the Greek and Roman models as the technology of the nineteenth century itself outstripped anything known in the past.

Instead of acquiring militarily defensible, geographically contiguous territories, the nineteenth-century empire builders sought economically advantageous colonies, wherever they were. Through large parts of Africa, European explorers wandered in trackless jungles to stake out claims for governments thousands of miles away. By 1914 virtually all of what we now call the Third World, outside of China and Latin America, was directly ruled from one of the European capitals.

Men like to consider themselves moral, and empire builders have always attempted to justify their activities. The starkest declaration of an imperial rationale comes to us from Thucydides, the great historian of the war between Athens and Sparta. Cleon, addressing the Athenian assembly, warned that "to feel pity, to be carried away by the pleasure of hearing a clever argument, to listen to the claims of decency, are three things that are entirely against the interest of an imperial power." He was speaking in favor of a proposal to massacre the adult male population of Mytilene and to sell the women and children as slaves. A few years later a weak neutral city appealed to Athenian delegates by reminding them that the gods favored justice and mercy. The Athenian reply to this naïve plea was a concise statement of the age-old principles of *Realpolitik*.

> So far as the favor of the gods is concerned, we think we have as much right to that as you have. Our aims and our actions are perfectly consistent with the beliefs men hold about the gods and with the principles which govern their own conduct. Our opinion of the gods and our knowledge of men lead us to conclude that it is a general and necessary law of nature to rule whatever one can. This is not a law that we made ourselves, nor were we the first to act upon it when it was made. We found it already in existence, and we shall leave it to exist for ever among those who come after us. We are merely acting in accordance with it, and we know that

you or anybody else with the same power as ours would be acting in precisely the same way.[1]

This kind of self-justification can be found in every age and culture and represents the clearest if not the most comfortable rationale for empire. Yet people do not like such a naked statement of the will to exercise power. Even the Athenians consoled themselves with reflections on the superiority of their culture and their historical right to a leading place among the Greeks.

The British also excelled at discovering reasons that obligated them to conquer the world. British rule brought missionaries and sanitation to the benighted and the diseased. The British established order and built railroads. They introduced incorruptible administration and the common law. The white race — and especially the Anglo-Saxons, whitest of the white — had a God-given responsibility to civilize and Christianize their darker brethren. When the unappreciative heathen began to agitate for independence, the British were quick to find reasons that made it impossible for them to leave. Ireland would fall into chaos without the steadying hand of Britain. After all, had not Ireland's history been eight hundred years of anarchy and rebellion? Winston Churchill, the last great British imperialist, broke with the Conservative leadership over policy toward India in 1931, specifically over the release of Gandhi from what Churchill called his "commodious internment."

"I felt sure we should lose India in the final result," Churchill wrote, "and that measureless disasters would come upon the Indian peoples."[2] It was impossible for Churchill to understand that for the Indians, as for the Irish, it was the arrival of the British that had been the measureless disaster — as it had been for the original Australians, the Zulu, the Cherokee, the Hausa, the Iroquois, the Chinese, and so many others. For himself and his own country Churchill scornfully rejected foreign domination; he won greatness by his defiance of Hitler. Yet he never understood that even small and poor countries ruled by Britain loved freedom.

It is easy for Americans to be objective about the claims of Athens, Rome, and even Britain to moral justification for their empires. Athenian culture, Roman law, and British administration all made contributions, none of which will be soon forgotten. Nevertheless, we can look at these societies with some objectivity and see that while they shone, they also stank. We can see their strengths and their weaknesses and note that the virtues and the vices of these three great historical systems were inextricably mixed.

We can also remain reasonably indifferent to the rise and fall of these empires. That great empires should fall as well as rise seems perfectly natural when we consider the land of the pharaohs or ancient Babylon. That the American Empire could suffer such a fate is more disturbing. And that the decline, and ultimately the fall, of the American Empire is the basic political fact of the present period in world history is more disturbing still. We cannot sit back and observe the fall of the American Empire with the detachment with which we view Rome; our hopes and fears are too closely bound up in the fate of the American Empire.

But if we cannot be neutral in action, there is all the more reason for us to be clear in thought. Because the stakes are so high, because the decline of the empire is the background for the other political and personal events in our lives, we need to examine the forces at work in the world with as much insight as possible. This means that we must avoid the pieties of conventional thought and see the world as it is, not as we wish it were. Especially because the present is so difficult a period of history, we cannot attempt to shape our world without first coming to understand it.

This book is intended as a contribution to an awareness of the state of the American Empire and of the choices that confront it.

THE RISE OF
THE AMERICAN EMPIRE

"Westward the Sun of Empire takes its way," wrote Bishop Berkeley in the generation before the American Revolution. "Time's noblest offspring is the last."[1] From the earliest days observers foretold that a day would come when the United States would be one of the world's great powers.

Americans themselves were not slow to believe it. The doctrine of Manifest Destiny in the nineteenth century maintained that God clearly intended the United States to stretch from the Atlantic to the Pacific and from the North Pole to the tropics. Otherwise, people reasoned, He would surely have put someone more powerful than the Indians and Mexicans in our path. As it happened, the Canadians remained perversely blind to their historical responsibilities, and the Mexicans proved too numerous and too obstinate to be incorporated into the Republic — but God's plans for the Indians reached their fruition, and His will was done from east to west, if not from north to south.

The founding fathers and the revolutionary generation were firmly convinced that the new nation was destined for glory. Alexis de Tocqueville predicted that glory, honor, and wealth inevitably awaited the Americans; European statesmen consoled themselves that America would not reach its zenith until some time in the far distant future — much as statesmen today look at China.

The grounds for these prophecies are not hard to find. The land that became the United States is located in the temperate zone, the most productive portion of the earth's surface. The great valley between the Appalachians and the Rocky Mountains is fertile, well watered, and provided with one of the world's most conveniently navigable river systems. In de Tocqueville's words, it is "the noblest habitation prepared by God for man." The United States, then as now, had no powerful enemies in its own hemisphere. Its people were united in religion — Protestant — and in their ideas — democratic.

America's first wars of conquest were against the aboriginal inhabitants — the Indians. After a series of wars lasting almost three centuries, the Indians were confined to tiny reservations, and their population shrank from approximately 1.5 million at the time of Jamestown to an estimated 237,000 in 1900.[2] Because the Indians were disunited and soon hopelessly outnumbered in the zones of conflict, the wars were one-sided, and the European settlers never seriously had to marshal their resources for the struggle. Indian resistance proved so ineffectual that the United States ended up with territory larger than Western Europe and with a belief that Americans were unusually peace-loving and idealistic.

After this painless conquest, the United States was not slow to make its appearance on the world scene. Historians often cite 1890 as the year when census figures showed the end of the American frontier; by the close of the 1890s American forces were subduing the Filipinos. The last quarter of the nineteenth century was the great period of imperial expansion by the European powers; coming late to the feast, the Americans nevertheless managed to acquire such choice possessions as Hawaii, the Philippines, and Puerto Rico. Led by men like Theodore Roosevelt, who were not shy about either their racism or their imperialism, the United States penetrated more deeply into the Caribbean and interfered more frequently in Latin American affairs. Although Teddy Roosevelt yearned for Canada, he contented himself with the opportunities history gave him, and acquired the site for the Panama Canal — "stole it fair and square," in Barry Goldwater's words.

Contemporary observers noted at this time that the United States already had the capacity to be the strongest power on earth. The industrial revolution that took place in this country during the generation after the Civil War saw America leap to the head of the world in miles of railbed construction, steel production, coal extraction, and almost every other indicator of military and economic might.

Participation in the two world wars made the United States the leading world power; essentially, the United States inherited the British Empire and Britain's position in world affairs and added to that foundation to create its own kind of empire.

The process began in the 1914–1918 war, but it was during the century's second great conflict that the country entered a major new phase. Although its rise had long been foreseen, the actual arrival of the American Empire was one of the most astonishing and rapid developments in history. In 1939 the United States was a potentially dominant power at the fringe of world affairs. Six years later it had become the most powerful state in the history of the human race. Having defeated or absorbed its enemies and friends alike, America faced only one truly independent state in the world — the exhausted and depleted Soviet Union. France, Britain, Germany, and Japan had all collapsed and depended on American aid for, literally, their daily bread.

World War II was the child of the Depression, an international financial crisis that began roughly with the American stock market crash of 1929 and gained momentum when the world's financial system collapsed two years later. The Depression was not just another dip in the boom-and-bust cycle of a private enterprise economy; it was a crisis that revealed the inadequacy of the world's political institutions and their economic policies. The great nations of Europe — Britain, France, Germany, and the USSR — had pursued uncoordinated policies of national self-interest. Britain and France built high protective walls around their colonial empires while extracting reparations from Germany and pretending that Russia had ceased to exist. As times grew more difficult in the late 1920s, the Western nations grew less and less cooperative, and each pursued beggar-my-neighbor policies in an atmosphere of gathering gloom.

World War II revealed as clearly as the Depression that the scale of world politics had changed. The three Western European powers — France, Britain, and Germany — all proved too small and too weak for the stresses of war. Only the United States and the USSR, countries the size of continents, were strong enough to emerge from the war as major powers. The system of completely independent European states and empires, for two centuries the basis of world power politics, lay in ruins. In 1945 the world was divided into two zones: the Anglo-American (rapidly becoming the American) and the Soviet. The Soviet zone included the USSR and Eastern Europe; the Anglo-American zone included virtually everything else.

As the organization of the Anglo-American zone proceeded, the British role sank toward insignificance. During the war Britain had slowly yielded more strategic power to the Americans, and after the war the process continued. In the 1940s Britain withdrew from the Middle East (with minor exceptions), from Greece, and from India. By 1983 Britain had relinquished almost all of its empire and was scheduled to surrender its remaining significant colony, Hong Kong, by the end of the century. The U.S. invasion of Grenada, a member of the British Commonwealth whose governor general represents the queen, was undertaken against the advice and the wishes of the British government.

The erosion of Britain's hold on its colonies had already begun during World War II. To pay for its massive purchases of arms and supplies in the United States, Britain liquidated much of its foreign investments at fire-sale prices. Under the "cash-and-carry" policy Britain was allowed to buy all the American arms it could pay for in gold or in dollars — as long as it could hire or purchase shipping to ferry the supplies over the U-boat-infested ocean to its shores.

In December 1940, when Britain was standing alone against Germany, Churchill sent Roosevelt a long message, reviewing the prospects of the coming year.

> Last of all, I come to the question of Finance. The more rapid and abundant the flow of munitions and ships which you are able to send us, the sooner will our dollar credits be exhausted. They are already, as you know, very heavily drawn upon by the payments we have made to date. . . . The moment approaches when we shall no longer be able to make payments for shipping and other supplies. While we will do our utmost, and shrink from no proper sacrifice to make payments across the Exchange, I believe you will agree that it would be wrong in principle and mutually disadvantageous in effect if at the height of this struggle Great Britain were to be divested of all saleable assets, so that after the victory was won with our blood, civilization saved, and the time gained for the United States to be fully armed against all eventualities, we should stand stripped to the bone.[3]

In fact, Britain sold over $5.9 billion in foreign investments and capital assets to meet the costs of the war. Its income from such investments was halved during the same period, and the costs of maintaining a military presence rose approximately 500 percent after the war.[4]

When Britain was no longer able to pay, President Franklin D. Roosevelt introduced the policy of Lend-Lease, by which America undertook to provide Britain with the means it required to carry on the war. A grateful Churchill hailed it as "the most unsordid act in the history of war," but he did not neglect to quote in his memoirs from Roosevelt's remarks to the American press:

> Quite aside from our historic and current interest in the survival of Democracy in the world as a whole it is equally important from a selfish point of view and of American defense that we should do everything possible to help the British Empire to defend itself.[5]

The lease to Britain of fifty overage destroyers in return for ninety-nine-year leases on some British possessions gave Britain desperately needed ships in a critical phase of the Battle of the Atlantic, but it was not the kind of bargain that the British Empire had ever contemplated making.

In addition to these well-publicized transactions, there was movement by American banks and corporations. Since dollars were the currency everyone wanted, banks with huge dollar deposits were able to meet the needs of their customers far more effectively than could their British cousins, and American banks replaced British ones as the clearinghouses for much of world trade. American oil companies assumed a higher profile in the Middle East as the British yielded ground.

During most of the war, Britain's entire effort had been concentrated on physical survival. The trade patterns of empire were disrupted not only by the Japanese occupation of Britain's Pacific territories, but by the need for Britain to use every available ton of shipping for the supply of the home island. Almost all of the country's productive capacity was harnessed to war industry; the United States was the one country able to produce goods for the world market.

It became evident that Britain had lost more to the United States than its economic position. Specifically, the United States inherited the geopolitical position that had enabled Britain to rise. For hundreds of years Britain had prospered in European politics precisely because it was an island. Spared the expense of maintaining a great standing army, Britain was able to concentrate on ruling the waves. The harvest of wealth it gathered from around the world during these centuries allowed it to maintain a balance of power on the continent by raising and funding coalitions against whatever land power seemed on the verge of dominating the European land mass. Britain systematically stripped its rivals of their colonies, thereby strengthening its own position, while the nations of Europe exhausted themselves in bloody, destructive, and usually indecisive land wars. Thus, in North America alone, Britain acquired New York from the Dutch, Quebec from the French, and New Jersey from the Swedes. It picked the French clean in India and as recently as World War I cleared the Germans out of Africa.

It was a wonderful way to make a living — while it lasted. Unfortunately for Britain, World War I marked the beginning of the end. Germany was so strong that Britain's influence was not enough to tip the scales against it; if America had not entered the war in 1917, Germany might well have won. Britain's balance-of-power diplomacy required a policy that was insulated from popular pressures, but in order to win the war Britain had to stir up the population with mostly fictitious stories of German atrocities. This popular hatred, once roused, could not be satisfied by a moderate peace. Although some British diplomats attempted to follow a conciliatory policy at Versailles in 1919, political pressure from home was so strong that they ended up with the worst of all possible results: a treaty that embittered Germany and made it long for revenge.

At the same time that the rulers of Britain lost their political maneuverability, their military position worsened. In 1940, when Germany crushed France in six weeks and launched the Battle of Britain, war came to England for the first time in centuries.

America fought the Second World War with Russian blood and British gold. Total American casualties in both theaters of war were slightly over 300,000 dead. The Soviets lost an estimated seven million men in combat and perhaps twice that many in civilian deaths. There were more Russian civilian deaths in Leningrad than American military deaths in the whole war.[6] America funneled supplies to both Britain and the Soviet Union; those countries made the greatest sacrifices. Britain emerged financially exhausted from the war; the United States was more prosperous in 1945 than it had been in 1939.

In 1945 Europe and Japan were starving and in ruins. The merchant marine of every country on earth had been sunk, militarized, or confiscated; the United States alone possessed food, industrial capacity, and the means of transportation. With a stable political system, a huge internal market, and a rich endowment of natural resources, America was in a position to assume the leadership of the world. It is small wonder that Americans and foreigners agreed that the world had entered something called the American Century.

American statesmen on the whole made the most of their opportunities. They scrupulously avoided the mistakes of Versailles and the interwar period, and they correctly understood that American hegemony would rest most securely on the basis of international cooperation. The Marshall Plan was only the most prominent of the means employed to guarantee America's position. By providing Europe with the dollars it needed to eat and rebuild, the Marshall Plan brought social stability to Western Europe and foiled the Communist parties of that region. Just as important, the Marshall Plan assured American businesses of orders from European customers.

Meanwhile, America increasingly assumed the responsibility for world political stability and for the world economic system. The United States made no effort to take over, physically, the possessions of the European empires; rather, it integrated these possessions into its economic system. American public opinion had long opposed European colonialism; after the war American diplomats concurred that colonialism was not only unpleasant — it was economically unnecessary. Although America helped France fight its war in Indochina, it cut off Marshall Plan aid to the

Netherlands to force that country to give Indonesia independence, and it humiliated Britain and France when those countries tried to assert their traditional power in the Middle East at the time of the Suez crisis in 1956.

During the late 1940s, the United States extended on a global scale the Open Door policy it had advocated for China during the late nineteenth century. It proposed that instead of each European country fighting for special concessions in China, all should combine their influence to ensure free, equal, and favorable terms of treatment for the white powers.

The postwar period saw the first truly global organization of the world's economy — under American hegemony. In corporate terms, Britain Ltd and France SA rejected a hostile takeover bid from Germany and called in the United States as a "white knight" suitor. If we compare these opponents during World War II with the participants in today's corporate takeover battles, it was as if the managements of Britain and France were allowed to stay in place, and even exercised considerable autonomy within a framework largely devised in Washington and New York. German and Japanese companies were reorganized under American supervision, following America's "hostile takeover," and were given new roles in the American system.

This new system was both larger and more sophisticated than the old ones. The United States actively encouraged the formation of the European Economic Community in Western Europe. Control over the underdeveloped countries was increasingly exercised by native elites as colonialism yielded to neocolonialism around the world. This second change made no serious difference in world power relationships. The West still owned the ball, the bats, the bases, and the umpires; if the underdeveloped countries wished to participate in the global economy, they did so on terms dictated by the West — in the end, chiefly by the United States.

The crisis of World War II had been resolved. The day of the European nation-state and its colonial empire had come to an end. In politics as in economics, the world — except for the USSR and its bloc — took its cues from the United States. Americans, who hardly knew what had happened, soon grew used to this new state of affairs. It seemed the most natural thing in the world for the United States to enjoy unchallenged supremacy in world affairs. For three centuries the American people had labored to settle their continent and put its affairs in order; this new assignment, to police the world, seemed to them the logical next step for the United States. Few appreciated the magnitude of America's victory, and fewer still understood how shaky were the foundations of American power.

THE STRUCTURE OF EMPIRE

L IKE ALL SUCCESSFUL EMPIRES, the American empire ruled by consent and cooperation when it could. The benefits of empire were scattered widely, if unevenly, around the globe. The stable currency, political security, and enlightened administration of the empire allowed for a rapid worldwide recovery from the war. The transition from colonial rule to national independence — even if this turned out to be less than met the eye in the long run — benefited the countries at the bottom of the world order; the countries at the top needed American aid and American muscle to get them through the postwar period.

The British Empire, with its dazzling array of territories, was in many respects the prototype of the American Empire. Churchill proposed a union between the British and American empires during the war, but Roosevelt had other plans. The union was consummated, but on America's terms. The British dominions now rely on the United States for defense, and rally, grumbling, to the American side in a conflict, as they used to do with Britain. Thus the former ANZUS pact (or Pacific Security Treaty), signed in 1951, provided for mutual defense among Australia, New Zealand, and the United States and omitted the mother country of them all. Both Australia and New Zealand supported American efforts in Korea and Vietnam.

Unlike its British predecessor, the American Empire does not usually assign different formal ranks to its possessions and allies. Instead, its allies and dependencies are arrayed in three tiers, with an additional category for the two so-called settler states of Israel and South Africa.

The first-tier countries, like Britain, France, Germany, and the British dominions, rank as junior partners in the empire. Their opinions on important issues are usually solicited — if not always deferred to. Except for Japan, they are ethnically European. The second tier contains countries like Greece, Turkey, Chile, and Argentina — countries whose economic and political situations hover between first- and third-tier conditions.

The third tier includes countries like Guatemala, Haiti, Zaire, and so on. These countries have minimal representation in the councils of empire; their national governments in many cases are solely the representatives of foreign powers. The American ambassador (or, in some cases, the French) has more to say about the form of government and the policies of the state than any citizen of the country itself. It is sobering for inhabitants of the United States to realize that the greater the amount of direct American influence within a country, the more wretched the state of the mass of the people, but we must beware of simplistic conclusions.

There is, of course, no hard-and-fast line between each of the tiers. Countries like Italy and Brazil blur the distinctions between the various levels. Even so, the division into tiers allows us to understand its structure more clearly and helps to illuminate the confused domestic debates in the United States about the options for imperial policy.

THE FIRST TIER

The first tier includes the NATO allies minus Spain, Portugal, Greece, and Turkey, plus Japan and the old British dominions. Countries that are nominally neutral, like Sweden, Switzerland, and Austria, can also be considered part of the economic empire of the United States. These countries would face a turbulent future without the support and structure provided by U.S. economic and security arrangements.

For all their differences, the first-tier countries have a number of features in common. They are all liberal democracies with well-developed welfare states. Many indeed have more liberal systems and more lavish welfare programs than the United States. The system of proportional representation, for example, results in legislative assemblies more representative of popular sentiment than the constituency systems of Britain and the United States. The first-tier countries are well aware that their destinies are, for now, tied firmly to the fortunes of the United States. This condition breeds both resentment and a certain air of unreality in European politics. As a general rule, the first-tier countries have active and vigorous parliamentary lefts, but these left parties mount no serious challenge to the existing social order, and they actively support it when they are in the government. It was, after all, the German Socialists who first called for Pershing missiles in Europe, and French Socialists who ordered the destruction of the *Rainbow Warrior*, a civilian ship, sponsored by the environmental group Greenpeace, in the harbor of a friendly country.

In the generation since the war, after the original communist challenge was beaten back, no major left party has threatened the first-tier status quo. Political questions gradually became questions of administration: What should interest rates be? How many weeks of unemployment benefits should workers receive? The European left enjoys the luxury of attacking the worst excesses of the American state. The Social Democratic parties of Europe outdid themselves in tsk-tsking over Vietnam, the Dominican Republic, the invasion of Grenada, and, more recently, the mining of Corinto in Nicaragua and the bombing of Libya. They will ceaselessly protest apartheid and vote on the side of the angels (and the Palestinians) in the UN General Assembly and miss no chance to denounce the cowboy diplomacy of the Reaganauts. Yet the observer of world affairs will look long and hard to find even one example of effective European action against any Third World government, however repulsive, that enjoyed the backing of the United States. Talk, diplomatic notes, eloquent hand wringing, yes — but the leadership of the European left is too deeply committed to the privileges of empire to take serious steps against the imperial order.

One feature of the American Empire is that remnants of the old colonial empires of Europe, somewhat retooled, continue to exist under its aegis. The French position in West Africa is little weaker — or less obvious — than it was before "independence." A Franco-Belgian expedition intervened in Zaire (formerly the Belgian Congo) to ensure that the citizens of that happy land continued to enjoy the benefits of Mobutu's government. Britain continues to exercise special influence in some of its former African colonies, and Japan has been able to revive some aspects of the Greater East Asia Co-Prosperity Sphere under American control.

The United States is no more concerned about domestic legislation in the first-tier countries than Augustus cared about the dietary laws of the Jews. As long as they remain in NATO and defer to American leadership on the essential matters of international relations, the United States lets them be. American hegemony over its first-tier allies is not perpetuated by the use of force or even its threat; the state of the world is such that these countries depend on the American connection to maintain their prosperity and military security. The United States can usually sit back and let facts do the talking in disputes with these allies. It is also true that the Western allies are paralyzed when it comes to constructing effective combinations against the United States. They can combine on certain specific issues, like the Siberian pipeline, but the area of common efforts against the United States has strict limits. Any German initiative to relax tensions in Europe worries the French, who contemplate the prospect of a united Germany with the same feelings as does the Kremlin. Similarly, French enthusiasm for a greater "European" presence and voice in world affairs evaporates when the European voice begins to speak with a German accent.

Present conditions condemn Europe to sterility. The verdict of World War II still applies: the traditional European powers are too small, too weak, and too divided to maintain full independence in world affairs.

American liberals and social democrats sometimes look enviously on the Europeans and their chains of gold. The European societies seem much more advanced than America. Their welfare states are better developed; their electoral systems look cleaner and more representative; their governments lack the awkwardness that the United States labors under as the price of its constitutional continuity.

There are two primary reasons for the disparity between Europe and America — for the disparity that is not merely the haze of liberal illusion. First, and most important, America cannot properly be compared with any one European country; it must be compared with the entire continent west of the Elbe. Unlike the neat little democracies of Northwestern Europe, the United States contains vast populations and regions not far removed from conditions in the Third World. Despite recent immigrations of guest workers into the principal European states, these countries have no counterpart of Appalachia, Mississippi, or Watts. Whole areas of the United States entered the modern economy only in the last generation. It is in these regions — the South and the West — that the strongest opposition to the welfare state makes its home. If left to its own devices, the most industrial and urban section of the United States — from Maine to Minnesota as far south as Missouri and Maryland — would adopt social democratic policies like those of Europe, and the South and the West might dismantle much of what already exists.

The second reason that social democracy flourishes more abundantly in Europe than in the United States is that it depends on the empire. It is one thing for Sweden to wax wroth over American imperialism. Yet Swedish politics could not go on as smoothly as they do if the Third World actually set up a new world economic order, under which small Nordic manufacturing nations would be unlikely to flourish as they do now. Because Europe has only a secondary responsibility to maintain the empire, European politics can disengage themselves from the unpleasant realities of world power. The European social democrats can romanticize the Sandinistas to their hearts' content without ever giving a moment's thought to "losing" Central America. It was never theirs to keep.

American liberals, on the other hand, can never escape their historical responsibility to "do something" about Marxism-Leninism in the Caribbean. Even in Europe the social democrats are more dovish out of power than in it; once in government, they begin to sound like the more muted chorus of American liberals.

A related, and important, factor is that the United States, as the primary imperial power, must maintain higher levels of military spending and of social militarization than do the European countries. Besides limiting the financial resources available for the welfare state, the American military machine requires that society be oriented to its needs. Senators must reflect on the consequences of the Pentagon budget for their home states; the necessities of military recruiting cast a shadow over government programs for youth. American liberalism must operate in a harsher, more realistic environment than European social democracy; in the long run this makes the United States a more important seedbed for progressive programs and ideas than Western Europe, the insulated, isolated junior partner of empire.

THE SECOND TIER

The second tier of countries within the American hegemony includes Greece, Spain, Argentina, and others that are wealthier than the third tier but poorer than the first. The second-tier countries get no invitations to fancy summits; their representatives are not admitted into the inner councils of empire. They offer their people fewer benefits than the first-tier countries can afford. Wages are generally lower and opportunities more restricted.

These countries enjoy much less freedom from external intervention in their domestic affairs. They are more vulnerable to economic coercion from foreign governments or foreign enterprises. While they characteristically have a significant locally controlled sector in the economy, the more important firms operating within the country are generally foreign-based.

Democracy in the second-tier countries is a sometime thing. Greece, Turkey, Spain, Portugal, Chile, Argentina, and Brazil have all lived under both democratic and military regimes in the last generation, and many of these countries have experienced outright fascism. The moral indignation evoked by the regime of martial law in Poland is greatly attenuated in the case of these countries; no American president appears on a TV show titled "Let Chile Be Chile."

In general, these societies hover on the brink of modernization. The power of feudal oligarchies has been weakened but not dismantled; an urban middle class forces the ruling powers to acknowledge its interests. Large sectors of the population would like their countries to adopt the liberal democracy of the first-tier countries.

It would be pleasant to claim that these societies as a group are progressing toward democracy. Unfortunately, that is only intermittently the case. Although Spain and Greece seem to be edging toward more stable democracies, Chile and Turkey have regressed. Half a century ago Argentina looked more like Canada than like Bolivia. The 1980s have not been kind to Mexico. Optimism is difficult to summon up when contemplating events in Korea. It is as if the second-tier countries, as a group, wished to move toward liberal democracy but their progress is blocked by an invisible hand. And this is precisely the case.

One of the most widely accepted maxims of political science states that a liberal democracy of the Western type requires, above all, a strong middle class. Doctors, lawyers, bankers, teachers, professors, independent businessmen, and white-collar workers must not only exist, but exist in such numbers as to play the decisive role in the political evolution of society. People from this social stratum often form the democratic opposition to second-tier military dictatorships, and do so with heroism and devotion. Argentina's Jacobo Timerman, Manila's Benigno Aquino, Somoza's Pedro Joaquín Chamorro, won the admiration of the world, and deservedly so. (Soviet dissidents come from a similar stratum.)

But this middle class does not appear out of thin air. Its numbers depend on the overall wealth of the domestic economy. Lawyers cannot prosper without clients; professors need universities and students need money; bankers need clients; businessmen need customers. In societies where wealth is concentrated in the hands of a tiny oligarchy and the rest of the population is desperately poor, the middle class can grow to only a limited extent. In these societies — typical of the third-tier countries like Haiti — the middle class never escapes its primary role as a servant class to the oligarchy.

In second-tier countries, the base for the middle class is more substantial than in Haiti or Guatemala, but it is not large enough to give the middle class a secure role at the center of the social order. Its influence remains marginal; it is vulnerable on the one hand to military overthrow and on the other to overthrow by revolutionary elements of the lower classes. Spain and Greece show the pattern. Since 1935 both countries have experienced oligarchies, communist insurrections, monarchies, and republican fascist regimes. Both countries have also preserved a strong democratic movement that at times — most conspicuously and, one hopes, definitively in the present — has been able to take over the state. Even then, however, the democratic elements in these societies must continue to look nervously over their shoulders at the army in a way totally alien to those in more established democracies. Variations on this theme characterize the political history of second-tier countries in general.

To understand why development freezes in this pattern in so many countries, it is necessary to consider what happens to the wealth generated in the society. After all, most of the present first-tier countries have political pasts that look something like the present-day reality of the second-tier states. Seventeenth-century Britain was torn between monarchy, military dictatorship, parliamentary rule, and commercial republicanism. The century after the storming of the Bastille saw the same conflicts in France, with three republics, two empires, a communist rising, and three monarchies under two competing royal houses. In these countries and in others, the oscillations ultimately subsided into liberal democracy. Why should this not happen in the second tier?

In today's first-tier countries, the impetus for the development of a strong middle class came as the economy developed vast new sources of wealth. In the first vigor of their industrial and commercial expansion, these societies reached out and transformed the world to meet their own economic needs. The accumulated wealth was reinvested at home and abroad, creating the need for a large middle class that could manage this wealth, and providing the means to pay its salary.

Like the first-tier countries, those in the second tier developed an internal network of profitable and modern economic relationships, but they have been unable to organize the world beyond their borders for their own benefit. Furthermore, a considerable share of their own national product goes to foreign investors or creditors, enriching the first-tier countries and strengthening their democracy but weakening it at home. The second-tier countries as a group have reached a limit. They cannot follow the "natural course" of economic development and bring other, less advanced countries under their sway, because there is no room at the top. They are like saplings, permanently stunted by the shade of older, more established trees.

THE THIRD TIER

The third-tier countries constitute most of what we commonly call the Third World. In these countries democracy is rare; their societies are marked by great extremes of wealth and poverty. A single strongman depends for support on the armed forces, on the local semifeudal oligarchy, and on foreign interests. The examples are numerous: Trujillo, both Duvaliers, Somoza, Mobutu. . . . The role of these countries in the world economy is to be hewers of wood and drawers of water. They are sources of such raw materials as timber, minerals, and agricultural products. Because wages are low, they have lately become industrial workshops as well. Production is skewed overwhelmingly toward export to the first-tier countries; domestic markets are small because the populace is so poor.

Two forces keep wages low: high unemployment and draconian labor laws. Secret police and goon squads, which sometimes turn into death squads, keep labor weak and divided. Strikes are broken by the military if necessary. The inhabitants of these countries enjoy few if any human rights, among them the most basic rights — to food, shelter, literacy, and medical treatment.

As with the second-tier countries, one would like to think that the third-tier countries are evolving into something better, and that Haiti will evolve into something more like Argentina, and that Argentina will evolve into something like the Netherlands. Our free enterprise buffs never tire of depicting the utopias that these authoritarian states will become in just a short time.

That would be all very well if so many third-tier countries weren't already hardened veterans of market economics. Supply and demand reigned supreme throughout Africa during the days of the slave trade, after all, and until the nineteenth century there were no tiresome government regulations to prevent the beneficial effects of the market from spreading through society.

"Underdevelopment" in the end turns out to be not so much the absence of sufficient development as the presence of a specific type of development. To illustrate the concept, we can examine a hypothetical country: Agraria. For many years technology and economics changed only slowly in Agraria. Most of the land is owned by a few wealthy landowners and is worked by many peasants. The peasants grow crops for their own use and pay rent in the form of labor or produce. Then somebody, somewhere, it hardly matters where, realizes that long-neglected Agraria is the perfect place to grow a cash crop — cotton, tobacco, sugar, cocoa, or bananas — it hardly matters what. Landlords either sell out to foreign interests offering unheard-of prices for their land, or, farsightedly, make the conversion themselves to cash-crop farming. The cash crops require cultivation on a large scale but need a smaller work force than subsistence farming, so the peasants are driven off the land. A few stay on as hired laborers, and more get seasonal employment. Most, however, must fend for themselves. In many countries like Agraria, the displaced peasants try to cultivate previously uninhabited mountain ranges, where the soil is too poor for cash crops. In others, the homeless flock to newly swollen cities, where they fill the shantytowns and search desperately for work. From twentieth-century Latin America, as from nineteenth-century Europe, they flee to the United States.

In England during the fifteenth century, the cash crop was wool. The peasants forced off the land roamed the country until the notorious "poor laws" confined them to the parish and the workhouse. The wealth that went to the landowners who sold their wool to Flemish merchants was the basis for the commercial — and later industrial — advances that eventually propelled Britain to world leadership.

Things don't work quite that way in Agraria. English, French, and American companies already control world markets. The foreign interests make arrangements with the local feudal elites, dividing the profits between them. The money from cash-crop farming scarcely trickles down to the Agrarian masses. Instead, rich Agrarian oligarchs fill the casinos and discos of the advanced countries. Their children receive expensive foreign private educations. As the starving masses grow more restive, the Agrarian rich realize how important it is to move their capital into Swiss and American banks.

Foreign interests end up controlling the country's wealth. A team of foreign geologists surveys the country and finds useful mineral deposits. The rights to these are purchased by the foreigners, with, of course, a cut to the Agrarian elite. There is no shortage of miners; the landless peasants will labor for almost any wage, no matter how dangerous the work.

During all this time, Agraria's statistics look better and better. With the changeover to a cash-crop economy, the gross national product rises sharply. The mining industry brightens the picture even more. Entrepreneurs and multinational corporations set up a few factories, lured by the low wages and the "favorable regulatory climate" — that is, the absence of almost all health, safety, child labor, overtime, and pollution regulations. They prosper, selling products in the markets of the foreign countries where the companies have their home bases; more and more factories spring up in the cities. The GNP shoots up; first-tier economists and journalists point to Agraria as a glittering showcase of free enterprise at work.

Only the sprawling shantytowns, where few journalists and no economists venture, and the intense misery of the rural populations contradict these glowing pictures. "Overpopulation," say the experts, and write proposals for expensive programs to instruct the Agrarian masses in the fine art of prophylaxis. But although the GNP has risen, the actual living standard of the people declines. Life as an illiterate peasant scratching a bare subsistence under semifeudal conditions of bondage is nobody's idea of the perfect life for a human being, but the alternative for an Agrarian peasant is life as an illiterate slum dweller without access to enough land for a vegetable garden.

The third-tier countries, like those of the second tier, suffer from *blocked* development. It is not that through sloth or stupidity their inhabitants never learned modern technology or organization; not a fault of the Latin or African temperament or family structure that dark-skinned people cannot organize viable societies even with the example of white success staring them in the face. The wealth and resources of some countries have been organized by other countries. Corrupt local oligarchies have entered into partnership with foreigners to strip their countries bare.

The third-tier countries lack even the small middle class of the second tier. The few lonely voices raised to favor a modern democracy find little response. Each country divides between fiercely reactionary supporters of the status quo and fierce revolutionaries determined to overthrow it. The conditions for a liberal democracy of the Western type do not exist. A hundred years would not breed the conditions for democracy as long as the country's economy is firmly in the hands of foreign interests.

Since third-tier countries are such a striking feature of the American Empire, a number of efforts have been made to square support of third-tier oligarchies with the American devotion to democracy. Most of these attempts rely on the idea that these countries are child states, "little brothers" growing toward democracy. A more recent attempt centers on the so-called distinction between authoritarian and totalitarian regimes. The idea behind this distinction is not a strong one, but it deserves attention because it is seriously presented as a justification for American policy by some who help shape it.

An authoritarian government, according to theory, is one that represents the traditional leadership of a traditional society. It is socially conservative — because its position rests on traditional social relationships. Although it uses coercion and sometimes even murder and torture to retain its position, the authoritarian regime is embedded in traditional society, with its long-established values and customs. These provide a basis for tolerance and limited human rights in the private sphere even when public life is closed. In contrast, totalitarian regimes attempt to reshape society in a new image. Traditional relationships are destroyed and people lose their private as well as their public freedoms. Furthermore, authoritarian regimes are open to evolution; witness post-Franco Spain. Totalitarian regimes do not change; they remain odious and tyrannical forever. For this reason, it is not only morally tolerable to support an authoritarian regime; in some cases it may be morally necessary.

Actually, the concept of authoritarianism does have a limited utility. It can be used to describe the England of Edward II or the France of Louis XII. It can be used also to describe Japan's government before that nation opened to the West and began to modernize. But the government that presides over the transformation of an agrarian peasant society into a cash-crop society is as totalitarian as any. The government that presides over the society that emerges from this transformation is profoundly destructive of traditional values and relationships. The "authoritarian" governments of El Salvador and Guatemala have been much more murderous than "totalitarian" Poland.

The misery of underdevelopment should not be confused with the age-old misery of human poverty and ignorance. The slums of Manila and Mexico City are signs of modernism, not of primitive squalor. People have been poor and sick for millennia; they died by thousands and millions when crops failed or plagues came; but the scourges of endemic malnutrition, unemployment, urbanization, and consequent social decay are relatively new phenomena.

Underdevelopment should not be understood as the first stage in development, leading inevitably to the higher stages. Some countries have been frozen in underdevelopment for centuries; others passed through a painful but rapid transition on their way to the first tier.

In any case, underdevelopment is the lot of much of the world today. From the thirty million homeless children in the cities of the free world to the hundreds of millions who live without enough food or hope, these people make up a major proportion of the American Empire. The same forces that create prosperity and freedom here create misery and slavery there. Awareness of this disturbing reality is no doubt a contributing cause of the superficiality, unease, and general bad conscience that mark so much of life in those would-be paradises, the countries of the first tier, and the imperial homeland itself.

The two settler states, Israel and South Africa, have an importance that far outweighs their size. Israel, with its strategic importance and the ties that link it with the first-tier nations, presents the world with the spectacle of a first-tier population directly confronting a second- and third-tier collection of enemies. Power relationships that are usually mercifully disguised by distance appear in sharp relief on the West Bank of the Jordan River.

Moreover, the Zionist experiment of social democracy for the dominant group and displacement for the weak represents the worm at the core of European social democracy. The ideals of the kibbutz were formed in the same milieu as the ideals of the European labor and peace movements; those ideals have failed to create a just world order either in the Middle East or in the whole world. Israel is a mirror in which Europe and America see themselves, exemplifying the hopes and the failures of contemporary civilization.

South Africa is even more graphic. The Boers never tire of attacking the hypocrisy of their Western critics, and they have a point. The Dutch, after all, have been in South Africa as long as the British have been in North America. If the Dutch had been willing or able to exterminate the native blacks with the same thoroughness they employed against the Hottentots, that the Australians employed against the Tasmanians, or that the Americans expended on the Indians, no one would now question their claim to the land. There is nothing like genocide for settling territorial disputes. The Boers find themselves criticized on moral grounds because there is less blood on their hands than on ours.

The moral basis for American self-righteousness over the homelands policy is also difficult to understand. There are differences between our system of Indian reservations and the Boers' system of tribal homelands, but injustice is the cornerstone of both.

The resemblance between South African society and the American Empire is not merely casual. South Africa is a microcosm of the empire as a whole, and the struggle over its future is inextricably involved with the broader crisis that affects the entire empire.

South Africa's whites, its first-tier population, enjoy relative freedom and absolute affluence. The economy is designed to work for its benefit, although it is a minority of the population, and by and large the design works. With the passing of time, however, the system shows more and more strain.

The whites themselves are divided into two principal groups. The dominant Boers are more conservative and more seriously concerned with the defense of the status quo. The English-speaking minority of the white minority bears an uncanny resemblance to the first-tier population of Europe. This group is more liberal than the Boers, more willing to consider various compromises with the majority. Because the Boers seem to be in power to stay, the English speakers are free to indulge in fantasies about impossible compromises and utopian schemes. They are given to more liberal posturing and hand wringing about the state of affairs, but, except in the case of unusual individuals, this is mostly a pose. The interests of the English-speaking whites are firmly tied to those of the Boers, and although their politics are superficially more progressive and interesting than those of the Afrikaaners, they are also more futile.

South Africa also has a second tier — the mixed-race coloreds and the Indians. In general the second tier enjoys conditions better than those of the majority and worse than those of the whites. The Boers make the real decisions; the English-speaking whites are at least permitted to speak their minds on vital matters; the coloreds and Indians participate in a largely sham parliamentary system; the majority has no voice whatever. Here we see the whole panoply of empire reproduced within one state.

The condition of the African majority is also most instructive. To an outside observer, South Africa is a political and economic unit. Only a web of invidious and discriminatory legal fictions prevents the majority from enjoying full citizenship rights. The blacks are declared citizens of artificial homelands, puppet states without resources or legitimacy, with governments tightly under the thumb of the real rulers in Pretoria. "Immigration" police seek to discover and "deport" illegal aliens; the fictional distinctions are held to overrule the real unity of the South African economy and power structure. As a matter of fact the majority in South Africa is inseparably united with the South African state; by a legal fiction they are cut off from access to its mechanisms. The slow growth of armed resistance, the slow insinuation of black and colored South Africans into the political processes of the state, and the growing anger and organization of the once-voiceless majority are nothing more or less than the slow but inevitable triumph of fact over fiction.

The similarities between the American Empire and the Republic of South Africa are numerous and, to tender consciences, painful. In the empire, as in the republic, a minority exercises power over a majority denied representation. The citizen of Haiti lives in a country with no more real independence than that of Bophuthatswana. The third-tier state is as often as not an entity created by the empire, with boundaries determined by the empire, with an economy dominated by the empire, and with a government whose policies, form, and personnel are chosen by and for the empire. In some cases, paid imperial civil servants — representatives of the International Monetary Fund, for example — bring the imperial edicts to the nominal rulers of the client state; in other instances, diplomatic representatives of the ruling power make their wishes known behind the scenes.

The peoples of the American Empire live in a single economic and political entity that is more interdependent than the thirteen colonies were in 1776 — but most of the empire's inhabitants are excluded from any say in the government. For some, the empire means freedom and peace; to others, it brings misery and war.

The day of reckoning looms large in South Africa; the future already casts its shadow over daily life. For the larger empire, that day of reckoning is more distant, but it too is approaching, and visibly so. As is the case in South Africa, there is no assurance that the fall of the empire will result in a change for the better in the short run. The violence, turmoil, and passion sweeping South Africa may lead to mass bloodshed, anarchy, and the destruction of everything all its peoples have built over centuries; the same fate or worse may await the American Empire. The Boers have formed a *laager*. Will the Americans draw the wagons into a circle?

Like it or not, the inhabitants of the American Empire will build their future together — as will Jews and Palestinians, and South Africans of all races, for better or for worse. That future can work only if it is built on a foundation of practical justice. The child born south of the Rio Grande must have the same rights and opportunities as the child born north of it; the child born in Port-au-Prince must be as free to grow and develop as the child born in Westchester County. The facts of human interdependence must triumph over the fiction of lines on maps. "A nation cannot exist half slave, half free," said Abraham Lincoln. "A house divided against itself cannot stand." In those words lies the key to the future of the American Empire.

✺ 4 ✺

THE LIBERAL EMPIRE

ONE OF THE REASONS that *empire* has become a dirty word, even among imperialists, is the belief that empires and democracies are bitter foes. Living in an age when everyone must pay lip service to democracy, our leaders find it necessary to disguise facts that in earlier ages they would have celebrated. But oddly enough we find that history is filled with examples of empires and democracies fighting side by side — and even of societies that became more democratic as their empires expanded.

We can begin with Athens. For the Athenians there was no difficulty in seeing their city-state as both democracy and empire.

As Pericles boasted:

> Let me say that our system of government does not copy the institutions of our neighbors. It is more the case of our being a model to others, than of our imitating anyone else. Our constitution is called a democracy because power is in the hands not of a minority but of the whole people. . . . When it is a question of putting one person before another in positions of public responsibility, what counts is not membership in a particular class, but the actual ability which the man possesses.[1]

Far from contenting itself with establishing democracy within its walls, Athens allied itself with the democratic factions in other Greek states. The protection of democracy may have been a fig leaf for Athens' pursuit of its own imperial interests, but the Athenians often managed to serve both imperial and democratic interests with the same policy.

In Rome the expansion of the empire went hand in hand with the democratization of the republic. Rome's constitution, like that of the United States, was considered "mixed"; it contained aristocratic, monarchic, and democratic elements. The popular, democratic element was at first relatively small, but it expanded under the pressure of military necessity. With the city perpetually endangered, the upper classes were in constant need of military help from the plebeian masses, and the plebeians soon learned to translate their military importance into political power, and won successively greater rights by riots, agitations, and strikes.

Some of the wealth that came from the empire went to the lower classes. We have already noted that Rome established an early "welfare state" with the proceeds of empire; it also instituted public works, like the aqueducts, whose benefits were available to all. Land confiscated from vanquished enemies was distributed to veterans and citizens. The protection of Roman law was extended to every citizen wherever he traveled.

In modern times, the same correlations are evident. France, Britain, and Germany all progressed simultaneously along the roads to democracy and empire. The British widened the franchise at the same time that they extended the boundaries of their domains; the Third Republic of France built the bulk of the French Empire. Germany, with less democracy and a smaller empire than its two western rivals, nevertheless followed the same pattern.

The United States was no exception to the rule. In examining the causes for the growth of freedom in the United States, historians are almost unanimous in placing great weight on the frontier. Those who were discontented with the existing order of society were always free to strike out for themselves. The wide open western states were always more populist and democratic than the cramped, hemmed-in colonies along the East Coast. Even today the constitutions of the western states as a rule contain more popular features than those of the eastern states.

Yet it cannot be denied that the frontier was the child of imperialism, that American democracy nourished itself on the confiscation of Native American lands and aggression against Mexico. As empires have done throughout history, the United States offered freedom for its citizens and subjugation by conquest to those who stood in its way. Both the freedom and the conquest were real; frontier society "shone and stank."

As America widened its horizons from the continent to the globe, American freedoms expanded in proportion. The years after World War II that saw the United States buckle down to the problems and responsibilities of global hegemony also witnessed a series of social movements and legal changes that enabled minority groups and individual citizens to live with more freedom than ever before.

In modern times, imperialism and democracy have met most often in the ideas we usually call "liberal." Often enough, liberalism has provided the best justification for empire building as well as for democratization. So pervasive has been the influence of these ideas that we could call the American Empire the Liberal Empire par excellence. Like imperialism and democracy, liberalism is one of the words that everybody uses and nobody understands, partly because liberalism seems to change its meaning in each generation.

Liberalism almost deserves to be called a chameleon ideology. Over the years it has subsumed so many views on so many subjects that some claim there is no such thing as liberalism, only liberals. In the seventeenth century, English liberals believed in a limited monarchy checked by a Parliament elected by the rich. A hundred years later, American liberals believed in a republic — but still held to the idea of a restricted right to vote. During the nineteenth century, liberals gradually adapted themselves to the idea that all adult men should have the vote; in the twentieth century came the admission of women to the magic circle. There was a time when liberals believed in eliminating welfare and dismantling the bureaucratic state. Today they are chiefly known for the opposite opinions.

In spite of this bewildering diversity, there has been an inner consistency to liberal thought. In every age, the liberal spirit has sought an enlightened compromise between the claims of existing traditional institutions and the abstract claims of justice. The specific content of such a compromise changes with changing times, but not the habit of mind that seeks to reconcile progress and tradition. New eras create new possibilities, and the liberal spirit remains eager to exploit new opportunities. Liberalism is open to science and progress; it conceives of history as a continuing process of development. In its earlier years, liberalism took the lead in battles whose results we now take for granted: it shattered the feudal monarchies of Europe; it broke the monopoly of the church on education; it ushered in an age of human freedom everywhere it penetrated.

What is just as important, liberalism has opposed the violent overthrow of traditional institutions. It is far more conservative than some conservatives understand. Liberalism is based on the belief that the best way to preserve what is essential and valuable in existing societies is to cast off what is inessential. Thus, Roosevelt's New Deal is widely credited with preserving the essence of American capitalism by reforming particular problems.

In other words, liberalism is founded on *reasonable reason*. Like more radical world views, it is an attempt to analyze and evaluate society according to the criteria of critical intelligence; but it also places value on keeping a level head.

The other great tenet of liberalism is its faith in the operation of the market. This statement may surprise some contemporary conservatives, who criticize liberals on the grounds that they wish to stifle the market by excessive regulation, but such a view oversimplifies the liberal position.

As Garry Wills pointed out in his perceptive *Nixon Agonistes*, the American liberal sees the market as a metaphor for all of life, not merely as a means of economic exchange. Just as in the free market of Adam Smith an invisible hand seems to direct the individual exchanges to produce, in the end, the greatest good for the greatest number, so does a free political market produce the best political leaders, and a free ideological market produce the best ideas. But liberals do more than admire the market; they ask what makes it work, how a market becomes free, and how it can be kept that way.

Historically, the economic market led not to the development of more and more small businesses in a freer and freer environment, but to the development of the trusts, great monopolistic corporations. Once the market had been invaded by trusts, it could no longer be considered free in the old sense. The trusts could and did use their great power to crush competition, rather than by "competing honestly" with it. Railroads had a monopoly on transporting farm produce from the Middle West to the East; this meant they could charge whatever freight rates they liked. They did not need to fear competition in the short run, because the lines were prohibitively expensive and took years to build.

Those espousing a radical approach might have called for nationalization of the railroads, saying that the market had failed and needed to be replaced by the state. A laissez-faire conservative would have done nothing, believing that nothing could improve the situation except possibly the invisible hand. The liberal response was neither to do nothing nor to abandon the market; liberals regulated the railroads. Where the market did not provide enough competition, the government would step in: it would prevent or regulate the monopolies that seemed to gain power over the dynamics of the market.

The liberal view of the market holds that various forces that act on the market distort it, and that the intervention of an outside force is needed to restore balance. Regulation was introduced into the American economy to shore up the market, not to weaken it.

Liberals also recognized that the market inevitably creates short-term injustices and suffering. The business cycle of a market economy normally alternates between booms and busts — recessions and recoveries, in the euphemisms of today. Once again, liberals seek a compromise between abandoning the unemployed and other victims of a slump to their own devices and demolishing the market entirely.

Liberals also believe that the market did not work according to form where blacks and certain other minorities were concerned. Affirmative action programs were designed to compensate for this failure by stimulating the market to provide jobs for talented people — even if they were black or Hispanic.

Liberal support for free speech, free artistic expression, and tolerance for socially deviant behavior also springs from liberalism's profound reverence for the market. Only if all ideas have the opportunity to be heard can the best ones emerge in the marketplace. No matter how outrageous an idea may seem at first glance, we need to hear it out and give it its chance in open debate. If the idea has merit, it will make its own way, sooner or later. If not, there is no need to suppress it; a bad idea will wither away on its own.

Liberalism opposes absolutes of any kind. Claims of religious or political apologists to speak for an absolute truth are given a hearing but are ruled out of order. Once the true religion has been discovered, after all, we would have to close down the market of religious ideas or convert it into a temple. We would no longer be willing to entertain new concepts, and this liberalism will never accept. "To travel hopefully is better than to arrive" could serve as a motto for liberalism in the realm of ideas. Liberals do not recognize the possibility of the discovery of an absolute truth; all human knowledge must be continually re-evaluated in the light of new information, and so no new idea can ever be judged to have won the market competition once and for all, and no old idea can ever be judged to have lost.

Liberals also believe that all conflicts can ultimately be resolved; if not once and for all, they can be compromised enough for the here and now. The idea of an irreconcilable conflict of any kind is foreign to an ideology that embraces the peaceful competition of the marketplace of ideas. Liberals shy away from the idea of a permanent conflict in human ideas, whether the subject is the class conflict of Karl Marx, the race struggle of Adolf Hitler, or the religious conflict between absolute good and absolute evil. So, although liberals are notoriously willing to borrow ideas from any source, and especially from the Marxist left, they reject the left's belief that class struggle cannot be compromised.

The convinced liberal believes that he or she opposes the left and the right because both extremes mire themselves in unscientific dogma. The left has its Marxism, and the right has its own ideologies, usually religious. It is a classic liberal argument to maintain that fascism and communism are really two forms of the same thing.

MODERN AMERICAN LIBERALISM

Whatever the liberal programs of past generations, since World War II modern American liberals have backed a cluster of programs in the United States and abroad that have dominated national and international politics. This liberal agenda more than any other factor shaped the American Empire at home and abroad during the years of its greatest power.

We can say that since 1945 liberalism in the United States has meant social leveling and economic management. Both of these trends had as their goal the strengthening of the free market that liberals continued to regard as the ideal means to achieve progress in society.

Social leveling is the erosion of the traditional distinctions between people based on anything other than individual performance. Liberal politics since 1933 have resulted in the gradual abolition of Jewish quotas in most of American life and the integration of more black Americans, other minorities, and women into the economic mainstream. All of this, we should note, is fully compatible with the free market. Liberalism tries to exclude extraneous considerations — nationality, gender, race, sexual preference — so that market decisions for employment and housing are based solely on economic factors. Most Americans regard the increased opportunity and freedom resulting from this approach as good in themselves; and for many, liberalism has made a lasting contribution to American life by bringing American reality closer to the beliefs expressed in the Declaration of Independence.

There is another side to social leveling, however, one that draws the fire of conservative critics. In the traditional American society, the individual was wrapped in a network of institutions that shaped identity and gave meaning to life. Although family and church were weaker in America than in Europe, nevertheless these institutions gave shape to life for millions of Americans. The effect of liberalism on these and other identity structures (regional and ethnic identifications, for example) has been extremely corrosive. It can hardly have been otherwise. To the extent that liberalism creates a world where each person stands or falls on his or her own merits, liberalism has weakened the intermediary forces of society. Every woman who is financially independent of her husband is a woman who can, if she chooses, leave the family. Marriages that cross ethnic and racial lines reflect greater social tolerance and greater individual freedom; they also show the weakened power of traditional identity structures. Greater social tolerance for various religious beliefs also reflects a diminished power of churches (and synagogues and mosques) over the world views of their memberships.

Large numbers of Americans now live alone or in nontraditional households. Even larger numbers are cut off from most of the traditional social structures that once defined and gave meaning to life. Increasingly, Americans define themselves by their jobs or such self-selected identities as hobbies, professional groups, or other chosen affiliations. More and more of us spend more and more time in superficial relationships, and intimacy, once taken for granted, becomes something difficult to achieve.

The values that liberalism offers as replacements for those it destroys are freedom and tolerance — very good things, but not in themselves enough for human beings to live by. Liberalism itself is incapable of providing new identities and ties to replace those which are lost; it leaves a society composed of lonely, isolated individuals. The resulting alienation and despair can end up being profoundly subversive of the tolerance and freedom created by liberalism. People turn, individually and en masse, to religious cults, revivals, or to virtually any ideology that offers the prospect of positive values.

While the "meritocracy" benefits from liberalism in its professional life, not everyone in society can join this elect. For the great majority of the population, liberalism can seem only a negative force, destroying the structures that give shape, meaning, and security to life but substituting nothing new, not even career opportunities. The sexual revolution and the advent of feminism mean one thing to a young woman from the upper middle class with access to professional training; they mean something else entirely to a divorced mother of two in a dead-end, pink-collar job.

Postwar liberalism stressed the involvement of government in managing the economy. Before the Depression, American society generally believed that the proper role of government was to act as an umpire, setting and enforcing the rules of fair competition. Although the populists and other radicals called for active government intervention, it was not until the 1930s that the federal government accepted responsibility for managing the economy and relieving distress. The technique of government intervention — besides regulation of the economy's component parts — has been chiefly the stimulation of demand. A combination of income transfer, subsidy, and targeted government spending is used to prevent the recurrence of another Depression.

The income transfer programs include everything from Social Security to food stamps. The welfare state has two purposes. One, of course, is to relieve poverty. Thanks to the welfare state, millions of people are eating better, living longer, and living with a little dignity. Just as important, the welfare state contributes to the overall health of the economy. The characteristic problem of a free enterprise economy is *overproduction* — not the production of more goods than are needed or wanted, but of more goods than can be sold. By putting money into the pockets of would-be consumers, the government stimulates private spending and therefore helps keep the wheels of the economy turning.

Despite all the horror stories of welfare queens getting rich on government benefits, the chief beneficiaries of social programs are not the poor themselves, but those who sell them things. Landlords cannot rent to people who cannot pay; supermarkets cannot sell to the starving. The most vigorous lobbyists for welfare programs tend not to be the poor or their radical representatives; the most active advocates for social spending turn out to be in the employ of those who make their living by meeting the needs of the poor.

Social Security, by enabling millions of older people to escape absolute destitution, has also vastly increased the domestic market for consumer goods. Traditionalists like to look back on the good old days, when children were responsible for their parents' financial well-being, but a return to that virtuous era would bankrupt the economy. If grown children suddenly had to pick up the bills for their parents' support, their own disposable income would instantly vanish. What would happen then to makers of cameras and barbecue grills? Automobile manufacturers? And to their employees?

The same thing is true of unemployment compensation and disability insurance. They cushion the blows of life not only for the unemployed and the disabled, but for those who would otherwise pay their bills and those whose incomes depend on servicing their needs. Far from being the drag on private enterprise that conservatives like to suppose, the liberal welfare state has helped to fuel one of the great economic expansions in history.

The government has also stimulated demand by massive, selected subsidies to various industries. Some of these, such as the farm subsidy program, take the form of direct payments or price supports. In other cases, subsidies come disguised as tax exemptions or tax credits. The exemptions for interest payments, for example, subsidize not only the construction industry but also the banks. With government picking up a significant share of the interest, banks can almost print money at will.

When interest rates peaked over 20 percent in the early 1980s, the shock
was considerably lessened by the tax exemptions for interest payments,
which cut the real cost of interest in half for those in the 50 percent
bracket. This subsidy, a keystone of the postwar economic order, greased
the wheels of the credit industry and helped to sustain economic growth
for a full generation.

Finally, massive public works programs and military spending keep
demand high. The interstate highway program employed tens of thousands and created profits for construction companies and equipment makers on an unheard-of scale. Those paychecks and profits did not sleep in
the pockets of those who received them; they went out into the economy,
determined to do good and spread demand for consumer goods wherever
they went.

Military spending, while unproductive for the civilian economy, also
generates consumer demand. The space program has spent billions, employed hundreds of thousands, and provided seed money for the high-
tech industry.

This is a brief, very brief, survey of a generation of liberal achievement
in the years after World War II. From this thumbnail sketch we can see
that the liberal era in American life has brought about simultaneous
increases in economic prosperity and the size of the government. Although the marriage of the federal system and a growing bureaucracy
has not always been a happy one, the liberal programs of the last fifty
years have made such sweeping and fundamental improvements in the
lives of most Americans that only the most hard-nosed warriors of the
right would want to see them rolled back.

Yet even liberals now concede that as the bureaucracy has grown
bulkier, the programs aren't working as well. Transfer payments continue to alleviate distress, but they no longer work as effectively to ensure
overall economic growth. Neither liberals nor conservatives have been
able to offer alternatives to a state of affairs that both groups find un-
satisfactory; after a generation of liberal rule American politics has become stale and blocked.

Internationally, the hallmarks of American liberalism have been anticommunism, multilateralism, free trade, and flexibility. These marks
were not arbitrary selections; they expressed an inner unity of purpose
and vision of the future. It was the genius of American statesmen to
understand that their empire could best be served by these liberal policies.
As time began to run out on the empire, the old liberal policies began
to fail — but no other policies showed any more promise.

Liberalism is often perceived as "softer" on communism than is conservatism. Nothing could be farther from the truth. The liberal John F. Kennedy ferociously attacked Republican softness over Castro and China. The most effective, as well as the fiercest, attacks on communism in American postwar history — the Truman Doctrine, the Marshall Plan, the Bay of Pigs, and the Vietnam War, to name a few — were organized by liberals. It was Richard Nixon who withdrew from Vietnam and recognized China, not Lyndon Johnson. Nixon initiated the SALT process, and Gerald Ford accepted SALT I; it was Jimmy Carter who withdrew SALT II from the Senate — and Ronald Reagan who grudgingly observed it for six years.

Liberals prefer a flexible response to communism — but this is a question of tactics, not strategy. Kennedy abandoned the idea of massive retaliation for that of flexible response because he perceived that the greatest danger of communist advance came from guerrilla campaigns, not from ICBMs. John Foster Dulles offered France's premier Pierre Mendès-France two atomic bombs for use in Vietnam; it was Kennedy who sent in the Green Berets. Neither response can be called soft. Liberals condemned Reagan's descriptions of the Soviet Union as an evil empire and his claim that the snake in the Garden of Eden was the historical founder of Marxist ideology because liberals consider that kind of rhetoric counterproductive, not because they like Lenin.

The liberal instinct for negotiation, far from being a supine capitulation to the enemies of capitalism, rests on a shrewd appreciation for how capitalism can best be defended under current conditions. The capitalism of the late twentieth century differs from the cutthroat entrepreneurial world of a hundred years ago. Coordination has become more important than competition, or, more accurately, the coordination of enterprises and industries that span the whole globe has become the chief field for economic competition in the modern world. The more hard-boiled the approach of the United States toward the USSR, the more America's allies look nevously for an exit. The more visibly America intervenes in the Third World, the more communist insurgents benefit from national patriotic resentment of the foreign intervention.

The liberal preference for multilateral approaches to foreign problems is an example of the liberal genius for compromise. The great advantage of a multilateral approach to international problems is that it commands wide support. The disadvantage of such an approach is that it relies on compromise with one's negotiating partners. Multilateral negotiations and multilateral institutions like the IMF have generally served basic American interests well and have spared this country the necessity of imposing its will in an infinite series of bitter bilateral negotiations. Despite the strains, the NATO alliance survives in part because Americans have thus far refrained — most of the time — from converting it into a modern version of the Athenians' Delian League, an ostensible alliance that is actually an instrument of subjugation.

Free trade is another mark of the liberal empire. American influence has been used to reduce tariff barriers and to promote the international flow of goods, services, information, and money. Such a flow, not coincidentally, tends to favor rich and highly developed countries. In the years after 1945, cheap American goods penetrated the world's markets. Even today the United States commands a strong position in world trade. Free trade may no longer have the broad appeal it enjoyed a decade ago, but it remains a cornerstone of the empire's economy. Above all, the free flow of money, services, and information is crucial to the functioning of the great multinational corporations. Although not all of these are based in the United States, most of them are, and American policy must inevitably reflect — or at least respect — their basic interests. When Ford builds a car in Europe with parts made in Latin America and Asia, and plans to repatriate its profits to the United States for investment in Brazil, it is clear that free trade on an international scale is vital to its plans. In the late 1970s RCA was the single largest exporter of manufactured goods from Taiwan.[2]

This world market, with its economics of scale and production, is what the American Empire made possible when it absorbed the earlier national empires. Any movement in the direction of higher tariffs or other trade barriers undermines the ability of the world's economy to benefit from advancing technology and integration.

Finally, the liberal American Empire is marked by flexibility. Steps that fill traditionalists with horror are taken almost casually by the liberal guardians and managers of empire. If the gold standard gets in the way of development, so much for the gold standard. Shibboleths like balanced budgets and fixed exchange rates are blithely ignored in the liberal empire when they serve no rational purpose. If the establishment of a Marxist government in Zimbabwe is good for the liberal world, then Robert Mugabe can take power with Anglo-American blessings.

Liberals seek to replace superstition and fetishism by pragmatism wherever possible. They will negotiate with anybody; they recognize in the end no value but success. They understand the difference between appearance and reality — that, for example, a Third World country can be integrated more securely into an empire with political independence than one without it.

The ideology of the American Empire is simpler and more appealing than the cumbersome ideologies of the past. The French *mission civilisatrice*, Kipling's white man's burden, Nazi race fantasies, limited the flexibility and global appeal of past imperial cultures; the American Empire escapes limitations like these. Beyond the operation of the market — in a word, beyond efficiency — it has no agenda: no way of life to spread, no religion, nothing. It does not rely on a presumed cultural or racial superiority to the rest of the world. It needs no fancy mottoes or phony religious justifications. The basis of the American Empire is pragmatic: it works.

THE GOLDEN AGE OF EMPIRE

With hindsight, we can see that the 1960s marked the high-water mark of liberalism at home and abroad. The two principal thrusts of liberalism within the United States were social leveling and economic management by the national government. In both fields the United States took momentous and apparently irreversible steps during the Kennedy-Johnson years.

The progress made in civil rights during the period was epochal. If for no other reason, the 1960s deserve to be honored. Three hundred years of cruelty and hypocrisy toward American blacks were finally opposed by the weight of the federal government. The century after the Civil War had been a chronicle of shameful betrayal of blacks and their rights. The Constitution of the United States specifies that any state which denied its citizens the right to vote on racial grounds would lose congressional representation in proportion to the percentage of the state's population that suffered from voting discrimination, but not once in fifty years of lynch law, terror, and fraud was this provision invoked against the guilty states. The Supreme Court blandly agreed that "separate but equal" educational and public facilities met constitutional tests for fairness as it transferred the protections of the Fourteenth Amendment from oppressed people to wealthy corporations. Antimiscegenation laws, the envy of Nazis and South African whites, held sway through much of the United States. The 1960s did not witness the end of discrimination and racism, but they did see more progress in a shorter time than any period since the false spring of Reconstruction.

The welfare state made similarly astounding progress. The government declared war on hunger in America, and the food stamp program looked like the instrument of victory. Project Head Start, a federally funded program for preschool children of the needy, made a measurable difference in the educational outlook for a generation of participants. An enormous expansion of postsecondary educational facilities and of financial aid resources opened the doors of higher education to millions of young people. Supplemental benefits to older citizens and the nation's first comprehensive program of medical assistance resulted in a steady improvement in the lives of the elderly.

The art of economic management was, people believed, nearly perfected during those years. The Kennedy tax cuts nipped a recession in the bud, giving a classroom demonstration of effective government management. Economists believed that the fundamental economic problems had been solved; from the 1960s on, they thought, government needed to follow a few simple rules to ensure steady economic growth, with unemployment and inflation hovering at or below 4 percent a year.

Finally, the Apollo program, perhaps the most dramatic government undertaking in human history, put a man on the moon within Kennedy's ten-year timetable. It was a feat comparable with Babe Ruth's signaling a home run in the World Series. NASA accelerated the development of computer technology, stimulated the economy, and provided useful and challenging jobs to hundreds of talented scientists and engineers.

These years also witnessed the development of characteristically liberal programs abroad. The so-called Kennedy round of tariff cuts resulted in the closest approach to pure free trade that the world had ever known. The inflexible doctrine of massive retaliation was scrapped in favor of flexible response, a move that theoretically reduced the danger of nuclear war while increasing the ability of the American Empire to defend itself from communist subversion. Competition with the Soviets was stiff, but negotiations on matters of common concern continued to reduce the risks of war over Berlin and Cuba. The first meaningful arms treaty of the nuclear age banned tests in the atmosphere and removed a growing threat to the health of the world. In Latin America, straightforward support for dictatorships was, at least in theory, replaced by the Alliance for Progress, a combination of aid and trade measures designed to strengthen the South and Central American middle class and to create openings for democracy and social progress. The Kennedy Doctrine, the most sweeping statement ever offered by an American president, announced the nation's determination to "pay any price and bear any burden" in the defense of liberty around the world.

The Kennedy-Johnson years ended in the debacle of 1968, a year of unprecedented trauma for the American Empire. The assassination of Dr. Martin Luther King, Jr., explosive riots in the cities and on college

campuses, and the shock of the Tet offensive shook the liberal order to
its foundations. The most aggressive pursuit of social justice and international security in American histoiy had ended with riots in the streets
and the looming probability of America's first unambiguous military
defeat in two hundred years. Two ghosts from what liberals had hoped
was the past — Richard Nixon and George Wallace — seemed to be
riding the wave of the future, and Hubert Humphrey, one of the great
liberals of the century, looked passé and forlorn. What happened? Why
did a decade of racial progress lead to racist outbreaks among so many
whites and urban riots in so many black neighborhoods? How did the
doctrine of flexible response mire us in an inflexible commitment to fight
in the Vietnamese quicksand? Why did liberalism fail in the 1960s?

To understand the consequences of the 1960s for American race relations, it is necessary to understand the limits of the liberal response to
the civil rights movement. Liberal ideology is, in part, an attempt to
reconcile the needs of a private enterprise economy with the aspirations
of the human beings who live in that economy. Liberals are committed
to the abolition of abuses in the existing system and believe that the attack
of abuses is the most effective method to preserve the system as a whole.
From the liberal perspective, the denial of basic human rights to American
blacks was a classic example of an abuse in the system. There is nothing
about private enterprise that necessarily restricts the participation of blacks
at all levels of the economy in numbers proportionate to their presence
in the population. The American government had been officially committed to voting rights for more than a century. Removing the legal
obstacles to full black participation in the existing system was precisely
the type of action that liberalism was capable of and saw the need for.
By assimilating the twenty million American blacks into the economic
and political mainstream, liberals reasoned, America would become more
stable and free.

But liberals and blacks together made a startling discovery in the 1960s.
The removal of abuses has only a limited value if the system itself is
abusive. As presently constituted, the American economy is incapable
of generating jobs for all the people who want to work; its ability to
create interesting jobs that pay decent wages is even more limited. Racial
discrimination means that a disproportionate number of blacks live on
the margin of society, but the abolition of racial discrimination, even if
it could be completely accomplished, would not lead to a decent standard
of living for every black who was eager to work.

Most working blacks in the 1960s had badly paid, low-status jobs.
Either they were in doomed fields like agricultural labor, or they worked

in low-paid service jobs. It was argued that efforts to improve their access to better-paid lines of work might result in an improvement for the next generation, but the adults of the 1960s were already in the occupations in which most of them would spend their working lives. Furthermore, efforts to open doors to future generations would suffer because of the inability of today's low-income parents to provide the schooling and socialization needed for their children's upward mobility. The movement for legal equality moved naturally into an economic struggle on behalf of the poorly paid and the unemployed of all races, and into demands for affirmative action to redress existing injustices as quickly as possible.

From the liberal perspective, the huge and systematic wage differentials in American society are hardly an abuse in the system. It would be closer to say that the disparity in material rewards constitutes the essence of the system. When blacks turned from demanding the vote to demanding a decent living wage, they were asking for something the system could not give.

Requests for equal access to a competitive process can be accommo- dated, with strains, by the U.S. system; requests for full employment at reasonable wages apparently cannot. Similarly, after thirty years of resistance by school boards, most American school systems have under- gone formal desegregation. But the provision of high-quality free edu- cation to the majority of American children, whatever their race, remains a dream. The school desegregation controversy is an instructive example of the limits of the liberal approach. The courts first removed the formal barriers to integrated education and then went a step farther, requiring actions up to and including busing to assure integration. Yet at no point in the resulting controversy were the root problems of education in a democracy attacked. Education is the single most important aid to a child seeking to rise from a poor background to achieve wealth, prominence, or the normal ease and amenities of life. The public schools are the core of this education and are vital in the relationship between government and individual, and government and the family. Inequality in educational opportunity cuts to the heart of the American dream and the American system. Yet the public schools are underfunded, understaffed, and un- dersupervised.

When the tremendous burden of desegregation was placed on the school systems, concerned citizens of both races put in long hours, as volunteers, in many communities across the country. Courageous South- erners risked ostracism and violence to form interracial parents' com- mittees to make the programs work. But the governments, state and federal, did almost nothing. Young children were sent across town in buses to strange schools, far from home, there to be faced with untrained, unprepared, and sometimes unsympathetic teachers. Small wonder that the public schools frequently became dumping grounds for problem children and the poor while more affluent parents lobbied for tuition tax credits for private schools. Small wonder that the collapse of the parochial school system was at least temporarily averted by hordes of families fleeing the chaos of desegregation and decay. Small wonder that teacher morale dropped, that racial conflicts multiplied, and that educational quality deteriorated.

The children of the wealthy do not usually attend public schools. They go to country day schools, prep schools, church schools, and other private academies. Paying tuitions of up to $10,000 a year, these families expect and receive for their children individual instruction and academic excellence. The faculty members themselves usually come from better colleges than teachers in public schools. Textbooks are often better, and facilities like science labs, computers, and art studios are, in most cases, incomparably superior. There are good public schools — isolated examples in large cities, whole systems in wealthy suburbs — but the experience of most American children in school is a twelve-year bath in, at best, mediocrity.

Liberalism was able to give blacks more access to the competition for better jobs; it was also able to enforce school desegregation. Yet given the real constraints of the availability of jobs and schools, these victories proved hollow to most blacks. Liberals shrank from the social changes that would be required if good jobs were offered to all adults or good schools to all children.

While the liberal programs brought hollow victories to some, they brought real defeats to others. If the number of good jobs remains relatively stable, and the number of aspirants increases, somebody will suffer. Opposition among some Jewish groups to what looked like a new quota system reflected an awareness of the arithmetic of opportunity. Mounting anger and frustration among whites — particularly among those who themselves had not won many prizes in the American struggle for success — was another consequence of this numbers game.

The chaos and disintegration of so many public schools unprepared for desegregation also created white losers. Whites had to sit on buses for hours to get to schools that were worse than the ones they left behind; even those who were not bused themselves suffered from the all too common consequences of large groups of children from different backgrounds being put together in a setting where family and other forces of social control were weak or insensitive.

The liberal solutions to racial discrimination largely involved forcing working-class whites to assume part of the burden previously carried by blacks. Societal inequality and discrimination — of which racial discrimination is simply the most virulent form — were not touched at all. Wealth, in the liberal utopia of the 1960s, was the means for avoiding the disagreeable consequences of liberal initiatives against racism.

Black leaders went beyond the liberal program. They consistently called for full employment, decent wages for all who were willing to work, and sufficient resources for the public school system. Their calls were dismissed as unrealistic by politicians who were willing to pay lip service to such noble goals but who understood all too well that the American economy was in no shape to pay for the programs.

Liberal racial policies in the 1960s ended by alienating blacks, who saw more and more clearly that their minimal aspirations would not be met by the Great Society; working-class whites, on whom the burden of change chiefly fell; and those conservatives who claimed to have seen it all coming. "Alabama has not joined the nation," boasted George Wallace. "The nation has joined Alabama!"

A fine epitaph for a liberal decade.

THE QUAGMIRE

The catastrophe of liberal social policy was matched by the fiasco of liberal security policies. There is little point in going back over the long trail of false hopes and broken promises that led the United States into and finally out of a devastated Indochina. It is necessary only to see that Vietnam was far from a horrible aberration of American policy in the imperial era. Rather, the intervention there was the logical consequence of such policy.

America's military position in the world since 1950 has rested on a growing network of multilateral defense treaties, from NATO to ANZUS. These treaties replaced the previous method of ensuring the allegiance of small states around the world — the outright conversion of foreign countries into a juridical empire. When Hitler called an inconvenient treaty a "scrap of paper," he was no doubt expressing the opinion of many statesmen, but the United States was not in a position in the 1960s openly to flout its principal security treaties, the cement of its empire.

A peculiar feature of world politics since Hiroshima is that the Great Powers so far have been unable to go to war with each other. Brushfire wars around the world become much more charged with Great Power connotations; intangible factors in diplomacy also become more important when the resort to war is so problematic. U.S. policymakers reflected on these facts and concluded that the national interest required that client regimes "perceived" that the United States was a strong and reliable ally.

Having made a commitment to the Diem regime in 1954, the United States was trapped into fulfilling that commitment even after, apparently, condoning the murder of the man to whom the original guarantee had been given. Vietnam, a country of almost no intrinsic interest to the United States, became the object of one of the most sustained military initiatives in all of American history. This huge expenditure of blood and treasure brought no useful return to the United States and only worsened Vietnam's situation. Intending to demonstrate its reliability as an ally, the United States instead proved to the whole world that the American people lack the stomach for long guerrilla wars. Morale in the armed forces sank to its lowest level; the American population was bitterly divided against itself.

After years of slowly, then rapidly, escalating involvement, after a deluge of official lies and false hopes, the breaking point for public opinion came with the Tet offensive of 1968. Although the generals claimed that Tet was a military victory for the United States, the public no longer believed them. If the U.S. Army, with its overwhelming advantages, could not guarantee the security of the U.S. Embassy in Saigon, and if U.S. intelligence had failed to predict the offensive, what reason was there to accept the generals' estimates of the military situation?

After a decade of self-confident advance on the international and domestic scenes, American liberalism suddenly found itself on the defensive. After only twenty-three years, the American Century was showing its age. After Tet, the American political issue was not how to win the war in Vietnam, but how to escape it. After Dr. King's assassination, the subsequent riots, and Wallace's showing of support in the Democratic primaries, the country began to look to the Republican Party — written off after 1964 — for new solutions.

In search of peace with honor and law and order, America turned to Richard Milhous Nixon.

PART TWO

Peace with Honor:
The Nixon Years

~ 5 ~

NIXON'S CHALLENGE

A
FTER the stunning and tumultuous events of 1968, when pitched
battles raged in the cities of both Vietnam and the United States,
Nixon took over, resolved to put the United States back on an
even keel. Believing that Kennedy and Johnson had pursued policies of
reckless adventurism, Nixon determined to make American policy at
home and abroad more moderate and to place it on a durable foundation.
The ignominious end of the Nixon era, leaving him in disgrace and
ruining the causes for which he had ruined himself, was an anomaly in
American politics. Previous administrations that left office in disarray
were those like Grant's or Harding's — administrations that had simply
not taken statecraft seriously. Serious American statesmen had failed
before — Woodrow Wilson and Lyndon Johnson spring to mind — but
none had been hounded from office as a crook. That Nixon was widely
respected overseas even after his resignation makes the contrast more
striking still.

Richard Nixon and Henry Kissinger understood that the United States
no longer stood alone in the world. The Soviet Union had recovered
from the Second World War, built up its economic potential, and was
in a position to challenge the United States around the world. The economic basis for American supremacy was quietly but steadily eroding
year by year. During the Nixon era a series of currency fluctuations
forced the United States to devalue the dollar and take it off the gold
standard. Unrest in the Third World assumed increasingly menacing
proportions. There was a military challenge in Indochina and an economic challenge in the Middle East. It was Nixon's task to manage the
retreat of the United States from its lonely pre-eminence in world affairs
back to a status more like first among equals. More than the personal
qualities for which he has been often attacked, it was the difficulties of
this task that laid him low.

THE ROOTS OF DECLINE

The tides of history created the American Empire. For most of its history the United States has not had outstanding leadership in its government, yet this lack did not prevent America's rise to power. Once tides began to flow against the empire, no president and no Congress could stop them.

The basis of the American Empire after 1945 was economic. The military might that seems so awesome is not the result of superior valor or intelligence, but of wealth. America rose to power not because it overpowered the rest of the world, but because the rest of the world exhausted itself. As the world recovered from the war, it was inevitable that America's relative power would weaken. The postwar position of the United States rested on its industrial pre-eminence, its dominance of world markets, and its control over the world's finances.

The decline of American industrial pre-eminence was unavoidable. It was impossible for American industry to remain prosperous after the war unless there was somebody out there who could buy American products. The Marshall Plan loans assured the United States of a market for industrial and agricultural goods — but only as the Europeans rebuilt their economies. Inevitably, they rebuilt their bombed-out factories with the most modern technologies available, but the Americans continued to use their existing plants. European products recaptured their home markets and then began to compete with American products in the Third World and in the United States itself. Japanese products followed suit, and the results are all too plain today.

Additionally, the countries devastated by the war recovered on the basis of national economic planning. Although our free enterprise purists scoff at the idea, the evidence demonstrates that intelligent national planning can lead to substantial results; witness Germany and Japan.

After the war, American suppliers had a near monopoly and could name their price. For American society, this had vital implications. It meant that there could be full employment with high wages at a time of low inflation and high profits. Inside the United States, the class struggle over economic issues seemed to turn into a question of management. Rapid economic growth led to a generally rising standard of living, financed the social programs of the modern era, and left the wealthy to enjoy their riches in peace. It was the best of all possible worlds, or seemed to be.

But with the growth of foreign competition, price competition in world markets again became a factor. The United States was no longer in the enviable position of being the only consumer of raw materials and therefore able to set their prices while, as the monopoly supplier of finished goods, it could set prices at the other end of the market, too. Commodity suppliers could charge more, and industrial goods suppliers could charge less. The squeeze intensified — most spectacularly in the case of oil — and brought an end to the easy years. Growth was slower; it was harder to achieve and was accompanied by more inflation. Competitive forces intensified within the economy, and the government could no longer claim to satisfy the basic needs of every social group.

Another outcome of the price competition also had dramatic effects. "Buy low, sell high" is the motto of any successful business, and as American wages rose, many manufacturers realized that they could enhance their profits by moving their factories abroad. Third World countries had low wages, weak labor movements, low taxes, and few vexing pollution and safety regulations. American businessmen did not need Ph.D.s in economics to understand the consequences.

At first these consequences were limited to light industries like textiles. Workers did not require much training and the machinery did not require sophisticated maintenance. Such industries were suited to areas where the work force was not well educated or completely acclimatized to the work rhythms of industry. Inevitably, the success of these industries lured others into the Third World until American high-wage industrial production faced low-wage competition in virtually every field. Protectionism, a dead issue after the fiasco of high tariffs during the Depression, returned from the grave to haunt contemporary political debate.

Third World manufacturing was not all bad for the American economy. Besides lowering prices for many goods, it provided favorable investment opportunitites for American corporations willing to diversify their production overseas. It assisted the efforts of American-based multinational corporations to compete in world markets where competition was steadily rising. But as the industries of Europe and Japan continued to thrive, those countries began to invest in low-wage, off-shore production. Real wages stagnated in the United States and peaked in 1973. Depressed by world competition, they began to decline, from an average of slightly over $200 per week in 1973 to $171 (in constant dollars) in 1986.[1]

Feeling the pinch, American workers and spokesmen for some industries have agitated for protection from "unfair" foreign competition. The pain of these people is real, but protectionism can only raise new problems for the American economy. Since many Third World producers are actually American corporations, or joint United States–Third World ventures, any attempt to strike at "foreign" competition will harm the balance sheets of American companies. Lower profits for American corporations will not finance higher wages for American workers or higher taxes to balance the American budget. Furthermore, these Third World countries are vital export markets for the United States. There is no way that they can finance imports from the United States — except by exports *to* the United States.

The failure to protect American jobs, however, leads to rising unemployment in the United States and to a steady decline in the wages of those who keep their jobs. This intensifies the price pressure on those who produce consumer goods, because consumers have less money to spend. And this, in turn, strengthens the competitive advantage of low-wage manufacturing countries and thereby accelerates the flight of jobs to off-shore sites.

In the decades since the war, America's role as the principal support of the world banking system turned from a strength to a weakness in the natural course of events. One vital key to American strength after 1945 was the supremacy of the dollar. The dollar was backed not only, or even primarily, by that enormous and glittering hoard in Fort Knox, but also by the huge productive power of the American economy. The world's desperate need for American products led to an unbounded demand for the dollars with which those goods could be purchased. The dollar became an official reserve currency; other countries backed their own currencies with dollars as well as with gold. In the end, this made American financial policy a hostage to foreign governments. Dollar surpluses began to accumulate in Europe, exerting a downward pressure on the dollar's value. To defend the dollar, America was forced to deploy its gold reserves, and as this trend continued, speculative pressures weakened the greenback even more. Nixon was forced to take the dollar off the international gold standard, devalue it, and allow exchange rates to float.

The results of the devaluation of the dollar were numerous and mostly bad for the American economy. While reduced dollar values made exports from America a better buy, the devaluation seriously weakened the ability of the United States to control the other Western economies. It strengthened foreign banks and assisted the resurgence of European capital markets and export capital. The increase in the price of imports, especially of oil, helped fuel the inflation that ravaged the American economy during the 1970s.

Meanwhile, the dollar remained a principal currency for international settlements. Oil prices particularly were indexed in dollars, and the major oil producers demanded payment in dollars. This cushioned the impact of the oil shock on the United States and kept the Europeans and the Japanese tied to the American economy to a certain extent, but it also required a disproportionately large role for American banks in recycling the dollar surpluses of the OPEC countries in their glory days. Third World countries borrowed billions to pay for their fuel. The dollars came from OPEC countries looking for a return on their money. In the short term, there were fat commissions and healthy profits for banks willing to make these loans; the long-term result was a critical overextension of the banking system into dubious loans.

In summary, the predominance of the American economy after the war led to the acceptance of the dollar as a reserve world currency. As overseas dollar holdings increased, the American government lost control over the value and the flow of dollars. The usurious interest rates of the late 1970s and early 1980s were in part required to reassert American monetary control over the dollar supply. Because the returns on dollar-denominated investments were almost insanely attractive, the dollar once again became a strong currency, but at the cost of greater foreign ownership of American assets, the elimination of thousands of American small businesses, and a dangerous overexposure of the banks.

None of these problems peaked during the Nixon-Kissinger era, but all of them made themselves felt. Between 1949 and 1975, West Germany's industrial production rose by more than 500 percent, France's production by 400 percent, and even Britain doubled its output of industrial goods.[2] Japan grew even faster, accompanied by the other Pacific Rim producers — Taiwan, Hong Kong, South Korea, and Singapore. Clearly, the U.S. world role in 1975 could not be what it had been in 1945 or even 1965; self-confident allies and trading partners were unwilling to follow Washington's lead. It was against this backdrop that Nixon and Kissinger attempted to extricate the United States from Vietnam on favorable terms and to construct what both hoped would be a durable foundation for peace.

THE REAL WORLD

Six years after Nixon left office, he published what he called a *cri de coeur*, an appeal to the leadership elite of the United States — the media, big business, and the leading intelligentsia. This elite, he said, "sets the limits of the possible" for elected officials and bears the primary responsibility for the nation's future. With a coldly realistic sense of America's social stratification, Nixon reminded this elite of America's immediate problem: "While the common man fights America's wars, the intellectual elite sets its agenda."[3]

Evidently, if the common man is to go on fighting the nation's wars, the power elite must stop giving him mixed signals. The media must stop derogating the nation's elected officials; big business must stop trying to appease liberal critics, and the intelligentsia must remember their responsibility to the social order.

Nixon sought to recall the power elite to its duty by reviewing the rise of the American Empire and the nature of its challenges. The United States had inherited Britain's role as the world's great maritime power, and with that role came the necessity of maintaining the balance of power against the strongest land power in Eurasia. The United States had to oppose the Soviet Union for the same reasons that Marlborough fought Louis XIV.

The United States had a more difficult assignment than Britain did, Nixon argued, and it was less prepared for global responsibilities than the once-sceptered isle. While Britain operated in a multipolar world, in which there were many Great Powers to play off against her leading rival, the United States faced the Soviet Union without allies of equal rank. Moreover, in Soviet communism the rulers of the Kremlin had found an ideology far more persuasive than tsarist orthodoxy. New commissar was but old tsar writ large for Nixon; Brezhnev's predecessors were Catherine, Peter, and Ivan, not Saint-Simon and Karl Marx.

In attempting to understand Russian behavior, Nixon returned to the Middle Ages and found that when Britain was embarking on the path that led from Magna Carta to the Reform Bill of 1832, Russia had already begun to sink beneath the Asiatic scourges of ruin and tyranny. The Mongol invasions left a deep imprint on the Russians; they became xenophobes and were habituated to slavery. Succeeding years of tsarist brutality, emphasized by the knout, atrophied the Russians' sense of personal liberty. Geographic isolation and their long fight in defense of their religion against the Muslims to the south and the Mongols to the east endowed the Russians with a strong sense of national mission. Poland is not the only Slavic country that thinks of itself as the Christ among nations.

Noticeable throughout Russian history has been a slow and steady, glacierlike slide from the heartland to the south, east, and west. Generations of tsars intrigued and schemed to take Constantinople; in the east Russian settlers traversed Siberia on the road to California; to the west they slowly and systematically nibbled at Poland and the Baltic littoral.

Marxism-Leninism, in Nixon's view, merely changed the mask under which Russia pursued its age-old ambitions. Nixon felt that communism, as an ideology, is suited to the Russian character: xenophobic, messianic, by turns cruel and fawning. He believed that Stalin's foreign and domestic policies merely carried forward Russia's traditional policies: brutal repression at home, opportunistic conquest on the frontiers.

The Soviet Union threat for Nixon did not mean a swift military strike through Central Europe. The threat was more subtle, harder to deal with, and more serious. Nixon believed that the Russians foment and support agitation in the Third World with the ultimate aim of cutting off the West from the natural resources on which its prosperity depends. He quoted from an exchange said to have occurred between Brezhnev and the president of Somalia, in which Brezhnev was reported as saying:

> Our aim is to gain control of the two great treasure houses on which the West depends — the energy treasure house of the Persian Gulf and the mineral treasure house of Central and Southern Africa.[4]

To accomplish their goal, wrote Nixon, the Soviets exacerbate local problems and rivalries, usually without regard for ideology or morals: "When they go to take a bite out of the world, the Soviets are not fussy eaters."[5] In order to advance their interests they will switch sides at a moment's notice, as they did with Somalia and Ethiopia.

Nixon's characterizations of the Soviet Union are sometimes odd but always vivid. He variously compared it to a lion stalking its prey, an insidiously subtle chess master, and the "chairman of the rush committee" for the international fraternity of terrorists.[6]

Geography itself becomes charged with emotion where the Soviets are concerned. Iran's oil treasures are "lying provocatively exposed to lustful Russian eyes," and the Horn of Africa is a "claw" whose pincers threaten the innocent Arabian peninsula.[7]

The greatest problem for the United States, Nixon contended, was the naïveté of both the power elite and the cannon fodder among the population. He argued that this innocence had its genesis during the nineteenth century, when a long isolation from the sordid world of European power politics convinced Americans that it was their moral purity that kept them aloof from the struggles of the Old World. In reality, wrote Nixon, it was the British navy that insulated the New World from the Old, and the end of British power left the United States ill prepared politically to exercise its new responsibilities. Nixon wrote longingly of the élan and the cohesion of the old British ruling class, and wished that our American power elite was more like it.

The weak and divided American elite failed the nation during his term of office, Nixon charged. The Indochinese War was lost in the jungles of Washington, not the jungles of Asia. Big business, the media, the directors of major foundations. . . . Except for big labor, all the national elites failed in their responsibilities. America was stabbed in the back.

Enough, wrote Nixon, of the squeamishness of a Robert McNamara, and the senile innocence of our Establishmentarian Nestors. We must become as ruthless, as duplicitous, and even as brutal as our opposition. Will power is the key to success in foreign affairs. If we dare, we can do; if we flinch, we shall fail. These were the sentiments that Nixon brought to the task of guiding the foreign policy of the United States.[8]

Nixon and Kissinger agreed that what the nation required was a consistent, bipartisan (if possible) view of the national interest. Such a view necessarily involved the maintenance of the balance of power against the efforts of the Soviet Union. Opening relations with China was a major step in this direction. From then on, the Soviets could never rule out the possibility of Sino-American cooperation.

Strengthening ties with non-European allies was another important element in the Nixon strategy. Candidates for such strengthened ties were the settler states — Israel and South Africa — and regional strongmen like Ferdinand Marcos, the shah, and South Vietnam's President Nguyen Van Thieu.

The Nixon program raised hackles on the left and the right. The right was flabbergasted by Nixon's betrayal of Taiwan. The left objected to the ties with dictators around the world. The tilt toward Pakistan during the secession of Bangladesh found the United States siding with a military regime that had massacred civilians by the hundreds of thousands and created approximately ten million refugees. But India, though the most stable democracy in the Third World, is a long-standing partner of the Soviet Union, and Pakistan is a client of the United States.

Nixon also initiated the policy of détente, best defined as the regulation of the competition between the United States and the Soviet Union. Nixon's hope was that both countries would recognize certain basic realities about their relationship, and that this mutual recognition would itself act to limit the competition. The United States recognized, for the first time, that the USSR had reached parity as a Great Power and carried out arms negotiations on the premise that both sides were entitled to equal amounts of strategic weaponry. The United States accepted the post–1945 boundaries in Europe, formally acknowledging the new boundaries of Poland and the Soviet Union.

Nixon was far from believing that the lustful and avaricious Soviet bear had become a lamb. *Détente*, an understanding reached among adversaries, differs from *entente*, an understanding among friends. Nevertheless, he felt that the recognition of facts by both sides and the definition of areas of mutual interest would lead to a relaxation of world tensions.

Détente required a strong United States. The understanding behind détente rested on the existing balance of forces in the world; if that balance were to change, relationships between the United States and the USSR would also have to change to reflect the new conditions. The result put Nixon in a political quandary. In order to relax tensions, he needed a strong foreign policy. Détente and his visits to Peking and Moscow angered conservatives; those who supported détente generally thought that its existence meant an end to the Cold War. Nixon adopted détente as a strategy for the Cold War, but there were many who hailed it or feared it in the belief that it was a substitution for the Cold War. It was a distinction Nixon was never able to communicate.

Crucial to Nixon's strategy of détente was what he called the "credibility" of the United States. The United States had security agreements with approximately fifty countries. Détente would take one shape if the United States had the means and the will to enforce these agreements and to protect its clients and its allies. If domestic political constraints blocked the United States from action, then these guarantees were worth virtually nothing — and détente was a collection of pious and insincere phrases.

The test case for American credibility in the Nixon era was Vietnam.

✑ 6 ✑

THE INDOCHINESE WAR

I N 1969, Richard Nixon inherited an unpopular war in Indochina. Five hundred thousand American soldiers were locked in an apparently interminable struggle with Vietnamese communist forces armed and supplied by China and the Soviet Union. Progress at the negotiating table and on the battlefield was urgently needed. Although American planners believed that the Viet Cong — the communist guerrilla army made up of rebellious South Vietnamese — had been smashed, its place on the battlefield had been taken by regular units of North Vietnam's army. Opposition to the war in the United States was vocal, bitter, and widespread. It was generally credited with forcing Lyndon Johnson to abandon the race for the presidency in 1968 and for blocking the election of his vice-president, Hubert Humphrey. The passions that had wrecked one administration seemed perfectly capable of breaking another; Nixon knew from his first day in office that his principal task was to end the American involvement in the war by any honorable means.

Unfortunately for Nixon, the Vietnamese understood the situation as well as he did. Well aware that time was on their side, the North Vietnamese were able to play a waiting game, negotiating with excruciating slowness and watching as Americans grew less and less willing to sustain the war, even by indirect means.

Yet knowing this, Nixon was unable simply to withdraw American forces. An admission of defeat on such a vast scale would remove any Soviet incentive to negotiate a détente acceptable to the United States. Revolutionary movements around the world would take heart from the victory, and nervous American clients would re-examine their options. The effect on the Pacific Rim — where Indonesia had only recently slaughtered hundreds of thousands of communists, suspected communists, and other malcontents, and where Thailand, the Philippines, and Burma all faced persistent communist insurrections — could not be predicted. The fall of Vietnam might have profound consequences as well in Japan, a country that placed all its confidence in security guarantees of the American government. There was the possibility that success in Vietnam would encourage the Korean communists to move again in the south. With forty thousand American troops permanently stationed in Korea, the United States might retreat from Vietnam only to find that it had exchanged one land war in Asia for another.

There was another factor in Nixon's thinking. Nuclear deterrence rests ultimately on a threat that may or may not be a bluff. If the Soviets believed that America's threat to retaliate was a bluff, they might have been tempted to undertake risky adventures. Every president, Nixon believed, undergoes a time of testing by the Kremlin. The commonly cited example is John Kennedy. The young president's failure to impress Nikita Khrushchev at the Vienna summit conference encouraged Khrushchev to order the construction of the missile bases in Cuba — a decision that brought the world closer to the nuclear abyss than at any time before or, so far, since. Nixon was not unnaturally concerned that a display of weakness, or even indecision, on his part in Vietnam would have far-reaching and potentially catastrophic consequences. It is easy to criticize this view, but the reader should reflect that there is no truly sane way to approach the subject of MAD, mutual assured destruction, and that at least some of Nixon's concerns may have been well founded.

If there had really been a national commitment to fight on in Vietnam, Nixon's task would have been simpler. North Vietnam, in the face of a genuine determination on the part of the United States, might have made an agreement earlier and adhered to it more closely, and the United States might have been prepared to enforce it. As it was, there was no American resolve to carry the war to a successful conclusion. Morale in the armed forces sank to ominous levels; drug use, indiscipline, and racial conflict spread through army units not only in Vietnam, but in Europe as well, where the NATO allies observed the condition of the U.S. Army and drew their own conclusions about its military potential.

Given the absence of an American commitment to fight to the finish, North Vietnam's problems were radically simplified. Convinced that the Thieu government could not survive unless it was propped up by outside forces, North Vietnam had only to avoid defeat to ensure ultimate victory. This was bad enough in itself for American policymakers; worse, the lesson was one not to be lost on other Third World insurgencies. The people of Angola and Mozambique took note, as did the guerrillas in the bush fighting Ian Smith's regime in what would soon become Zimbabwe. If, as Nixon believed, the Soviet Union was engaged in a vast flanking attack on capitalism through its "treasure houses" in the

Third World, it had no reason to doubt its ultimate success. From Rangoon to Rio, the Third World was becoming a tinderbox, needing only a spark here or there to burst into flame. The defeat of a guerrilla army in Indochina might make other insurgencies more vulnerable later and would at least convince the American people that such contests were winnable.

But desirable as a national commitment to victory in Vietnam would have been for Nixon, there was no such commitment. Had there been, Nixon would not have been in the White House, and Lyndon Johnson would never have been driven from office. In these circumstances, Nixon's one serious strategy was to buy time for South Vietnam by slowly reducing the American presence; diplomatically and politically, he had no choices other than unilateral withdrawal or the pursuit of a policy based on bluff — or, less politely, systematic deceit.

He had to convince the North Vietnamese, against all probability, that the United States was prepared to carry military action in Indochina into the indefinite future to protect its interests and those of its clients. Nixon fought a delaying action against congressional efforts to end the war once and for all. He could win congressional funding for the war only by exaggerating the chances for agreement and by playing down the commitment necessary to implement any agreement that might be reached. Such a commitment implied that the United States would return in force to Indochina to attack anyone who violated the treaty that ended the war.

There was little likelihood that Congress would support an agreement of this sort, so Nixon found himself having to lie to the South Vietnamese, too, inducing them to believe in an American commitment to their future that simply did not exist.

THE OPPOSITION TO THE WAR

The Indochinese War was not the first war to divide American society. In the Revolution and the Civil War, Americans fought in both armies. New England's leaders debated secession during the War of 1812. Thoreau, John Quincy Adams, and Abraham Lincoln denounced the Mexican War as an immoral aggression. The attack on the Philippines after Spain's capitulation in the Spanish-American War gave rise to fierce protests around the country and inspired Mark Twain to indite some of his bitterest prose. Yet in none of these conflicts did mass opposition reach the pitch or have the impact on the outcome of the war that it did in the

Nixon years. Here is Kissinger on the reaction to the invasion of Cambodia, an act he insists "was *not* a moral issue."

> Some two hundred and fifty State Department employees, including fifty Foreign Service Officers, signed a statement objecting to Administration policy. The ill-concealed disagreement of Cabinet members showed that the Executive Branch was nearly as divided as the country. . . . A group of employees seized the Peace Corps building and flew a Viet Cong flag from it.[1]

This opposition had many sources. There were a few, a very few, convinced supporters of the communist regime in North Vietnam. There were blacks who echoed Muhammad Ali's sentiments: "I ain't got no quarrel with no Viet Cong." Martin Luther King, Jr., the only American born in this century whose birthday has become a national holiday, lent his immense moral authority and his oratorical gifts to the antiwar, antidraft movement. Millions of young men had career plans that emphatically did not include dodging enemy fire in the snake-infested jungles of Indochina. Echoes of earlier isolationism were heard across the country. Sections of the nation that had traditionally opposed foreign entanglements, especially the Midwest, returned to their old stance and elected fierce antiwar partisans to the House and the Senate. Operating without a sophisticated understanding of international affairs, and convinced that for America to be great it was necessary only for her to be good, idealists of every description came to oppose the war.

Worse, from Nixon's point of view, the Establishment itself concluded that the war was lost. One by one the "onlie true begetters" of the war — the Democratic "wise men" of the last two decades — stepped forward and said, "We goofed." Men like Daniel Ellsberg, with long-standing ties to the policymaking community, emerged as determined dissidents. For most of these men, Kissinger was right. Cambodia, even Vietnam itself, "was *not* a moral issue." Few of them reflected at any length on the morality of fomenting civil war in another country. For the elite, those who, as Nixon says in his book, "set the limits of the possible for Presidents and Congress," the cost-benefit ratio had changed, and Vietnam was no longer a viable venture. The mounting economic and, more important, the social cost of the war no longer served any proportionate, rational end. It was time to take a write-off on Indochina.

It was easier for these men to turn against Nixon's war than Johnson's. A sense of their own responsibility to Johnson — a fitting sense, as it was on their advice that he had committed troops to the conflict — stopped their mouths while he was in power; but, in Kissinger's words, "once out of office the Democratic Party found it easy and tempting to unite in opposition to a Republican President on the issue of Vietnam."[2] That the Republican president in question happened to be Nixon made the transition easier still. Nixon had begun his career as a brash Sun Belt outsider, attacking the eastern Establishment for its pusillanimity and its sympathy for communism. He made his name by pursuing the case of Alger Hiss, a protégé of the eastern Establishment who was accused of passing secrets to communist agents. Nixon's inflammatory rhetoric during the McCarthy era, in the early 1950s, had also deeply angered the foreign policy Establishment, especially his attacks on the State Department, which he called "Dean Acheson's cowardly college of communist appeasement."[3] In vain did Nixon and Kissinger plead that it was the Establishment "whose maxims had produced the war." In vain did Nixon present himself as a "new" Nixon, no longer the upstart and outsider on the prowl for striped-pants pinkos in the corridors of power.

In fact, the Nixon-Kissinger claim to represent a continuation of the Truman-Marshall-Acheson policy that had created NATO and the Marshall Plan was somewhat disingenuous. It was true that in opening a door to Red China, Nixon was tacitly conceding that he and the Republican know-nothings of the early 1950s had been wrong to purge the China hands in the State Department, wrong to press for the "unleashing" of Chiang Kai-shek, wrong to assume that the triumph of Mao was a triumph for Moscow, wrong even to support MacArthur's policy of provocation in Korea. As Nixon later acknowledged, Secretary of State John Foster Dulles was wrong to refuse to shake Chou En-lai's hand in Geneva. In effect, Nixon was admitting that the Republican anticommunism of the Eisenhower era had been too moralistic, not responsive enough to the ambiguities and opportunities of real life. What Nixon would not, perhaps could not, acknowledge was the implication that all the issues around which he built his entrance into public life were a tissue of misunderstandings exaggerated by demagogues — that, in effect, Eisenhower should have had the courage to insist on a more principled and intelligent running mate in 1952, and that in allowing the nomination of Nixon, the general had appeased a misguided political faction whose impact on public life was almost wholly negative and destructive.

Although Nixon claimed, and perhaps believed, that his years of participation in public life had broadened his perspectives, beneath the new dedication to supple diplomacy lay a deep, apparently ineradicable substratum of naïveté. Having decided to play a Machiavellian game, Nixon could not shake his belief that, at some level, relations between states are governed by rules of conduct. He became in a sense the Woodrow Wilson of evil, and the moral ideas he brought to world leadership were more appropriate to the leadership of a Boy Scout troop than to the likes of Thieu, Mobutu, Marcos, Duvalier, and the shah.

Thus, to gain the respect of these figures, it was first necessary for the scoutmaster to earn their trust by keeping his word. Boys will not tolerate a scoutmaster who fails to do what he has promised. The scoutmaster must show himself to be firm yet fair, slow to anger but quick to defend his charges. The scoutmaster understands that his charges are young and immature, and he tailors his expectations of the boys to their actual capacity.

Nixon was no more able to gauge the depths of depravity of a Marcos or a Thieu than a do-gooding liberal juvenile judge can plumb the cynicism of the young hood before him. That the delinquent and the dictator take a savage joy in stealing is the one thing that neither the liberal judge nor the pseudocynical president can quite comprehend. In private meetings Marcos might lean forward and tell Nixon, with tears in his eyes, how much he valued the Judeo-Christian ethic and loved the American system. Imelda might sing "God Bless America," and both would tell him of the importance of a world anticommunist front. Nixon was as helpless in meetings of this kind as Neville Chamberlain at Munich or as Wilson at Versailles. Nixon is a sincere anticommunist; his passion burns with a gemlike flame; he could not believe that his negotiating partners were unmoved by considerations that to him were so important and immediate. Like him, they sometimes did immoral and ugly things, but, also like him, it was only because the unpleasant realities of life forced them to make concessions. He could not believe that a noncommunist head of state could be a basically immoral person who just happened to be smart enough to understand that the international communist menace was good for practically unlimited American Aid. The Truman-era diplomats understood this and concluded that Chiang's government was a rat hole into which infinite sums could be poured; it was the innocent trustfulness of the right that converted this traditionally unscrupulous warlord into a symbol of freedom.

Petty tyrants, particularly those dependent on foreign support, generally have a sharply bounded range of concerns: they want to stay in power as long as possible, they want to make as much money as they can while power lasts, and, when the game is played out, they want to escape with as much of it as they can carry off. Their enormous and world-weary cynicism makes it impossible for them to take seriously the progress of something as abstract as the world communist movement;

in any case, they see it as only one of many potential threats to their power. The most immediate threats to their power have nothing to do with bandit armies blowing up radio transmitters in the boondocks; the dictators are worried about the colonels in the air force barracks on the outskirts of the capital. A reasonably sized communist insurgency in the outlying provinces is not so bad; the Americans will spend billions on such things, much of which any ruler with a gram of good sense can divert to Switzerland. The rest goes for new warplanes and international junkets for the air force colonels. The only communist threat that could seriously energize people of this type would be a Red Army assault on the Bank of Geneva, and even then, if the price was right, one of them could be found to guide the Soviet tanks to the vault.

It was the recognition that South Vietnam was another kleptocracy, a state governed by an elite dedicated solely to plunder, that gradually drove even the most hawkish of the old Democrats to look for ways out. They saw taking shape in Vietnam the humiliation they had avoided in China — the inevitable defeat of a power the United States had backed with armed force — and they began to cast about for alternatives. In their minds, the new Nixon of 1972 was the same old Nixon who had called Acheson a cowardly appeaser in 1952. Ideologically rigid, strategically naïve, and tactically unscrupulous, Nixon still embodied the xenophobic moralism that, in the opinion of the Democratic foreign policy community, represented the worst side of the American character. Vietnam *and* Nixon were expendable in the minds of the Establishment, and they were not sorry to see Nixon destroy himself for the sake of a war that the Democrats had started.

The movement to end the war, then, drew its strength from popular opposition and a growing Establishment consensus. These upper and nether millstones between them slowly ground the administration to pulp. Under fire and under pressure, engaged simultaneously in deceit on all fronts, the Nixon administration slowly disintegrated.

THE COLLAPSE OF THE ADMINISTRATION

A policy dependent on bluffing requires confidentiality above all. "No doubt," admits Kissinger, "there was an element of braggadocio in our pronouncements. But if the bluff did not work, what then was to be our policy?"[4] No one has yet invented the neutron press release, one that addresses itself to the enemy but leaves one's friends unaffected. Faced with the difficulty of convincing the American people that it was winding down the war while convincing North and South Vietnam that America would soldier on as long as it had to, the administration was forced to resort to news management on an unprecedented scale. The "secret bombing of Cambodia" was a case in point. The enemy could not but notice that he was being bombed. The secret bombing was a secret from political opponents, not from military foes.

Normally in wartime, democracies limit the exercise of constitutional rights. This limitation is tolerable because the population as a whole supports the war effort. The press does not have to be bludgeoned into submission; it leaps to comply. When Ronald Reagan consoled Nixon with the thought that CBS might have been tried for treason in World War II if it had acted as it had during the Indochinese War,[5] it was an indication of the difference between that war and previous conflicts.

Unable to curb liberty with the consent of the people, Nixon was driven to other methods. The Ellsberg case seems to have been a catalyst in his thinking. The so-called Pentagon Papers, classified documents concerning the early stages of the war, were copied illegally by Ellsberg and made available to the *New York Times,* the *Washington Post,* and the *Boston Globe.* Their publication solidified opposition to the war by pointing out the contrast between the rationales offered for public consumption and the ones that carried actual weight with policymakers, and by documenting the conscious deceit that surrounded every stage of American policy in Vietnam from the early 1950s.

The Pentagon Papers were not a specific problem for Nixon; he had had little to do with the crucial decisions of the early 1960s. But since Nixon had assumed the burden of the war, the demonstration that the government had lied about its origin and roots weakened his ability to fight it. When Ellsberg became a hero, Nixon had problems. He felt like the long-suffering David in Dryden's *Absalom and Achitophel,* with the media cast in the role of Shimei.

> When two or three were gather'd to declaim
> Against the Monarch of *Jerusalem*
> *Shimei* was always in the midst of them. . . .
> If any durst his Factious Friends accuse,
> He pact a jury of dissenting *Jews:*
> Whose fellow-feeling, in the godly cause
> Would free the suff'ring Saint from Humane Laws.
> For Laws are only made to Punish those
> Who serve the King, and to protect his Foes.[6]

The entire foreign policy apparatus of the government was riddled with opponents of the war. On any morning Nixon could wake up and discover the inner workings of his own administration headlined in the newspapers for the interested readers of Washington, Moscow, and Hanoi. Kissinger's National Security Council staff leaked like a colander; dovish congressional staffers poked each other in the ribs as they pawed through intelligence material. Even the CIA was unreliable. According to Kissinger, its analysts were "liberals [who] usually erred on the side of the interpretation fashionable in the Washington Establishment."[7] When J. Edgar Hoover gave signs of using knowledge of improper wiretaps to blackmail Nixon into keeping him in office, there was really no choice but to create a White House–based extralegal investigative body. By the time of the Watergate burglary, the White House was involved in so many illegal and quasi-legal operations that it was impossible for Nixon to make a clean breast of his activities.

There was, as Nixon correctly tried to argue, nothing new about Watergate. The Keystone Cops of the Cuban diaspora had been around since 1961, and they had never been hobbled by an excessive reverence for the laws of the country that gave them asylum. Wiretaps and tape-recorded presidential conversations had been heard of before. No one remotely familiar with the careers of Lyndon Johnson or John Kennedy could suppose that Nixon was the first president to consider the obstruction of justice a patriotic responsibility.

Unlike Johnson, Nixon seems not to have engaged in these activities to further petty personal or even partisan ends. Unlike Kennedy, who grew up in a milieu in which bootlegging and political corruption were laws of nature that superseded any edicts of mere legislatures, and "civics" was a subject for suckers, Nixon seems to have believed that only the overriding national interest justified his indifference to the nation's laws. He employed illegal methods as tools of state, hoping to erect his "generation of peace" on a foundation of criminal acts. Even the scale of deceit used by Nixon was less than that of Roosevelt in 1940 or Johnson in 1964, both of whom conducted explicit peace campaigns while secretly preparing for war.

Since 1917, when America first became a major player in world politics, foreign policy has been formulated, and often carried out, behind the scenes. A smoke screen of policy rationales has been laid down for public consumption: Truth, Justice, and the American Way. But the serious players have always known that the game was much more complex. To quote again from the Kissinger memoirs:

> Our entry into World War One was the inevitable result of our geopolitical interest in maintaining freedom of the seas and preventing Europe's domination by a hostile power. But true to our tradition, we chose to interpret our participation in legal and idealistic terms.[8]

Until the Indochinese War, popular ignorance about the basis of American foreign policy was, if anything, an asset to the conduct of that policy. Major wars were presented as crusades forced on a pacific United States. Anyone saying what Kissinger said about World War I while the war was in progress would have been locked up if not lynched — particularly if the speaker had been a German-Jewish immigrant and a Harvard professor, to boot. During World War I Kissinger himself would have said nothing of the kind; he would have joined in the effort to present the war as a moral crusade — as, indeed, he did during the Indochinese War and as he continues to do with respect to the situation in Central America.

Indochina, however, revealed a flaw in the system. What Washington hoped would be a minor police operation grew into a full-scale war. With 500,000 troops involved, the conflict was too big to ignore, but no convincing justification for the involvement could be advanced that did not admit to a cynicism the American people were not prepared to encounter in their government officials. The rational calculations that led Nixon — and, for much of the period, the entire foreign policy apparatus minus a few dissenters — to conclude that Vietnam was an essential security concern of the United States were based on sober assessments of national interest and the traditional balance-of-power diplomacy. Suntzu and Machiavelli would have had no problem understanding the policy and its necessity from that point of view.

But for generations Americans had believed, and been trained to believe, that their country "stood for something" other than naked self-interest in world affairs. Patriotic and even chauvinistic feeling was based on idealistic misconceptions about American history. To have openly acknowledged the interest-based policies that led to the war would have presented a logical, cogent reason for involvement — at the cost of shattering popular illusions and public faith in the government. The public would not have sacrificed its idealism so easily; the spirit of Woodrow Wilson has not yet entirely disappeared. An open admission by the government that the United States was the center of a world empire (as opposed to being the leader of a coalition of free countries fighting for peace, democracy, and the right of neutral Belgian nuns not to be raped, as alleged in World War I) would have put powerful new weapons in the hands of the antiwar movement. The American people were far more likely to believe that their country used to be pacific and idealistic, until the present gang of cynical thugs hijacked the government, than to accept such a disclosure.

Rather than endure the trauma, the Establishment was prepared to sacrifice both Nixon and Indochina. In Georgia, a former peanut farmer decided that there was room on the national stage for a politician dedicated to the "restoration" of the traditional American idealism in world affairs — an idealism so warmly admired by all the peoples of the hemisphere, from the Sioux to the Panamanians.

Meanwhile, Kissinger lied gamely while the administration collapsed around his ears. In 1972–1973 he pressured the South Vietnamese to accept terms he felt meant their eventual isolation and defeat:

> The South Vietnamese . . . simply did not feel ready to confront Hanoi without our direct involvement. Their nightmare was not this or that clause but the fear of being left alone. For Saigon's leaders a cease-fire meant the departure of our remaining forces; they could not believe that Hanoi would abandon its implacable quest for the domination of Indochina. . . . And they were not wrong. . . . It was not Thieu's fault that we had simply come to the end of our road.[9]

It was George McGovern who had the last word on the Indochinese War. "Saying America will leave Vietnam if we can do it with honor," he said in the course of the 1972 campaign, "is like a prostitute offering to quit — if she can do it as a virgin." In August 1974, a helicopter flew Nixon out of the White House and into retirement. Less than a year later, another helicopter made the last trip from Saigon.

The verdict of history on the Nixon-Kissinger policies is not yet in. The unprecedented national loathing that drove Nixon from office has yielded to a vague feeling that he was harshly, if not unjustly, treated. The passions connected with the Indochinese War, newly inflamed by the prospect of conflict in Central America, remain alive, and the wounds of Vietnam are still open.

We cannot say how future generations will look on Richard Nixon — perhaps he will seem like Richard III, commonly regarded as an egregious blackguard, staunchly defended by a few. But this much is certain: neither he nor Kissinger can complain of injustice if, after they sacrificed everything on the altar of pragmatism, history casts a cold light on their ignominious defeat. It is all very well for them to argue from the fringes of public life that their policies would have succeeded had they not been foiled by shortsighted opponents, but history will retort that the careful calculation of the strength of the opposition is the responsibility of all statesmen, and most clearly of those who acknowledge no law but success.

THE MARKET IN CRISIS

ARRY WILLS called Nixon "the last liberal," but he did not mean
it as a compliment. Wills meant that Nixon stood for the ideology
of the free market — the economic market, the marketplace of
ideas, and the political market. That a man like Nixon should serve as
its standard bearer was, to Wills, a sign of liberalism's bankruptcy by
1968.

Wills's basic criticism of the market ideology is that the market does
not work. In wartime, when the government needs economic production
to be as efficient as possible, the free market is jettisoned for a planned
economy. If the market were really the best way to organize production,
Wills argues, then wartime would presumably be when government
should deregulate in order to mobilize for the national emergency.

Defenders of the free market theory argue that the American economy
grew because of its free enterprise system. Wills makes the counterar-
gument that government and business were in close partnership during
the nineteenth century and that this partnership had as much to do with
economic development as the market. The transcontinental railroads are
a case in point. Without massive government land grants, the railroads
could not have been built.

In general, the more important an industry, the more heavily regulated
it becomes, and this is true not only in the United States, but in all the
advanced countries. No serious person would argue that pharmaceutical
companies should be left to the market. In the long run, perhaps, only
the companies whose products were unadulterated and thoroughly tested
would survive; before then, however, millions might suffer.

What the free market produces when left to itself is a monopoly or an
oligopoly that functions in much the same way. In politics it led to the
oligopoly of the Republican and Democratic parties, an oligopoly the
parties were not slow to exploit by stacking the laws against third-party
contenders. In business the market produced the multinational corpo-

rations; in the realm of ideas it produces the academic orthodoxies that reign on university campuses and the conventional wisdoms that reign beyond them.

Sophisticated apologists for marketplace theory have developed methods for controlling, if not explaining, the cases where Adam Smith's invisible hand fails to order things properly. To counter monopoly, regulatory and antitrust legislation was developed. The government launched programs to subsidize small businesses that might otherwise have been forced out of the market entirely. The collapse of the family farm was temporarily slowed by an enormous variety of subsidies, price supports, credit guarantees, and other devices. We have seen that government also stepped in to regulate the most persistent feature of the free market economy — the periodic boom-and-bust cycle. Market purists might argue in the long run that this cycle is the inevitable method for shaking inflation out of the economy and creating permanent prosperity — but people don't eat, pay rent, or educate their children in the long run.

The result of the waves of reform was the creation of a jerrybuilt society, one in which government and private enterprise often work at cross purposes while the government often works at cross purposes with itself. With one hand society tries to strengthen market forces, to provide "incentives," and with the other it takes them away. It keeps food prices high with subsidies, and tries to lower them with anti-inflationary measures.

Moreover, as Wills points out, a chasm opens up between the American dream of the self-made man, the lone entrepreneur, and the reality of the harassed small businessman or farmer. The small businessman generally exists in the nooks and crannies of the economy, where the crumbs are too small for big business to make the effort to gather them, or where government regulations or subsidies allow small business to survive. It is inconsistent, to say the least, for such people to denounce the hand that feeds them, but market ideology remains deeply embedded. The awareness that they depend on government robs the small businessmen of much of the savor of their achievements. Believing that individual achievement gives life meaning, they find that achievement today cannot help being communal. The result is a frustrated people, one tempted to lash out, but with no clear idea in which direction to strike.

BEYOND THE LAST LIBERAL

Wills's *Nixon Agonistes,* published in 1969, remains a valuable book, filled with uncanny insight into the Nixon era, even though it was written before the Watergate scandal. Its treatment of the failure of American ideas, politics, and economics to meet the needs of the American people is outstanding. But the real challenge to the ideology of the liberal market came from outside the United States and only gradually made its real weight felt. This challenge was posed not by disgruntled small businessmen, radical students, angry blacks, or any other domestic interest; the challenge came from the Third World, and it was not a criticism of the outcomes of the liberal market but an assault on its preconditions.

The Wealth of Nations was published in 1776; in it, Adam Smith traced the hidden sources of national prosperity. The near-universal human propensity "to truck, to barter, and to trade" turned out to be the road to national wealth. Smith and his school believed that government should eliminate the regulations that remained from the medieval and mercantilist eras and confine itself to the role of an umpire, enforcing laws of contract and protecting the rights of private property.

What market theory never addressed was the question of why some found themselves (in, say, 1776) with money to invest while others had nothing to sell but their skins and their labor. One man started a sugar plantation in the West Indies while another worked in a Lancashire coal mine. Why? Was it the market?

Revolutionary America gave one answer to this question. Europe, the home of a decadent and corrupt aristocracy, was also the home of special privilege and oppression. There it might be true that the market could never be free, because most men were born poor and were held back by the laws. In America, on the other hand, there was enough opportunity and enough land for every person to rise as high as his talents and industry could take him.

That is, if he was a he.

And if he was white.

If Smith's market theory gave insufficient weight to the question of aristocratic and commercial privilege, the American variation on it ignored the importation of slaves and the theft of the land itself. In neither the Old World nor the New did the market descend shiny and spotless from Heaven like the New Jerusalem. It emerged in both places from the mud and the muck of human history, and like the rest of that history it was shaped as much by force as by anything else.

For nearly two hundred years this remained a purely theoretical objection as far as most Americans were concerned. In those two hundred years whites fanned out across the world in such a way that the world's riches flowed to Europe and the United States. When the other peoples of the earth resisted, and they did, they were beaten down by sheer force of arms. There is no need to recapitulate here the long history of European conquest and compulsion in the Third World. The point is that only recently were the non-Europeans able to do anything about it.

The Third World challenge to the market system took two forms. In Indochina the Vietnamese demonstrated that determined resistance could drive out even the greatest of the white Western powers. OPEC showed something else: the terms of trade between the First and Third Worlds could, under some conditions, be changed. For years the West benefited from cheap oil. Suddenly, OPEC showed that there was nothing sacred or eternal about this relationship. The world supply of oil had not changed dramatically between 1970 and 1975, nor had demand. But the price of oil skyrocketed.

There was nothing effective that the Nixon administration could do about these challenges to the basic world order. It was unable to put down Vietnamese resistance, unable to seize the oil fields, and unable to break the OPEC cartel. The balance of forces in the world had shifted decisively against the United States and the coalition it headed. The Third World was no longer in the position of having to appeal to American charity and forbearance; some of its members had learned to put their requests across as demands that had to be met. There is no need to romanticize this process; neither the Vietnamese nor the sheikhs were saints — but so what? Neither were the European explorers, traders, and conquistadors.

The consequences of this newly effective Third World resistance were both moral and practical. Morally, Vietnamese resistance delegitimated the existing world order. Many Americans came to believe that their country was behaving in a ruthless and imperial manner in Indochina. They began to question the myths of American history and frequently found them wanting. It became harder and harder for the government to defend its policies in Vietnam, and the infection began to spread. Americans had always more or less assumed that the liberal marketplace was a just and humane method for building a just and humane world order. The sight of young children being napalmed to put down resistance to that just and humane world order was deeply unsettling. Americans were not ready to abandon market ideology, but they were less willing to fight to defend it.

The war and OPEC also had marked effects on the economy. Both acted to increase inflationary forces. In the years after 1973 the United States never enjoyed anything like the easy prosperity to which it had grown accustomed. The economy staggered and reeled — and with it, the mood of the American people.

Worse, OPEC vitiated the assumptions on which American economic planners depended. Since the end of World War II, the economy had sailed on serenely, with little disturbance from international events. This state of affairs continued so long, particularly in the years after the Korean War, that even economists forgot how unusual it was. U.S. government economic policy assumed implicitly that the economy existed in a sheltered environment where it would not be drastically thrown out of whack by interruptions in the supply of raw materials, catastrophic crop failures, boycotts, or the like. In other words, American economics assumed American omnipotence. When omnipotence failed, the resulting economic problems fundamentally weakened the American economy and forced the administration into a series of dubious policy moves that satisfied no one and failed to address the basic, noneconomic problems of OPEC. Economists gloomily revised their "optimum performance" indicators to say that the best sustainable levels of inflation and unemployment were no longer 4 percent and 4 percent as in the 1960s, but now stood at 6 percent and 6 percent. By the end of the 1970s, 8 percent and 8 percent looked more realistic.

The huge dollar surpluses that began to accumulate in the OPEC nations were another consequence of the new power relationship. Recycling the OPEC surpluses was a problem that was never satisfactorily solved. Part of the balance was absorbed by expensive new development projects in the OPEC countries. Arms sales on an unprecedented scale were also helpful in recycling the money — though not in building a generation of peace. Finally, as is well known, the banks rose to the occasion by lending money to Third World countries unable to pay their new energy bills. The consequences of all three recycling strategies could only mature with the passing of time. After a decade, the Third World's debt was a growing, perennial worry; the Middle East was armed to the teeth, and the war between Iran and Iraq threatened to plunge the whole region into chaos; and the wild swings in energy prices were still causing massive dislocations in the world economy.

These events were not in the script for the American Century.

Nor were the military consequences of the debacle in Vietnam. The once-derided domino theory received new credibility after the fall of Saigon. Not only did the other two countries of Indochina turn communist; communists made rapid gains in Africa and Latin America. The dominoes newly at risk in the post-Indochina world included, according to some, the "big enchilada" on the south side of the Rio Grande.

Both the adherents and the opponents of the domino theory often oversimplify it. It is not simply a matter of military pressure and Soviet intervention. The spread of communism in the Third World is not synonymous with the spread of Soviet power. Stalin's monolithic control over the Marxist-Leninist parties of the world has been smashed. A communist China has given the Soviet Union more trouble than Chiang Kai-shek ever dreamed of. The leaders of today's Soviet Union must sit still at world conferences and listen to attacks on their policies from the Italian, Rumanian, Spanish, and other parties with what must at times seem a tedious regularity. Although the Soviet Union remains the world's strongest communist state, its proportional influence diminishes as the communist world grows.

The complicated nature of the Soviet-Cuban relationship typifies the new state of affairs. Cuba depends on Russian guarantees and on its economic assistance, but the Cuban government cannot be considered a puppet of the Kremlin. Castro, like Tito before him, has his own base and his own stature in the world independent of his ties to Moscow. Mikhail Gorbachev would never dream of updating Stalin's boast: "I will shake my little finger and Tito will fall." World communism is incomparably stronger now than it was in the 1940s; the position of the USSR within that movement is not.

Nevertheless, no matter how the spread of communist movements affects the USSR, it poses a threat to the American Empire. Third World communism strikes at the ability of the empire to function smoothly. It threatens American interests with possible nationalization of property, the repudiation of national debts, and the restriction of investment opportunities. Although the communist or Marxist states of 1970s vintage have shown great willingness to accommodate their policies to the requirements of the capitalist corporations with which they hope to do business, the process of revolution alone is extremely disruptive to the free flow of goods and money through the American sphere. Prolonged civil strife closes mines and farms, ruins businesses, and creates a general nuisance in the revolutionary country and its trading partners. The economy of the modern capitalist world is too delicate and too dependent on the rest of the world to tolerate an indefinite series of revolutionary shocks.

The mere threat of communism forces Third World governments to adopt the kind of nationalistic economic policies that are abhorrent to the managers of empire. Regimes worried about popular insurrections make trouble for the IMF. "Sound" investment and development policies have to be sacrificed on the altar of pacification of the general populace. Inefficient subsidies must be paid to keep food prices low so that the slum dwellers don't set up barricades on the streets; public sector spending remains high even though the financial experts of the world's leading banks prove conclusively that debtors could pay more money to the banks if the price of wheat — and ultimately of bread — were allowed to rise. Economically less efficient small agricultural holdings are created from cash-crop-oriented latifundia — all to deprive guerrillas of their popular support and to keep the surplus population from flocking to the cities.

Characteristically, even when they go on doing business with the Western world, communist and other radical governments in the Third World alter social consumption patterns so that they do not reflect the priorities of the advanced market economies. The absence of vast quantities of cheap consumer goods in these countries reflects their leaders' decision to emphasize investment at the expense of consumption. These countries close their borders to Palmolive soap, to Cottonelle toilet tissue, and to gourmet pet foods. Items like Coca-Cola become curiosities in many communist countries. National income goes to establishing a national educational and material infrastructure rather than being spent on the import of consumer goods. Programs that are directed to the dispossessed majority of the population, whether or not they improve the lot of this group, also contribute to diminishing the market for Western and Japanese consumer goods.

We are not concerned here to argue that communist governments in the Third World have generally succeeded in improving the standard of living of most of their citizens, or even that the advanced countries ruthlessly exploit the Third World. To understand the communist threat to the American position, it is necessary only to see the consequences of a drop in consumer consumption in an international economy devoted largely to the profitable production and sale of precisely these commodities.

Finally, in thinking about the domino theory, we must once again see that it refers primarily to political and economic matters, and only secondarily to the military balance of power. Partisans and opponents of the domino theory share the tendency to identify it too closely with the military strength of communist governments. The image of toppling dominoes reinforces the idea of communism coming from outside a given society, and seizing power by use of bayonets of foreign troops. Such a theory cannot explain the Bolshevik Revolution itself, or the Chinese, Vietnamese or Cuban movements. Considered from the purely military perspective, the domino theory leads to the "so what?" response.

If Vietnam fails, then so will Cambodia. So what? Well, then Laos will fall. So what? The chain of events that leads from Hué to San Diego is too improbable to create much anxiety.

The popular understanding of the domino theory leads to a simultaneous overestimation of the military importance of communist gains and to an undervaluation of the political and economic consequences of such gains. The domino theory actually works in the sense that a communist victory in one country can strengthen communists in another one. If the Sandinistas can win, this gives new inspiration and hope to communist insurgents all over the world. If Vietnam can defeat the United States, so can other countries. If majority rule can come to Zimbabwe, then Azania's day of liberation cannot be far off.

Also, as the empire contracts, what remains must be ever more intensively cultivated. Cash-crop agriculture must be introduced more extensively in already shaky societies; mineral resources must be exploited with greater intensity. The contraction of markets resulting from communist success can lead to intensified price competition, thereby putting pressure on wages. All these forces strengthen communist movements where they exist and foster their creation where they do not.

These factors are more important than the addition to the military firepower that can result when the neighbor of an unstable country goes communist. Only rarely have anticommunist forces been outgunned and outarmed by their communist adversaries. Except for Eastern Europe, where the Red Army played a key role in postwar political developments, communism has usually won its victories with less firepower than its opponents. Less firepower and more determination. Cuba and Nicaragua have relatively little ability to alter the balance of forces in the Western Hemisphere by military means, but the contagion of their example cannot be overestimated in a region where the living standard has fallen steadily throughout recent history, and where people of all political persuasions and in all walks of life are accustomed to consider the United States the great enemy of national freedom.

THE DYNAMICS OF DEVELOPMENT

The cause of American decline in the Third World is not Soviet machinations; if it were, it could be dealt with. Rather, it is the tendency, apparently inevitable, of the American system to generate domestic resistance.

We have already seen that the second- and third-tier countries suffer from frozen political and economic development. Their economies have grown up in the shadow of more powerful countries; the social basis for a modern democracy on the Western model never developed. The money that, in theory, could have underwritten such a development has gone to Europe, America, and Japan, muting social conflict in those countries and strengthening democracy where it already exists.

A great many Third World countries have seen a burst of industrial activity since 1970. Thousands of factories have opened in countries that until recently were almost entirely agricultural. The manufacturers migrate to these countries to escape taxes and pollution and safety controls and to cut costs by uniting the acquisition of raw materials and the production of finished goods — but the basic reason for most of this activity can be summed up in two words: cheap labor. With minimum wages in the advanced countries at around $25 per day — and an additional social wage in the form of various government services and benefits, paid for by taxes — the contrast with the developing world, where wages are often less than 10 percent of those in the advanced countries, cannot be exaggerated.

If the underdeveloped countries were following essentially the same path as the liberal Western democracies, a process of economic and political struggle between the haves and the have-nots would begin. That struggle would ultimately evolve into a relationship embracing conflict and accommodation; wages would rise and working conditions would improve, and the growing middle class would press for and win a greater degree of freedom in the overall political system.

Unfortunately, this process cannot go forward very far in the contemporary world. Any increase in wages or social costs eliminates or reduces the competitive advantage of one country vis-à-vis others. If workers in one Third World country win too many concessions, manufacturers will stop coming to the country, and some factories that already exist will close down. Capital, following economic laws as compelling in their way as the laws of nature, will migrate toward the cheapest labor sources. The most mobile industries — textiles and other light consumer goods' manufacturing — are the quickest to go. These industries are labor-intensive rather than capital-intensive, so they take advantage of cheap labor. Equipment is cheap, too, and is easily repaired and can be operated by unskilled workers. Having moved from New England to the Carolinas, from the Carolinas to East Asia, the textile makers are ready to pick up and move again if need be.

This kind of mobility was not possible for industry when today's advanced countries were at the stage of development comparable with underdeveloped lands. Communications facilities and the global information network were so primitive that the distance from plant to market was a significant factor in the decision about location. Such natural features as proximity to deep-water ports and sources of cheap fuel, usually coal, were also determining factors. The advanced technology of the contemporary world has lessened their importance. Transport costs are so low, and international transport so effective, that a shirt maker in Taiwan can use cotton from India, dyes from Indonesia, and oil from Saudi Arabia to make shirts for Peoria. The head office in New York can order design changes over the telephone and coordinate the entire process over distances of thousands of miles. A worldwide financial network, similarly connected by electronic communications, can provide instant financing for all phases of manufacture. For these reasons, wage rates are often the most significant if not the only differential between a number of otherwise equally convenient manufacturing locations.

We have already seen that contemporary developing countries are blocked in their evolution toward democracy because the profits from industry that could support a rising middle class must be returned to foreign investors. Society is left split into a small elite of wealthy owners, a small and fluctuating middle segment, and great masses of poor people in the cities and in the countryside. The foreign interests, naturally enough, enter an alliance with the elite to bring the country into the world economy. It is an extremely comfortable arrangement for the people at the top of the developing country; they will do anything to keep it going. If this means repressing unions and democratic parties, so be it. In countries like Zaire, Haiti, and Indonesia, the process takes place almost invisibly. The democratic forces in society are so weak that voices of protest remain ineffective. Americans and Europeans are most moved when, tragically, democratic aspirations are strong enough to be felt by the professionals of a second- or third-tier country, yet this group remains condemned to a role of permanent, impotent protester against cruelty and injustice.

Here is the script for political and ultimately armed resistance: huge masses of poor workers and unemployed kept at or below a basic subsistence. A tiny elite linked to foreign interests. A small middle class unable to mediate the conflict. Peaceful means for change are blocked — but existing conditions are intolerable. The story is repeated in country after country without urging by the Soviets, the Cubans, or anybody else. True, once resistance is under way, or once people have decided they want to fight, they can turn to these countries for help, and they sometimes receive it. But whether they seek foreign assistance has to do with the relative strength of the forces once conflict has begun — and our inquiry is into the roots of popular resistance to the American Empire, not the course of civil wars once they begin.

Given that the operation of the market economy as it affects the Third World breeds resistance to it, we can see that, with or without foreign help, some insurgencies will win. The Chinese communists had little help from Stalin; Castro won his war on his own; North Vietnam never received the logistical and military support from the communist world that the United States gave South Vietnam. The guerrillas in El Salvador similarly get less aid from Nicaragua, Cuba, and the USSR put together than the government gets from the United States.

The success of one revolutionary movement prepares the way for others elsewhere. It saps the will of antirevolutionary forces. It disrupts the smooth working of the free world's economy, creating tensions and distortions that breed yet more trouble. We should perhaps speak not of a domino effect but of a ripple effect from one country to others. Whatever terms we use, we should recognize that the primary opponent of the American system of hegemony is the operation of that system itself, not the armed power of the Soviet Union.

The Nixon administration tried and failed to deal with these conditions; its successors tried and failed to deal with their consequences.

PART THREE

Why Not the Best?
The Carter Era

‿ 8 ‿

THE POLITICS
OF COMPROMISE

THE YEARS after Nixon's resignation witnessed a rapid retreat of
American power. Kissinger watched in bitter frustration as Congress blocked aid to the struggling Thieu regime and to Jonas
Savimbi's "freedom fighters" in Angola. Marxist regimes came to power
in Asia, Africa, and Latin America in the most rapid chain of revolution
since 1917. Unlike the communist regimes in Eastern Europe, the new
regimes owed relatively little to outside support and almost nothing to
the Red Army, at least initially. American impotence seemed graphically
demonstrated when Castro thumbed his nose at the pitiful, helpless giant
and sent his troops to Africa and his advisers to Nicaragua and Grenada.
Although the American media continued the litany of stories about the
impending collapse of the Soviet Union (one briefly popular book asked
in its title, *Will the Soviet Union Survive Until 1984?*), the Soviet economy
perversely continued to gain on America and its military strength mounted
in absolute and relative terms.[1] The chief ideological challenge to Moscow's perspective within world communism — Maoism — faltered and
failed. The increased independence of the Western Communist parties
did not create the hoped-for split in the world communist camp.

The United States was not without gains of its own in this period, the
largest being the accession of Anwar el-Sadat's Egypt to the Western
camp. But against this had to be set the sudden and terrifying fall of the
shah of Iran. At the same time, the world economy went into a tailspin.
Throughout the advanced industrial countries growth slowed or stopped;
unemployment and inflation both rose. Interest rates and currency values
fluctuated wildly; commodity prices raced up and down, disrupting the
markets whichever way they moved. The ominous increase in Third
World debt hung over the scene like a thickening storm cloud. The IMF
found itself in the position of dictating austerity programs to sovereign
nations in order to protect the standing of the great commercial banks.

As President Gerald Ford struggled gamely to pick up the pieces from the Nixon catastrophe, he was hampered by unfavorable international and domestic trends. Crippled by the political error of the Nixon pardon, without an effective mandate (Ford was never elected by any constituency beyond his congressional district in Michigan and was the first person to hold the vice-presidency and the presidency without being elected to either one), there was little he could have done, and he managed to accomplish even less. It was an administration that may be best remembered for the fall of Saigon, WIN (Whip Inflation Now) buttons, the Nixon pardon, and Ford's impromptu "liberation" of Poland in his debate with Carter.

The Bicentennial election brought into office a former nuclear engineer, peanut farmer, governor of Georgia, and member of the Trilateral Commission. For the first time, the United States had a president who openly proclaimed the advent of political and economic decline. Nixon and Kissinger spoke of a return to a "multipolar," as opposed to a bipolar, world, but that conception did not necessarily mean that the United States was on the wane — merely that other powers were on the rise. Carter spoke more bluntly about an "age of limits." He believed that his task in the Oval Office was to help America begin the adjustment to reduced expectations at home and to introduce it to an era of accommodation abroad.

What Carter's policies shared with the Nixon and Kissinger world view was that the process, if not the fact, of change in the world could be managed in a fashion that was acceptable to the United States. Nixon and Kissinger had attempted to exert control in Indochina even as they retreated from it. Carter sought an accommodation with the forces of change in the world, believing that the interests of the United States and of the "progressive forces" around the world were compatible.

Nixon's domestic policy had been to slow the growth of liberal programs and to curb agencies, like the Office of Economic Opportunity, that showed too much zeal for their low-income clients. (Few government agencies in American history have ever been disciplined for showing too much zeal for the interests of high-income clients.) Carter came into office denouncing the fiscal irresponsibility of Ford's $66 billion deficit, and calling himself a political liberal and a fiscal conservative — and making no secret of his belief that domestic spending had to be cut.

The question of a permanent lowering of expectations had never come to the fore in the Nixon years. Prosperity was assumed to be the norm for the American economy. The inflation and stagnation of the Nixon years were deemed to be aberrations, variously attributed to the fiscal consequences of the Indochinese War, to policy errors on the part of the Nixon team, or to the malice of OPEC. Only the gloomiest believed that the permanent prosperity of the postwar era was fading into the past, but their pessimism spread as the decade wore on, until it became the consensus by the Bicentennial year.

The Ford and Carter years saw the beginning of a major, sustained drop in the standard of living. From 1970 to 1980, average weekly earnings in constant dollars for private nonagricultural workers fell 8 percent, with most of the damage coming after 1973. The real income of households also fell during this period, and though a larger proportion of the adult population was employed in 1980 than in 1973, the share of national income going to wage earners as wages or fringe benefits actually fell.[2] As real wages fell, the social wage also declined, because government services were cut back. The basic elements of the welfare state remained in place during these years, and in some cases actually expanded, but services depending on many state and local governments rapidly deteriorated. The New York City financial crisis resulted in a serious deterioration in basic services, and the nation's other major cities experienced similar, if less dramatic, problems. Public hospitals were closed or suffered cuts in budgets; tuition in state-supported colleges jumped; the condition of the nation's infrastructure deteriorated.

The migration from the old industrial Northeast and Middle West to the Sun Belt during the 1970s was also a sign of deep economic trouble. The migration of industrial workers to the South and Southwest was no more a sign of good times than the Okie migrations of the Depression. When economics cause family and neighborhood breakups, dissolving well-knit communities and disrupting individual lives, then the economy has failed to deliver the essential minimum for human beings. Families forced to move lost much of their house equity as prices fell in the blight zones, and they had to start over at new, usually lower-paying jobs in a different part of the country, where they had no network of connections, no community support, and little or no prospect of returning to their former standard of living. Many of these families were to face new upheavals in the next decade, when the gyration of the world's oil prices sent the Sun Belt into a regional depression.

Imports from Japan and the Third World created new kinds of unemployment. We have already seen how low-wage labor overseas can crowd American goods out of national and international markets; investments in American factories declined as more investors sought rewarding opportunities overseas. Giant American industrial corporations began to diversify their holdings in the hope of surviving the coming crunch; steel, railroad, and auto companies were frantically searching for other, more profitable lines of work. The result of this disinvestment was that American industry continued to lose its one remaining edge — technological prowess. The new unemployment counted formerly well-paid, unionized industrial workers among its principal victims. It was an unemployment that would, analysts said, be eliminated only when the service sector of the economy could absorb former production workers. Because fast-food chains pay substantially less than car manufacturers, the implications for the middle class were both clear and disturbing. In fact, wages for employees in the service sector fell much more rapidly than wages in mining and manufacturing. From 1975 to 1980, average weekly wages in manufacturing fell by 1.7 percent; they rose in mining. By contrast, workers in retail sales saw their wages fall 12 percent, and construction workers lost 15 percent of their 1975 income in five years.[3]

Carter had nothing to offer in the way of halting or reversing these changes. The causes of America's problems, he said, were world history trends that American action could not hold back. Unwilling to attack either OPEC or the oil companies, for instance, Carter advised Americans to turn their thermostats down and wear sweaters in the house. He argued that the new age of limits need not be intolerably painful; that with "honest and competent management" the American government and people could function on less. Such arguments weakened his support among traditionally Democratic circles and failed to win him any Republican friends. For more than a century Americans had accepted the many drawbacks of life in an industrial market economy in the belief that by and large such an economy would deliver greater benefits to all classes. The Democratic Party, from Roosevelt on, claimed to be the party that would bring about economic growth to benefit working people; now the president of that party seemed to be saying that this was no longer the case. Moreover, the experience of many millions told them that the economy was not merely stagnant; it was shrinking. Spreading unemployment and weakening industrial performance sent waves of well-founded fear through the American working class.

Inflation-ravaged paychecks forced millions to ask where their "keep-even" raises would come from — where but from the expanding economy they were now told was a thing of the past? Carter's humiliating defeat in 1980 (Herbert Hoover received more electoral votes in 1932) came about in part because Carter had so little to offer his constituency.

Yet Carter's policies had seemed realistic and sober in 1976. At the end of his term his view of a future with limited growth and limited power still seemed more realistic than the "voodoo economics" of the

Reagan team. A closer look at the Carter policies shows that their failure was a symptom of a much deeper trouble — a crisis that went to the heart of the American experiment.

INTERNATIONAL COMPROMISE

Carter inherited a nation that was still deeply divided over Vietnam and Watergate. Much of the country had been shocked and disheartened by the revelations about the Nixon administration. As Nixon, in his vain efforts to salvage his mandate, broadcast discreditable information about his predecessors, many sincere and idealistic people began to lose faith in the system itself. Carter believed that if the government was ever to be effective, particularly in the field of foreign policy, it was necessary first of all for it to regain the trust of the American people.

Another development that Carter and his team accepted as irreversible was the increase in the importance of the Third World. Looking at the direction of U.S. trade and at the growing importance of Third World natural resources, President Carter and Secretary of State Cyrus Vance concluded that north-south relations were as important to the United States as the east-west polarity. It followed from this new appreciation of the Third World that the administration would also make an attempt to look at Third World aspirations on their own terms, not as outgrowths of United States–Soviet rivalry.

Insofar as competition between the United States and the USSR mattered in the Third World, the new administration expected that it would be able to outmaneuver the Soviet Union. The greater economic resources of the United States, its more sensitive political process, and, above all, its "true self," progressive and pacific, would rout the Soviets from the Third World. The United States would, in a sense, repeat Disraeli's political feat on a larger scale — it would "dish the Whigs" and seize the mantle of progressive world leadership from communist shoulders.

Such a policy would meet the key requirements of U.S. foreign policy, Carter hoped. Its progressive and humanistic content would restore faith in the government at home, it would stymie the Soviets overseas, and it would avoid the necessity of defending American interests in more Vietnams.

Human rights was the first, as it remained the most prominent, application of the Carter theory to foreign policy. It had its roots in a painful and perplexing development. Since the death of Stalin, the human rights situation had shown slow improvement throughout the Soviet bloc. In Latin America unfortunately there had been a general deterioration during the same period. Murder and torture became common in those regimes whose police and military were largely trained and equipped by the United States. It became difficult to reconcile the reality of American complicity and responsibility for the crimes of the military regime of Augusto Pinochet in Chile with the oft-proclaimed idealism of the United States government and its policy.

With a great deal of fanfare, the new policy was announced. Under Carter, the United States would use its influence to press its allies to move toward democracy, or at least to restrain themselves from excessive reliance on torture and terror. Early on, the policy ran into snags. Carter quickly discovered that client regimes were not prepared to change their ways at his request. These regimes were not always convinced that Carter meant what he said, and they were also aware that not all the organs of the United States government agreed with the new policy. It was also true that, though client regimes were willing to accept American leadership when that leadership was exerted to preserve their power, they were not so eager to follow a man who seemed to view their potential overthrow with complacency.

On the other hand, there were countries where the situation was so explosive, the regime so weak, or the external dangers so pressing that it was useless to urge the leaders to change their ways. Carter could threaten Argentina with a cut-off of American aid; he could not make the same kind of threats to Korea.

"Moral" impulses toward reform in the empire visibly struggled with the empire's security needs during Carter's term. The desire to disentangle America from the bloody embraces of tyrants and thugs turned inevitably into a search for scapegoats. Carter's policy needed tyrants so strong that they could survive highly public demonstrations of American disapproval or tyrants who were situated in countries where the alternative to their rule seemed to be something more like a democracy. Tyrants in strategic countries had to be supported no matter what the cost in consistency or credibility.

In the end, the campaign degenerated into something like public relations. Bilateral aid would be ostentatiously cut — while American officials on world bodies like the IMF or the World Bank saw to it that multilateral bodies took up the slack. In other cases Israel eagerly stepped in to supply weapons to such countries as Argentina and Guatemala.

Besides the campaign for human rights, Carter sought to make real the long-time liberal dream that the United States would be the ally and not the opponent of progressive forces around the world. To the extent that this was sincere policy and not window dressing, it reflected a fundamental misconception about the state of the world. Advocates of a progressive strategy for the United States generally believe that only the blind obstinance of the United States stands between democracy and the developing countries. If the United States would abandon its timid, self-limiting policy of supporting corrupt and reactionary feudal elites, and would encourage the democratic forces in these countries, then the Marxists would be either co-opted or marginalized. Thus, reason the advocates of the opening to the democratic center, the United States should have listened to Ho Chi Minh in 1946, when he appealed for American aid against the French. True, Ho Chi Minh was already an experienced communist in 1946, but a friendlier American attitude might have changed all that. He would have seen that greater gains were possible "within the system." Further confusing the issue, the example of American support of decolonization in the French, British, and Dutch empires can be a model for the new opening, say its advocates. America won the "friendship" of these colonial peoples by giving this support. Can't we do something similar now?

The problems with this approach are numerous. We have already touched on the most significant: the failure of the developing world to grow more democratic has to do with the basic structure of economic power in the world, and this is something not easily changed by the reshuffling of political leaders.

As for the American role in decolonization, that is neither as new nor as progressive as the idealists like to think. Britain played a somewhat similar role in the decolonization of Latin America in the nineteenth century, effectively blocking Spain's efforts to reassert its authority. Britain supported the Monroe Doctrine (without British support it would have amounted to nothing) to open up Latin America to the developed world of the time and to end Spain's system of preferential trade relations. Naturally, as the leading economic and trading power, Britain expected to benefit more than any other nation from free trade in Latin America, and it did.

In any case, the liberation movements in the Third World today do not have as their targets the direct representatives of European rule. Today's guerrillas are fighting neocolonialism, not colonialism. These neocolonial regimes are unpopular not only or even primarily because they are not democratic in the liberal sense; they are unpopular because they allow foreigners to exploit the resources, natural and human, of their societies.

The Carter policy of rapprochement with "democratic" forces in the Third World also failed to take into account the weakness of these forces. Like Alexsandr Kerensky's Provisional Government during the Russian Revolution, the "democratic" forces in much of the world are too weak to seize and hold power on their own. Thus, in Nicaragua the Marxist elements in the insurrectionary coalition quickly dominated the liberal democrats. In the far more depressing political world of El Salvador, the liberal democrats, split themselves, are the junior partners of the two warring social groups. The right democrats provide an illusion of re- spectability for the murderous oligarchs who control the security forces, and the left democrats tail helplessly behind the Marxist guerrillas. It is a configuration that should have been familiar to us from Vietnam.

In Iran the "moderates," as they were called, the pro-Western forces, proved no match for the Ayatollah Khomeini and the radical theocrats. In Iran and other countries the lawyers, newspaper editors, and would- be members of legislatures are unable to hold political power on their own.

Carter policy in South Africa attempted to create an opening toward the majority. As a policy it was more consistently planned and better executed than the administration's dismal fumblings in Latin America and Iran. The choice of Andrew Young as ambassador to the United Nations was courageous and wise. Few people in American public life understood as well as Young the aspirations of the South African ma- jority.

Yet while Carter policies in Latin America and Iran were sandbagged by nationalist, anti-American feeling there, his Africa policy was castrated by nationalist, right-wing feeling here. Young's statements about the constructive role of Cuban troops in Angola and his sympathy for the Palestinians were close to the minimum required of a United States that hoped to be taken seriously in the world as an ally of peoples aspiring to freedom and nationhood. Yet even these mild and tentative speeches by Young were savaged by the American press and the political lead- ership. Although Young's views are center-right by world standards, he was portrayed in this country as an extremist.

Behind the public relations problems of Young's tenure were the very real difficulties in the way of Carter's Africa policy. Although in 1976 white rule in South Africa appeared doomed, it was clearly entrenched for the indefinite future. To sacrifice relations with an existing govern- ment in firm command of its country's resources for the sake of "good relations" with a hypothetical future regime is a controversial course of action under the best of circumstances. It is extremely unlikely that the

United States could win a bidding war with the Soviet Union for the friendship of the African National Congress. The result of Carter policy in South Africa, even if it had succeeded in winning a role for the United States in the transfer of power to majority rule at some undefined point in the future, would have weakened forces disposed to cooperate with the United States and strengthened an oppositon that, while not a hardened Leninist movement, could not be counted on as a bulwark of international capitalism.

The situation of neocolonial Africa also creates problems for an American policy based on support for national liberation struggles in the continent. The governing elites in the black African states occupy an ambiguous place in relation to the anticolonial movement. While the ideology of national independence provides them with a mantle of legitimacy for governments that are often incompetent, corrupt, and autocratic, their continued power depends on close ties with the former imperial states or with the Americans. They must pay lip service to the struggle against neocolonialism, even though most of the African governments hope that this struggle remains far from their own borders. Although always ready to gain popularity by denouncing imperialism and the imperialists, the last thing such puppet regimes want is to see their own protests taken seriously.

Carter pushed the South African government to its limits without defusing the hostility between majority and minority in the region. The Americans hoped that the Zimbabwe agreement, which brought majority rule to the former white state of Rhodesia, would open the door to an agreement over Namibia, the former German colony under South African control since World War I. In the scenario favored by Carter's State Department, the successful transition to majority rule in Zimbabwe would encourage South Africa to agree to independence for Namibia. This in turn would build the confidence of the ANC in the American-sponsored program of peaceful change in the region as a whole.

But the most that the South Africans were willing to give — majority rule in Zimbabwe — was less than the minimum that the liberation movements were willing to accept, and Carter's diplomacy, for all its good intentions, was never able to bridge this wide difference.

The Camp David negotiations that led to the peace treaty between Israel and Egypt showed the same pattern. Carter extracted all the concessions that Menachem Begin was willing to make without succeeding in shaping an offer that the Arab world would find acceptable. No Israeli government would accept the right of the inhabitants of the West Bank to determine their own future; no Arab consensus would give it up. As

in South Africa and as in so many Third World countries, there is no
effective center in the Middle East, no common ground on which Zionists
and Palestinians can meet.

Under Carter, American foreign policy was like a sinner in search of
what theologians call "cheap grace" — like a brothel owner offering to
improve working conditions and wages to gain respectability. The United
States would put itself at the head of the world's genuinely progressive
forces — at no cost to the United States. Absent from American rhetoric
was any specific idea about what the United States would *do* to meet the
aspirations of the peoples in revolt. Would it adopt a strict code of conduct
for American corporations in the Third World? Join the West German
Social Democrat Willy Brandt's strategy for international development?
Help impoverished countries compensate foreign owners for nationalized
assets?

In fairness to the Carter administration, it must be said that some steps,
even difficult ones, were taken to end legitimate and long-standing grievances. The Panama Canal Treaties were an example of such a step —
but an example, also, of the narrow limits of this policy. With bipartisan
support at the top, the Canal treaties barely squeaked through the Senate.
The New Right used the Canal controversy to build networks of committed supporters and mounted a campaign that in 1978 defeated eight
senators who had voted for the treaties. The struggle left the administration weakened and therefore less able to press for further steps along
the road to compromise. Once again, a move that had tested the outer
limits of the United States to make concessions fell far short of the
minimum changes required to win over the forces that opposed the
empire.

It may be that Carter himself never understood the difficulty of what
he was attempting. Like many Americans, he contrasted the cynical
diplomacy of the Nixon era with what he supposed was the more idealistic diplomacy of an earlier day. He longed for a return to the idealism
of a Wilson or a Jefferson in foreign affairs — odd choices, as neither
man is generally held to have succeeded in the field of world politics.
Yet here is Franklin Roosevelt, Wilson's secretary of the navy, speaking
a week after leaving office:

> Until last week I had two [votes in the proposed League of Nations] myself,
> and now Secretary [of the Navy Josephus] Daniels has them. You know
> I had something to do with the running of a couple of little republics. The
> facts are that I wrote Haiti's Constitution myself and, if I do say it, I think
> it a pretty good Constitution.[4]

According to Carter, "Our country has been the strongest and most effective when morality and a commitment to freedom and democracy have been most clearly emphasized in our foreign policy."[5] To be great, we must first be good. It seemed not to trouble Carter that the other nations in the hemisphere were unable to recall any such epochs of morality and generosity in American history. Perhaps they were simply uninformed.

In his memoirs, Carter himself cites the Truman administration as an example of a time when "morality and a commitment to freedom and democracy" were clearly evident in American policy. He singles out the Marshall Plan and the decision not to punish Germany and Japan as classic instances of American generosity. Without wishing to detract in any way from the achievements of the Marshall Plan, we must still conclude that only in the most superficial sense could it be presented as a disinterested policy — or even one that consciously sought to embody "morality" in Carter's sense. Immediately following the war — a war in which the terror bombing of cities caused unparalleled violence against purely civilian targets — both Germany and Japan were punished — and punished severely. American occupation troops in Germany were issued orders to remind the people that they were there as "conquerors, not liberators." In much of Germany rations under American occupation fell to eight hundred calories per day, and the inhabitants were forbidden to travel or use the mails. As epidemics spread among the weakened population, even hardened observers who had seen the effects of Nazi brutality in Dachau and Bergen-Belsen were shocked by conditions in Germany a year after the war.[6]

As for generosity, American aid was used systematically to control the economic and political policies of former Allies and enemies alike. The British were shocked, and their economy sank into a crisis, when Lend-Lease was abruptly canceled in August 1945.[7] When the Netherlands refused to follow American dictates on decolonization in Indonesia, its Marshall Plan aid was suddenly suspended.[8]

What underlay American policy in postwar Europe was not a sudden attack of agape — pure Christian love — but two practical considerations. First, economic opinion was unanimous that American prosperity depended in the long run on a prosperous Europe. The end of every war since the start of the Industrial Revolution had seen serious depressions — and in 1945 memories of the 1930s were still sharp. Second, the balance of power in Europe required a shift in American policy. Germany was no longer the strongest land power in Eurasia; that distinction now belonged to the Soviet Union. The consequences of this shift led the

United States to take a number of actions, some of which would pass muster by a board of moral accountants, some of which would not.

Germany was permitted to revive and rearm. This is normally considered to have been a moral step, particularly by the Germans. On the other side of the ledger, the United States gave shelter and employment to war criminals and, with their aid, constructed an intelligence network to operate in formerly German-occupied Eastern Europe. No one considers this moral, except for the Nazis, but the policy was in every way the logical extension and inseparable companion of the "generosity" toward defeated Germany that has won so much praise. When the United States determined that its own interests required a strong Germany rather than a good one, denazification was consciously subordinated to the task of reconstruction.

As for granting Marshall Plan aid to former Allies and to Italy, balance-of-power factors entered into that decision as well. The nightmare of American planners in the troubled postwar years was the prospect of Communist Party power in Italy and France. In both countries Communist participation in government was indispensable in the immediate aftermath of the war. How to ease these parties out of power and develop a stable political consensus that would exclude them was the constant preoccupation of American diplomats. In the short run, the CIA covertly funded the Christian Democrats in Italy. Marshall Plan aid was to help turn back the red tide by restoring prosperity in the slightly longer run. It worked, but in both Italy and France the "benevolent" aspect of American policy went hand in hand with a less admirable side: political figures tainted by association with Mussolini and the collaborationist Vichy regime in France found their paths back to public life considerably smoothed by the invisible influence of the United States. This policy also made room for active fascists and Hitler sympathizers like Franco in the grand coalition against the new land power in Eurasia.

Meanwhile, American influence was exerted to drive its wartime Allies out of their empires in order to extend the American sphere. American aid to Britain was explicitly tied to Britain's willingness to dismantle the system of imperial preferences that had held together the British Empire. American intervention in Iran helped the American oil companies strengthen their power in the Middle East vis-à-vis their British rivals, and America forced the British to abandon the Suez Canal in 1956 when the Federal Reserve Bank mounted an attack on the British pound. Americans scoffed at the claims of British and French governments that in opposing national liberation movements they were defending Western interests against communism, yet when America intervened in the Third World, as in

Guatemala, in 1954, and Iran, it insisted that its motives were purely idealistic. Britain, France, the Netherlands, and Belgium were and are unconvinced.

If there is one thing that proponents and opponents of the Vietnam adventure have agreed on, it is that the war was the logical extension of American policy since World War II. The NATO experience was the model for CENTO and SEATO, the collective security organizations that brought the United States into Asian politics. The balance-of-power logic was the same in both cases, as was the willingness to make common cause with former enemies and unsavory elements to ward off what was believed to be the chief threat. Nixon's Vietnam and Truman's Korea were not so very far apart.

But if secrecy, cynicism, and balance-of-power politics prevailed during the Truman administration, can the golden age of American democracy that Carter evokes in his book be found earlier in the past? The Sioux, the Cherokee, the Apache, and the Ibo think not. From Lenin to Kissinger, twentieth-century statesmen have praised the sophisticated *Realpolitik* of the founding fathers.

Carter opens his discussion of foreign policy with a moving reference to what he learned from the civil rights movement:

I grew up in south Georgia within a legally segregated society . . . and never gave a thought to the lack of equality inherent in the separatedness. Neither did the adults who managed the education system, nor the lawyers and judges in our courts, nor the governor, nor those who led our government in Washington and were responsible for the administration of justice in our great and free nation.[9]

But this story had a happy ending, and Carter believes that this experience of moral awakening can serve as a guide for the development of American foreign policy — presumably with the Third World cast in the role of American blacks.

There is something evasive and disingenuous in Carter's implied claim that neither he nor anybody else in the South ever thought that its racial policies were unjust. Evidently slavery and segregation came about by accident, without anyone's ever happening to notice that they were wrong. Here again we see the search for cheap grace, the quest for salvation without real repentance; not "I have sinned," but "I made a mistake in good faith."

The analogy led him to a fatal miscalculation. While it is certainly true that the American nation as a whole remains blind to the structural inequality in the world economy, there are key differences. Most important of all, blacks are a minority in the South, but the Third World includes the vast majority of the earth's population. Satisfying the just demands of these peoples would require enormous adjustments on the part of the minority, adjustments that the minority is clearly unwilling to make.

Moreover, the grievances of the Third World are more complex and, in some cases, greater than those of American blacks. Twenty years after the Civil Rights and Voting Rights Acts of the 1960s, the United States was still unwilling or unable to offer blacks equality with whites. The most spectacular failure was the failure of black income to match white income. How would Carter have proposed to address this issue on a global level? Would he have expected the Third World to accept anything less than equality with the advanced countries? Or believed that the peoples of the Third World would accept the United States' ideas about the proper pace of change?

The military overconfidence of the Kennedy-Johnson years led the United States to a military impasse in Indochina. The moral overconfidence of the Carter team had a similar result. Like Carter himself, the American people were unwilling to pursue a cynical policy of exploitation and aggression around the world. Like Carter, they did not understand that it was impossible to maintain their position by any other means. Like Carter, they preferred to comfort themselves with illusion — to believe that the truly hard choices need never be made.

LESS IS MORE: THE POLITICS OF SACRIFICE

In foreign policy Carter hoped that the consequences of American decline could be alleviated by a compromise with the forces of change. Within the United States the consequences of decline as Carter saw them were primarily financial: the federal government could no longer afford the growing welfare state. He came to office committed to cuts in military and social spending, denouncing the "special interests" that for too long had grown fat at the federal trough.

Given the international situation and its domestic political consequences, the military cuts could not be sustained. By the end of his administration Carter was calling for annual increases of 5 percent in the Pentagon budget, a level nominally equal to the actual numbers under Reagan. As for the domestic cuts, he soon found that the special interests were a match for any administration. Carter went into office calling for fundamental reform of the income tax, a collection of laws, regulations, and administrative and judicial precedents that had grown so complicated that by 1976 not one person in the entire country could claim to understand it all. Taxpayers looking for guidance from the Internal Revenue Service found that the IRS would not guarantee the accuracy of returns prepared with its assistance. Although the dense thicket of regulations and the manifold loopholes infuriated most taxpayers, they generally worked in favor of those rich enough to retain lobbyists, lawyers, and accountants; each year the press carried stories of wealthy people and corporations that paid little or no tax. Injustices so general and so widely publicized threatened the legitimacy of the entire tax system. Calling it a "disgrace to the human race," Carter vowed to bring order and justice into the system.

He rapidly discovered that the system was unwilling to be reformed. The most notorious deduction that Carter attacked was the so-called three-martini lunch, a provision that allows salesmen, executives, lobbyists, and others to deduct the cost of entertaining prospective clients or contacts in the normal course of business. Many firms keep season tickets at sporting events, hunting lodges, and other "perks" to sweeten potential clients and favored employees. Carter not unreasonably considered that the taxpayers had no obligation to subsidize these facilities beyond a certain minimum, but his far-from-draconian proposal met with howls of rage. Restaurant associations warned of their impending destruction and foresaw millions of unemployed waiters and chefs starving on the streets. Ashen-faced executives warned that the measure would mean the end of business as we know it.

As it happened, virtually every tax loophole had its own constituency. Worse, as soon as a tax bill — even one labeled a "reform" tax bill — hit the Congress, hordes of lobbyists emerged from the woodwork with plans for new loopholes to redress this or that injustice.

Energy legislation presented many of the same problems. Producers, consumers, wholesalers, and retailers all had conflicting interests, and all organized into effective and competing lobbies. The 1977 session of Congress was largely devoted to maneuvers over Carter's energy bills, but they did not finally pass until October 1978 — and only after an intensive campaign by Carter that in his own estimation used up so much of his political capital that it significantly affected his ability to achieve other goals.

Carter had been elected on a pledge to balance the budget within four years. It was a pledge he was unable to keep, in part because it sparked such bitter opposition from Democrats on Capitol Hill. Supporters of programs from food stamps to water projects were all armed with explanations, usually backed with statistics, to show that their particular program was in the national interest. All of them agreed in the abstract that fiscal responsibility was necessary for a government running $66 billion in the red; all of them agreed, too, that their own programs were so important that *true* fiscal responsibility would find a way somehow to fund them. "The lobbies are a growing menace to our democratic system of government,"[10] wrote Carter from retirement in Plains, and he sourly noted that some of the most outrageous proposals he fought became law under his successor.

It was not surprising that Carter and the Democratic Party split over the question of special interests. Long before Carter's time, many candidates of both parties owed their seats to the efforts of special interests and their campaign contributions. Some politicians — Lyndon Johnson foremost among them — made their way in Washington because of their close ties to interest groups and their financial resources. If Carter was looking back to a golden age in which democracy reigned, when politicians consulted the general interest and not special interests, he was to have a long search, one that was no more fruitful than his quest for the golden age of idealistic foreign policy.

The New Deal, the political consensus that shaped the modern Democratic Party, was an affair of special interests. Farmers needed price supports. The unemployed needed relief. Business needed federal assistance. Roosevelt cemented the loyalty of whole regions to himself and his programs by the most generous distribution of pork barrel projects in American history. Millions of people blessed Roosevelt for bringing electricity to their homes, and millions of others were grateful for the jobs or the Social Security checks that came from Washington during his era. The Tennessee Valley Authority was not only one of the greatest public works in world history; it was also a colossal boondoggle that fed private interests with public funds. There was pie for everyone under Roosevelt. Unions got the minimum wage, the Wagner Act, and a sympathetic National Labor Relations Board. Business got the National Recovery Act; big business got new credit through the reformed and subsidized banking system; small business and the farmers got special credit assistance from new government agencies. Migrant workers, veterans, even writers and painters, got something from the New Deal.

What kept the New Deal from turning into a feeding frenzy for lobbyists was the widely shared belief that society was made up of special interests, and that the general interest was something like the sum of the special ones. Farmers, workers, entrepreneurs, teachers — all of these groups were part of the nation, and it was government's job to help each of society's component parts make its unique and necessary contribution to the common good. Labor leaders neither were, nor did they resemble, shortsighted and greedy thugs out to fleece the public; they were recognized as the democratically elected representatives of working people, expressing the need of the workers for a living wage. And that need was legitimate in Roosevelt's view. Unless the workers made decent wages, how could they buy the products of the farmers and the businessmen?

The Democratic coalition, as far as it continues to exist, still shares this view of the general interest. The nation is the sum of its parts, and the national government exists to assist the various parts in making their contributions to the whole. When Thomas P. (Tip) O'Neill put together a farmer-labor coalition for food stamps, he did not believe he was organizing a cynical raid on the Treasury. Farmers and grocers needed customers; hungry people needed food: *voila!* food stamps.

Only sustained economic growth can support a program of this kind. The rationale for building New Deal–type coalitions is that each of the interests involved can and will make a positive contribution to the overall development of the country — a rationale that assumes that further development is possible and desirable. Although the New Deal was put together from a hodgepodge of sometimes contradictory proposals, it was informed by a coherent vision of growth through national cooperation.

The age of limits proclaimed by Carter transformed the special interests from natural allies to natural enemies. Who was going to get that federal dollar — the farmer or the welfare client? Was it to be bridges or B-1s? It made the task of Democratic leadership in Congress and in the Executive Branch next to impossible. It set in motion a Darwinian process in which only the most efficient and powerful lobbies could protect the interests of their clients. The most powerful lobbies tend to be the best funded, and since corporations and industries are better funded than unions and populist causes, the influence of wealth and power in politics is always magnified in a time of economic stagnation.

The new influence of oil companies and defense contractors seems to have alarmed Carter most, though he had few kind words for other powerful lobbies. Oil company lobbyists roamed the halls of Congress with proposed revisions to his energy legislation that were, Carter charges in his book, written in the law offices of the energy companies. Defense lobbyists gained greater and greater influence over procurement decisions in Congress and the Pentagon. Beyond these specific abuses, Carter attacks the consequences of the special interest state for the formulation of government policy. Special interests can block legislation or hold it hostage. The committee system in Congress gives them the leverage at vital points to control the movement of legislation. Extremists from both sides can combine to block centrist, compromise proposals. The real threat to democratic government from special interests is not so much that they distort the decisions of government, although they do, but that they paralyze government's ability to act at all.

Carter, during his presidency, was not alone in apprehending this danger. From people in all bands of the political spectrum came cries that the system was in crisis, that the government no longer "worked." There was no coherent view of the national interest — only the babble of conflicting regional and economic interests. Rarely was Congress able to act on important legislation. Greek lobbies and Israeli lobbies held a veto power over crucial foreign policy decisions. The two-party system was falling apart. Single-issue voting blocs and regional alliances were undermining the party structure. Party leadership no longer maintained effective control over the representatives and the senators. There were 435 parties in the House and 100 parties in the Senate, and every politician voted on every issue without fear of the leadership.

Carter was not the only person in public life to fear the consequences of these developments. The succession of blows — beginning with the 1963 assassination of President Kennedy — was having an effect. Not since Eisenhower had an American president completed his full term of office retaining the respect and affection of his countrymen. Vietnam, Watergate, and the failed Carter presidency led many to wonder whether the system had not, in some basic way, broken down.

Actually, what was happening was even more disturbing. The national malaise identified by Carter was not the result of a breakdown in the system. It was the system itself that was causing most of the problems in the Carter years. The system was working — and that was the problem.

THE CONSTITUTIONAL CRISIS

WITH THE POSSIBLE EXCEPTION of the Bible, no document in the United States is so widely revered and so poorly understood as the Constitution. Virtually all Americans consider it a marvel of political science, the shaper of our national institutions, and the guarantor of our personal freedoms — and almost no one can give a coherent account of the political theory behind it.

An important source of this confusion is the series of changes that have revolutionized American political ideology while leaving the Constitution nearly unchanged. Since the nineteenth century, most Americans have assumed that democracy is good in and of itself. Since the American government is democratic, people reason, and since the Constitution is the foundation of that government, the Constitution must be a democratic document.

This is far from the case. The men who wrote — designed — the Constitution did not consider democracy to be good in itself. On the contrary, they feared nothing so much as an unbridled democracy, even an unbridled representative democracy. Political theory in the eighteenth century still looked back to the ancient world, and the observations of Aristotle and Polybius seemed to have been amply confirmed by events since their era. Classical political philosophy distinguished three basic forms of government and taught that each form had a characteristic corruption. Some thinkers postulated a cycle of government — from monarchy to aristocracy to democracy to tyranny. The tendency of democracy to evolve into tyranny was widely noted in the ancient world, perhaps because there were so many examples. A strong leader caters to the prejudices or gratifies the passions of the uneducated, unreflective mob, and so is freely given the highest offices in the democratic state. He consolidates this power, fortifies his position, and ends by subjugating the state to his will.

This pattern has recurred often enough in history. Julius Caesar began his political career as the leader of the popular, democratic party in Rome. The history of the Italian city-states — now largely forgotten among the general educated public in English-speaking countries but still quite vivid in the eighteenth century — gave more bloody examples. The records of Robespierre and Napoleon confirmed the founding fathers in their fears of democracy in the first years of constitutional government. In more recent times the careers of Hitler, Juan Perón, and Marcos show that mass popularity in a democratic state can still serve as the stepping-stone for what we call dictators and what the ancients called tyrants. The bitter opposition to Franklin Roosevelt had at its core a fear that he had designs of this kind; his proposal to pack the Supreme Court and his apparent determination to enjoy life tenure in office drove not a few of his opponents to despair for American democracy. The Twenty-Second Amendment to the Constitution, limiting presidents to two terms in office, was adopted to prevent any other man from gaining this kind of power.

The founders of the Constitution did not believe that they could create an eternal system, but they hoped to design a long-lived one. In order to counteract the negative effects of each of the three major systems of government — monarchy, aristocracy, and democracy — political writers recommended a "mixed" constitution, one in which each type of government would be checked by the others. The Roman Republic, although it ultimately decayed into tyranny, was the longest-lived and most successful system known to antiquity, and it was admired because its constitutional structure had room for the monarchical element (the executive consuls), the aristocratic element (the Senate), and the popular element (the tribunes and the assemblies of the people).

The American Constitution was designed to emulate Rome's mixed constitution, and monarchic, democratic, and aristocratic elements were carefully blended. The president represented the monarchic element, the Senate and the Supreme Court were aristocratic, and the House of Representatives was popular. The visible interplay and rivalry of the three branches of government, which Americans habitually call the system of checks and balances, is only one of the systems of checks and balances built into the Constitution. Besides balancing the powers and the ambitions of the three branches of government, the founding fathers also attempted to design a system of checks and balances to govern relations between the states and the national government and to govern the relations among the various social classes of American society.

To maintain the states against the national government, the U.S. Senate and the president were originally to be elected directly by the state governments. The national government was unable to levy direct taxes on the states or their inhabitants, and its economic jurisdiction was restricted to interstate commerce at a time when many of the states were still independent economies. A small number of states could block any constitutional change, and Article V provides that "no State, without its consent, shall be deprived of its equal suffrage in the Senate."

The checks and balances used to keep the various classes in society equilibrated were the most complex of all, and perhaps the least understood today. The founders believed that each class in the community would be tempted to press its interests too far, leading to general ruin, unless there was some kind of built-in institutional check on its power. Left to themselves, the rich would yield to their avarice and drive the poor into open rebellion. On the other hand the poor — the "rabble" — would, left to themselves, quickly subvert all order and morality by an assault on private property. Besides the numberless examples of such class struggles that history offered for their inspection, the framers of the Constitution had discovered for themselves that popular majorities, unless checked, were all too willing to inflate currencies and to annul or repudiate debts. Because history showed that in the long run the popular element in any state was usually the strongest force, and because the founders themselves were all well-to-do and naturally consulted their own interests in designing a government, the Constitution originally contained far more checks on the rabble than on any other element. The most popularly responsive body in the federal government — the House of Representatives — was the most restricted in its powers.

From 1789 to 1913, well over half the period of its existence to date, the Constitution provided that only the House of Representatives would be chosen by direct popular vote. (The Senate was elected by state legislatures until 1913. The president is still elected by the Electoral College.) Even the House of Representatives was not originally intended to represent the unpropertied rabble. The thirteen colonies had property qualifications for voters, and the United States Constitution specifically guaranteed their right to establish these qualifications as they saw fit. As late as the 1830s, when de Tocqueville visited, property qualifications remained high — in some states, higher than the requirements in Britain. While the new western states had universal (white) male suffrage, de Tocqueville reported that the original colonies maintained voting qualifications ranging from owning fifty acres of land (South Carolina) to paying taxes, serving in the militia, or simply staying off the list of registered paupers (Maine and New Hampshire). Massachusetts required

an income of £3 or a fortune of £60; Rhode Island required landed property worth $133.[1]

As an additional limit on the popular character of the House, the slave
states received a "credit" for three fifths of their slave populations when
seats were apportioned after each census.

While all poor people were potential dangers to the security of the
state, eighteenth-century political theory considered the urban rabble the
most dangerous of all. Their great concentration and the lack of any way
for them to gain the subsistence that rural poor people could get from
the land made them extremely dangerous. Any fears the founders had
of urban rabble based on their reading of ancient Roman, modern Italian,
and even British history was reinforced by the French Reign of Terror
early in the life of the American Republic. The streets of Washington
were designed to allow cannons an ample field of fire on any urban mob
that might aspire to direct action; fear of the rabble was a contributing
factor in the apportionment of congressional representation as well. The
"large state–small state" compromise that guarantees equal representation in the Senate also guarantees each state at least one seat in the House,
regardless of its population. These provisions weight both houses toward
rural and against urban populations. Since state legislatures often preserved the same imbalance (until the 1960s, when the Supreme Court
decided after 180 years that "one man, one vote" was a constitutional
right), the urban masses were kept effectively in check.

The consequence of these provisions becomes evident when we compare the weighting of votes in California, the most populous state, with
Wyoming, the least populous. Each eligible voter in Wyoming has seventy-five times the weight of a California voter in determining the make-
up of the United States Senate. Because electoral votes are assigned on
the basis of congressional representation, the Wyoming resident's vote
for president has about five times the weight of the Californian's. (Wyoming has about 1/75 of California's population and 1/15 of its electoral
vote.)

In the Electoral College, which elects the president of the United States,
each state receives a number of votes equal to its congressional representation. Legally, the national vote in November is a nonbinding primary, a beauty contest. The electors not only *are* free to vote for whomever
they wish; in some cases they do. In three of the four presidential elections
between 1968 and 1980, an elector voted for a candidate other than one
he was pledged to support. If the Electoral College is deadlocked, the
election goes to the House of Representatives in a profoundly undem-
ocratic procedure that gives each state one vote, regardless of its population.

Nowhere does the Constitution even require that the members of the Electoral College be chosen by popular majorities within each state. Legally, each state legislature can decide how the state will choose its electors. The election of 1824 was the first in which popular votes predominated in selecting the Electoral College, and in that year the winner of the election, John Quincy Adams, received one-third *fewer* votes than his unsuccessful rival.

As if all this would not suffice to keep the urban rabble in check, the Constitution provided that the appointment of federal judges be completely isolated from popular direct vote — along with foreign policy and the selection of the Cabinet. Judges are appointed for life by the (indirectly elected) president and confirmed by the (indirectly elected until 1913) Senate. Treaties must be approved by two thirds of the Senate. In all these cases, the House has no constitutional voice. Similarly, while the House can vote to impeach a president or a judge, only the vote of two thirds of the Senate will remove either from office. The House was deprived of even the one weapon the colonial legislatures found effective against British officials before the Revolution: it cannot vote to lower the salaries of federal judges.

Finally, the process of amendment was made exceptionally difficult. Two thirds of the states must ratify any amendment, and some states require a two-thirds vote by both houses of their own legislatures. The defeat of the Equal Rights Amendment, consistently backed in polls by more than 70 percent of the population, was an example not of a breakdown of the system, but rather of its success. The urban rabble, with its dangerous and innovative ideas, was foiled in its efforts to lay grubby and radical hands on the Constitution.

The supposed golden age of popular rule, when democratic American institutions worked to promote the general as opposed to the special interests, turns out to be as historically elusive as the golden age of American diplomacy. Liberals in the 1970s devoted huge amounts of effort to reform the system in a way that would restore it to its true nature — and what they ended up with was a system that resisted populist pressures as intensely as ever, with the added wrinkle that the reformed institutions were less suited to the actual conditions of modern life than the jerrybuilt, unregenerate structures they were intended to replace.

In the two centuries since the Constitutional Convention, such fundamental changes have taken place in the nation and the world that much of the Constitution simply makes no sense as written. The division of war powers between the president and Congress is one troubling example. Under modern conditions, a war between the United States and the USSR might last half an hour and wipe out humanity. The president has the authority — must have the authority — to launch a nuclear strike without congressional consultation, much less a declaration of war. Congress thus retains the power to declare minor wars, as the Roman Senate retained control over copper coinage even when the emperors took over gold and silver. Even this power is limited by the president's right — under the supposedly restrictive War Powers Act — to order U.S. forces into combat for thirty days without congressional approval. An act of war that Congress never approved can commit the nation to hostilities that Congress would be powerless to terminate.

Carter's attempt to dismantle the imperial presidency was a well-intentioned but futile effort to return to the pristine nature of American constitutional forms, an effort made impossible by the unwieldiness of the old system. Since 1941 the United States has been in a permanent state of crisis in its foreign relations — either at war or on the edge of it. The constitutional process of treaty ratification has become largely irrelevant to the conduct of policy. The SALT II Treaty, for example, was never ratified but was scrupulously observed; the Organization of American States treaties and the UN Charter were solemnly ratified and frequently flouted.

The Constitution was designed to prevent sudden upsets or rash actions. The system of checks and balances among regions, classes, interests, and the branches of government aims to ensure that one coalition will not be able to impose its will on the others to any great extent. Had it not been for the Civil War, for example, the slave states and territories of 1860 would still be able to block the abolition of slavery by constitutional amendment. In 1789 the founders reasoned that, once a basic and sound framework had been established, action posed many more dangers for the new Republic than inaction. Geographically isolated and militarily secure, the American Republic could afford a limited, even a chaotic state; efficiency was the last thing the founders wanted to see in the national government. The system of checks and balances was *designed* to produce frequent deadlocks in government. The system worked well during the Carter years.

CRACKS IN THE SYSTEM: THE INVISIBLE REVOLUTION

A number of factors have combined to change the actual form of American government while leaving its outer trappings unchanged. The sheer size of the United States today, compared with the 3.9 million residents in 1790, has produced some of the most far-reaching changes. In the original Constitution, each member in the House represented a constituency of about thirty thousand inhabitants. Half of those inhabitants were women, who did not vote. Of the remaining fifteen thousand, up to 50 percent were underage or noncitizens (this does not take into account slaves), and of the remaining potential voters as few as one fifth may have met the property qualifications. John Quincy Adams was elected president of the United States in 1824 with fewer popular votes than Clint Roberts received in his unsuccessful bid in 1980 for South Dakota's seat in the House of Representatives.

Clearly the relationship of a representative to one of two thousand voters was different from today's system, in which one congressional district may have 500,000 constituents — meaning that each district today would be more populous than all but one of the thirteen original states in the first census. (The entire United States of 1790 would rank as a middle-size state today; in the 1980 census it would rank twenty-second in population, between Michigan and Alabama.) California today has a population equal to the total United States population as late as 1850 — and California's 23,667,947 people in 1980 had exactly as many senators as Delaware's 59,096 had in 1790.

Related to this population growth, and compounding its effect, is the growing size of the federal government. Not only does each representative represent more people; each representative has less influence. There were sixty-one members of the first House of Representatives (sixty-seven after representatives from North Carolina and Rhode Island were seated); today's representative speaks for a hundred times as many voters and is one of 435 members of the House.

Meanwhile, the government has grown out of all recognition. There were more than 2.9 million federal employees in 1985; this is larger than the population of the largest state in the Union at the time of the Civil War. The federal budget in 1985 was larger than the gross national product before World War II. Each state and the District of Columbia spent more money in 1985 than the federal government spent in 1905.

No representative, however conscientious, can be expected to become familiar with all the operations of government today. Under the committee system, representatives specialize. Districts whose representatives occupy places on major committees are represented far more effectively than other districts — and the individual citizen has no voice in the matter. Speaker O'Neill's Massachusetts constituents never took him to task for committee assignments to Utah's delegation; this crucial government function escapes almost all popular control.

The tortuous path of a piece of legislation on its way to the statute books takes it through several committees in the House and the Senate, then occasionally to a conference committee, and finally back onto both floors for passage. It then faces a possible presidential veto and perhaps partial amendment or total repeal at the hands of a federal district court. From there it may wind its way up to the Supreme Court in a process that routinely takes years before its ultimate fate is known.

Even if the bill becomes law, and the courts do not strike it down in whole or in part, it usually requires a set of regulations written to translate congressional intent into executive policy. The average citizen is either unwilling or unable to follow this process in the detail that would allow him or her to understand what the government is up to. Subcommittee votes on small but often crucial changes in the wording of a bill may in fact be far more important than the final roll call vote, yet only rarely do these votes receive substantial publicity. The most important congressional activity on a bill can take place when a subcommittee chairman gets briefed by a member of his staff about the Executive Branch's regulations for implementing a new law. Nine hundred and ninety-nine times out of a thousand, this process takes place far from any public scrutiny. Even where there is such scrutiny, the actual changes in wording and the regulations themselves are couched in dense legalese, language the reader cannot understand without special training.

This legislative process readily lends itself to abuse. The volume of legislation, together with the intricacy of the process, guarantees that the public is effectively excluded from watching the legislative process. Such a system favors the "Christmas tree" bill, a bill with special breaks and provisions hung on it like ornaments. Voters have no way of knowing that their congressman's vote, on, say, a food stamp appropriation was also a vote on a $10 million giveaway for distressed tuna fleets or some other worthy cause.

Only highly publicized issues bring representatives before the public eye to be held accountable for their stands. However, even on emotional issues, like abortion and the nuclear freeze, representatives can alter the wording of a proposal in such a way as to confuse many voters. Only the naïve will deny that representatives prefer to fudge this sort of touchy issue much of the time. There is nothing that a politician dreads as much as a straight up-or-down vote on an issue of great political importance.

The remarkable foliation of the U.S. tax code provides an example of these forces at work. The tax code has, as Carter noted, become a "disgrace to the human race," which can be neither understood nor defended. It is common knowledge that the tax code favors wealth and influence;

that a plethora of loopholes have largely annulled any progressive features it once contained. Public anger about the tax system has been growing for a generation — and so has the tax code. Tax breaks are almost habitually attached to unrelated legislation or are presented in such disguised form that virtually no voter in America can describe his representative's voting record on tax questions. How many readers of this book know what their senators and representatives have contributed to the creation and elaboration of the tax system? How would one go about obtaining this information? Or publicizing it?

There has been a series of publicized votes in almost every Congress on the tax system. These debates are among the most disingenuous processes in American politics, with congressmen of both parties rising to proclaim their undying opposition to the evils they themselves created in the past — and intend to go on creating into the future. Fortunately for the politicians, the tax system is so complicated that the effects of a change can seldom be clearly assessed by accounting firms, much less by the average voter. The situation is ideal for the frequent "compromises" (most notably the two thousand–page "tax simplification law" of 1986) that satisfy public longing for change with fine phrases while leaving the key features of the tax system unchanged. How can a public that cannot calculate its own tax liabilities gauge the effect of some new provision in the tax code? The answer, of course, is that we cannot. The legislative process, in many of its most important features, has entirely escaped from popular oversight, and the American people today can say, as James Otis said in 1763, that they suffer from a system of taxation without representation.

RED TAPE: THE GROWTH OF THE BUREAUCRACY

The generation after the Civil War witnessed spectacular changes in American life. Huge corporations grew up, dwarfing anything that had existed before. Railroads, enriched by generous government land grants, enjoyed monopoly control over the economies of whole states; the oil, banking, and steel trusts came to dominate their respective industries. The scale of these enterprises nullified the attempts of the states to regulate them. The corporations were able to either buy the necessary votes or fight the state governments and win.

Clearly national action was called for, but what kind? Congress had no experience in regulating industry, and the regulatory process did not lend itself to Congress's slow, deliberative pace. Would each schedule of railway freight charges have to be submitted for approval by congressional vote? Was Congress going to set timetables, standardize track and car measurements, and regulate competition by passing laws? Obviously, such a procedure would have been hideously unwieldy. On the other hand, giving authority to presidents to set rates for major industries by executive fiat would have been efficient, but it would have overturned the constitutional separation of powers; the president would have been able to pass laws by decree. Then there was the further problem of adjudication. The federal courts would quickly have become clogged if every dispute over train fares had to go to a full civil trial. (And the Bill of Rights guarantees the right to a jury trial in federal actions that involve $20 or more.) How were disputes to be resolved? By acts of Congress — impossibly inefficient. And the resulting laws could *still* have been challenged in the courts. By presidential decision? Then the executive would have been prosecutor, lawmaker, and judge, all in one.

The solution was to set up the so-called fourth branch of government, the regulatory agency. Each agency is empowered by Congress to make regulations governing a specific activity within guidelines established by law. It is empowered to enforce these regulations and to resolve disputes through administrative procedures, though the affected parties have recourse to federal courts after exhausting their appeals within the system. Agency commissioners are appointed by the president for fixed terms and must be confirmed by the Senate.

The fourth branch of government has multiplied and divided since the creation of the Interstate Commerce Commission in 1887. The SEC, FTC, FDA, EPA, NLRB, FCC, FAA, and their alphabetical brethren total sixty-two federal agencies, with responsibilities ranging from the Library of Congress to the banking system. There is no single pattern for the chartering or function of these agencies; each must be understood on its own. Each, from the mighty CIA to the little-known Railroad Retirement Board, has its own charter, its own regulations, and its own set of internal guidelines and precedents. The federal agencies affect the lives of Americans in more direct ways than almost any Cabinet department or other institution specifically named in the Constitution.

Along with the federal agencies, another important section of the government in a sense belongs to the fourth branch of government. At the same time that the first federal agencies were being constructed, there was a movement calling for the adoption of the so-called merit system for civil servants. The unappetizing spectacle of wholesale firings of government employees every time power changed hands, and the even less appetizing spectacle of government employees working and contributing to re-elect machine politicians, resulted in a deep and lasting popular revulsion. A cry went round the country — to get "politics" out of government by ensuring that federal employees would have secure tenure regardless of the outcome of any election.

Any time the citizens of a democracy start distrusting politics, the student of democracy pays close attention. What do people mean by *politics?* What do they consider to be a nonpolitical process in the government? With the simultaneous development of the Civil Service and the federal agencies, a new and wonderful creation appeared on the historical stage: the federal bureaucracy. "Nonpolitically" appointed and "nonpolitically" administered, the bureaucracy has insinuated itself ever more deeply into the nooks and crannies of American life. Governors of great states tremble at and obey the edicts of anonymous bureaucrats lurking deep in the federal agencies. Administrations come and go, but the bureaucrats remain, secure in their ability to wage guerrilla war against orders passed down by the few remaining political appointees.

Politicians and the populace alike complain about the resulting situation. Bureaucrats often show little or no concern for a public that stands in long lines, fuming and steaming, while bureaucrats pass out sixty-page forms to be filled out in triplicate. Nixon was driven to a frenzy by the entrenched resistance of the bureaucracy to his proposals; every president has been horrified by the sabotage of which the bureaucracy is capable.

The only surprise is that anyone is surprised. What do people think the point of a nonpolitical civil service system is, if not to insulate the bureaucrats from popular and official wrath?

The fourth branch of government is intentionally insulated from popular pressure. Presidential appointments to many agencies are intentionally staggered *not* to coincide with elections or the terms of other office holders. A senator gets a six-year term to make him or her more independent of constituents (that is, less responsive); fourteen years is not an unheard-of term for a federal commissioner.

The activities of the federal agencies lie shrouded in obscurity. Some, like the CIA and the Federal Reserve Board, take secret decisions for reasons of state. Others, like the Federal Maritime Commission, operate in near-total secrecy as far as the general public is concerned because their operations are both stupefyingly boring and exquisitely complex. The only people willing and able to follow the operations of the agencies are those who have an immediate, major stake in the decisions being taken. Thus the Teamsters Union and the trucking industry find the activities of the ICC deeply fascinating. They retain lawyers to understand the activities of the commission and the decisions it hands down, and they hire lobbyists to change the decisions they don't like. The general public is unable to name any members of these commissions, much less know anything substantive about their work. As we saw earlier in the case of Congress, the fourth branch of government operates in a series of small and occasionally interlocking "communities," composed of parties with interests in the subjects at hand.

To evaluate, even to understand, the work of many of these agencies is beyond the ability of most citizens. Reading federal regulations is a painful process even for the initiated. To understand them it is often necessary for a person to have a background both in general law and in the specific case law of the agency involved. Furthermore, to evaluate the impact of new regulations on an industry one needs a solid, indeed an encyclopedic, knowledge of the industry itself. Will proposed deregulation in the bus industry, for example, favor Trailways over Greyhound? Reduce or enhance bus service to isolated rural communities? Favor large or small carriers? How healthy is the bus industry anyway? Is it tending toward greater competition or greater diversity? Whom do existing regulations favor, and why were they adopted? How effectively have they worked? Have they had any unintended consequences? Have conditions in the industry changed so much since they were first drafted that the existing regulations no longer serve their original purpose?

A citizen needs this kind of knowledge simply to have an informed opinion about the activity of one regulatory agency of one industry. As far as having an impact on the decision, what is the ordinary citizen to do? Write a letter to each member of the commission? But why should the commissioners pay heed? They are not running for anything, and the citizen's elected representatives may not even sit on the congressional committees that oversee the agency in question. And in any case, commissioners tend to be insulated from most congressional pressure; they deal only with the members of the pertinent oversight committees. Even so, few commissioners dream of being named to term after term where they are. Far better to return to the private sector and use the contacts and experience developed in government service to earn five times their former salary.

In some extreme cases, Congress can and does intervene to correct glaring injustices — or, sometimes, glaring justices. Yet the process of congressional oversight usually revolves around committees and subcommittees. The elected officials, busy attending bean suppers given by the American Legion in their home districts, inevitably delegate much of the responsibility to paid staff members. While lobbyists make it their business to know who these staff members are, and how each can best be made to see reason, the average American citizen would not know how to begin seeking out these people, much less how to communicate effectively with them.

It is possible to isolate an agency from the electoral process; it is impossible to insulate one from the influence of wealth. The net result of the establishment of the fourth branch of government has been to reduce dramatically the power of the voter over government and its decisions. The process of casting a vote every two, four, or six years for or against an elected official bears no actual relation to the behavior of the federal agencies or the federal bureaucracy.

Members of the House of Representatives only rarely win or lose elections on the basis of particular stands. (Incumbents rarely lose for any reason whatever.) They are judged more by the voters on their efficacy as advocates for their constituents, and by the campaign contributors as advocates for particular constituencies. If a representative can bring home the bacon from Washington, he is considered an effective legislator; if he can help a widow straighten out her problems with Social Security, he is a local hero. Bureaucrats and commissioners who wish to endear themselves to Congress can do so far more readily by granting individual exceptions and making judicious use of the agency budget to direct the pork into appropriate districts than by any other method.

Mention should be made here of two agencies set up to shield the activities under their jurisdiction from political pressure: the Central Intelligence Agency and the Federal Reserve Board. The Fed can influence — to some extent, control — interest rates, and it can affect the availability of credit to both business and consumers through a variety of policies. Any study of American history shows that the fight between tight-credit forces (those who have plenty of money already and want to get good interest for it) and easy-money forces (those who owe or want to borrow money) was one of the major forces in American politics. From the struggles over the financing of the Revolution to the free silver controversy, the desire of banks to maintain a sound-money policy was opposed by legions of small businessmen, farmers, and debtors who had more to gain than to lose from inflation. When the crisis of 1933 brought the American banking system to a complete collapse (every bank in the country was closed on March 4 of that year), it was evident that the system could not continue without massive and continuous federal assistance, and the sound-money forces faced a problem. They needed the power of the government to continue operations, but they were terrified that government support of banking could lead to popular control over the banks and especially over the money supply.

The solution was to extend the powers of the Federal Reserve and to keep it insulated from popular control. Members of the Federal Reserve Board are appointed at staggered intervals for fourteen-year terms. Decisions about Fed policy are made at private meetings, with no review or approval by elected officials before they take hold. Politicians can thunder about the Fed's insensitivity all they want; they can bluster and bluff; but within broad limits they have little influence over its behavior. As in the other regulatory agencies, the members of the Federal Reserve are hardly in need of their jobs. A stint in the government at a five-figure salary is the banker's equivalent of a citizen's jury duty; it is an onerous, underpaid, but necessary form of public service.

It is easy to attack the Fed for being un- or antidemocratic, but this is to ignore a serious point. The U.S. economy is a uniquely complex system. To understand its operation requires much study, the kind of study that the general public shows few signs of undertaking. To translate poll results into national economic policy would be a recipe for disaster. If elected officials were directly responsible for making the policy decisions now handled by the Fed, they would find themselves in an impossible position — besieged by powerful interests with conflicting views and faced with the alternatives of catering to popular whims regarding interest rates or courting political disaster by opposing them.

One further observation: most of the financial community believes with reason that most elected officials themselves, never mind the electorate, have an exceedingly feeble grasp of economics and would be unable to formulate a coherent policy even if they could find the political courage to do so.

The CIA is another key government agency whose deliberations are intentionally shielded from the view of the public and its elected representatives. The curtain of secrecy around the CIA is even more opaque than the one around the Fed; not only its deliberations but even its activities take place out of the glare of publicity. The reasons have something in common with the reasons that govern the regulations of the Federal Reserve. Technical reasons, different in each agency but similar in their urgency, require that both agencies be able to function in secrecy and often operate by surprise. Additionally, the CIA carries out some functions that the government cannot openly sponsor — either because of embarrassment to allies or because the activities in question violate international law or other treaty commitments. The Vietnam experience and public reaction to the ensuing revelations suggest that if the public were better informed regarding certain operations of the agency, it would not support many, perhaps most of them. In some cases the opposition would flow from an outraged sense of Wilsonian morality; in others, from a simplistic cost-benefit analysis. There are some who might think it morally wrong to bribe King Hussein; others might feel that Hussein wasn't doing enough singing to pay for his supper. Aside from the impact on the politics of foreign countries of detailed revelations concerning CIA intervention in their affairs, the American public might have a difficult time understanding why its government was subsidizing the careers of foreign figures who regularly denounce the United States in public forums. The tedious task of explaining that the bribes and the retainers keep the opposition to the United States merely verbal would consume a great deal of energy and cause even more embarrassment, without necessarily building a popular consensus in favor of this activity. A public more aware of the financial backing of various European, Middle Eastern, and Latin American public figures would want a great deal more bang for its buck.

At present, the majority of Americans appear to be as ill prepared to exercise thoughtful responsibility in foreign affairs as they are in the direction of the domestic economy. Furthermore, they seem to have little interest in educating themselves about modern economics or in deepening their understanding of world affairs.

Significantly, neither economic management nor foreign relations were expected to be national preoccupations at the time when the Constitution was drafted. Although the federal government was charged with responsibility for foreign affairs, in 1789 they were not expected to dominate American life. The country's remoteness and its security led the founders to hope that foreign affairs, the traditional bane of republics, would continue to rate low among the priorities of the people.

Economic management, in the sense of governmental responsibility for the health of the economy, was a foreign concept to the founders. The late eighteenth century was an era when governments were moving out of economic management — particularly in a country like the United States, where British mercantilism had stunted economic growth. The government established by the Constitution was designed at most to charter a central bank and to undertake public works projects, not to regulate and subsidize a modern economy.

As a result of the factors we have examined, the United States of the 1980s has altered the substance of its government without changing its form. From a small Republic with an even smaller electorate, the United States has grown into a mass state in which the actual processes of government bear little relation to public debate. The average citizen, when he or she votes at all (and only about half of those eligible to vote take the trouble), more or less blindly entrusts his or her vote to candidates who collect millions of dollars from various interest groups and spend the money in an effort to gain support by blurring the issues.

In the original American Republic the informed consent of a small number of electors held the system together; the contemporary Republic counts on the uninformed acquiescence of a vast number of voters. The citizen has been replaced by the consumer of government as the building block of the state. The citizen helps shape the state by actively participating in its affairs; the consumer accepts or refuses a package prepared for him or her by others.

The resulting lack of substance in political life appears on every side. In the extreme, one sees the figures of Johnson and Nixon preaching peace while preparing to widen a war. From day to day there are endless arguments over prayer in schools, tax reform, and other issues dear to the hearts of P. T. Barnum's latter-day descendants and spiritual heirs. A Gresham's law of political discourse seems to be at work; bad political discourse drives out good. Political life increasingly revolves around the state of the economy, a preoccupation that differs little from the "bread and circus" politics of the declining years of the Roman Republic. The circus acts are provided by a political system that has deliberately and knowingly turned over much of its policymaking authority to unelected boards of experts and officials.

The consumers of the Republic are willing to accept the system so long as nothing serious is demanded of them. But where consumers are still asked to fulfill even the most trivial responsibilities of citizenship, a noticeable weakening of commitment is observed. Thus, voluntary tax compliance, voter turnout, and draft registration have all undergone measurable declines. The presidential election of 1980 saw an expenditure of $1.2 billion on all races; voter turnout was 54 percent of those eligible, a record low. Reagan's mandate came from 26 percent of the eligible voters. Nineteen eighty-four saw another fall in voter participation — to 53 percent. In ten states and the District of Columbia fewer than half of those eligible bothered to vote.

THE POWER OF WEALTH

The balance between the unpropertied rabble and the more substantial members of the community envisioned by the Constitution has changed in unexpected ways. The independent producer in a free market was the centerpiece of the Jeffersonian system in his incarnation as a farmer; in his mercantile form this same producer was the center of Hamilton's system. This figure has been driven to the fringes of American life, but not by the rabble. Instead, a new class of superproprietors has grown up and eclipsed the farmer, merchant, and laborer together.

In the early days of the American Republic, there were many rich men, but the influence of wealth was checked by numerous forces. The most important economic check on wealth was its form: most wealth was tied up in houses, lands, slaves, ships, and other commodities. The great Southern planters like Washington might own enough land to form a European princedom, but they were as cash-poor as they were land-rich.

The interests of the rich were linked to the interests of the rest of society by apparently indissoluble bonds. While the rich and the poor might disagree over the distribution of wealth, all classes in society united in a common concern for the interests of their state or their region as a whole. For entirely selfish reasons, a tobacco planter in Virginia was concerned for the welfare of the whole state. The prosperity of the commonwealth was the precondition of his own affluence. It was in his interest to make the rivers more navigable, the roads more serviceable, and to support the progress of the arts and sciences. It was difficult for such a planter to dispose of his landed property and slaves and to reinvest the proceeds in another lucrative enterprise. Money was more or less tightly bound to its region; property, whether landed or commercial, was the dominant form of wealth.

Today, this is no longer the case. An advanced economy has made assets more easily interchangeable. People whose wealth is invested in stocks or other financial assets can easily move them from one company — or one continent — to another. Many Americans still own the property that produces their incomes, and they would not easily be able to sell out and reinvest, but this is no longer the dominant form of wealth.

This change can make it difficult to understand the eighteenth-century conception of liberty embodied in the Constitution. For the founders, private property was the best guarantee of the public good, because the richest members of society were the ones with the strongest interest in its prosperity. The richest merchants in New York would have the most public spirit when it came to improving the harbor. The largest planters would care the most about improving communications and agriculture. And the rich of all kinds would have the greatest interest in governing society in such a way as to avoid provoking rebellion by excessive laxity or severity in law and administration.

The theory is precisely that of the public corporation in which those who have the largest stake have the largest say. As a system of government, it appeared eminently natural during most of the last two centuries. Many constitutions in Europe divided voters into classes based on their tax assessments and weighted the votes of the various classes to produce majorities that reflected the interests of the more well-to-do. As late as 1948 Great Britain maintained a system of plural suffrage that allowed the owners of businesses to vote once from their home and once from their business addresses.[2]

Laws and views in revolutionary America had more in common with England's feudal past than we commonly recognize. Although the eighteenth century believed, in the abstract, in the brotherhood of man, in politics property determined being. American law at the time of the Constitution still recognized a number of classes into which the brotherhood was divided. (The sisterhood of man was also divided into classes and, where possible, bound to the brothers.) Slaves were chattels, with no more standing in a court of law than cows. Next came paupers, those dependent on public assistance for their means of support. The Articles of Confederation — echoing the provisions of England's notorious poor laws — specifically granted each state the right to refuse admittance to paupers coming from another jurisdiction.[3] Apprentices and indentured servants came next, followed by a category called freemen in Massachusetts, men not bound to serve another but too poor to vote. Finally came the freeholders, the only class with the right to vote. (The names and the numbers of the classes varied from colony to colony. North Carolina, for example, exercised its constitutional privilege to maintain two classes of voters — one able to vote for the state House and the state Senate, and one able to vote for the House only. The system did not disappear until well into the nineteenth century.[4])

In such a society, one's claim to liberty could not be separated from one's right to property, and the Bill of Rights shows a healthy concern for the property of the freeholders. Of the ten amendments that make up the Bill of Rights, six guarantee rights based in or pertaining to private property. Thus, the Bill of Rights forbids the quartering of troops except in war; guarantees a jury trial in suits involving $20 or more (a more democratic provision in today's depreciated currency); prohibits "excessive" bail or fines; specifies that an individual cannot be deprived of life, liberty, or property without due process; and safeguards the individual's home and property from warrantless searches and seizures.

The Constitution prohibits the "establishment" of religion (its maintenance by public funds) before guaranteeing its free exercise. Freedom of the press, then as now, was an affair for those who owned presses. The Constitution allows anyone to publish whatever he can afford to publish; it does not guarantee that all should have access to the means of propagating political opinions. The main body of the Constitution also shows a healthy regard for private property, guaranteeing the sanctity of contract and prohibiting the bill of attainder — once popular in England as a means by which a parliamentary majority could confiscate the property and end the life of an unpopular person without the trouble of proving facts in a court of law.

The government envisaged by the founders of the American system did not last long. A movement toward greater democracy took shape under the leadership of Jefferson and, in a more radical form, took control of the government when Andrew Jackson entered the White House. This movement smashed many of the delicate checks and balances written into the original Constitution and reached its climax when Lincoln, by an executive order issued under the emergency of wartime, overthrew the due process doctrine, ignored the sanctity of contract, trampled on the procedure for amending the Constitution, and — in a genuinely revolutionary proclamation — freed the slaves.

American democrats in the nineteenth century believed that the problem of wealth versus popular power was solved by American abundance. The size of the continent — and the military weakness of its aboriginal inhabitants — encouraged Americans to believe that, unlike Europe, the United States would never undergo the horrors and decadence associated with the urban rabble and the grim politics of scarcity. Americans watched European wars and revolutions with the smug certainty that it would be many years before such ills could take root in the New World.

Any American who wanted a farm could have one — provided only that he was white. This was the primary fact that shaped political thought during the generations between 1789 and 1868 (the year when the Constitution was amended to make universal manhood suffrage the law of the land), when the process of democratization was overthrowing the conservative Republic of the founding fathers. The settled, sensible property interest could only grow, absolutely and relatively, as long as more and more people owned their own land. Too poor to oppress his neighbors, the family farmer was rich enough to have a stake in an orderly administration of the laws and in the protection of private property. Instead of a sober, sensible republic resting on an elite of the privileged, America could have a sober, sensible republic that rested on the mass of the people.

Democracy was an odious word to the nation's founders. At best, most of them saw it as a necessary evil in the organization of the state. While an element of democracy was necessary to give the masses some form of representation, the mob was the great enemy of freedom, and they guarded against it as best they could.

The sea change that swept over the country in the next fifty years was revealed in the election of Andrew Jackson. By this time, democracy was the chief political value of the American people. A few old-fashioned Federalists still shuddered at the danger of the democratic excess, but they were confined to the political fringe. It was an article of faith that the common man was qualified for any government post — and the few surviving Federalists must have considered many nineteenth-century presidents common men indeed.

The speeches of Lincoln, the poetry of Whitman, and the sentiments of the Civil War show the elevation of democracy into a good in itself. Participation as one free man among many in the shaping of government, self-government, was not only or even not primarily a prudent method for ordering the affairs of a large and growing nation; it was one of the major paths of human self-development. The democratic Republic was the political expression of the brotherhood of man, and to oppose democracy was not only an error of political science; it was the sign of a defective moral sense.

Americans had come to believe that the absence of class politics — either in the old Roman form of the struggle between plebeians and patricians or in the new, Marxist form — was the rule, the norm. The stable, settled world of the thirteen colonies, compressed between the mountains and the sea for 150 years, had vanished into air. Not for the last time, Americans reinvented their past. They exaggerated the democratic elements in the past and ignored the hierarchical. The Pilgrims became seekers after freedom, homesteaders in funny hats. The Constitution itself was reimagined. Since America was the democratic country par excellence, and America's government rested on the federal Constitution, that Constitution must be a democratic document.

As it happened, the triumph of the democratic ideology coincided with the maturity of a new threat — the great wealth that accumulated as the nation expanded. The American industrial revolution created new and larger cities, cities that soon began to fill with a new and more menacing rabble — industrial laborers from all parts of the Old World, many Catholic, many Jewish, most unable to speak English.

But the faith remained strong even as problems multiplied. America could still be a Paradise if the trusts could be controlled . . . if the power of wealth could be blocked, and the people restored to full control of their institutions . . . if free silver coinage could only be restored . . . if women could just get the vote . . . if the liquor trust and the rum vote could be excluded from politics.

Popular politics in the generation after the Civil War consisted of an effort to return to a classless society and to prevent the rise of a new ruling class. The effort was doomed from the beginning. First, preindustrial America had never been the classless society imagined by its nostalgic supporters. Its abundance depended on the theft of Native Americans' land and the use of black labor. The populist movement in American politics during this democratic golden age was always aware of these facts and always on its guard to prevent sentimentality from admitting blacks or Native Americans to real political equality. It was Jackson who defied the Supreme Court to drive the Cherokee from their rightful, treaty-recognized homes, and though Lincoln was the Great Emancipator, it was his ultimate desire to send the blacks to Africa.

A second factor that doomed the attempted return to a classless society was geographic: the land area of the United States is finite. More than one American politician cast an occasional glance up north; God Himself seemed to be saying that the Arctic Ocean was America's natural frontier, but the British remained deaf to the divine prompting. In a surprisingly short time, the good land in the West was all taken.

Third, great wealth developed by the natural process of the market economy. The same railroads that made settling the continent possible made great fortunes possible. A small price to pay for Averell Harriman, say the liberal elitists of the eastern seaboard, but the price was too high for western farmers. Though the farmers owned their property, the monopoly power of the railroads meant that they were no longer masters of their destiny.

In the new struggles between wealth and popular power, wealth began to change its nature. In the eighteenth century wealth took the form of productive property; in the nineteenth century that productive property mushroomed into enormous trusts. The eighteenth-century society was a society of many masters who devised the Republic to guarantee their mutual interests. In the nineteenth century the forms of the old Republic were used by the trust builders and the robber barons for much the same purpose. The trusts may have been more efficent than the smaller enterprises they replaced, but they were further removed from local interests and local control. They dissolved the commercial and agrarian small producers who were the traditional guarantors of the democratic state. They formed a large urban work force that rapidly organized itself into big-city political machines and labor unions, and that showed signs of un-American tendencies toward Marxian socialism, anarchy, and the

Roman Catholic Church. A society that based itself on the paramount importance of the individual turned irresistibly into a society of mass politics. Masses of men confronted masses of money.

These developments went farthest in the Northeast and the Middle West, the most heavily industrialized sections of the country. The predominantly rural regions of the nation remained closer to the ideals of the nineteenth-century populists — and inherited their astigmatism about the rights of nonwhite peoples. The slow decline of the fortunes of the family farmer was reflected in the decline of the political fortunes of the William Jennings Bryan wing of the Democratic Party — dry, rural, and WASP — and the rise of the wet, urban, and Catholic Al Smith wing.

The new republic, the third, began to take shape early in the twentieth century and reached maturity under the New Deal. Big labor, big business, and big government reached an accommodation — uneasy but real. As we have seen, its central tenet was that a painless compromise among the nation's principal special interests could be reached if reasonable economic growth could be achieved.

The third republic was unraveling during the Carter era. Carter's desire to return to an earlier, more democratic, and virtuous America was rooted in his Southern background. Carter's prescription for the national malaise was a purified populism along the lines of the nineteenth-century movement for democracy. He believed that this democracy was somehow inherent in American institutions; that it would re-emerge if structures like the imperial presidency could be dismantled and if the power of the special interests could be broken. He knew that big business and big labor were here to stay, but he was suspicious of both. He appealed from them to the "general public" — a public he seems to have imagined as being something like a collection of independent farmers and small businessmen from the populist past.

What actually happened during this period was that wealth, once again, was changing its shape. As that happened, the populist forces in American politics were, once again, groping for new ways to assert their interests. Wealth was gradually becoming more abstract. The long peace throughout much of the world since 1945 and the continued consolidation of the world economy into one unit were internationalizing and generalizing wealth. In the eighteenth century wealth was tied to a region, an industry, a trade. In the nineteenth century it was national in scope, but was still confined to a particular industry — the steel trust, the oil trust, the railroads, and so on. In the twentieth century, wealth became much more purely financial. Money moved freely across national boundaries as conglomerates and multinational corporations flowered. The Mellons still had a connection with Pittsburgh early in the century; the Fords were tied to Detroit; but all such ties grew more tenuous in the postwar period. America's great industrial families tended to move their money out of the smokestack industries, to diversify their portfolios. The robber barons and trust builders yielded to nearly anonymous CEOs and boards of directors.

Wealth was less and less intimately tied to its country of origin. Money managers sprang up; their purpose was to find the best investments not only in the United States, but all around the world. The smokestack industries themselves diversified — into other industries and into new parts of the world. John D. Rockefeller, Sr., was primarily interested in building Standard Oil. He was willing to sacrifice short-term profits for the long-term growth of his company. In today's volatile world, corporate management rarely owns much of the corporate stock. Managers are rewarded for short-term profitability, regardless of the long-term effects on the company.

The gradual divergence between the interest of wealth and the general good has deepened with the development of the market economy. The more perfect — that is, flexible, international, and quick moving — the market becomes, the less wealth has in common with what was once the national interest.

As in the early populist era, the response of the rabble and its allies was at first to attempt to turn back the clock. Labor unions fought to protect their existing positions and to restore their political power. Civil rights groups, farmers, and other elements of the collection of interests calling itself the Democratic Party invoked the spirit of Franklin Roosevelt as their predecessors had invoked Andrew Jackson.

Meanwhile, the influence of money in politics grew. Organized popular power blocs like the labor unions were weakened by the economic changes under way, but those who initiated the changes were making more money than ever. The 1978 elections saw unprecedented funding for conservative candidates; prominent liberals, pillars of the postwar order, toppled all across the nation. The regulatory commissions and the national bureaucracy, hallmarks of the third republic, came under intense fire.

The weakening of the popular institutions in relation to the power of wealth led, during the Carter years, to a bizarre revival of the original function of parts of the original constitutional system. Since the time of Franklin D. Roosevelt, the imperial presidency had overshadowed the other interests in society, taking the leadership in resolving disputes. Under Carter, the United States experienced something similar to the preimperial presidency as envisioned by the founding fathers. It didn't work.

Without the firm hand of a masterful president, government rapidly became deadlocked. Regional differences and conflicts among special interests slowed energy legislation until a painstaking compromise was worked out. It was a classic case of constitutional checks and balances preventing the dominance of the underpopulated energy-producing states by the overpopulated energy-consuming states. Similarly, the popular outcry against the tax system was barely heard. The vested interests and lobbyists overpowered the representatives of the urban rabble and the rural poor. A triumph for the Constitution — and a disaster for the Republic.

Even the decay of the party system and the decline of voter participation would not have displeased the founders. They considered the party system the bane of English politics and the enemy of true republicanism. Mass parties they would have regarded as the symptoms of a republic in terminal decay. The development of machines in politics was opposed to everything that the founders believed in.

During the Carter years the nation writhed as neither the Executive nor the Legislative Branch of government could take effective action to respond to crisis and near-crisis conditions. But this again was a triumph of the constitutional system. A slow-moving, deliberative Congress primarily responsive to vested economic interests was precisely what the founders thought the United States should have. A relatively weak president without a secure grip on a political mass machine was exactly what the Constitution was designed to produce.

The first republic, the constitutional republic, was produced under the stresses of the Revolution and the early years of independence. The second republic established itself under Jackson, and the third reached maturity under Roosevelt. Under Carter, the nation was groping its way toward a fourth. It was a process still in its early stages, marked more by discomfort with the old structures than by creative insights into how to build new ones. If history was any precedent, the search for a fourth republic would be a long one, marked by many false starts and blind alleys. And because the United States and the world were in such a delicate and complex situation, the search for the fourth republic was likely to be more difficult and to require more sweeping changes than the previous efforts to remake America.

In the Carter years, this crisis in historical development looked like a crisis of liberalism.

THE LIBERAL CRISIS

B Y 1980, liberalism was in the midst of a full-fledged crisis. Reagan openly proclaimed his hostility to the welfare state; liberals were hopelessly divided among themselves, uncertain, and weak. Many commentators spoke of an end of the Roosevelt era.

There was no single cause of the liberal crisis, and among liberals there was no consensus on how to overcome it. The attacks and the difficulties came from all sides. The economic policies on which liberals prided themselves no longer seemed to work; on social and cultural issues they found themselves retreating in the face of a many-sided and complex reaction; and the ability of liberals to form effective political coalitions seemed to have disappeared.

The economic crisis of liberalism was a crisis of Keynesianism and a crisis of free trade. Keynesianism, as practiced in the United States for the last fifty years, has meant relying on the federal government to support the economy through recessions. So-called countercyclical programs, like public works employment and heavy government borrowing, cushioned the effects of recession and hastened recovery. The increased productivity of the economy was expected to raise government revenues, compensating (or nearly compensating) for the deficit spending required to get the economy going. Previously, governments cut spending when times were bad and revenues down; the result usually was to exacerbate the situation.

Keynesianism is an economics of "demand management." Like Marxism, it posits that capitalism is not the self-regulating system of conservative economic theory. For Keynesians the Achilles' heel of the economy is the relationship between savings, investment, and consumer demand. Everything produced by the economy must be sold, and sold at a profit. But if consumers decide to save their income instead of spending it, then overall demand drops, and not every good can find its market. Corporate executives, noticing this, will cut back on their plans for new investment;

when they cannot sell their existing output, they see little point in increasing their productive capacity. With investment dropping, demand for economic goods falls even further. With no new factories being built, there are fewer jobs for construction workers, less demand for steel, and so on.

Economists of the old school believed that any such disturbances were temporary. Sooner or later — sooner if the government and associated liberal do-gooders kept their hands to themselves, later if misguided humanitarians interfered with the operations of the free market — the economy would right itself.

It was John Maynard Keynes who advanced the troubling idea that the economy might right itself, but at a permanently higher level of unemployment. He suggested that when economic activity began to fall off, there would be less demand for labor and so, in the classic operation of the market, the price for labor would fall. This would reduce the ability of people to save money, thereby restoring the balance between supply and demand in the economy as a whole. Now everything is at an equilibrium again, but wages are lower, production is down, and unemployment is higher than before.

The world of the early 1930s looked very Keynesian. The solution that he proposed — that government stimulate demand to raise prices, wages, and production to a higher equilibrium — was politically popular because it turned the government into Santa Claus. Franklin Roosevelt, who had campaigned against the irresponsible budget deficits of the big-spending Hoover administration, resigned himself to the biggest peacetime budget deficits in history, and by 1934 the economy began to crawl back from the depths. Unemployment slowly receded from a high of 25 percent, and in 1937 a relieved government decided that it was safe to abandon the dangerous experiment of Keynesian policies and cut the budget deficit. The result was another slump that threatened to return the country to the worst conditions of the Depression, and the place of Keynesian economics in government and academia was secured for a generation.

The policy seemed to work well. The economy prospered after 1939; World War II provided a major Keynesian stimulus, and the combination of military spending and social welfare and public works projects in the years after the war continued to keep demand high. The national debt rose sharply during those years, but it rose more slowly than the GNP. Postwar recessions were mild and short; recoveries were long and robust.

During the 1970s, these policies were not working as well. Inflation persisted even through recessions. More and more countercyclical spending, accompanied by higher and higher deficits, yielded less and less in the way of prosperity. Keynesian economic management seemed to have reached a point of diminishing returns.

Free trade, the other pillar of liberal orthodoxy, was in no healthier state. Free trade turned out to mean free fall for a number of American industries. Most of America's developed trading partners had introduced extensive national economic planning in the years after the war. Such practices made it harder to say what free trade was. Were the European state-subsidized steel companies dumping steel in the U.S. market? Did Japanese policies of encouraging industrial growth in certain areas amount to a subsidy for key industries? What about Third World tax breaks for industries that set up shop there? Wasn't this a form of state support for industry?

Germany and Japan argued that America's anarchic approach to its own economic future had created a competitive disadvantage for American industry. Americans claimed that the monopolistic, state-subsidized, and centrally planned economies of our trading partners distorted economic realities and subverted the concept of the free market.

Meanwhile, although the United States continued to advocate free trade in public, it built up its own complex system of subsidies and incentives to underwrite production and make its industries more competitive in world markets. The defense industry and the needs of the air force gave American corporations the financial muscle to corner the world's market in civil aviation. American farm price supports, linkages of foreign aid to purchases from American manufacturers, and other indirect subsidies for exports also made free trade less a policy than a slogan as the postwar era moved on.

One implication of free trade is the free flight of capital from country to country. It is only natural under those conditions for investors to seek the most profitable locations for investment. Within the United States there was a movement by corporations away from the unionized, high-wage regions of the country toward the unorganized, low-wage regions; internationally, the same movement took place on what became a much greater scale.

The unions, never happy with free trade, were joined by a chorus of manufacturing representatives as the competition tightened. While everyone recognized the harmful side effects of protectionism, many seemed to feel that protection was still required. Chemotherapy may make you bald, but better bald than dead.

The primary cause of the problem was a worldwide revival of national economic rivalry. Itself a sign of the slow collapse of the postwar American hegemony, the renewed conflict among the advanced countries threatened disastrous consequences. International cooperation was more essential than ever in the explosive economic conditions of the 1980s. Unless, for example, exports from Third World countries to the advanced countries could substantially rise, those Third World nations would be unable to pay even the interest on their huge debts. With one hand, the advanced countries encouraged the Third World to concentrate on export-oriented growth and investment in order to earn the foreign exchange to service their debts. With the other hand, the advanced countries were closing their domestic markets to Third World goods. Far from agreeing on ways to salvage the economies of the Third World and thereby restore stability to the world's financial system, the advanced countries became involved in squabbles among themselves over market shares and export dumping.

Besides its economic problems, liberalism faced pressure from the right on the social issues ranging from abortion to prayer in schools to gay rights to the teaching of evolution in public schools. Facing grave economic and, ultimately, military problems, the public turned to sources of religious comfort and certainty. The pragmatic, nondogmatic liberal approach — the "value-free" management of social conflict, tolerant individualism, and such — offered few inner resources to deal with mass terror. Best-selling books warned of the imminent return of Christ and traced the Middle East conflict to biblical prophecies. The liberal agenda for women and blacks was on the verge of total victory in the late 1970s, yet popular feeling against this agenda was mounting. The prospects of a declining economy emphasized the conflict between social and economic groups competing for a limited number of slots in the economy. As the public lost confidence in liberal promises of growth and prosperity, it recalculated the cost of affirmative action.

The liberal coalition lost all coherent sense of political purpose. Its stock-in-trade, a better future through compromise, seemed shopworn and unrealistic. Liberalism is an ideology of growth, not of retreat. When the economy threatened to impose hardships on the population at large, the liberal coalition suddenly dissolved. When forced to make choices — when history asked "Butter or guns?" — the liberals' instinct was always to say "Butter the guns!" The liberal coalition was united around the demand that Samuel Gompers made central to the American labor movement: "More!" Nothing in liberal experience or theory lent itself easily to the development of a program around "Less!" Less for whom? Labor? Management? The North? The South? Farmers? The rich? The poor? Women? Men? The middle class?

THE LIBERAL SPIRIT

It is often observed that the liberalism of yesterday is the conservatism of today. As political clichés go, this one has merit. We observed early on that liberalism is a state of mind, not a set of dogmas. The English Whigs in the seventeenth century believed in a monarchy subordinated to a Parliament that represented agricultural and mercantile interests. The founders of the American constitutional system believed in a republican government with a limited franchise. Nineteenth-century liberals extended the franchise to all adult white men; twentieth-century liberals extended the franchise further and brought government into the economy. The golden thread that ties these positions together is that liberalism in each era supported an enlightened compromise between traditional institutions and the conditions of contemporary society.

Liberalism is open to science and progress; its proponents conceive of history as a continuing process of development — preferably a uniformitarian process of development without wasteful and destructive upheavals. Liberals believe that the conflicts in society can be solved — if only everyone will be reasonable. In American history, liberals specifically sought a compromise in the clash between wealth and popular power by developing structures to protect the essential interests of both in as humane a fashion as possible. The Constitution was a classic example of a liberal initiative; its reliance on the system of checks and balances was an effort to find a rational replacement for the superstitious views of government once prevalent in Europe — that without kings, anointed by God to rule, and without feudal lords, similarly blessed, society would rapidly decay into anarchy.

At the same time, liberals oppose the violent overthrow of traditional institutions. Liberals opposed slavery, but they did not favor a war to end it. French liberals wanted to subject Louis XVI to elected assemblies, but they did not want his queen beheaded in the public square. American New Deal liberals wanted to reform the abuses of American capitalism, but they did not want to fly the red flag over Congress.

The affairs of the spiritual world give us perhaps the clearest insight into the liberal dilemma in the last quarter of the twentieth century. In theology we are free to deal with ideas set loose from many of the historical links that complicate political life. In politics even an ultraconservative like Jesse Helms will support a colossally wasteful government giveaway to tobacco farmers in the interests of a filthy and destructive habit because, well, because he needs the votes. In theology people are more free to follow their ideas to logical conclusions.

Christianity, we are told, is a *revealed* religion. God communicated absolute truth directly (through Scripture, Scripture and Tradition, Scripture and the Book of Mormon, or Scripture and the Reverend Mr. Moon, depending on whom you ask) to mankind. Unlike science, revelation does not depend on experiments, analysis, and observation to establish its truth; revelation gets its validity from the Author of revelation.

As scientific information began to conflict with traditionally received religious views, it seemed at first that people would have to reject either science or religion. Either the Bible was right and Galileo was wrong, or vice versa. If Galileo's instruments told him something different from what God told the church in the Bible, then the devil had obviously bewitched Galileo's telescope.

A third way opened up, however: something analogous to liberalism in politics — modern theology. Liberal theology in the broadest, non-technical sense is based on the assumption that ultimately science and religion are not in conflict. Any apparent conflicts are the result of misunderstandings, either of science or of religion. The account of creation in Genesis was interpreted as an allegory, or, alternatively, as divinely inspired folklore that presents an essential truth — that God made the world — in the mythological terms that were current among the people who first heard the story. After an initial period of agonized hesitation, most of today's so-called mainline Protestant churches as well as the Catholic Church swallowed hard and abandoned their traditional readings of Genesis for the new, "liberal" interpretation.

But though the new theologies were able to accommodate the scientific exegeses of traditional Western religions, they were less successful in meeting the religious needs of believers. People turn to religion for solace, for companionship, and for reassurance that life's suffering means something. People expect from their churches a coherent statement about what life means, and they want an ethical explanation for the freedoms and limitations they experience in daily life.

The harder life is, the greater the need of many human beings for religious comfort and structure. Yet what we can call, speaking loosely, liberal theology offers nothing of the kind. It proposes a nebulous faith, an evolving moral law in which today's sin is tomorrow's natural impulse, and a complex idea of religious truth whose greatest enemy is the black-or-white approach of most people to questions of truth or falsehood. The liberal churches find themselves in the anomalous position of having the least to offer those who need religion most, and the most to offer those least interested. The churches spend much of their time informing people that the idea of religion that drew them into the church was wrong — and then proposing another, more difficult idea of religion to keep them there.

Under the circumstances, it is not surprising that the fastest-growing religious groups are the fundamentalist churches and the unchurched. Fundamentalism has little to offer educated, scientifically minded skeptics, yet fundamentalist preachers know that people come to church for reasons other than to hear advanced lectures on the philosophy of religion. Those who need religion get the old-fashioned kind; those who don't need it stay away altogether.

Sooner or later, the progress of liberal theology leads to a conflict among its supporters. Those who thought liberalism would preserve the past by accommodating the future in certain limited respects feel that liberalism has gone too far. Those who valued liberalism because it was opening up the closed, musty museums of the past to the fresh winds of change want to go forward. In denomination after denomination, religious order after order, a point comes where some kind of decision has to be made. Where and how the line is drawn reflects the specific quality and experience of each religious group. Among the Methodists, the Lutherans, the Catholics, and the Presbyterians, the lines have been drawn in different places. In most churches, the forward movement of liberalism has stopped while the hierarchies grope for alternatives — so far, without much success.

Liberalism in politics led to a similar result. In the 1970s reform Democrats were split between those who wanted reform in order to change the orientation of the Democratic Party and those who wanted to reform the Democratic Party to make it more effective but otherwise unchanged.

In other areas of national life liberal reforms ended in the same kind of impasse. Government regulation, which had once enhanced the operation of American business, began to interfere. Popular involvement in foreign policy threatened to make it impossible for the U.S. government to conduct any foreign policy at all. Liberal reforms to make Congress more democratic by weakening the power of the leadership and dismantling the seniority system resulted in a Congress that looked scarcely capable of functioning at all.

With liberals splitting between those who wanted to stop and those who wanted to press forward, liberalism found itself vulnerable to a challenge from the right — the first conservative resurgence of measurable strength since the McCarthy era.

In politics, liberalism performs a desacralizing function similar to its work in religion. The self-confident spirit of a young liberalism dissolves belief in the divine right of kings with the acid of its skepticism. "But without kingship," said the tories, "good government is impossible."

"Nonsense," said the liberals. "Good government rests on the critical analysis of political theory. We can devise a constitution that protects the essential features of liberty and order without subjecting ourselves to a rubbishy old monarchy."

And the process continues. Traditionalists continually seek to vest an existing social order with a legitimacy that is ultimately derived from some nonhistorical — and usually religious — source. Liberalism says that effectiveness is its own legitimacy and needs no divine sanction. Political theory once sounded like theology and was filled with appeals to natural law and the Bible. Liberalism asks instead, "How is the economy doing?"

Against radicals, especially Marxists, liberalism has a similar effect. Liberalism borrows extensively from Marxism — as it does from conservative ideologies — for the sake of its practical programs as well as its theory. But what liberalism balks at in Marxism is its "dogmatism," its "ideological ossification." At the center of this dogmatism is Marx's insistence on class struggle as the basis of history. Liberals consider any form of absolutism in ideas abhorrent, and the idea of an absolute and irreconcilable class conflict offends liberal sensibility as much as the idea of an absolutely ordained divine right of kings. Liberals see no more irreconcilable conflict between the classes than between science and religion, and they aim to reconcile social classes on a liberal middle ground in the same way that they attempt to reconcile scientific and religious thinking.

All conflict, say liberals, is manageable conflict, and the real job of government is to keep conflict within manageable bounds. The answers to political questions cannot be brought in from ideas outside the political process — not the Bible, not *Das Kapital*. Any dogma in politics must sooner or later go wrong.

But liberal politics like liberal religion works best for those who need it least. Liberalism in politics and religion is an ideology for the comfortable — those whose lives occupy that pleasant middle ground where life offers no hideous dilemmas. People who are in the midst of an overwhelming personal crisis, or people who are hungry and oppressed, are seldom satisfied by blandly phrased appeals to enlightenment and moderation. The success of liberalism depends on its success in maintaining a world where it can flourish — where most aspirations are met and most people can live decently. Successful management of the economy is the bottom line for liberalism for two reasons. First, successful economic management is the criterion that liberalism itself proposes as the true test for political legitimacy. Second, only successful economic management can create the conditions for liberalism.

The classic case in recent American history was the New Deal. Ideologically the New Deal was slapdash and sloppy. It took its ideas from the far left and the far right and displayed a serene indifference to its own inconsistencies. Ideologies on the left and the right were frustrated and infuriated by Roosevelt, and they tore him apart in the learned journals. Yet Roosevelt could always answer, with Galileo, *"Eppur si muove."* Nevertheless it moves. It works.

Moved. Worked. Liberalism in the 1980s had lost its vision, its self-confidence, and its mandate. Its supporters were divided and perplexed; its adversaries confident and united. The ideologues were back, and the liberals retreated in dismay. The conservatives returned from the political wilderness, and they were loaded for bear.

PART FOUR

*On the Beach
with Canute*

THE DAWN OF THE DEAD

R ONALD REAGAN'S election in 1980 was the greatest humiliation of a sitting American president in history. After more than a decade of failure, humiliation, and retreat, after hearing for four years that the future held little or no growth, the American people — or at least the 26 percent of those eligible who cast their votes for Reagan — opted for a candidate who promised to restore America's military strength, redeem its global position, and reignite its economy. In one of Reagan's most effective speeches, he spoke of seeing Jimmy Carter in a dream.

"You want my job," said Carter.

"I don't want *your* job," said Ronald Reagan. "I want to be president of the United States."

Jimmy Carter was the accountant of decline, the manager of retreat; Reagan hoped to be the man on horseback leading the nation into a brighter future. Comparisons with Jack Kennedy are not amiss. Like Kennedy, Reagan felt that it was time to get the country moving again; he felt that his predecessor was soft on Cuba; he feared a missile gap. Where these two gifted and charismatic politicians differed was on means. Kennedy believed that America's future would be assured by an extension of the New Deal and related programs; Reagan believed that these programs themselves limited the country's forward progress.

Reagan's brand of conservatism had been considered dead as recently as 1964. Vats of ink were spilled by dull gray Establishmentarians to hail the "newfound maturity" of the American voter after 1964. The voters, said these pundits, instinctively repudiated ideological extremes; any party captured by its extremists would be pushed out of power. The path to power in American politics lay up the middle of the road.

When McGovern lost in 1972, the sages of the center elaborated their theory of politics. Each party has a radical, ideological wing, one that unfortunately is overrepresented in the primary process. The responsible elements in the party (all too often this means those in each party who have no binding principles beyond personal ambition) work to overcome the opposition of the ideologues to choose a centrist candidate who will appeal to the other party. The party that best resists its own principles is rewarded by political success for betraying its inner beliefs.

Much less has been heard of this conventional wisdom since the election, in 1980 and 1984, of the most ideological candidate in modern American history.

For liberals there was something uncanny about the political atmosphere of the mid to late 1970s. Forces long dead, or thought dead, were heard from again. The unwashed fundamentalism of the kind laughed out of court by Clarence Darrow reappeared, forcing new "monkey laws" through state legislatures. The chairman of the John Birch Society took a seat in the United States Congress. The internal security committees of the House and the Senate stirred in their sleep. Liberals can be excused for feeling that they had fallen into George Romero's film *The Dawn of the Dead,* that they were a dwindling band of survivors watching the zombies stumble through malls in search of new prey.

Conservative groups formed with bewildering speed — the Moral Majority, the Conservative Caucus, NCPAC (the National Conservative Political Action Committee), the Religious Roundtable — and set about not only to block liberal proposals, but to agitate for their own agendas. Conservatives demonstrated a magical ability to use the new campaign finance laws for their purposes and to target liberal officeholders for elimination. "We're ready to lead" was the boast of Richard Viguerie, the direct-mail fund raiser who found millions of dollars for the issues of his choice.

THE DOMESTIC AGENDA: THE MARKET AND ITS FOES

The New Right came to the fore with a consistent world view and political agenda. In this sense, it was the most ideologically committed movement ever to capture the American presidency. Franklin Roosevelt, the last president to initiate sweeping changes in national life, had no ideology but pragmatism. He would accept any idea that showed promise. The New Right had higher standards.

The core of the right's analysis was its belief in the market. But just as the religion of the right was the old-time religion, without any of this newfangled criticism and relativism, so was its faith in the market the old kind of faith. By the free market the right did not mean the gigantic multinational corporations and their oligopolistic practices. The right believed that the early capitalist market, the kind described by Adam Smith in 1776, not only still existed, but was the cutting edge of American capitalism in the late twentieth century. From new entrepreneurs came the breakthroughs in technology, the new products and services, that would transform the American economy and re-create an era of prosperity. Citing statistics to show that new jobs were created in the small companies and enterprises, not in the great ones, the New Right theorists like George Gilder, Arthur Laffer, and Jude Wanniski argued that the market remained, as in 1776, the most efficient possible means for the production and distribution of commodities.

But though the unregulated market served as a cornucopia for all of society, the market itself needed protection. Competition is the mainspring of the market, and competition means winners and losers. In general, the theoreticians of the New Right favored policies that reinforced the economic consequences of competition. Taxes on the earnings and capital gains of the winners were to be lowered, but losers like Chrysler were to be allowed to die.

One nagging weakness in capitalist apologetics is the system's foundation in greed. From Adam Smith to the present, capitalism's defenders have struggled with the task of demonstrating that the anarchically self-seeking activities of greedy people can result in a just and humane social order. Moreover, though the invisible hand of the market may, in the long run, create a harmonious social order out of the discords and janglings of competitive economic life, in the process many innocent people suffer. It has not always been easy for the defenders of the market to show why this suffering is justified.

Adam Smith's halfhearted defense of the morality of the market was not enough for George Gilder. Far from conceding that capitalism has its origin in greed, he claimed that it begins in generosity. "Not from greed, avarice, or even self-love can one expect the rewards of commerce, but from a spirit closely akin to altruism, a regard for the needs of others, a benevolent, outgoing and courageous temper of mind."[1]

John D. Rockefeller could not have said it any better, and Rockefeller, unlike Gilder, would not have been able to cite Levi Strauss in support of his claim. Gilder confidently traces capitalism back to the potlatch of certain Pacific and Native American peoples. In a potlatch culture, leaders compete in giving. With each distribution of goods, rival leaders try to emulate the generosity of the first donor and to surpass it. As these leaders (*mumis*) strive to make ever-larger gifts to their communities, the economy expands, specialization sets in, and capital begins to accumulate within a given society.

To the casual observer, big-spending liberal congressmen look as much like these leaders who gain power by giving as do entrepreneurs, but this doesn't bother Gilder. Nor does it disturb him that he is unable to put forward any example of a society that potlatched its way to capitalism. The similarity of the entrepreneur and the mumi of the Pacific isles needs nothing so vulgar as a visible causal link to establish it.

The New Right considers the marketplace an eminently moral institution. The best men win. Leading a successful business requires the finest human characteristics. Not merely Gilder's altruism, but self-control (our mumi begins his own rise by "limiting his consumption of meat and coconuts"), moderation, tolerance, intelligence, and faith all go into the making of the entrepreneur.

In this moral market, however, competition in generosity must still be protected. If government, or any other force, steps between the entrepreneur and his just reward, the moral balance of the universe is upset. The thrifty lose their just deserts, and the shiftless prosper unduly. Inflation, with its systematic bias toward feckless debtors and against generous, conscientious, *moral* creditors, is not only poor policy; it is immoral.

Entirely vanished from this ideology is the revisionist market doctrine introduced by the nineteenth-century progressives. The market cannot be improved; we can only interfere. The social safety net of the New Right was intended to catch only the most pitiable of social cripples, and in order to preserve the moral health of society, it was better to err on the side of stringency than of generosity in awarding government aid. Better that a deserving food stamp recipient or a truly disabled person lose benefits than that an undeserving applicant get them. Better that a child go hungry than an adult, somewhere, live too well. After all, if an undeserving person gets benefits, the whole moral structure of society obscurely trembles. If on the other hand a deserving person is unable to collect, the only result is a little individual hardship, and, who knows, this may be just the incentive required to shock that person into making the effort to overcome the disability.

So, armed with the arguments of Gradgrind, Pecksniff, Podsnap, and Murdstone, the right set about to reconstruct the welfare state.

ENEMIES OF THE PEOPLE

The concept of class struggle was banished from American life while liberalism reigned. All conflicts were negotiable, all interests reconcilable. The right had no such illusions. From its earliest days, the theoreticians of the New Right identified specific class enemies and hoped to develop programs to drive their opponents out of power and smash the economic bases of their support. Gilder and others have divided their enemies into three sometimes overlapping classes: the clients of the welfare state, the new class of social administrators and bureaucrats, and the decadent offspring of the old rich. Opposed to these groups are the entrepreneurs, the backbone of the American economy, and honest working people who, the New Right believes, are eager to work for the entrepreneurs without all those union work rules and OSHA (Occupational Safety and Health Administration) regulations.

The New Right does not believe that the aspirations of all these classes can be met simultaneously, and it follows that society must choose between a doomed effort to gratify the insatiable appetites of its drones and an attempt to smash the drones' power to use the political process for directing the distribution of the national product. Although the drones lack all talent for managing the economy, they are past masters of the art of politics — but it is in this arena that the New Right intends to challenge its enemies.

The note of class enmity sounds in Viguerie's *The New Right: We're Ready to Lead*. He quotes Paul Weyrich, a man credited with helping Jerry Falwell make up his mind to enter politics:

> In fact, Paul likes to argue that we are at war. "It may not be with bullets," he concedes, "and it may not be with rockets and missiles, but it is a war nevertheless. It is a war of ideology, it's a war of ideas, and it's a war about our way of life. And it has to be fought with the same intensity, I think, and dedication as you would fight a shooting war."[2]

This war in which "we" find ourselves is a war against liberals and their allies, mostly those in the elite. With a precision honed in dozens of direct-mail fund-raising campaigns, Viguerie identifies this "we." Small businessmen being strangled with government red tape, fundamentalists appalled at the explicit sex on television, anti-abortion and antibusing activists, and all those "unwilling to accept the liberal line that America has had her day in the sun."[3]

Gilder identifies the upwardly mobile groups in American society more clearly still. Hard-working ethnics, mostly Catholic and often "of short heritage on these shores," are striving to reach the pinnacles of American society. Gilder is fond of statistics that show that Greeks, Irish, Jews, and Poles earn more than WASPs (although he neglects to add that WASP earners include a disproportionate number of poor Southern and Appalachian whites). These ethnics are the group Michael Novak calls the PIGS (Poles, Italians, Greeks, Slavs), and they are the basis for the northern wing of the new Republican majority first proclaimed in the Nixon administration. This group and its allies must take power from what Jerry Falwell has called "the godless minority of treacherous individuals who have been permitted to formulate national policy."[4]

An unholy — in Falwell's view, literally godless — alliance opposes the hard-working Christians, the backbone of the country. The class enemy already alluded to comprises the decadent old rich, the beneficiaries of the welfare state, and its administrators. Special interest groups in this broad coalition are feminists, gay and lesbian rights advocates, and those who foster the delusion among blacks that racism is a pervasive force in the United States.

In Gilder's view these enemies of the people have committed many crimes, but the worst thing they have done is opt out of the economic market. These groups choose security over risk, government over economics. Welfare clients seek to increase their benefits; bureaucrats seek larger appropriations for their wretched agencies. They siphon money from the virtuous and the productive in order to give it to the drones. Gilder argues that such struggles can never win any substantial benefits. To the extent that the dones manage to increase their share of the national income, they undermine the potential of the system to generate new wealth. In the long run, their own success defeats them. But as long as these groups persist in their misguided raids on the Treasury, they remain enemies of the American people. The drones and the productive have nothing more in common with one another than the vampire has with his victim.

THE PRESCRIPTION

The New Right's prescription for the economy is simple: strengthen the productive classes and weaken the drones. The economy will then right itself. The market will work, and all will be well.

Gilder, one of the committed supply siders, takes issue with a central contention of Keynes — that recessions and depressions can be caused by an excess of supply in relation to demand. This doctrine is at the heart of contemporary liberalism and provides the economic justification for the liberal welfare state. Liberals believe that by redistributing income from savers to spenders, they are keeping demand high enough to ensure that the goods that are produced can be sold, and that the economy will therefore continue to expand.

But the supply siders return to the older concept that supply generates demand. It seems to them self-evident that production generates sufficient demand. The cost in wages, rent, and raw materials that go to produce something is always enough to buy that product. Keynes never argued that this was untrue in principle, but he maintained that not all of the money made every year is spent. Some of it is saved, and though some of what is saved gets invested, there is no automatic mechanism that keeps savings and investment in balance. If savers put "too much" in the bank, and investors put too little back into the economy, an imbalance can result, say the Keynesians.

The supply siders agree that savings and investment need to be balanced, but they argue that it is better to stimulate investment directly than to redistribute income to stimulate demand. Giving money to the welfare cheats and bureaucrats means taking the money out of the hands of the productive. The taxes necessary to pay for social programs — or to service the national debt — reduce the incentives for investment, so they may exacerbate the "underinvestment" problem that government spending is supposed to cure.

The Reagan tax cuts were designed to address this problem. They were intended to make investment more rewarding, thereby overcoming the problem of excess savings. A 30 percent tax cut would, hoped the supply siders, encourage more investment and move the economy ahead.

The other economic goals of the new administration had the same purposes. The attack on inflation was necessary to restore predictability to the economy. Investment could not be predictably profitable if the payoff came in depreciated dollars. Opening federal lands for economic exploitation was designed also to open up profitable horizons for investors. The same was true of the military buildup. There is nothing better for making investment profitable than defense spending; nothing is safer than a government contract. In the era of the $600 hammer, few lines of work were more profitable.

Deregulation was introduced to open hitherto closed fields to new entrants. Controls on pollution, occupational safety, and affirmative action were also relaxed — all to the end of making investment more profitable and consequently more common. It was an economic program designed to benefit the productive classes; the supply siders were sincere in their belief that the new prosperity would eventually trickle down.

The right was not only interested in strengthening its allies; it also intended to cripple its foes. This again was a new development in postwar American politics. Conservatives set about attacking the institutions and organizations that they believed sustained their political opponents — "defunding the left," as some of them put it. One obvious target was the new class of bureaucrats with a vested interest in liberal programs. Nests of liberalism like the Legal Aid Society, the Civil Rights Commission, and the National Endowment for the Humanities were subjected to purges and, where possible, cutbacks. Lists of appointees to key posts throughout government were scrutinized by hard-eyed conservatives for names of unreliable people. Departments like Health and Human Services, which once served as funding conduits to such liberal groups as Planned Parenthood, had their money rerouted. Regulations for government studies and programs were rewritten to attract applications from the right. The welfare state was curtailed. Some programs were eliminated; some were cut; some were burdened with regulations intended to frustrate possible beneficiaries. Waves of layoffs roiled the liberal swamps of the bureaucracy.

The Reagan revolution was under way.

FOREIGN AFFAIRS AND
THE NEW RIGHT

I F THE NEW RIGHT saw domestic affairs as a class struggle between
the productive and the unproductive, it brought a no less clear view
to world affairs. It visualized international relations as a global class
struggle between the forces of free market society and an international
communist movement with its headquarters in Moscow. Among the
heroes of his youth, Richard Viguerie includes "the two Macs" — the
Big Mac, who fought the communists in Korea, and the Little Mac, who
fought them in the Senate.[1] With these two figures hovering in the back
of his mind, it is small wonder that Viguerie, like many others of the
right, viewed Nixon's détente as a sell-out, a capitulation that MacArthur
would have scorned and McCarthy investigated.

In November 1979, Jeane Kirkpatrick published an essay in *Commentary*
titled "Dictatorships and Double Standards." According to legend, Reagan read it, was impressed, and invited her to join his administration as
ambassador to the United Nations. Whatever its role in her appointment,
the article lays out very clearly the views that would play a significant
role in shaping the Reagan foreign policy.

Carter's emphasis on human rights, she writes, was doomed from the
start. Because communist nations are unmoved by American appeals for
human rights, Carter's policy could work only against American allies —
Third World countries under friendly but authoritarian regimes or the
settler states of Israel and South Africa. She points out that the transition
from nondemocratic to democratic regimes is a difficult one. It requires
the material base we have discussed earlier — a large and comfortable
middle class — but that material base needs time for society to develop
the traditions of accommodation and compromise that make democracy
possible. Democracy will not work until current leaders learn to tolerate
dissent and until the dissenters, when they take power, learn to tolerate
their former rulers. Kirkpatrick observes that Britain's development of

democratic government took six centuries, and that our own was also an affair of generations.

When the Carter administration eyed guerrillas opposed to the Somoza regime, it was too willing to consider the Sandinistas a bunch of agrarian reformers, a sort of armed Latin American Grange. "Armed intellectuals citing Marx" are probably not democratic socialists, Kirkpatrick notes. While a long slow process toward democratization may be possible in some authoritarian societies (she cites Spain and Portugal), Carter's policies were incapable of fostering it. The worst time to urge a regime toward liberalization is when it is under strong pressure from the outside. Any concessions at such a time are likely only to whet the appetite of the opposition; they increase tension rather than reducing it. Any attempt of the United States to dissociate itself from the regime under attack will only encourage those who hate both the regime and the United States to step up their offensive.

She argues that the doctrine of noninterference in the affairs of sovereign states represents an unattainable aspiration rather than constituting a guide for the conduct of foreign policy. The Carter administration, she notes, loudly proclaimed its devotion to noninterference but used its muscle to intervene directly in Iran, Nicaragua, and the country that briefly called itself Zimbabwe-Rhodesia. Why, she asks, does noninterference apply to the Sandinistas but not to Somoza? Why, if the Cubans are to work out their destiny without outside interference, should not the South Africans enjoy the same privilege? The Carter people were unable to give an answer that satisfied the American people; Kirkpatrick attempts to understand, without trying to defend, their policies by examining the assumptions about history that lay behind them.

She argues that Carter's philosophy of history presupposed historical progress, an idea now widespread but one not shared by all men at all times. The specific kind of progress in which Carter believed can be called "modernization," a long-term process by which the world's societies become progressively more interdependent, more "advanced," and more like one another.

This set of beliefs is close to the heart of liberalism but, as Kirkpatrick observes, every one of its elements has been questioned or refuted in recent years. She contends that, used as a framework for foreign policy, the "modernization paradigm" leads to the belief that there is very little a government can do to shape events in desired ways. The best it can do is align itself with the progressive forces of history and then try to nudge the process in its favor here and there.

"In such a world," writes fellow neoconservative Irving Kristol, foreign policy — the defense of one's national interests — would cease to exist, having been completely replaced by a diplomacy aiming to reconcile the interests of all. Our State Department acts most of the time as if that world were already at hand, as if diplomacy were no longer the handmaiden of foreign policy but its master.[2]

Carter's belief that the world was progressing led to another conclusion — that the wicked would not prosper for long. Progress, the handmaid of the Lord, would bring them low and smite all those who sided with them. In the words of the Psalmist,

They will soon fade like the grass,
and wither like the green herb. . . .
Yet a little while, and the wicked will be no more;
though you look well at his place, he will not be there.[3]

In propping up the shah, Somoza, or the South African whites, the United States was taking on not only the populations of those countries, but the Lord Himself. If we wished to be great, we first had to learn to be good.

The conservatives dourly observed that the Psalms were written a long time ago, and not *all* of the wicked had yet perished. Those who wait upon the Lord may, in the words of Isaiah, renew their youth like eagles, but they will need as much youth as they can get, because they have a long wait ahead of them.

Kirkpatrick observes that we do not need to be good in order to be great; being good can sometimes be a hindrance to the pursuit of greatness and in this sad world; it usually is. She is not overwhelmed by the evidence of progress. Most of the world, now as ever, is under the rule of authoritarian dictators. Most people are, now as ever, poor, hungry, and without much hope that things will get better. Kirkpatrick argues that the task of a statesman is to defend the interests of his compatriots so as to ensure that they are not doomed to wait upon the Lord for their vindication. She can endorse Winston Churchill's dictum in *The Gathering Storm:* "The Sermon on the Mount is the last word in Christian ethics. Everyone respects the Quakers. Still, it is not on these terms that Ministers assume their responsibilities of guiding states."[4]

Carter's refusal to resort to force to determine the outcome of political struggles in other countries strikes Kirkpatrick as another example of woolly thinking. She quotes Carter's assertion that the result of an application of force would be only "superficial" and cites officials who argued that the use of force against the Sandinistas was "unthinkable." In office, the new team would show that the use of force in foreign

relations was eminently thinkable. Kirkpatrick attributes Carter's reluctance to use force to the "Vietnam syndrome," a craven belief that
because the United States lost one war, it should never fight another.

The arguments put forward by Kirkpatrick and her fellow conservatives of both the neo and the paleo persuasions struck a chord in the
America of the late 1970s. Liberals were as confused and demoralized by
foreign policy as they were by domestic events. Having diagnosed the
"Carter disease," the new conservative movement was ready to implement its own policies to restore respect for the United States and to stop
the spread of communism.

THE PRESCRIPTION

America needed to assert itself once more in foreign affairs. That was
the primary feeling of the right at the dawn of the Reagan era. Viguerie's
chapter on foreign policy bears the simple, direct title "Our Goal: Military Superiority." And that says it all.

Although they disliked détente, most of the right accepted the traditional power politics put forward by Nixon in *The Real War*. There were
differences in emphasis, some of them critical, but few contested Nixon's
assertion that the Soviet Union was a ruthlessly expansionist power and
that to the United States fell the historical responsibility of opposing its
ambitions by any means necessary.

The right generally had less use for NATO and Europe than the center
did. In the years after 1945, the eastern Establishment considered the
Atlantic partnership the keystone of American defense policy. For the
right, this was less true. There was a long-standing division of American
opinion on the question of the relative importance of the Atlantic and
the Pacific to the future of the United States. Eastern Establishment types
had strong ties to Europe. The West Coast naturally enough looked
toward the Pacific.

Geographic divisions of this kind were nothing new. In the nineteenth
century, New England was largely indifferent to expansion. Opposition
to the Mexican War was strong there, but support in the South was
almost overwhelming. The South dreamed of annexing Cuba; the North
didn't want any more slave states. New England had almost seceded
over the War of 1812; maritime interests considered war with a major
trading partner who also ruled the seas to be a form of madness.

In the twentieth century, isolationist sentiment was strongest in the
Middle West and weakest along the Atlantic seaboard. The cause of

Taiwan interested Los Angeles and bored Boston. Texas was more interested in Mexico than was Oregon.

The right wing of the Republican Party was the veteran of many years of warfare against the Establishment, largely liberal and largely eastern. In the 1950s an angry Robert Taft had charged that First National City Bank (now Citicorp) had nominated every Republican candidate since 1936. Reagan's victory in the 1980 campaign was a triumph of West over East and of the right over the center. It was to be expected that the new administration would take more interest in the Pacific and pay less attention to European allies, which it considered somewhat senile.

The issue of the containment versus the rollback of communism was another bone of contention in American politics. The liberal consensus, which prevailed until 1980, held that if communism could be contained long enough, communist societies would begin to show signs of convergence, of evolving into social democracies. Failing that, they would fall apart under the weight of their own unpopularity and economic insufficiency. To those who favored rollback, containment bordered on pusillanimity. In practice, it meant conceding to the Soviets the right to go fishing in capitalist waters without fearing any incursions into their own. The New Right wanted to show that the Brezhnev Doctrine, so-called, did not limit the ability of the United States to strike at communist regimes, especially those at a convenient distance from the Soviet heartland. Simultaneously, the right urged a strong propaganda campaign against communism through such existing channels as Radio Free Europe and Radio Liberty, as well as the creation of a Radio Martí for Cuba. Where mere persuasion was not enough, covert activity aimed at the destabilization of foreign communist regimes was also not to be excluded from the arsenal of policymakers.

In the Third World generally, the United States was to assume a higher profile in the pursuit of its interests. Allies in trouble, however unsavory, were not to be abandoned or discouraged. A future shah or Somoza would not be abandoned by his friends when he needed them most. Policymakers would consider a contest between a future shah and his opposition to be a struggle between two autocratic factions, one favorable to U.S. interests, one opposed. Nor, if worst came to worst, would the new administration rule out the use of force in international relations.

As for the United Nations and the obligations imposed by its charter, the right has never accepted them. Kristol derides the commitment of the American foreign policy Establishment to the "utopian notion that the ultimate and governing purpose of American foreign policy is to establish a world community of nations all living amiably under the rule of law." He characterizes support for the UN Charter at the State Department as "sanctimonious but not self-serving" and considers it an example of "debased and vulgarized Wilsonianism" and of "callow, even childish notions of what foreign policy is all about."[5]

Strong support of the settler states was to be another pillar of right-wing foreign policy. Far from distancing itself from South Africa, the United States should expand its constructive relations with it. Kirkpatrick was not alone in urging recognition for the Smith-Muzorewa regime in Zimbabwe-Rhodesia. The right was not likely to view the establishment of a SWAPO-backed government in Namibia as a triumph of American diplomacy. Israel, too, would be supported — though with the reservations inherent in America's partial dependence on Arab oil.

The United States is, after all, a settler state. To admire our past is to admire the present of Israel and South Africa. What is wrong with depriving the indigenous population of political rights and deporting them to tiny, inadequate homelands? The Boers fought for their freedom against the British army; they crossed their country in covered wagons; they fought epic campaigns against savages incapable of appreciating the advantages that would accrue to them from the spread of Christian civilization. What is so terrible about that?

As for South Africa's race problems, the American right can sympathize. The impetus for desegregation did not come from the American right. Far from it. Many prominent members of the conservative movement grew up opposing civil rights tooth and nail. Strom Thurmond and Jesse Helms made careers out of supporting race laws not entirely dissimilar from those of Pretoria. Such people see nothing unnatural or immoral in an alliance between South Africa and the United States. To speak of shared values and a shared culture of the two countries makes all the sense in the world. Sympathy with those defending themselves against the communist-backed African National Congress comes naturally to those who attacked Martin Luther King, Jr., for his alleged communist ties.

In any case, South Africa is a strategically placed and valuable ally. The ties between the Boer and the Zionist states are close and mutually beneficial; the United States can only benefit from a closer relationship among all three. This was the policy of the New Right.

Rearmament was another aspect of the new conservative strategy. Most obviously, this called for a massive military buildup. The Soviet Union was believed to have closed the gap between its own capabilities and those of the United States; the right aimed to mobilize the superior power of the West to provoke an arms race in which the Soviet Union would either be ruined or be forced to accept a level of strength acceptable to Western conservatives — a level that could never be confused with parity. Besides building up strategic nuclear arms, the right intended to restore the American navy to levels sufficient to overcome any conceivable challenge by the USSR. Conventional strength would be upgraded to levels that permitted the United States to wage simultaneous wars in the Atlantic, Pacific, and Middle Eastern theaters.

Although the military budget made the most apparent changes in the economic and political atmosphere, an important goal of the right was to "rearm" the CIA and the other clandestine agencies of American power. The restrictions imposed on those agencies following the Watergate revelations were dismantled; their charters and budgets were expanded. Early in the Reagan era, the CIA was back in the business of "covertly" carrying on wars.

But rearmament for the right was not simply a question of bombs and guns. The United States always had military superiority throughout Indochina. Since 1945 the United States had been far more powerful than the Soviet Union, but in the view of the right, it was the Soviet Union that had made all the gains. Like Nixon, the right believed that power equals manpower plus economic power times will power. By will power, however, the New Right did not mean the isolated determination of a clique in the White House; the right saw the need for a new national will to use military power — a kind of moral, social rearmament. Blessed with a coterie of intellectuals who had thought deeply about how to create a national consensus for an aggressive foreign policy (part of what the social theorists of the right often called the "moral fiber" of society), the right sought to strengthen the elements in the American polity that would support a policy inviting war. Those Jerry Falwell described as "pro-family, pro-moral, pro-life and pro-American, who have integrity and believe in hard work, those who pledge allegiance to the flag and proudly sing our national anthem,"[6] were to be prepared for a policy that risks war to support some of the less appetizing regimes around the world. That Viguerie, who issued the call to arms just cited, is aware of these implications is evident when we discover other measures he proposes for reaching what his book calls "Our Goal: Military Superiority."

Viguerie calls for a World War II–style emergency war preparedness for the United States defense industry. This mighty Gulliver must pull free from the restraints in which Lilliputian bureaucrats have entangled him. Purchasing requirements, arms control considerations, time-wasting low-bid regulations, and the irritating, useless rules of OSHA and the EPA must be cast aside. The workers must get on a war footing —

and presumably this means giving up the right to strike for the duration of this ill-defined war.[7]

Preparations for war on such a scale, to support such a collection of allies, and, even more, the outbreak of war itself, would inevitably provoke domestic opposition of the kind that, in the end, made the prosecution of war in Indochina impossible. The right is aware of this and calls for a rearmament of domestic intelligence as well as of the international variety.

A social rearmament would have to include a new relationship between the press and U.S. armed forces in combat. The outlines of this relationship began to emerge during the invasion of Grenada, when the forces of the United States actually turned back, with threats, reporters who found their own means of transportation to the war zone.

Future wars in Latin America are likely to be much more divisive of American opinion than the Indochinese War ever was; logically, the willingness to defend American interests by force in the hemisphere presumes the willingness to take the necessary domestic measures to see that the application of force is not prematurely curtailed by domestic dissent. The "stab in the back" theorists of Vietnam will guard their rear more carefully the second time around.

Another aspect of social rearmament is the restoration of the powers of the imperial presidency. The president's ability to engage American troops, make binding promises of support to foreign leaders, and respond quickly to real or perceived emergencies — all without congressional approval — is crucial to the will power necessary to win World War III, a war that the right believes is already being fought. Steps would be taken to defang the Freedom of Information Act and to impose on government officials restrictions that Nixon never dreamed of. Aided by a convenient Supreme Court ruling that struck down the legislative veto, that administration made no secret of its belief that it was not really bound to observe the War Powers Act.

The invasion of Grenada can serve as an illustration of the principles that activated moral rearmament and as practice for other, more complicated uses of force down the road. The decision to intervene, clearly an act of war, was taken without congressional consultation. The press was ruthlessly disinformed and then denied, as long as possible, access to the war zone and facilities to report from the conquered island. Massive pressure was applied to domestic critics; reasons given for the intervention were conflicting, hazy, and shifting.

In the aftermath, it was clear that none of the rationales accounted for the action. The threat to American citizens was minimal, and the invasion plan was not designed to rescue them. One of the two campuses of the medical school with American students was not even among the original primary targets, and American students remained in areas under control of Grenadian forces during much of the fighting — giving the Grenadians ample time to murder the students, had they been so inclined. The information coming from Havana about the number of Cubans on the island, their role in the fighting, and their original mission in Grenada proved to be accurate — unlike the frequently changing information that emanated from Washington as the Pentagon attempted to attribute continued resistance to Cuban, not Grenadian forces. The treaty under which the United States claimed that its intervention was legal had never been signed by the United States, and its provisions in any case were not legally invoked. The request from six states for American intervention had been drafted in Washington by the State Department.[8]

What was involved was a battle in World War III. The right, believing itself engaged in a life-and-death struggle with the evil empire, struck a blow with no regard for conventional international law — yet felt no more remorse for the action than the British did for their raid on neutral Copenhagen during the Napoleonic Wars or for their attack on the French fleet in the Second World War. Necessity may, as Milton said, be "the tyrant's plea," but it recognizes no lesser laws.

The invasion of Grenada was a short war and called for no really heroic acts of will. Requiring only a week to conquer an island twice the size of the District of Columbia with a population equal to that of Cedar Rapids, Iowa, the administration had no need to take the kinds of protective measures against domestic dissent that a longer — and therefore inevitably less popular — intervention would have necessitated. But the logic of history is clear for those who will see it. If the elimination of communism in this hemisphere is a vital national interest, necessary to the preservation of American power, independence, and freedom, then those who oppose the measures required to eliminate communism must, in the end, be treated with the same resolve and forcefulness used against the communists themselves. And those who will not deal with opponents of the war with the necessary firmness are as big a danger to the nation as the original opponents, and therefore as dangerous as the communists themselves, and they too must be dealt with firmly and with the utmost resolve. And so it goes.

The American conservative movement that took power in 1980 is nothing if not logical.

THE END OF THE LIBERAL EMPIRE

To the extent that Reaganite policies remain dominant in the thinking of foreign policymakers, the era of the liberal empire can be said to have ended. The builders of the liberal empire said, and many believed, that they were constructing an international road on which the peoples of the earth would be able to advance into the modern era. Any alliances with reactionary dictators and concessions to oligarchs were temporary, brief halts on the march to peace and progress for all. The vision, so contemptuously dismissed by Kristol, of "a world community of nations all living amiably under the rule of law" was the central vision of the liberal empire. Without it, the dodges and shifts of American policy since 1945 looked terrible.

Kristol and the right, or some of it, had the moral fortitude to gaze unmoved on the spectacle of naked greed — no vulgarized Wilsonianism here. The basic moral justification for their policy — that communism is so bad that anything up to the threat of, and perhaps the actual outbreak of, nuclear war is preferable — must cover not only the sacrifices we impose on ourselves, but also the sacrifices we impose on others, without their consent. It is just too bad for them that South African blacks can't have much freedom; they should console themselves with the reflection that Americans are more free because they are less so. The millions of homeless children in the slums of Manila and Latin America should rejoice to be part of the free world, even if their own part of it isn't so exciting.

As policy twists and turns, it becomes necessary to support communist countries to fight communism. Some cases, like Yugoslavia, are easy, but not all. Rapprochement with China, for example, began when that country was still in the midst of the Cultural Revolution. The United States continued to support the claim of Pol Pot's regime to a seat in the United Nations. Supporting communists to smash communists is a policy that can be explained only with difficulty, especially when one ends up supporting the totalitarian Gang of Four and Pol Pot against the authoritarians in the Kremlin.

A policy of supporting dictators to defend freedom and supporting communists to defeat communism requires an adroit and supple defense, one that, for the present, the right can provide. But it is a policy vulnerable to attack when it leads to serious sacrifice — to war or the danger of war. Because of its many contradictions, its supporters find themselves engaged in not a few embarrassing arguments — arguments that were turned against their predecessors in the Indochina debates and have the same potential now.

On the other hand, the right's attitude toward communism has one significant advantage over the liberal alternative: like the Soviets, the right believes that there is an international struggle in progress between the world proletariat and the world bourgeoisie. The Soviets believe the proletariat must inevitably win and, as former Trotskyite Irving Kristol observes, "so far, there is precious little evidence to prove them wrong."[9]

In any case, the Soviets view an agreement with the United States as an episode in the class struggle, not as the conclusion to it. The liberal hope, forever renewed, that every round of negotiation will lead to a new and less conflicted era in superpower relations has been frustrated from the time of Ambassador William Bullitt's experiences with Stalin.

Liberal attempts at détente or at simple containment have at their heart some form of convergence theory. With the passage of time, reason the convergency theorists, capitalist countries will introduce more state planning and increase social spending. Communist countries, for their part, will gradually loosen up, and the world will edge into a social democratic utopia.

In fact, there has been some convergence, but much of it has been perverse. While the communist countries have loosened their control over their populations and permitted more diversity in their economic systems, capitalist countries in the developing world have become much more repressive since 1945. One has only to compare the human rights records of Eastern Europe and Latin America in the years from Stalin to Pinochet to grasp the pattern. Eighteen months of martial law in Poland brought fewer deaths than a week of death squad activity in El Salvador during the same period.

One frequent complaint from the Reagan right is that the Establishment has been too pacific toward the Soviet Union. The evident failure of convergence to reduce East-West rivalry after forty years lends weight to the charge, but the situation is more complex. The eastern Establishment represents the section of American society that is the most fully integrated into the world economy and has the closest relations with the European allies. With a great deal of its money linked to the harmonious meshing of the economies of the advanced countries, the Establishment is not eager to rock the boat of international diplomacy. The prospect of even limited nuclear war in Europe depresses the Establishment almost as much as it does the Europeans.

The Establishment would like to resolve the crisis of American foreign policy, if possible, by forming a consortium of its leading trading partners. Only through international coordination can serious economic and security issues be addressed, says the Establishment. But to build such relationships would require more, not less American sensitivity to the interests of its allies. A close working relationship with Germany, for example, would have to respect West Germany's desire to see tensions relaxed in Europe to facilitate pan-German cooperation. Trade relations with the Soviet Union could not be held hostage to American political storms.

The right looks at trade with the Soviet Union as a fulfillment of Lenin's prophecy that the capitalists would sell rope to their Soviet hangman. It rejects the charge that putting U.S. economic and security interests ahead of those of the allies constitutes narrow nationalism, and it points out that a healthy United States economy is the rock on which Western security rests. The right also argues that if the Europeans want to dither and tut-tut while America fights communism around the world, that is their decision, but the United States has the same right to consult its interests as do the Europeans.

Convergence with the communists and cooperation with the Europeans do not go down well with the right. Reagan and the communists may not understand each other perfectly, but both sides agree that their conflict is fundamental and cannot be compromised. Although nuclear weapons make a direct attack of one superpower on the other unthinkable, at least for now, both systems are doomed to fight each other where they can. Resolved not to see his system lose ground "on his watch," Reagan has been determined to go over to the offensive, inaugurating the rollback of communism with the invasion of Grenada, working openly to overthrow the Sandinistas, and aiming, apparently, at the "liberation" of Cuba.

The Kennedy people, in accord with the postwar consensus, believed that American strength lay in the liberalism of the American Empire at home and abroad. They liberalized America to strengthen it; they buttered the guns. They sought a more consultative relationship with the Europeans, and they extended civil rights at home. Reagan has shown no intention of seeking a compromise solution in foreign policy. He has not attempted to implement a global policy of counterrevolution with a program of reform. A civil war between communists and oligarchs is not a foreign war for Reagan and the right. One cannot choose whether to get involved — the international character of the struggle supplies the links between various fronts.

Liberals love to caricature this point of view, reducing it to a simple paranoid fear of Soviet manipulation. They feel they have refuted it by observing that the world communist movement is no longer "mono-lithic," if it ever was. With a tolerant air of weary patience, they point out that Third World insurgencies are locally based and that foreign aid plays only a secondary role. Without injustice, they point out, Central America would be as cool as a cucumber even if Castro covered it knee-deep in machine guns.

All very true, but, as Reagan could retort, in our actual world there is no real prospect for ending Central America's poverty and injustice any time soon. There is certainly no prospect of accomplishing this under conditions of insurrection and civil war. One thinks of the words from the evangelical hymn:

> Just as I am without one plea
> But that Thy blood was shed for me.

This was Thieu's theme, and today it is the song of the leaders of El Salvador and Honduras. Like the sinner in the song, Central America cannot reform itself before it is saved; good Protestant theology teaches us that reform comes after salvation, if then. Either one agrees to defend corrupt, murderous, and oligarchical regimes, or one decides not to fight communism. Without injustice, communism will not spread — but what prospects are there, pray, for eliminating injustice from the free world? Cutting off everyone's feet would eliminate the scourge of athlete's foot; eliminating injustice would halt the spread of communism. Kennedy, believing this, organized the Peace Corps; Reagan, seeing the same thing, has organized the Somocistas.

As for the end of monolithic communism, this is not as important as generally hoped. True, China, the USSR, and Vietnam are all paying through the nose to maintain armies on one another's frontiers; true, local Communist parties are not under the thumb of the Kremlin as much as they used to be. But the flexibility of the local parties has often made them more effective and has not deprived them of their Soviet support.

The triumph of communism worldwide need not be orchestrated by the puppet masters of Moscow to frighten those who identify their interests with what Marx called the bourgeoisie. It cannot greatly comfort rich Venezuelans, say, to hear that the local communist army prefers on the whole the East German model of rural electrification to the Soviet version. They do not necessarily rejoice in the bars of the international hotels to hear that the cadres seemed to prefer Antonio Gramsci to Nikolai Bukharin. If Ethiopia were to reduce its dependence on the USSR, and against all the odds to organize a working African communism, this "fragmentation" of world communism would only strengthen communism in Africa. It might well encourage more communist movements — movements that the Soviets perhaps would support despite considerable ideological differences.

Politics place their own limits on public discourse in the United States. The electoral process does not lend itself to the sophisticated expression of complicated views. With both parties constantly striving to broaden their base, ideological fuzziness can win more votes than plain speaking. The ins and outs of anticommunist strategies rarely receive wide discussion. Anticommunism in politics is often confused with a strong stand against the presumed geopolitical ambitions of the Soviet Union. The political, military, economic, and international aspects of the situation get blended into a mush.

Nevertheless, the Reagan administration started out with what was — given the distortions imposed on political expression by the nature of American politics — a consistent, logical, and relatively frank policy, something the Carter team had difficulty achieving. If the American people did not realize the ultimate costs and risks of the original Reagan policy, they did at least understand its orientation and purpose. This in itself must have come as a relief to millions baffled by the spectacle of drift and decline during the preceding years.

THE ANATOMY OF
THE AMERICAN RIGHT

AVING EXAMINED the foreign and domestic policies of the conservative movement that triumphed in 1980 and again in 1984, we inevitably ask whether these policies will "work" and to what extent. Can the conservatives consolidate their hold on power? Can the productive classes be unleashed to introduce a new era of prosperity and growth? Can firmness abroad coupled with rearmament halt the erosion of the American Empire — and if so, at what price?

We can begin these inquiries by analyzing the strands that contribute to the American right. One of the first features of Reagan's support to strike us is that it is split into two camps: a social right primarily concerned with social issues, and another group primarily interested in economics. These camps have some items in common, but their agendas and compositions are different enough to make them worth examining separately.

The social right concerns itself largely with intangible values — family values, moral values, and traditional values. We saw earlier that liberalism overwhelms these values and the intermediary structures that protect them, like churches, families, and ethnic groups. The social right is united in its opposition to liberalism, but it is divided by the nature of the traditions that various parts of it seek to preserve. While there are almost as many social right subgroups as there are in the wider society, we can lump them into three major groupings: a Catholic right, an evangelical or fundamentalist right, and a tory right.

Not long ago, toryism and fundamentalism were the dominant strains of thought in American politics. Episcopalian bankers upheld the traditions of their faith in the eastern cities; William Jennings Bryan spoke for the prairie and the Bible. Modern liberalism has affronted both traditions. Tories and fundamentalists are united in their dislike of liberal divorce laws, abortion on demand, the open practice of homosexuality, and the "secularist" ideology of the public schools. When the right is weak, these groups cohere; when it is strong, they split apart once more.

Tories possess a more sophisticated (indeed, liberal) theological apparatus, which allows them to assimilate much of contemporary thought; they tend to be wealthy, well educated, and they do not want so much to overthrow the Establishment as to convert it. When tories are swept away by romantic fantasies about the superiority of the thirteenth century to our own degenerate age (tories can be Catholic as well as Protestant), their social thought runs along the lines of Burke and Hobbes with a sprinkling of Locke. In private, romantic moments tory Anglophiles wonder whether the Revolution was really such a good thing; not a few of them consider Elizabeth II to be "our" queen in a way that no other monarch can be.

Toryism is a sentiment of the elite and, in the nature of the case, cannot be a large movement. It is a rich movement, however, and maintains an influence out of all proportion to its numbers. It exerts influence through its ties with prestigious educational and cultural institutions and its ability to call on the talents of a few articulate spokesmen (rarely women) in every generation.

Fundamentalism, on the other hand, is a mass movement. Its beginnings go back to the anti-Establishmentarian Baptist, Methodist, and Calvinistic Scots-Irish elements in the old West and South. The lost world that fundamentalism seeks to restore has nothing in common with the Barsetshire of Anthony Trollope; it looks back to the egalitarian American farming society of the nineteenth century. Tories are nostalgic Hamiltonians, and fundamentalists Jacksonian democrats. The historic links between what today is a right-wing fundamentalist movement and populism are deep and strong. The anti-elitism of George Wallace's campaigns was characteristic, not aberrational. Fundamentalism is anti-monopoly, nativist, and anti-elitist to the core.[1]

The close and continuing ties between some of the most progressive and some of the most rigid attitudes in American history are a constant source of interest to the historian and of confusion to the casual observer. That Americans of the nineteenth and early twentieth centuries regarded women's suffrage, the income tax, and Prohibition as allied crusades is bizarre enough; that the same people involved themselves in the Ku Klux Klan and some of the most genuinely progressive movements in American history seems incredible. We see something like this mixture of populism and racism among the Boers and in the Israeli Sephardic Jews.

Movements of this kind were all based on resistance to a dominant elite that was monopolistic and exclusive. In the American South, the resistance of small farmers to what some of them would not have hesitated to call Yankee imperialism was a determining factor in the shape of fundamentalist populism. Threatened from above by northern industrial interests that were steadily orienting national policy toward their own requirements, and from below by former slaves, southern farmers rallied their wagons into a circle, or, as the Boers say, formed a *laager,* and fought both enemies. We see a similar formation of Sephardic populism in Israel, united against the Ashkenazi threat from above and the Arabs below; at the turn of the century the Boers fought the British and the blacks; Protestant Unionists in Ulster are caught in a similar squeeze. In Germany, Nazi voters felt squeezed between international finance on the one hand and Bolshevism on the other.

The Catholic populist right is a younger phenomenon in American politics than its fundamentalist counterpart, but the two formations have much in common. The ancestors of today's Catholics did not receive a warm welcome from the forebears of the fundamentalists. The Klan hated Catholics as much as it loathed Jews and blacks; the nineteenth century is rich in the history of anti-Catholic panics and riots. Because the Catholic immigrants arrived in this country without any property, and remained unable to acquire much as long as they remained tied to the industrial economy, for many years their politics were staunchly trade unionist and in some cases socialist. While Protestant divines were still mumbling piously that unions actually undercut the freedom of the worker by limiting his freedom of contract, Catholic bishops were blessing assemblies of the Knights of Columbus and instructing the faithful in the rights of labor. This kind of Catholic politics captured the Democratic Party from the fundamentalist populists with the nomination of Al Smith in 1928.

As more Catholics achieved a measure of financial success, Catholic politics began to change. The success of the trade unions gave them something to protect; the migration of blacks from the rural South gave them someone to protect it from. Catholic politics began to take on the aspects of a struggle against a remote but all-powerful ruling class and a present and threatening underclass that marked the politics of similarly situated groups around the world.

Aggravating the reactionary element in Catholic politics was the success of subgroups within American Catholicism. The success of the Irish, symbolized by the election and subsequent apotheosis of John. F. Kennedy, was part of an immense and many-sided process of mutual accommodation between Irish and WASP elements in American society. Catholics moved into the professions and into the high ranks of the great corporations. Those who remained in the working class prospered, entrenching themselves in the better-organized and better-paid fields.

In the 1970s and 1980s, these groups were attacked or threatened from above and below in a social pincers movement. As we have already seen, basic economic and foreign policy was made behind the scenes by those Nixon calls the "leadership class." From the standpoint of urban, ethnic whites, the liberalizing initiatives — busing, fair housing, and affirmative action — of the nation's decision makers offered them nothing constructive and threatened to weaken their grip on what little property and security they had managed to obtain and achieve.

For the first time, large numbers of ethnic whites were ready to hear the message of the Republican Party, and they were far more interested in its more radical, populist wing than in its Establishment mouthpieces. These prospective new Republicans were not interested in the classic conservative issues; they were by no means anti–New Deal or antilabor. Their membership in unions was often their basic piece of economic "property" on which everything else rested. The higher wages and benefits in unionized industries — the fruits of the New Deal and a half century of liberal empire — were what they hoped the right would protect for them. They didn't want the building trades de-unionized; they merely wanted colored people kept out of them. The neighborhoods, parochial schools, and other institutions that they wished to protect all depended on a continuation of the old-fashioned, liberal wage structure.

Just as southern farmers effortlessly forget free market, limited government principles whenever it comes to the Preservation of the Family Farm, their northern counterparts would never be so conservative as to cut their own throats and destroy the unions.

It was not easy to forge a coalition between groups with interests and traditions so separated by history. The inclusion of newly conservative Jewish voters in the coalition raised even more problems, but necessity spoke more loudly on this occasion than did theology. God might not hear the prayer of a Jew, but Jerry Falwell would. God may have prepared for the Jews ovens in Hell hotter than anything in Auschwitz, but en route to this final destination they could serve the Lord's purposes by joining committees for the moral regeneration of the United States. Catholics might be papist idolaters under the Whore of Babylon, but the United States is not Northern Ireland, and the theological associates of Ian Paisley (a graduate of Bob Jones University) could fight abortion in league with American supporters of the IRA.

Both the tory and the fundamentalist movements are pessimistic, which is striking for movements that have had such major recent successes.

Popular evangelical religion stresses the ultimate futility of human endeavor. It rejects the possibility, so dear to the hearts of more liberal church people, that a gradual improvement in human affairs can bring about the millennium. According to popular evangelicalism, Antichrist will rise, perhaps soon, and wars and disasters will sweep the earth. A popular interpretation of biblical prophecy holds that today's Common Market is the "revived Roman Empire," symbolized by the beast with ten horns in the Book of Revelation. Antichrist will rise to the head of the Common Market and, among other things, establish a worldwide financial system that will require "the mark of the beast" — a tattoo of some kind for credit identification purposes.[2]

These sentiments cannot bring comfort to the members of the Trilateral Commission, whose aim in life is to establish a world economic system similar to that of the Antichrist. Apocalyptic thinking has spread rapidly through the United States, a significant portion of whose population prefers the Bible's theory of biological origins to Darwin's. The return of the Jews to Israel and the approach of the year 2000 — to say nothing of the bomb — give end-of-the-world thinking a wide appeal. When Secretary of Agriculture James Watt played down the importance of conservation because he believed the Second Coming was imminent, he was reflecting a mood prevalent in the heartland, among so-called trailer park Protestants.

Apocalyptic thinking is characteristic of social groups that see no clear way into the future; it is a world view characteristic of a dying class. Fundamentalist America finds itself in a strange and incomprehensible world. Rural and small-town America has dwindled into intellectual insignificance and political impotence. It cannot have confidence in even its own victories. The cities and the industrialism and giganticism they represent are anathema to traditional American populism. Yet they spread their influence to every American village and home, and there is no escaping them. Many millions of people, themselves caught up in the toils of the urban and suburban economy, attribute their alienation to the destruction of an imagined past. As they wander from K Mart to Pizza Hut, they look back to the good old days on Walton's Mountain, where God was in Heaven and Mom was in the kitchen, when families were happy, when all towns were small and all folks were good. Carter briefly captured their interest by evoking their love of this nonexistent past, but Reagan stole their hearts by pledging to restore it.

Yet they know, religiously and intuitively, that the dream cannot be realized. All human striving will end, at best, in the Rapture, when the true believers will fly to Heaven to wait out the Great Tribulation on earth. The turn to a politics of yesterday goes hand in hand with a return to the religion and to the science of yesterday. Modernism and liberalism, too, seem to go hand in hand — the scientific assault on biblical literalism and traditional piety is felt as part of the same movement that erodes family values, the free community of farmers, and small-town happiness. This perception is absolutely correct, as far as it goes. Those of the fundamentalist right are pessimistic because even they know that the advance of modernism and science is, humanly speaking, irreversible. Only some great and terrible intervention from the spirit world can restore the idyllic past. "Maranatha," says the fundamentalist, echoing St. John the Divine. "Come quickly, Lord Jesus."

Tory pessimism, if anything deeper and blacker than the fundamentalist version, is a somewhat more decorous affair. America is even less likely to turn into the rural parts of mid-Victorian England than into rural Kansas, vintage 1910. The goals of toryism, condemned to march behind the vanguard of fundamentalism in any crusade to restore the good old days, tend in politics to be rather low key — upgrading Latin curricula in private schools or defending the purity of the nation's boys' choirs from those who wish to make them co-ed. The American gentry faded early from a dominant role in national life. They were driven out of office by Jackson and his democrats, and then lost their economic primacy to the upstart industrialists after the Civil War. The newly wealthy families of the late nineteenth century endowed prep schools on the English model to provide training for the sons of the old gentry and the new industrialists. These efforts were crowned with a certain degree of success — one thinks of FDR, JFK, W. Averell Harriman, the Hamilton Fishes, William and McGeorge Bundy, Joseph and Stewart Alsop, among many others. An ingredient of the glamour of the Kennedy administration was the patina of culture many of its leading members had acquired in the old elite schools. The tory educational movement succeeded in polishing the surface of American politics, but an upper-class education never became a requirement for participation in public life. In many cases — George Bush's, for one — it remains a severe handicap. In any case, putting the great-grandsons of the robber barons in evening dress and teaching them French doesn't entirely exhaust the range of the tory vision.

Tories believe that tradition gives shape and meaning to life. The traditions specifically of Western Christian civilization embody the finest achievements of the human spirit. To prepare oneself to appreciate and pass on this tradition is the tory vocation. It is not actually necessary to read Latin oneself, but one must admire those who do. Traditions in manners, dress, religion, and family life are as important as intellectual tradition itself. The High Anglican preoccupation with liturgy is the quintessence of toryism. The complicated ceremonies of the liturgy draw their value from an affinity with tradition. The cadences of the traditional prayers and the repetition of the old, beautiful hymns and chants are not seen by tory worshipers as merely aesthetic experiences. Rather, the majesty of the liturgy has the power to lift up the participant to a new understanding of the majesty of God and the nature of man. The traditional aesthetic and spiritual values of Western Christian civilization have a unique ability to bring humanity closer to God; this is the heart of the tory conviction.

There is, of course, no prospect of reorienting American life in this direction and toward a worship of what the tory trinity all too often turns out to be: wealth, privilege, and the past. America broke decisively with the tory vision as early as the 1620 landing at Plymouth; toryism was based on a misreading not only of American culture, but of Western civilization itself. Change is far from foreign to the spirit of Western Christian civilization, insofar as it can be said to have a single spirit. Compared with other civilizations, it was not distinguished by the beauty of its art, the profundity of its philosophy, the conservatism of its cultural forms, and certainly not the sincerity of its religious profession. The chief mark of Western civilization seems to be its restlessness and rootlessness. Dissatisfaction with the status quo and a desire for change drove Westerners around the world and started a process, one that still continues, of social, political, and economic upheaval. Dynamic instability is the hallmark of the West. American iconoclasm is a product of European history. The teenager taking strange drugs and listening to rock-and-roll music, the elderly couple touring the continent in their Winnebago, and the Kansas City Kiwanians eating dim sum while visiting New York all have a surer sense of the pulse of Western civilization than does the pale and studious liturgist combing the Epistles of Clement for clues on the meaning of the Mass.

THE ECONOMIC RIGHT

The social constituencies of the right may be divided; its economic supporters are even more so. The division between Main Street and Wall Street is a familiar one in American politics; both groups found themselves supporting the conservative renaissance of the 1980s, but for different reasons.

Wall Street remains a convenient label for corporate America, even though only a minority of the nation's largest firms still have their head-quarters there. These great corporations have conflicting interests, of course, but as a group they have in common certain interests not shared by the rest of society, and these interests constitute the program of the big-business right.

For most of recent history, Wall Street was, on the whole, comfortable with the liberal, New Deal state. Although some (not all) of the pillars of corporate America denounced Franklin Roosevelt as a traitor to his class, he carried the younger men with him, and big business grew quite fond of Keynes, government intervention in the economy, and the new era of labor relations ushered in by the Wagner Act.

With interests on a national and international scale, these enterprises valued stability and predictability above all else. Paying somewhat higher wages to a unionized work force was less expensive for companies of this type than dealing with frequent wildcat strikes or other disruptions. These firms stood to gain by intelligent cooperation on some issues with the national unions.

Similarly, the firms welcomed the stability that government intervention brought to the economy. As John Kenneth Galbraith points out in *The New Industrial State,* the unpredictable and violent business cycles of laissez-faire capitalism represent an unacceptable risk for a company whose investment decisions involving billions of dollars must be made over multiyear spans. Ford does not want to see its new line of cars, repre-senting a $5 billion investment, roll off the assembly line in the midst of a recession.[3] The new role of the federal government under FDR may have brought about higher taxes, but they were in the nature of economic insurance premiums, and, in any case, the large corporations were well placed to ensure that the tax burden would not fall disproportionately (or even proportionately) on their shoulders.

Regulation, too, had a silver lining for the large corporation. It was Grover Cleveland's attorney general, Richard Olney, who first described it; he wrote to a disgruntled railroad owner that the new Interstate Com-merce Commission, far from destroying the railroads, would satisfy "the popular clamor for a government supervision of railroads, at the same time that that supervision is almost entirely nominal." It would, more-over, serve as "a sort of barrier between the railroad corporations and the people and a sort of protection against hasty and crude legislation hostile to railroad interests."[4]

There was more to regulation than even the sagacious Olney saw. For the large corporation seeking stability and predictability in its markets, regulation could take the guesswork out of pricing and planning. Regulation weakened the force of competition in the market, and it raised the entry costs borne by would-be entrants. In some cases, regulations limited the number of firms able to serve a given market and guaranteed prices that ensured profitability. These actions would have violated antitrust laws if undertaken by private companies on their own, but once an unelected and undersupervised regulatory agency sprinkled them with holy water, Uncle Sam smiled benignly on industrial cartels. The world of international trade showed how regulations allegedly designed to serve consumers and ensure quality could be used to protect domestic industries without messy and embarrassing tariffs. Such features of regulation benefited those firms already established in a given business, and Wall Street was not slow to perceive the consequences. Under the regulations of the 1930s, 1940s, and 1950s, America's major corporations enjoyed a generation of stable growth and high profits, and, despite occasional complaints, the postwar years were marked by an absence of movement by big business against regulation.

Free trade, another shibboleth of liberalism during the period of its supremacy, was also endorsed by big business. It is generally forgotten today that this marked a 180-degree turn from the historic position of corporate America. Nineteenth-century American businessmen considered free trade a dangerous economic heresy not far short of socialism. From 1860 to 1930 the Republican Party was proud of its heritage as the party of high tariffs that protected American workers and manufacturers, and orthodox American economists labored to reconcile the principles of Adam Smith with the imposition of tariffs that were among the world's highest. Only as American manufacturers became net exporters, and as America succeeded to Britain's position as the world's dominant economic power, did the charms of free trade appear to big business and its academic acolytes. By the end of World War II big business had thrown its weight behind the principles of free trade, and the wild and crazy heresy of yesteryear became the stable, solid, unquestioned orthodoxy of today.

Although Wall Street came to embrace the economics of the New Deal, Main Street — small business — remained more aloof. Companies with one or two factories realized no economies of scale from the establishment of labor unions; such companies remained fiercely anti-union. They were not major exporters; free trade never made many friends on Main Street. Main Street never saw the point of Keynesian economics; red ink is red ink to small business. The great corporation can see debt as an opportunity; for small business, debt is more often an evil, even when it is necessary.

Regulation also affected Main Street in a different, less favorable way.

The small or middle-size business desiring to expand into the national market was often hampered by regulations designed to protect the existing firms. Only by combining on a national scale in lobbying associations could small businesses have the same impact on regulators as the major corporation, and even then the individual businessman lacked the access and the clout of his larger competitor. Small business had a shorter horizon than the large corporation; it was more flexible and often better able to move quickly to take advantage of changing market conditions. But wage, price, and other regulations often prevented the small business from using its flexibility to fullest advantage, thus depriving it of its major weapon in the constant battle for survival and growth. Finally, regulations often added to overhead, and these costs were much more burdensome to small companies than to large corporations without cash flow problems.

The New Deal did not neglect small business. Farmers, the most numerous class of small businessmen in the nation, benefited from a variety of federal programs, ranging from improved credit access to rural electrification to price supports. Other small businesses benefited from similar programs. Local banks and savings-and-loans associations in particular were heavily supported by the national government. Laws against interstate banking blocked the giant banks from consolidating the industry into a few national bank chains, and the government's interventions in the credit markets were designed to enhance the health of smaller institutions. "Fair trade" laws limited the price competition that, during the 1920s, had helped the national chain stores establish themselves at the expense of independent retailers. State and national regulations of the New Deal defined "game preserves," in which small businesses could take shelter from the competitive pressure exerted by the giants, which had made the Roaring Twenties an era in which Wall Street swallowed up much of Main Street.

Yet these programs never helped the New Deal win the hearts and minds on Main Street. Farmers and other businessmen vociferously supported the federal programs that helped them out, but they rejected the theories of government and economics that those programs implied. By day the cattleman gazed out over his subsidized herds as they drank the water that came from the government irrigation project; at night he studied, by electricity that came from a government-sponsored rural electrification co-op, the figures on his government-provided, subsidized loan, and as he figured his taxes, he cursed the big government that swallowed his profits. The banker, the real estate developer, the insurance agent, and the automobile dealer shared his sentiments — and his dependence.

The surprise of the Reagan years was not that Main Street held fast to its old-time opposition to big-spending liberal government; the surprise was that the prime beneficiaries of the old system, the great financial and multinational corporations, turned away so suddenly from an economic regime under which they had prospered for a generation. Why was the First National City Bank, that great pillar of liberal, "me-too" Republicanism, born again as a fundamentalist laissez-faire institution — and how lasting was that conversion likely to be? The change of heart was especially striking because it came so soon after Nixon, placed on the Republican ticket in 1952 as a sop to the forces of McCarthy and Taft, formally abjured the old-time conservative religion. "We are all Keynesians now," Nixon said as he visited Red China, took the United States off the gold standard, and instituted wage and price controls.

We weren't all Keynesians for long. By 1980 Keynes was dead, monetarism was king, and every industry, from automobiles to finance to transport, was looking to deregulation as the wave of the future. Companies that had lived comfortably with their unions since 1936 suddenly turned on organized labor, liberal Republicanism faded into memory, and a hue and cry against do-gooding Democrats rose up in boardrooms across the land.

The cause of this massive and abrupt change of heart was the growing internationalization of the American economy. Foreign competitors, organized under different and sometimes more efficient economic systems than our own, began to challenge U.S. firms successfully here and abroad. At the same time, as we have seen, major American firms themselves became more international in their production and marketing. The relatively stable environment of the postwar era became more competitive, more challenging.

The evolution of the market economy since the nineteenth century had passed through earlier stages of cooperation and competition among business enterprises. Characteristically, new industries were born in competition and a multitude of ambitious producers dueled in the marketplace until the number of participants dropped and the survivors agreed among themselves to divide the market and to protect one another's margins from the consequences of unseemly price wars. In the nineteenth and early twentieth centuries the cooperative phase of industry resulted in combinations, trusts, and price-fixing schemes. From 1933 onward these cartels grew up under government auspices — openly, as provided for under Roosevelt's National Recovery Act, or implicitly, as the result of regulations.

By the 1960s, most major industries seemed locked into a cooperative structure, but with the intrusion of foreign competitors, that situation changed. As the world became integrated into a single economic unit, it was clear that there were too many firms in too many countries. The future would see fewer — but bigger — automobile companies, international banks, shipbuilders, and so on. The gentlemanly rules of conduct that maximized profits in a stable national cartel would not work during the new competitive phase, and American companies, like their foreign counterparts, demanded the freedom to compete for markets and capital.

For Wall Street, the evolving world market was both an opportunity and a threat. It offered new outlets, new and cheaper production facilities, and new sources of capital; it was also a source of potentially dangerous competition. But it was clear to Wall Street that American business had no choice but to participate in the global competition. If American banks refused to compete with new financial products in the Eurodollar markets, or were prevented by misguided regulators from doing so, then French, British, and Japanese bankers would gladly relegate the American banks to the backwaters of finance.

The old vocabulary of competition and free markets was once again appropriate for Wall Street; the old beliefs were once again dusted off, and in the decade after 1975, it seemed as if big business had returned to the economic orthodoxy of 1928. In the new atmosphere no proposal was too radical for consideration. Scholars solemnly discussed a return to the gold standard, and opposition to the progressive income tax reared its hoary head. Main Street pricked up its ears as it heard the sound of the old trumpets, and the economic conservative movement had pulled itself together.

Despite their adherence to a common set of slogans, however, Wall Street and Main Street held opposing views on the nature and purpose of their alliance. For Wall Street, where opinions are shaped by the movement of international markets, conservatism was a tactic, not a religion. The new era of international competition would, by an irresistible logic, lead ultimately to a new era of regulated cartels. Weak producers would be shaken out or bought up by the stronger ones, and a handful of multinational companies would dominate world markets as the national companies had earlier dominated national markets. The need of large companies for stability and predictability would assert itself once more, and a network of international and national regulations, policies, and gentlemen's agreements would once again create an environment in which the giants could flourish.

This was not the way Main Street looked at the economy. In the small-business view, deregulation and tax cuts should and would stimulate new entrepreneurs to transform the economic landscape. The corporate elite of Wall Street would be overcome by a smarter breed of high-tech entrepreneurs and independent businessmen. The bureaucratic age of gigantic institutions, in business and government, was ending.

There are few dreams so cherished, and so frequently disappointed, as the one that the age of the small entrepreneur and the independent professional is about to return. The love of bureaucracy, whether corporate or governmental, has no deep place in the heart of the American people, and even those who have spent their entire working lives successfully navigating the treacherous shoals of bureaucracies confess to a longing for the independent life. It is an unfortunate, deeply regrettable, but unavoidable conclusion, however, that the time when most businesses could be small and most folk could be independent ended some time in the last century. Since then Main Street and its allies on small and medium-size farms have stormed Heaven — and Washington — with prayers, but they have never been able to reverse the decline of their importance in the economy.

Main Street itself has not been able to put forward a coherent economic program that would work for the nation as a whole. Not only has Main Street remained mired in the nineteenth-century laissez-faire economics that has long been rejected as impractical; it has forgotten what the old economics was all about. The economic gospel being preached to Main Street by its favorite preachers would have been received with gales of laughter by any nineteenth-century economist. The idea that the "magic of the market" could achieve permanent prosperity, putting the nightmares of recessions, depressions, and bankruptcies behind us forever, has never been entertained by any serious thinker. Free market economics never held that the path of capitalism would be smooth and easy; it merely argued that any interference with the admittedly disruptive and painful operations of the economic system would in the long run create even worse problems.

The Main Street economics of the Reagan era mirrored the liberal confidence in Keynesianism of the Kennedy years. The proper government activities — intervention in one view, abstention in the other — would ensure economic growth. Recessions and depressions, according to both schools of thought, were caused by policy errors, not — as the *real* free market theorists of the past held — by the inner workings of the business cycle.

This touching but misplaced faith in the magic of the market left Main Street defenseless against the budgetary chicanery that characterized the first Reagan term. As deficits mounted to astronomic levels, taking real interest rates with them, the administration was able to allay Main Street's fears by producing the series of what David Stockman, then the budget director, called "rosy scenarios" — budgetary projections that showed how the deficit would be eliminated after a mere decade or so of *uninterrupted economic growth.* The administration, in other words, would be able to balance the budget if the economy performed better than it had at any time in history. Why a free market that produced violent crashes and profound depressions at regular intervals ever since the Industrial Revolution should suddenly change its nature was not a question that Main Street would ask, because Main Street worships a market that never existed.

The agendas of Main Street and Wall Street were to clash repeatedly during the Reagan years, and the administration would consistently demonstrate that, though its heart and lips were in Main Street, its brain was in lower Manhattan. Monetary, fiscal, and trade policy set Main Street and Wall Street against each other; in all of these areas, and also in its attitudes toward the critical financial industry, the administration came down solidly on the side of big business.

The administration paid lip service only, and precious little of that, to Main Street's desire to see real interest rates low. Smaller businesses have fewer financing options — and more expensive ones — than big businesses; with their more limited cash flows and their less exemplary credit ratings they find borrowing more difficult and repayment more burdensome. From colonial times small business has favored easy-money policies — and from the Federalist period small business has been opposed by more established and larger firms that benefit from sound money pegged closely to international money markets and rates. Paul Volcker reigned over the nation's money supply through six disinflationary years of Reagan's rule, pursuing policies that would have pleased every chairman of the Federal Reserve since the Wilson administration.

Fiscal policy also divided the two wings of the conservative coalition. Main Street has traditionally viewed government debt as a curse, but the interest-bearing debt of a stable government is a blessing to Wall Street, particularly when the world's most famous inflation fighter reigns supreme at the Fed. The skyrocketing debt of the Reagan years gave pause to the markets, but that debt had a shiny side for the banks and corporations whose financial possibilities were vastly expanded by the immense volume of liquid, interest-bearing obligations of the U.S. government, the world's most creditworthy borrower.

Trade is another issue over which big and small business disagree, and here again the administration demonstrated an overwhelming preference for the Wall Street point of view. The modern multinational corporation depends absolutely on a free flow of money, goods, and information across national frontiers. Economic nationalism in any form is a curse to an economic organization that thinks in international terms. An automobile company that buys steel from Korea, parts from Taiwan and Mexico, employs a European design, and sells its products in two dozen countries does not want its world constrained by tariffs and restrictions. It wants currencies to be freely interchangeable, profits to be mobile, and banks to be international. The last thing such a company wants is a trade war. Because the United States remains the world's largest market economy, big business fears economic nationalism and protection more acutely here than anywhere else. The United States has far more power than any of its partners to disrupt world trade.

Small business derives fewer benefits and suffers greater losses from international trade. Chase Manhattan has much more to gain from international finance than does East Pugwash Savings and Loan. Even large industrial companies under siege by foreign competition have more flexibility than small businesses in the same position. GM can move production overseas more easily than the local widget works can.

In fact, small and large business have as much in common as the trout and the fisherman. They are both in the same food chain, but they occupy different positions. The trout and the fisherman may agree, temporarily, on an economic program, but the trout will discover, too late, that the program was not just a mayfly for the trout; there was also the matter of a trout for the fisherman.

THE MYSTERY OF THE CONSERVATIVE MOVEMENT

The great paradox of the contemporary conservative movement is the alliance between its social and economic wings. As anyone who knows them can attest, the higher classes of American society are no more conservative in their personal habits than so many bunny rabbits — with a few exceptions. They regard fundamentalists as a mild variety of snake handler and would as soon see their children in Jonestown as at Oral Roberts University. What are these people doing sharing podiums with the Reverend Falwell? What is the Reverend Falwell doing sharing podiums with them? How did a divorced movie actor who hardly ever goes to church get to run against a Baptist Sunday school teacher as the Christian candidate?

The answer lies in a central tenet of American conservatism, one that marks it off from conservative movements in many other countries. Like liberalism, American conservatism is genuinely wedded to the idea of the free market. Pre-industrial society never really became the status quo in the United States except in the South, and the only semi-aristocratic ruling class the United States ever knew was crushed in the Civil War. There was therefore never any group in America that corresponded to the feudal nobility of Europe, a group that defined conservatism as an anti-industrial, anticommercial ideology. In the Vatican, "conservative" may label someone who thinks that the French Revolution was a terrible mistake; in Spain, it can mean someone who thinks that the Inquisition was the victim of a bad press. There are depths to conservatism around the world that American society can scarcely credit. American conservatives largely believe that if the Industrial Revolution was not altogether a good thing, it was at least a necessary one; they consider the ideas of English political philosophy as revealed to Adam Smith, John Locke, and John Stuart Mill to be close to Holy Writ. The older, more atavistic tendencies exist within the tory wing of the American conservative movement, but they are everywhere checked, shadowed, and rendered impotent by the overwhelming and dedicated allegiance to the free market and the private enterprise economy.

A hundred years of history have amply shown that the free market produces monopoly and oligopoly. Competition presupposes a winner; yesterday's winner does not compete on exactly equal terms with yesterday's loser. One is weaker; one is stronger. If one competes consistently better than the others, he will win and drive his rivals from the market. Eventually, the market will be dominated by a few successful producers who can, if they like, minimize their common risks by cooperatively sharing the proceeds.

Our concern here is with the social consequences of the free market and its transformation into a closed circle. American society during the nineteenth and twentieth centuries gradually turned from a society of many independent producers into one of a relatively small number of large producers. It became a collection of employees rather than entrepreneurs. The expansion of production favored the development of large cities. The needs of an industrial economy ended the usefulness of the family as an economic unit. Industrial work also brought women into the work force on a new and greater scale, paving the way for the financial independence of women and turning the family, de facto, into a voluntary institution.

All these things and more were brought about by the free market, with its emphasis on profit. The profit motive created the factories and filled them with workers; the profit motive concentrated the ownership of productive facilities in fewer and fewer hands.

The market closed down family grocery stores, mom-and-pop diners, and family pharmacies, and replaced them with national retail chains. The market favored companies that expanded their operations to a national and then international scale — meaning that first thousands and then millions of American wage earners left their extended families and their roots and human ties. The market sent millions of former agricultural workers to the North from the fields of the South and of Puerto Rico when it mechanized agriculture and moved from sharecropping to large estate agribusiness.

The natural and unavoidable activity of the market is to erode traditional social institutions and to weaken the hold of religion and family over individuals. The free market economy is not a stagnant thing; as with Western civilization itself, its most outstanding characteristic is dynamism, change. It is the most formidable instrument of social change ever seen on this planet.

Conservative economics overthrows conservative order; this is the central paradox of the American right. The free market is a market in which large producers are free to extinguish small farmers, storekeepers, and businessmen, the social pillars of traditional values. The longer and more freely the market operates, the more inexorably it destroys its political base.

THE ROD OF AARON

Historically, liberal society emerged from a conservative one; we see the process at work in the Wilson administration. Wilson's foreign and domestic policies bear an uncanny resemblance to FDR's — except that what seems green and unripe in the Wilson era looks powerful and mature under FDR. Wilson's banking and regulatory legislation laid the foundation for the New Deal, and his peace proposals in 1918 prefigured those of 1945. He was the first president to act as if the United States was the most powerful country in the world, and to attempt to give it an economic system that could support its global responsibilities. Wilson's programs seemed premature in 1919; isolation and laissez-faire triumphed in the 1920s, to enjoy an Indian summer until the Depression and another war ended their reign in American politics.

American conservatism was the ideology of a strong and progressive, but isolated, nation-state. It was an ideology that could not serve as the basis for a world empire — it was far too localized, restrictive, and eth-nocentric. Its evocation of traditional American values, of pioneers toiling across the prairies, of evangelical religion and the missionary spirit — that is, of the icons of a society on the rise or on the defensive — could not inspire an empire that was opulent, expansive, and effortlessly dom-inant. Like the Boers remembering their treks, the Americans drawing their ideology from the pioneers would never be able to deal well with the natives.

American conservatism also was the ideology for a nation that was still relatively close to the free market of its early industrial age. By 1932 this ideology was simply inappropriate. Its exponents were unable to grasp the events around them, much less to affect them. It was like a scientific hypothesis that works well enough on one set of facts, but falls apart when new data are introduced.

Liberal ideology reigned secure until the empire ran into trouble. Con-servatism, where it appeared, was anachronistic or crackpot in origin. Sections, like the South, that clung to it were seen as backward; a liberal orientation was almost a requirement for social acceptability in intellec-tual circles. Conservatives were on the defensive, unable to define issues in ways that brought them any support. Even within the Republican Party, conservatives shrank to a minority and watched Wendell Willkie, Thomas E. Dewey, Dwight Eisenhower, and Richard Nixon all run within the framework of the liberal state. When the conservatives finally ran one of their own, Barry Goldwater, in 1964, he suffered the worst electoral trouncing since the last conservative candidate — Alf Landon, in 1936.

Conservatism re-emerged only when the liberal empire came face to face with uncomfortable facts. Liberal economists could not account for stagflation (to use Paul Samuelson's word) any more than liberal tacticians could explain the stalemate in Indochina. The conservatives were more than eager to step forward with a response. As America slipped from its unchallenged pre-eminence toward a less dominant role in the Western alliance, it would have to fight harder for its interests. In the palmy days of empire, the Americans could say little and wait, knowing well that the facts would do the talking and bring the allies into line. As America became relatively weaker, it would have to push harder to get its way. Conservatism had worked well when America was one strong nation-state among many; perhaps it could succeed again.

The Reagan approach to allied relations is based on competition rather than hegemony. Superiority is something to be attained, not something to be administered. In this respect the conservative perspective corre-sponds more closely with the actual American position in the world than does the liberal view, which continues to lean toward a less assertive line in foreign affairs in the hope that circumstances will, in the end, bring the allies around to the American position.

On the domestic scene also conservatism has advantages over liberalism in an era like the present. Conservatism is far better adapted to a politics of scarcity and of class competition.

For these and other reasons, the American people decided to give the conservatives another chance in 1980 and confirmed that choice in 1984. Yet the election results indicated a certain caution — the House remained staunchly Democratic in the elections of 1980, 1982, and 1984 — and there are other clear indications that conservatism is incapable of regaining the kind of hegemony it once enjoyed.

First of all, the internationalization of everyday life undermines ethnocentrism and racism. The huge Asian immigration, for example, makes it impossible for most Americans to revert to the stereotypes of another era. The treatment of American citizens of Japanese origin during World War II now has a firm place on the nationally acknowledged roster of injustices, and marriages between whites and Asians are becoming more common. Whatever the remaining power of racism in American society, the shift in white attitudes toward blacks since 1963 cannot be reversed. Integration has proceeded too far; too many whites have black friends and co-workers who have demonstrated competence and humanity. Jim Crow is dead, and even if the racist view of history that gave him ideological support still lives on, it has received a crippling wound.

The cultures of non-Western societies can no longer be considered purely primitive. European and American culture has lost much of the inflated sense of superiority over the rest of the world that so disfigured it at the zenith of its conquest. Western visual and musical arts are saturated today with motifs that in past generations would have been incomprehensible. Americans listening to African tribal music today tap their feet and smile; we have developed an ear for African rhythm and harmonics. The rich traditions of the Orient have similarly penetrated Western culture. Knowledge of Oriental religion, philosophy, painting, poetry, even cuisine, has spread into general awareness. Oriental culture still strikes the Occident as exotic, but no longer as alien.

Moreover, there is a universal cultural expectation that as time goes by we shall become more familiar with and more admiring of the achievements of other cultures. We are willing now to suppose that things we find strange or unappealing will look better if we give them a try; we have grown from a nation of meat-and-potato eaters to a nation of sushi samplers, and we like it that way.

These developments undercut the conservative vision. American history no longer looks so much like the triumph of reason and order over chaos and war. It is no longer natural and therefore completely understandable for white people to exterminate reds, enslave blacks, and napalm yellows. The ideas of the city on the hill and Manifest Destiny have to be defended before they can be believed today, and when an idea has to be defended, much of its power is gone. Such an idea does not fade away all at once; it lingers on as a shadow of its former self. Creationism did not vanish after Darwin, and even today majorities prefer it to Darwin's theory in much of the country. Even so, "creation science" has lost its hegemony in the world of ideas; it has passed over into opposition in the parliament of thought.

Military reality also strikes at conservatism and puts the question of national defense on a different footing. One way or another, the bomb will end the present system of national sovereignty. Militant nationalism, not to say chauvinism, has become a suicidal impulse. This is a fact that conservatism in its present form simply cannot accommodate, yet it forces itself on the attention of every rational being as effectively, if not as immediately, as every other human biological urge. The instinct for self-preservation and the preservation of one's children is one of the strongest human emotions; in the past the conservative appeal to group tradition and solidarity against outsiders satisfied this need as well as anything else could. Today, chauvinism is a threat to humanity itself.

We have already seen that the conservative policy of letting the free market work its will leads to the undoing of all but a handful of producers, creating the world of impersonal corporations and big government that so many deplore. Conservative ideology is not capable of devising a way to restore the Jeffersonian Garden of Eden, nor can it insulate the American people from the developing global economy.

For all these reasons, we can assert with some confidence that conservatism cannot displace liberalism as America's ideology. Liberal weakness was the conservative opportunity: at sunset the lesser stars appear. This is not to say that the conservative mini-renaissance is necessarily headed for a rapid defeat. Barring a shock to the system, conservatism can remain a potent, if not effortlessly dominant, force on the political scene. Yet like its last period of dominance, the 1920s, conservatism's present period in the sunshine will not leave many traces when it ends.

George Bush, before he realized which side of his bread had the butter on it, ridiculed Reagan's program, asking "How do you balance the budget, raise military spending, and cut taxes all at the same time?" Bush's answer: "With mirrors." He was dead right, and that is precisely how conservatism can govern in the absence of a real ideological mandate.

Ronald Reagan is able to bring together the varied constituencies. He projects — or, rather, allows others to project onto him — an image of America as it never was but ought to have been. Easy grace, good humor, stern purpose, and relaxed attitude are the qualities he stands for in government. Reagan's real program is to be Reagan. Barring an absolutely unmitigated disaster — a banking crash, a return to depression, a Watergate-style scandal, or a long, meat-grinding war in Central America — Reagan will deliver on all his promises by smiling on television.

The national government is at a huge, incalculable distance from the average citizen. We depend on the media to feed us impressions, and we use these to help us assess the state of the country. Reagan's gift is that he can project a reassuring image of control, competence, and benevolence. He can get away with scandals that would have landed Nixon in prison; he can order foolhardy moves that have resulted in the death of more than two hundred Marines and placed every American in the world at increased risk; he can preside over a massive redistribution of income in favor of the rich while the middle class begins to dissolve — yet his mere presence makes it all irrelevant.

But though Reagan can sell himself, he cannot sell Reaganism. None of his allies or assistants shows any signs of being able to replace him. His closest political associates are, nationally speaking, still considered unpopular cranks. Reagan's programs without the Gipper are widely unpopular. The spell he casts is personal.

THE MYSTERY OF SIN

Conservatism — fundamentalist and tory, Wall Street and Main Street — assumes a world that is permanently in conflict. In theological terms, American conservatism sees the world according to the Calvinist doctrine of Original Sin — the utter depravity of man. According to this idea, human nature was so distorted by the Fall that human beings are incapable of any good act unless they have been born again.

Political philosophy for conservatives comes down to the question of how to govern unruly human beings in a manner that will bring out their better impulses and suppress their baser ones. Conservatives believe that no political solution will work perfectly; evil impulses are too deeply rooted in human nature for any social engineers to pull them up. Furthermore, conservatives observe, no system can be better than its operators in the long run. Those operators, being human, will abuse even the most perfect system. Darkly suspicious of human motives, conservatives at their best are quick to spot the flaws in the idealistic visions of optimistic liberals like Eleanor Roosevelt. Conservatism has the strength and consistency that come from a firm ideological point of view; liberals tend to flutter from hope to conjecture.

Conservatism is the gloomy voice of experience, the wet blanket of the past. The painfully gained knowledge of human history — that power corrupts, that institutions fail, that good intentions are not to be relied on — speaks through conservative ideology.

If the Calvinist view of human nature is correct, then humanity's days are numbered. Humanity will not, because it cannot, create a just world order, and reason will not prevail over passion. The bomb will fall — and if not the bomb, then the deadly synthetic virus or the particle-beam weapon or the supertoxin. Perhaps we will poison the planet beyond repair before we blow ourselves up. Perhaps not.

Religious ideologies that are based on Calvinism stress the Apocalypse, the final destruction of the world and the judgment of its inhabitants. Man is incapable of handling his own affairs, so God steps in to ring down the curtain. Until recently, Apocalypse was a purely religious notion. Those who believed in the impending end of the world looked for signs of extraordinary divine intervention; it would, in other words, take a miracle to end the world. Unfortunately, in today's world the depravity of man implies that it would take a miracle to save it. What was once an abstract idea, a piece of religious cosmology, has now entered the political field.

Conservatism must now oppose anything we might call the politics of survival — politics that starts from the assumption that human nature is malleable enough so that social conflicts can be contained, if not completely eliminated. Obviously the pre-eminent representative of this school of thought is socialism in its many forms, but conservatism is also doomed to combat any proposals on disarmament and East-West relations that proceed on a basis of mutual trust. Faced with a choice between terror and trust to ensure peace, conservatism must always choose terror.

Experience and reason may tell people that conservatives are right, and that arms control is a hopeless aspiration. Proposals ranging from verifiable freezes to unilateral reductions strike the conservative mind as naïvely optimistic, but for masses of people such proposals represent their only hope. Better a weak hope than a strong despair, they say. As the arms race mutates with the proliferation of new weapons and delivery systems, and as the inherent technical limits of Star Wars become more generally understood, these popular feelings can only grow.

Conservatism is doomed to offer the counsels of despair. At best, these are counsels of humanity and decency. If we are going down, let us keep our pride and behave like the band on the *Titanic*. At worst, the counsels of despair are "Eat, drink, and be merry"; they weaken the will to take even palliative measures to avert the catastrophe. It is unfortunate but true that the second reaction to despair typifies the mass response of our time.

In any case, the politics of despair is bad news for those who espouse it. Tactically, conservatives have to play down the seriousness of the human predicament — war, chaos, arms, and a damaged ecology — because conservatism offers no real remedies for these problems. Committed to rapid growth under capitalism, the administration would be in no position to impose the necessary regulations on private industry even if it wished to do so. The cost of proper disposal of chemical waste would be astronomical; to force companies to take responsibility for past pollution would be to force the chemical industry into a depression. The administration must therefore draw attention from the problem, making the eventual clean-up more difficult and more expensive. This is all very well until the bill comes due.

Similarly the Star Wars proposals for defense are intended to create the illusion of a conservative alternative to nuclear disarmament. Devoid of any serious scientific support, the system has been sold as if the most optimistic hopes of its most convinced supporters were realistic plans. As research work continues it becomes evident that neither Star Wars nor any other defense system can negate the ability of the superpowers to destroy civilization and perhaps humanity itself.

At the same time that conservatives endorse Star Wars, they are forced to minimize the danger of nuclear war. They must attack the findings of those who claim that a war would result in a nuclear winter that would threaten life on earth. They must argue for multiple scenarios allowing for the use of nuclear weapons below the threshold of a general nuclear war. They must underestimate the risks of an arms race, pooh-pooh fears of an accidental nuclear exchange, and turn a blind eye to the threat of proliferation.

The mask of false optimism with which much of the right covers its despair about everything from the fight against communism to the control of nuclear weapons will not give conservatives the "permanent majority" they dream of. Politics must offer hope, real hope, and in the long run this can be sustained only by real progress. By politics, of course, we mean democratic politics. It is possible for military regimes like those throughout the U.S. sphere of influence to enforce a conservative vision with bayonets; perhaps this is the direction in which American conservatism has to travel if it wishes to retain power. If so, there will be no shortage of leaders willing to travel that road or of intellectuals willing to rationalize that decision, defending torture and dictatorship while preening themselves on their hardheaded realism and their affinity for the eternal values of Western civilization.

THE MARKET AND THE RIGHT

IN NO COUNTRY is the free enterprise system so widely hailed and so little understood as in the United States. We have already seen that the free market is primarily responsible for the social developments unwelcome to American conservatives; there are two other areas where the invisible hand shapes institutions in ways that pain and surprise its supporters.

The New Right has no special love for big business and Wall Street. Its long struggle against the Rockefeller wing of the Republican Party left bad memories on both sides. But hostility toward the winners of economic competition is an uncomfortable position for competition's defenders. When Ronald Reagan, George Gilder, Barry Goldwater, Phyllis Schlafly, and others hymn the praises of free enterprise, they like to focus on the system's rewards for risk taking, for innovation, and for creativity. These qualities often do characterize small companies, and at one time, when such companies dominated the economy, they characterized the marketplace as a whole. While that marketplace was never quite the utopia later commentators made it out to be (do we really want to praise the entrepreneurial spirit of the slave traders and to memorialize the job opportunities created by the opium dealers?), today's market relies on different qualities for success.

Mature companies prosper not so much by taking risks as by avoiding them. People rise in corporate hierarchies by their bureaucratic skills, not their entrepreneurial abilities. Richard Vigurie complains that big business is all too often hand in glove with big government, and that this hampers the innovative entrepreneurs.[1] But so what? If it is acceptable for government policy to favor small entrepreneurs by generous tax breaks and other favors, should not the same favors be extended to those who have proven that they can succeed in the market?

Small entrepreneurs often think of themselves as the wave of the future — as the early mammals preparing to replace the dinosaurs. They

are smaller but smarter, and in time they will inherit the earth. This is
a pleasant self-image, but it would be more accurate to compare the new
entrepreneurs to baby dinosaurs than to the mammals. The infant bron-
tosaurus was no doubt more sportive and agile than his massive dam,
but had he defeated the odds and survived the hunger of the frisky baby
carnivores and the occasional unseeing foot of an uncle or aunt, he would
have grown up to become another slow, plodding, dull denizen of the
swamp.

In the same way, of course, the sleek, smart new company will, if it
survives and grows, become in time another bureaucratic and boring
large corporation. Many of today's most ossified companies were once
exciting high-tech ventures; railroads used to be glamour growth
stocks.

Ever since the rise of the great national trusts, entrepreneurial companies have played a marginal role in the economy. Some studies show
that small companies in recent years have created more jobs than have
large ones, but small business in this definition includes such enterprises
as fast-food franchises. The owner of a local Mcdonald's hires people
and looks good in the statistics, but behind him looms the parent company, the Big Mac itself. If the New Right wants to argue that the virtual
elimination of locally owned and managed independent diners and greasy
spoons, and their replacement by franchised Pizza Huts and Burger Kings,
is a triumph for diversity and the small entrepreneur, it is free to do so;
alternatively one can argue that large corporations have discovered a new
way to assign higher risks to small capitalists while keeping substantial
profits for themselves.

The proliferation of high-tech companies is also sometimes taken as a
sign of the revival of the classic free market of early capitalism. Such a
view, though cheering to the right, misses two important points. First,
it is normal for new industries to spawn large numbers of independent
producers. A few, a very few, of these producers may grow into major
corporations on their own; others will be bought out, and most will fail.
Billions of dinosaur eggs were laid every year; only a handful hatched
and fewer babies grew to maturity. The existing great corporations often
prefer to sit back and wait for the new industry to shake itself out before
making their moves. New products can be expensive to develop, and
the risk-averse giants like others to cope with the uncertainties of new
markets. Once the initial spate of new companies and new products has
begun to take definite shape, existing companies can buy out the producers with proven track records, or they can imitate successful products
at far less risk.

In mature industries there is still a role for the small independent producer. It would not be economically wise for large corporations to develop the productive capacity for filling every order at the peak of the business cycle. That capacity would lie idle for most of the time. Far better to let the small, hungry entrepreneur scavenge these marginal markets — but the small entrepreneur in this case is no more the leading edge of the economy than a hyena is the leader of a pride of lions.

The second feature of the high-tech marketplace that reinforces the oligopolistic nature of modern business is the role of finance capital in the new companies. In the early stages of the capitalist economy, entrepreneurs needed relatively little capital to start a new business. Equipment was cheap and so was labor. In the United States, almost anyone could assemble the capital needed to start a farm. Even technological research was easy to capitalize. The Wright brothers built their airplane in a bicycle shop.

Since those days it has grown steadily more expensive to start a new business. The clerk of yesteryear needed a goose quill pen, foolscap, and a whale oil lamp to produce effectively and competitively. Today's secretary needs telephones, a word processor, a copier, and an office that is well enough heated, cooled, and wired to keep all the machinery working. New products are more expensive to design and produce than they used to be — in most if not all cases. The frontiers of technology have advanced, and the reseacher who is designing computers or engaged in biological engineering needs much more equipment and money. An individual silicon chip may have a small unit cost, but that is only because it comes from an expensive, high-tech factory capable of turning out such chips by the hundreds of thousands. Every year these factories get more advanced and therefore more expensive to build and maintain. The start-up costs of business keep rising.

A result of this cost escalation is the rise of the venture capitalist — a person or institution that provides start-up money for new ventures in return for equity participation, a share of ownership in the new company. Although such an arrangement has long existed, it used to be easier for an aspiring capitalist to borrow his start-up money. Once the original loan was paid off, the businessman would own his company outright. Increasingly today's businessman must sell pieces of his company before he can open its doors. The chances are excellent in such a transaction that the investment bankers and venture capitalists are much better prepared to negotiate a good deal for themselves than is the cash-starved entrepreneur. Not only are there more hungry, would-be businessmen than there is capital, but the managers of investment capital have more information, more experience, and better legal advice than most entrepreneurs.

What we have in a process like this is a kind of financial franchising. In the same way that the parent fast-food company imposes regulations on its franchises, the financial franchisers require uniformity in business practices and management. They look for certain types of opportunity and have strict, uniform requirements about rate of return, additional financing, and corporate development. Often the biggest profits in starting a new business come when the corporation is ready to go public, to sell its stock on the open market. The old-fashioned entrepreneur aimed to build up a company for himself; the modern franchisee goes public as soon as his far from silent partner feels the time is ripe. The entrepreneur becomes a manager with equity participation — a well-paid and well-regarded employee, but not an independent owner. Many venture capitalists specifically reserve the right to replace the original entrepreneur with another manager if the entrepreneur is not as efficient, or as conformist, as they require.

The normal course of the economic cycle also works against the new entrepreneur. When the high-tech industry opened, new companies sprang up by the score. Great fortunes were made; new capital rushed into the business, here and overseas. Before long, whole sectors of the high-tech industry had been overbuilt; there were too many semiconductor factories, too many personal computer makers. With supply greater than demand, the price of the new products began to drop, and in the bitter competitive struggle that ensued, the winners were the companies with the deepest pockets. Large corporations were able to buy out high-tech companies at attractive prices, but dozens of smaller companies were forced out of business.

As has been the case for more than a century, free competition leads to a concentration of wealth and power. The free market is not a steady state phenomenon; it brings its own demise in its wake. Wall Street can afford to smile on the populists of the right when Main Street agitates for less regulation and less government supervision. Only strict and stifling controls can protect the salmon from the shark.

The coalition between big business and the small entrepreneur to open up the free market and to get rid of some federal regulation was like the dinner party described by Lewis Carroll:

> I passed by his garden, and marked, with one eye
> How the Owl and the Panther were sharing a pie:
> The Panther took pie-crust, and gravy, and meat,
> While the Owl had the dish as its share of the treat.
> When the pie was all finished, the Owl, as a boon,

Was kindly permitted to pocket the spoon:
While the Panther received knife and fork with a growl,
And concluded the banquet by————.[2]

THE RIGHT, THE MARKET, AND THE MINORITIES

The concentration of poverty among racial minorities, especially among blacks, has recently become a theoretical and practical problem for the right. In a genuinely free market one would expect wealth and poverty to be more or less equally distributed among groups that were otherwise similar in demographic make-up. The enormous gap between racial groups in the United States requires some kind of explanation.

In the past, the right had no difficulty accounting for the difference. Blacks were, quite simply, an inferior race. They lacked the intelligence, self-discipline, and capacity for management possessed by the white race. Providence had favored them with talents for singing and dancing, and doled out a generous helping of physical endurance, but for reasons best known to Himself, God had not seen fit to gift the black race with a capacity for what used to be called "white man's work."

Many leading figures in the American right of the 1980s once routinely took such positions in public, but the evolution of public morals, the Civil Rights Acts of 1964 and 1968, and the Voting Rights Act of 1965 have combined to restrict such conversation today to private places. Die-hard segregationists and Jim Crow apologists of yore now profess the most fervent devotion to the "true" principles of the same civil rights movement they once said was communist-inspired. (The "true" principles of the civil rights movement somehow always manage to be defined so as to forestall any actual or proposed measure to improve the lot of blacks today.)

Without for a moment questioning the sincerity of these conversions, we can observe that they raise a troublesome theoretical problem for the defenders of laissez-faire, laissez-tomber economics. If the market is not just in its operations, if a systematic racism denies rewards to some and gives them to others on noneconomic grounds, then the theory that the free market is the best and most equitable method for allocating the resources of society disappears into air. The door is opened to affirmative action and other programs to correct this systematic market bias. Such a statement also requires the admission that the United States is and always has been a cruelly racist society — an admission that ill suits the social rearmament the right believes necessary to human freedom.

Additionally, if the market can fail so conspicuously to achieve justice for such a large group of people, will it not have other failures as well? From a theoretical point of view, there is no solution that would satisfy the needs of contemporary right-wing ideology. Far from being a reliable and prudent governor of social well-being, the invisible hand turns into an arbitrary force that must be heavily regulated to be endured at all. The victims of the invisible hand, once dismissed as life's losers and malingerers, now press forward with claims to compensation and redress.

In order to avoid such a state of affairs, the partisans of the right have constructed another theory. Yes, they concede, America was a racist society *in the past.* But America is no longer racist. The civil rights laws ended all that. One is reminded of Aleksandr Solzhenitsyn's contemptuous description of Stalinist careerists defending the state from the charges of Stalin's victims:

> The distortion experts rushed unbidden into the breach! They might have been waiting all those years for just this: to cover the breach with their gray-winged bodies and with the joyous — yes, joyous! — flapping of their wings to hide the Archipelago in its nakedness from astonished spectators.
>
> Their first cry, which came to them instinctively, in a flash, was: *It will never happen again!*[3]

In the United States, these "cherubim of the lie" now proclaim the end of racism in order to avoid the necessity of fighting it. And this from the same people who argued against the civil rights laws on the grounds that morality cannot be legislated, that social customs of long standing cannot be extirpated by laws. Any stick will do to beat the blacks.

There is no really comfortable, consistent theoretical approach that the right can take toward black America. Every black face in the United States is a reminder of three centuries of oppression, theft, slavery, and neglect. It is a reminder to whites, reluctant or otherwise, that there is a vast blind spot in the national consciousness, a powerful argument that the United States may lack the qualifications for telling the rest of the world how to live, and a living testimony that the free market so beloved of conservative ideologues has never existed outside the pages of textbooks.

Nonetheless, blacks refuse to go away or to become invisible, and the social theorists of the right, like Adam and Eve, aware of their nakedness, seek to cover themselves with leaves of trees. George Gilder's efforts in *Wealth and Poverty* are particularly instructive.

He argues that the racism of the past accounted for the historically unequal position of blacks in American society, but now that we are in a postracism era, some new force must be at work. His candidate? "Liberalism, not racism, accounts for the enduring poverty of blacks in America."[4] Like most conservatives, Gilder chooses not to dwell on the respective roles played by liberals and conservatives in the supposed eradication of American racism between 1960 and 1980. Martin Luther King, Jr., was a hero, but we must never ever say anything about what he believed or whom he fought.

The crimes of liberalism against blacks have been numerous and heinous, he charges, but he has no doubt as to the most serious offense: "Here I choose my words as carefully as I can — a wreckage of broken lives and families worse than the aftermath of slavery."[5]

One can only marvel at the tremendous power of the Great Society; it took slavery almost 250 years of murder and oppression to do less damage than a handful of bureaucrats could accomplish in twenty years with a few food stamps.

But what can this statement, so carefully worded, mean? The aftermath of slavery was a terrible thing. Blacks had been kept illiterate by terror and law; after a lifetime of brutal and uncompensated toil, elderly men and women found themselves set adrift, without property or social insurance, in a world that despised them; families had been torn apart by the avarice of their owners; the former slaves had undergone the total (was it totalitarian or merely authoritarian?) and forced destruction of traditional tribal relationships, families, and even language; a defenseless people was abandoned to the tender mercies of their bitter enemies, who subjected them to lynching, terror, and systematic discrimination for most of the subsequent century.

No doubt millions of unsung blacks long nostalgically for the good old days of lynch law and the KKK, bad in their way of course, but not to be compared with the horrors of Project Head Start and child nutrition programs. One can only wonder at the cynicism of the liberal media, which cover up the existence of the vast silent majority of American blacks yearning for the return of Jim Crow to deliver them from the toils of the welfare state.

Gilder goes on, joyously flapping. There is no gulag. American leaders refuse "to tell the truth about blacks." They do nothing to counter the "false and invidious" proposition, "slanderous" of white Americans, that "racism and discrimination still explain the low incomes of blacks."[6] Gilder argues that family breakdown explains this much better. He points to the high percentage of black families headed by women and the high rate of divorce and separation that afflicts the urban centers. In another burst of carefully chosen phrases, Gilder gives his view of the process:

> Benefit levels destroy the father's key role and authority. He can no longer feel manly in his own home. At first he may try to maintain his power by the use of muscle and bluster. But to exert force against a woman is a confession of weakness. . . . His response to this reality is that very combination of resignation and rage, escapism and violence, short horizons and promiscuous sexuality that characterizes everywhere the life of the poor.[7]

One hardly knows where to start, but if this mixture of characteristics dominates the life of the poor "everywhere," if it applies to the slums of Manila as well as to those of Indiana, then must we not blame poverty, rather than the welfare state, for this condition?

In any case, Gilder does not address a far more crucial problem: Why do black men have so few opportunities to earn more income than welfare checks provide? With a minimum wage of $3.35 an hour (too high, in the opinion of most of the right), a forty-hour work week brings a weekly income of $134 before taxes, or an annual income of about $7000 — assuming no layoffs or unpaid vacations. It is not easy to see how a family can live on such a sum. If we make work more attractive by lowering benefits to a point where $134 per week looks like a princely sum, well worth forty hours of dangerous, difficult labor, we may be surprised by how few people — whatever their race — are willing to hail us as great philanthropists.

Unless the right is to abandon its reliance on the market altogether, it must come up with something besides racism to account for the disparity between the incomes of blacks and whites. Gilder follows the life history of a group of black men who were in their thirties in 1957. In that year, they were among the top 33 percent of wage earners; by 1971, they had fallen to the bottom third.

Gilder has a "clear" explanation for this result: credentialism. In the misguided effort to eliminate discrimination, paper qualifications were imposed, replacing the system of hunches and intuition relied on by employers. Blacks with experience but without degrees were denied promotions and opportunities to improve their positions.[8]

Another explanation, not even considered by Gilder, is that blacks in 1957 worked in jobs that required little education because they were systematically denied access to that prerequisite. Their jobs are heavily concentrated in blue-collar fields, and there is little gap between starting wages and peak wages in such jobs. Blacks ranked relatively high at the earlier stages because whites continued professional education or took entry-level white-collar jobs that had lower starting salaries than blue-collar ones. But the whites steadily progressed along their career track, and the blacks stagnated in theirs.

Discrimination in employment was not outlawed until 1964, the year when the thirty-five-year-old black laborer of 1957 was forty-two years old and past the point at which promotions from laborer to manager occur. Any system of credentialism spread only gradually through the economy during the next seven years, the period covered by Gilder's study. Only after lawsuits, the appointment of a Civil Rights Commission with clout, and a gradual trickle-down of new management practices to factory floors and employment offices across the United States could the new laws be said to have taken effect. It was by then much too late for men in their fifties to enter the junior executive programs that had welcomed their white peers twenty-five years earlier.

Blacks are not the only minority who give the New Right the theoretical heebie-jeebies. "Capitalism begins with giving,"[9] writes the ever-cheerful Gilder. The reader will recall that Gilder has argued that capitalism is a profoundly moral social system because it begins with generosity. This would make Squanto the first great capitalist of North America, and if the United States functioned like the benevolent potlatch society imagined by Gilder, whites would be scratching their brains to come up with a gift to repay the Indians for letting them have the continent.

Things haven't worked out quite that way for the Native Americans, and Gilder has a villain: government. Government action, Gilder charges, has reduced the native people to "a state of bitter dependency."[10] There is an undeniable historic truth to this charge, but Gilder is not thinking about the record of genocidal wars, broken treaties, or government's corrupt bargains with private enterprise to deny the tribes the benefit of any natural resources inadvertently included in the reservation lands.

Gilder does not seem to believe that this sort of government action has anything to do with the plight of the American Indian. What Gilder objects to is the pittance of aid and assistance given to the tribes that escaped the assault on their existence. That the tribes have failed to make much out of the deserts and wastelands to which they were relegated is the fault of government programs that destroyed their incentives — by preventing their outright mass starvation.

It is an interesting theory. One almost hopes that someone will practice it on Mr. Gilder. Perhaps he and his family could be deprived of their possessions and means of livelihood, set down in a distant and barren territory, made objects of general execration to their neighbors — with whom they could be forbidden to intermarry or trade. It would be fascinating to see what wonders of capitalist prosperity they could achieve. Perhaps in a spirit of generosity Mr. Gilder will agree to show the Indians how it is done. They, for their part, could take over his work and extol the generosity and humanity of the social system that sent him into the wilderness, and argue against any proposals to send Mr. Gilder and his relations any demeaning relief or assistance, on the grounds that it would only make them bitter and dependent.

In the meantime, one can hardly avoid the conclusion that the right can discuss the market only as an abstraction, as a utopian social system that can never exist. Deprived of the reliance on simple racism that served them so well for so long, market theorists spout idiocies when challenged on the historic record. Only those who ignore the facts of American history can find the simple market ideology of the American right at all plausible.

THE RIGHT, THE MARKET, AND THE THIRD WORLD

The inability of American market ideology to give a satisfactory account for the conditions of the American Indian is only a theoretical problem for the right. It has been a number of years since the indigenes of North America were in a position to compel respect for their views. The problem of blacks is thornier, because there are more blacks; the right's black problem has a practical as well as a theoretical side.

In the long run, the theoretical problem that the right faces when it tries to account for conditions in the Third World has the most serious implications of all. There are, after all, many more people in the Third World than in the United States, and history seems determined to give them a voice in shaping the future.

The theoretical problem in all three cases is the same: primitive accumulation. How did Western society — more specifically, certain groups within Western society — accumulate the capital that enabled it to develop in advance of the rest of the world? In the past, this question — like the domestic questions pertaining to blacks and Indians — was answered by references to race. The European had a restlessness, an urge to explore, to achieve, to invent, to think. Other races liked to lie in the sun and give no thought for the morrow. Europeans built cathedrals; Africans ate bananas. One must go to Israel and South Africa today to hear these sentiments in their pristine form, but within living memory they were the foundation of international political theory in Europe and North America.

Such answers were never popular in the Third World. Most of the world experienced the spread of European influence as the last and worst of the barbarian invasions. Every continent has its horror stories to tell; from Peru to Peking, people shuddered at the mention of invaders who were more greedy, more pitiless, and more destructive than any conquerors before them. A hundred million Africans were taken for the slave trade; the British in India (as in Ireland) did not shrink from famine as an instrument of policy; opium was forced at gunpoint on the Chinese; there were repeated episodes of genocide from the Americas to the antipodes. The Third World has a simple answer to the question of primitive accumulation: the West stole it.

The American right has little to offer the Third World, and little incentive to try. Never entranced by liberal illusions about the possibility for world compromise, the Reagan administration steadfastly rejects all calls for a new world economic order. It makes no secret of its intention to support any viable regime, however unsavory, that is willing to befriend the United States. By "befriending," the administration does not mean anything as simple as voting with the United States in the General Assembly. The right has too little respect for that body to attach a high price to victories there. Countries that are friends of the United States are countries that open their markets and their resources to foreign penetration and that, if asked, comply with American "requests" for military bases.

It is not enough for countries to do business with American firms. The Soviet Union, after all, has been doing business with Americans since 1918. Third World countries must be willing to do business with U.S. companies on terms that are favorable to those companies. The international corporations are looking for "friendly regulatory climates" — meaning that they do not wish to protect either their workers or their environment. They want the greatest possible freedom to buy and sell assets within national boundaries without regard for local interests. They do not want to be shackled by powerful unions that enjoy government backing. They do not want irritating restrictions on repatriation of profits. They do not want requirements on hiring local management, and they do not want a lot of red tape concerning joint ventures and local control. They want to buy low and sell high, and they have the muscle to get their way.

In American universities this process is sometimes praised as free enterprise and international development. Even when accompanied by a loss of political freedom, this process has its American admirers. Thus, a respectful Nixon praised the Pinochet government for its "daring gamble" with University of Chicago Business School economics, and concluded, "Rather than insisting on instant perfection from Chile, we should encourage the progress it is making."[11]

These words were written shortly before the collapse of the Chilean economy and the beginning of a long national depression; they illustrate the extent to which American politicians are willing to accept the destruction of real political freedom in exchange for hypothetical economic progress.

No less than American blacks, the people of the Third World are able to recognize their enemies. The right's economic program for the Third World can be summed up like this: pay off your foreign loans, cut back on your social spending, and allow the continued exploitation of your labor and raw materials by foreign-owned companies. It can be no surprise that a government with such a program is desperately worried about the spread of international terrorism; it also makes sense for such a program to go hand in hand with a trillion-dollar defense buildup. If we cannot call this policy prudent, we can at least acknowledge its consistency, and in that respect, perhaps, it is superior to a policy of liberal illusion.

In domestic politics, the administration chose a collision course with black America in the belief that it had little to lose. It has made the same judgment with respect to the Third World — an ill-defined but huge entity that grows better armed with every year. How long the United States can sustain this policy of unyielding hostility to the hopes of most of the world's people cannot be predicted; nor can we say what options, if any, we will have when events make this course untenable. A mistaken sense of America's invulnerability undergirds this policy of confrontation; here as in its economic policy the reliance of the right on inappropriate ideological thinking leads it into dangerous territory. With banners flying and trumpets sounding, the right charges on into the unknown, like Custer on the route to Little Big Horn.

✍ 15 ✍.

THE TRUMPETS SOUND RETREAT

SOME AMERICANS looked on the Reagan triumph with hope, others with fear, but events would show that both sentiments were exaggerated insofar as they arose from a perception that the "Reagan revolution" would produce an enduring change in American life. The objective, external constraints that had limited the freedom of action of his predecessors also forced Reagan to accept what had, for better or worse, established itself by default as the bipartisan policy of the American government. That policy was never enunciated by any political figure and never explicitly adopted by either Congress or the Executive Branch, but for almost two decades it has irresistibly dominated both branches of government and has frustrated any attempts to deviate from it, either to the left or to the right.

That policy can be summed up in one word, and it represented the wishes of neither party. The policy was retreat: retreat from the achievements of the liberal state, retreat from the beleaguered positions of the American Empire, retreat from the promises once made to the American people that their living standards would rise and their livelihoods become more secure with the passing of time.

The process of imperial decline, proceeding at a pace that statesmen could affect but not control, imposed its own timetable and priorities on successive administrations. Nixon attempted to outmaneuver the forces of decline; Carter tried to make peace with them; and in both cases the realities of American decline destroyed the political power of the administration. It fell to Reagan to discover how the United States could, temporarily, be governed, even as the process of decline accelerated.

What was to become Reagan's policy was first suggested by Vermont's Senator George Aiken during the dark days of the Indochinese War. America, said Senator Aiken, should simply declare victory and get out. Under Reagan, the retreat would go on, but it would be a Glorious Retreat, with victories proclaimed at every step. The standard of living might fall, the economy perform worse than that of the Soviet Union, key allies collapse, but no matter. America would stand tall once more to declare victory and get out.

The foreign position of the United States decayed rapidly during Reagan's tenure, reflecting a continuing erosion of the economic structure of the American Empire. Living standards in most of the Third World, and much of the First, continued to fall. Per capita GNP fell 8 percent in Latin America after 1980, and the trend in social services was even more alarming. In nine of fourteen countries reporting to the Inter-American Development Bank, per capita health expenditures fell during the 1980s; in some countries, health spending fell by 50 percent.[1] Real wages in the United States declined sharply in 1981 and 1982, rebounded briefly, then resumed their long decline.[2] The international debt problem, in addition to weakening American banks, blocked the development of most of Latin America and other important U.S. allies, including the Philippines. The resulting political crises affected the governments of countries whose stability was critical to the empire — notably, Mexico and Egypt.

The United States, which had briefly matched the growth rate of the Soviet Union during the Carter years, fell behind once again, even though the Soviet economy itself was slowing down. In four of Reagan's first five years in office, official U.S. government figures showed that the Soviet economy grew faster than ours.

The economic crisis was felt by the allies. Britain, the ally whose policies were closest to those of the Reagan team, suffered the worst, but Western Europe as a whole endured rising unemployment and poor growth. For the first time in twenty years, the communist countries of Eastern Europe posted faster economic growth than the Western market economies.[3]

Efforts by the administration and its ideological allies to establish uncompromising anticommunism as the linchpin of a new, more confrontational strategy made little headway. Far from carrying the war against communism into Cuba, the administration was barely able to get the funds to keep the contras alive in Nicaragua. Although American public opinion had recoiled from the spinelessness it associated with Carter, it was unwilling to abandon the key themes of his presidency in foreign affairs: human rights in the empire and majority rule in South Africa. By 1986 Tamar Jacoby, of the *New York Times*, could write in *Foreign Affairs* that there had been "a 150- if not a 180-degree change" in administration policy.[4] The team that had excoriated Carter for forcing out Somoza and the shah found itself giving Marcos and Duvalier their walking papers, nudging a reluctant and embattled Pinochet to return Chile to democracy, and even urging a policy of cautious reform on South Africa.

Forgotten, or at least disregarded, were the stern words from Kirkpatrick about the futility of forcing right-wing dictators to give ground in the face of opposition. Forgotten, too, the advice so frequently offered to Carter that, with all their warts, dictatorships of the right were preferable to the regimes most likely to succeed them. Reagan vowed to oppose dictatorships of the left and the right, and people like Jesse Helms, who remained faithful to the original goals of the crusade, found themselves out in the cold.

The hard-line conservatives were shocked by the revelation that their hero was a sheep in wolf's clothing. They oscillated between the anguished belief that Reagan was being deceived by his Establishmentarian staff — the tsar loves his people, but his ministers don't tell him the truth — and a disappointed sense that Reagan himself lacked the determination required to take the conservative course. The last thing they had expected was that Reagan would turn out to be like the Charles II depicted by the Earl of Rochester:

> Here lies our noble lord king
> Whose word no man relies on;
> Who never said a foolish thing
> Or ever did a wise one.[5]

It was no consolation to the conservatives that Reagan could answer them much as Charles II had replied to Rochester: that his words were wise because they were his own, but his acts were foolish because they came from the legislature. Conservatives discovered with Reagan what liberals had known for years: events beyond the president's control determine the limits within which he is free to pursue his policies, however sincere his views.

What happened in Lebanon demonstrated Reagan's moderation and, what amounted to the same thing, American impotence. A relative handful of Shi'ite militiamen forced the United States Marines to retreat under fire and demonstrated Reagan's inability to free American hostages in the Middle East. Wisely, Reagan took the advice of Senator Aiken: he declared victory and withdrew. The about-face in Beirut — a pointless involvement; spasmodic, random shelling; retreat under pressure — did little for American prestige.

Its allies began to treat the United States with contempt. Israel thumbed its nose at American weapons' restrictions, and embarrassing spy scandals revealed how little gratitude had been purchased by the billions of dollars in aid. Japan and Germany pursued economic policies with less and less deference to their conqueror. The administration's one reliable friend among its Western allies, Margaret Thatcher, found her pro-American reputation to be a serious political liability, and it was unlikely that future British prime ministers, of any party, would court political disaster by cooperating too closely with the United States.

The record of "constructive engagement" in southern Africa was little better. The administration seemed bent on discovering the real "lesson of Munich," something that had been forgotten by a generation of conservatives. The phrase "constructive engagement" had not yet been coined in the 1930s, but nothing better describes Neville Chamberlain's policy toward Germany. Appeasement was not a supine policy of giving Hitler territory in the hope that he would be nice in return. The goal of French and British policymakers during the 1930s was to turn Hitler toward the East — specifically, against the Soviet Union. They looked to the common heritage of Germany, Britain, and France, and their shared anti-communism, and they hoped to use Nazism as an anti-Soviet weapon.

This was what the Reagan administration hoped to do in South Africa, but to its intense and repeated embarrassment, it learned that P. W. Botha could no more be appeased into concessions and rationality than Hitler. Every gesture of sympathy and understanding from Washington only strengthened the hands of the more extreme elements in the South African leadership and convinced them that they were free to pursue their policies of domestic terror and international aggression.

The administration witnessed the same phenomenon in Argentina: its expressions of support for the military regime did not succeed in turning the Argentine military into a reliable, anticommunist ally. Instead, they encouraged the Argentine illusion that Washington would tolerate the invasion of the Falklands/Malvinas. Aggressive right-wing dictatorships make unreliable negotiating partners; this was the lesson of Munich, of Buenos Aires, and Pretoria. A common dislike of communism does not provide a sufficient basis for an alliance. As the Argentines were only too happy to sell grain to the Soviets, as Hitler was only too glad to sign the 1939 Nazi-Soviet pact, as white South Africa would be only too happy to come to terms with the Soviet Union if that country proved willing, so any right-wing dictatorship will swallow its distaste for communism if it can gain an advantage by doing so.

Domestically, the record was even more dismal. Six years of the largest deficits in the history of the species had created four years of economic recovery and even expansion, but the GNP statistics could not conceal the worsening economic situation. The economic expansion was relatively anemic. In 1984 the GNP rose a healthy 6.5 percent, but in no other year did growth reach the average growth level of 1961 to 1970. Overall, the average growth of the economy from 1981 to 1985 was 2.3 percent, only one tenth of a percent better than the dismal performance of 1971–1975, the years of war inflation and OPEC shocks.[6]

As usual, the American press was filled with accounts of the Soviets' economic disaster; the slow growth of their economy indicated a crisis of major proportions. Yet the even more dismal performance of the United States was hailed as an economic miracle, proof that our system was working better than ever.

Real wages continued their decline: the median family income fell by 5.7 percent from 1979 to 1984, and the poverty rate rose from 11.7 percent in 1979 to 14.4 percent five years later.[7] Minority enrollment in colleges and graduate programs fell; the "new poverty" of the Reagan years was suffered disproportionately by children; the $1 trillion deficit was not the only mortgage taken out on the nation's future. By almost every measurement, America in 1985 was worse off and more polarized than it had been in 1980. Homelessness and joblessness were both up; soup kitchens returned to the American scene; and growing numbers of beggars haunted the country's parks and streets.

Distress was not confined to the poor; a variety of surveys pointed to a slow shrinking of the middle class. In 1977, 25 percent of the nation's families held at least one share of stock; in 1983 that figure was down to 19 percent.[8] The numbers of people not covered by health insurance rose; the percentage of unemployed receiving benefits declined. The increase in service-producing jobs and the stagnation or decline in the goods-producing industries meant a fall in wages for formerly middle-class families. What was more insidious, it meant a loss of benefits. A study prepared by the Institute for Labor Research and Education found that the "old jobs" in the declining manufacturing sector provided pension plans for 86 percent of plant workers and offered more than nine paid holidays to 72 percent. The "new jobs" in services offered pensions to 48 percent of employees and more than nine paid holidays to 19 percent. A two-earner household in the new-jobs sector might well have less income and would almost certainly have fewer fringe benefits than a one-income household with one of the old jobs.[9]

Throughout the "expansion," banks collapsed at a rate not seen since the Great Depression, and the longer the expansion continued, the more acute became the financial crisis. One of the nation's ten largest banks failed, for all practical purposes, and others, including the mighty Bank of America, were weakening. In the financial-services sector generally, which was to replace manufacturing as the cutting edge of the American economy, American firms retreated before the onslaught of the Japanese.

Unemployment refused to drop significantly below 7 percent, even at the "peak" of the new prosperity; one could only speculate on the levels to be reached in the next, inevitable recession.

The United States had three traditional sources of economic strength: agriculture, manufacturing, and energy extraction. All of these sectors were depressed during the peculiar, fevered expansion of the Reagan years. The new high-tech industries, once hailed as the replacement for the dying industries of the past, were themselves in a slump, and layoffs swept through Silicon Valley. These difficulties all came during the much-heralded economic expansion. As to the course of events in a recession, one can only speculate, in the words of the Bible, "If they do these things in the green wood, what will they do in the dry?"

The failure of the economy at home contributed to the unraveling of the conservative agenda abroad. The country's apparently incurable economic woes were already affecting the administration's military strategies for restoring the clout of the country in foreign affairs. The bipartisan congressional coalition in favor of increased defense spending dissolved; in its place was a bipartisan coalition that urged cuts. The ambitious plans of the administration to bankrupt the Soviets with an expensive new arms race were stymied by the realization on both sides of the aisle in Congress that, whatever the effects on the Soviets, it was the United States that was unable to bear the costs of Star Wars.

Budgetary limits were cutting into foreign policy in other ways. The economic crises in the Philippines, Mexico, and Egypt were severe enough to destabilize regimes that were essential to the United States, but the billions of dollars required to give these countries an opportunity to recover would be hard to come by in an era of fiscal restraint. Furthermore, the deteriorating condition of the world economy, and the continuing fall in commodity prices, suggested that the ultimate requirements of these countries would dwarf the aid extended in the first half of the decade.

Reagan had staked much U.S. credibility in Europe on a policy of restricting trade with the Soviet Union. In 1982 the administration came close to an open break with the Europeans over the question of the Siberian gas pipeline. Even then the Europeans pointed out derisively that Reagan had lifted the grain sales embargo Carter had slapped on the Soviet Union — without getting anything in return. In the face-saving solution to the pipeline quandary, the Europeans and the Americans agreed that they would at least not subsidize trade with the Soviets. The news in 1986 that the United States had offered subsidized grain sales to the USSR was not calculated to impress the allies with the country's firmness of purpose or the reliability of the American government.

In international economic policy in general, the administration's flip-flops lowered the prestige of the United States to so low a level that recovery would take many years. For most of its first term the administration affected to despise the consultative institutions that had grown up after the Bretton Woods conference in 1944. When Europeans asked for help in dealing with an overvalued dollar or high U.S. interest rates, they were treated to insulting public lectures on the wisdom of the market and the iniquity of price fixing for currencies and interest rates. By Reagan's second term, the shoe was on the other foot. Then it was the United States that was asking for coordinated help from the other Western countries in driving down interest rates in their domestic markets. The Germans and Japanese were much too diplomatic to reply with the arrogant rudeness that the Reagan administration was accustomed to employ in its sermons to the allies; nevertheless, they made it clear that they lacked enough faith in the American government to base their economic decisions on its recommendations or to take its commitments at face value.

The administration appeared to have a share of the peculiar naïveté exhibited by the policymakers of the Nixon years. Masquerading as cold, hard-bitten cynicism, this view holds that foreigners are more impressed by saber rattling and military engagements than by anything else. Thus, Nixon could doom thousands of Americans, and perhaps a million Indochinese, to futile deaths, and he justified this appalling slaughter by saying it was necessary to demonstrate America's intention to abide by its international commitments. Yet this same Nixon, with a stroke of the pen, violated what the Europeans and Japanese considered a far more important U.S. commitment by devaluing the dollar and going off the gold standard. Had the resources and the energy expended on slaughter in Indochina gone into formulating intelligent policies either to defend the gold standard or to compensate the allies for their losses when it was abandoned, the United States and the world would have been much better off.

In the same way, Reagan thought that he could impress the world with hasty, ill-considered military adventures, even as his government abandoned itself to an erratic economic course, sacrificing its international obligations to short-term domestic considerations.

Unfortunately the administration conducted arms control negotiations with the same erratic disregard for the rights or the interests of allies. Star Wars, an initiative that was sprung on the allies by surprise, represented a break with four decades of American policy. To the extent that Star Wars might ever succeed, it would make the United States less vulnerable to nuclear attack while doing little or nothing for Europe and Japan. In the jargon of strategic planning, it "decouples" the defense of the United States from that of Western Europe, and it constitutes the clearest possible signal that NATO in its present form has at best a secondary importance to the American government.

The bizarre conduct of U.S. strategic arms policy entered the realm of the surreal at Rejkyavik in 1986. The Europeans could not fail to be impressed by the casual disregard for their interests displayed at the "nonsummit summit," nor could the world ignore the amateurish disarray within the American government on a subject of critical importance. In a wild binge of a weekend the president fanned popular hunger for complete nuclear disarmament, offered — without consultations — concessions to the Soviets that would fundamentally alter the strategic balance in Europe, and, by making Star Wars the sine qua non of American strategic planning, served Europe and Japan with a formal notification that the United States would abandon its promise to defend them with nuclear weapons under certain conditions. The consequences of that weekend will be felt for a long time, and Reagan's successors will have their work cut out for them in an effort to undo the impression of carelessness, ignorance, and unreliability created in Iceland.

But if the Reagan administration's record of solid accomplishment was as scanty as any since Warren Harding and Calvin Coolidge, Reagan and his staff demonstrated a profound grasp of the symbolic functions of the American presidency. The American president has two jobs: he is the head of government and head of state, Mrs. Thatcher and the queen. Reagan was a very bad Thatcher but a very good queen.

The head of government is a well-paid, but usually frustrated, civil servant; the head of state is the symbol of the nation. The head of government must disappoint all of the people some of the time; if he turns water into wine he offends the Temperance League, and if he walks on water he alienates the ferry lobby. The head of state can win the affectionate respect of millions by traveling around the nation opening shopping centers and dedicating parks.

To his considerable credit, Reagan never had any doubts about which role suited him best and, indeed, which was more important. The ideal American president gathers political strength in his role as chief of state and expends it to accomplish his goals as the chief executive. Reagan's success as the symbol of the nation gave him a political strength unmatched since the early years of the Johnson administration, but his inadequacy as head of government meant that the nation received little of lasting value from his tenure in office.

Carter understood the importance of symbolism in the presidency. His early months in office were filled with actions designed to establish what he considered the correct symbolic tone for his tenure, but the effort was misplaced. Carter, like Harry Truman and Lyndon Johnson, came from the South, and like them he grew up in a culture where Jacksonian populism still exercised a hold on the popular imagination. The three Southerners believed in old-fashioned republican simplicity, even plainness, and they despised the airs of aristocracy and the flashier trappings of office.

Time has dimmed the memory of the contempt in which Truman was held for much of his time in office, but it was not dissimilar to the feelings that people came to have for Carter and Johnson. The most damning fault attributed to these presidents by their contemporaries was a lack of dignity: they didn't look and act presidential enough.

The American people, members of a media-dominated mass society and conditioned from earliest youth to a diet of celebrities and glamour, want their presidents to be larger than life, and they get restless and frustrated if this expectation is not met. The patrician Roosevelt, the victorious Eisenhower, the glamorous Kennedy, and the glitzy Reagan have all known how to reign as well as to rule, and this talent gave them the ability to sail past catastrophes that would have capsized the plebeian Truman, the earthy Johnson, the maladroit Nixon, and the wimpy Carter.

Interestingly, the modern British tendency to venerate the head of state also began at about the time that Britain's empire stopped rising, stabilized briefly, and began to fall. The monarchs of the eighteenth and most of the nineteenth centuries were neither beloved nor admired; Victoria herself was deeply unpopular in the 1860s. Her apotheosis came in the 1880s and 1890s, particularly at the Golden and Diamond Jubilees. As British power and its relative economic position ebbed throughout the twentieth century, the pomp surrounding the Saxe-Coburg-Gothas (like many humbler families in the American Midwest, they changed their German surname during World War I) became more elaborate, and new "traditions" were invented at every opportunity, until today Mrs. Elizabeth Mountbatten exercises less power than a justice of the peace and celebrates her birthdays with more pomp than Louis XIV.

It may be that for both Britain and the United States the declining

international position of each country has increased the need for its citizens to find a personal focus for their feelings of loyalty and national
pride. Certainly since Eleanor Roosevelt became the first dowager first
lady in American history to maintain a political profile after the death
of her husband, we have seen a recurring tendency toward dynasticism
in the presidency. The elevation of the Kennedy clan into a quasi-royal
family, the typically awkward Nixonian attempt to create a rival Eisen-
hower-Nixon line, and the loyalty inspired by Ronald Reagan all suggest
that the symbolic functions of the American presidency have become
more important in these years of decline.

In any case, Reagan has mastered the art of the Glorious Retreat so
that a defeat can be presented as an affirmation of national values and
purpose — as a victory of sorts. The celebration of the successful extri-
cation of Americans from imprisonment abroad has become the great
national patriotic rite. The Nixon-era return of the POWs held by North
Vietnam was the first of these national celebrations; it was followed by
the return of the crew of the *Mayaguez* from Cambodia shortly after the
fall of Saigon and Phnom Penh, and the reception of the Iranian hostages.
These celebrations provide a focus for national pride, but they should
not be confused with the achievements of an empire on the rise.

Six years into the age of Reagan, the United States exhibited all the
characteristics of a nation hooked on cocaine. Each dose — the invasion
of Grenada, the Statue of Liberty extravaganza, the bicentennial of the
Constitution (appropriately opened at Disney World) — created a rush
of exhilaration, followed by depression, paranoia, and the restless craving
for more. Like the addict, whose fixation on the drug blinds him to the
deterioration of his life and character, the United States embraced the
illusion of well-being that comes from the drug and averted its gaze from
the signs of disaster. The course of such a disease can be predicted: the
addict requires more of the drug to get the same feeling; paranoia increases
as the patient's mood swings between exaltation and despair; the addict
withdraws from friends and family to live in a fantasy world; savings
and assets are exhausted in a desperate effort to get high.

By the end of 1986 the limits of Reaganism were becoming more
apparent. As revelations of illegal and amateurish behavior in the White
House poured forth, and as public concern over the future of the economy
grew, the growing disquiet over Reagan's performance as head of government began to diminish his standing as chief of state. "Pay no attention
to the little man behind the curtain!" thundered the White House public
relations machine, but the process of disenchantment, once fairly begun,
cannot easily be stopped.

The more Iranscam diminishes the standing of the administration, the more we can expect a cognitive shift to occur among the public. The other scandals of the Reagan regime, and the investigations of figures like Michael Deaver and Lyn Nofziger, once ignored by the public, are likely to gain new importance. The influence of corporate interests on government decisions — a striking feature of this administration — will appear both more sinister and more interesting.

Even if the Iran scandal fails to reach its full potential for embarrassment and worse, the end of the Glorious Retreat is at hand. Reagan's successor, of whatever party or ideological persuasion, will be forced to concentrate on the tasks of government. Reagan was not able to end the age of limits; in important respects his successors will face limits more narrow and choices less appealing because of Reagan's flight from reality.

Reagan's legacy to his successor is unlikely to be the "nation standing tall" that he dreamed of. Cynicism about the nation's government, distrust of politicians, and fear for the future were temporarily masked by the ideological "high" of Reaganism, but by December 1986 the party was ending, and all but the most boisterous guests — such as Pat Buchanan — were leaving. The post-Reagan era in American politics will not be the new era of unlimited greatness he so confidently expected; the *New Republic* aptly labeled the next period in American history "The Morning After in America."

Declining empires indulge in a politics of spectacle. Kevin Phillips compares Reagan with Napoleon III, the French mock-emperor who presided over an orgy of corruption and, until Prussian guns at Sedan destroyed the illusion, pretended to restore France to its former greatness. One also thinks of Queen Victoria's Diamond Jubilee, celebrated with lavish splendor as Britain's decline was becoming evident. Today that event is best remembered for the prophetic poem "Recessional," written for the occasion by Rudyard Kipling:

> Far-called, our navies melt away;
> On dune and headland sinks the fire:
> Lo, all our pomp of yesterday
> Is one with Nineveh and Tyre!

We cannot conclude our assessment of six years of the age of Reagan with any sentiment more appropriate than that with which Kipling closed his poem:

> For frantic boast and foolish word —
> Thy mercy on Thy People, Lord![10]

PART FIVE

Rake's Progress:
Politics
in an Age of Decline

16

RECESSIONAL

U P TO THIS POINT we have confined our attention to the present and past. Here we begin to peer into the future and to enter an area even less certain than the territory we have just traversed. Our governing assumption in this new venture, our compass, is that the decline will continue, regardless of the policies adopted by future American administrations. We have already put forward our reasons for this assumption. Coming disasters or triumphs can retard or accelerate the pace of decline, and we will not try to establish a timetable for the process. It is also irrelevant to our purposes here to attempt to decide whether this process is a Good Thing. It will benefit some and hurt others. In contemplating as dismal — for Americans — a topic as the erosion of our economy and power, we will perform the analysis as objectively as possible. This is not the time to gloat over the wreck of what radicals used to call Amerika (Amerikkka when they were particularly upset), nor is it a time to bemoan it. Serious people who are concerned for the well-being of the American people and humanity as a whole need to understand this phenomenon so that they can take the appropriate action. If we are correct in our belief that this decline is inevitable, our attitudes toward it matter no more than a pebble matters to the course of the Mississippi. If this belief is erroneous, history with its customary insolence will soon set about to demolish our fallacies.

On the domestic scene, the continued decline of the economy will take place against the backdrop of cyclical fluctuations. When the tide goes out, not every wave falls farther down the beach than its predecessor. But over a period of time the average level of water falls if the tide is truly receding, and that is what we have seen in the American economy since 1968 and what we forecast for the coming years.

The natural tendency of American wages during the present period is to sink toward world levels, but two factors will work against such a move. First, political considerations in the advanced countries will lead

to more protectionism to save jobs and keep wages high. To the extent
that protectionist measures are adopted, world trade will suffer. Exports
of capital, technology, and finished materials from the first-tier countries
to the third tier will be adversely affected; the ability of the developing
countries to repay their loans will be seriously compromised. In the end,
the economic disruption that attends protectionism will drive down the
purchasing power of wage earners in the advanced countries, but protectionism will slow down a process that is already under way.

Second, an assessment of growing political risk for foreign investments
in the Third World may keep more capital at home. Capital-intensive
production is safer in politically stable countries. Countries where wages
are low and the governments unstable are unattractive sites for investment
in automated production facilities. Furthermore, the disruptions of world
markets and exchange rates will affect production facilities in the underdeveloped countries more seriously than those in the advanced countries.
Factories in currency-poor Third World countries may find it difficult
to import needed raw materials. However, the automation of manufacturing in the advanced countries has effects almost as serious for employment and wages as the relocation of factories to the Third World.
And the economic disruptions in world trade that would make the Third
World a risky place for investment interfere with the economic process
in the rest of the world as well — reducing markets and injecting an
element of expensive chaos into the process of production.

Therefore we conclude that the relative importance of these factors
will determine the specific shape of the economy in the future — but
that, overall, the trend will be toward declining real wages in the advanced countries. The decline in wages, however it comes about, will
lead to a progressive shrinkage of the market in the advanced countries.
The consequences of the resulting marketing squeeze will be an accelerated flight of capital and a corresponding shrinkage in the government's
revenue base. These will bring about larger deficits and lead to a decline
in the social wage, as well as to a decline in the government's ability to
apply countercyclical economic stimulation. The first six deficits of the
Reagan era doubled the national debt; there are no signs that this process
is about to end. Such deficits can only lessen confidence in the security
of U.S. Treasury obligations, thereby raising payments on the national
debt. Since the value of paper currency ultimately rests on confidence in
a particular government, pressures for inflation seem destined to increase.
Inflation will have to be allowed free rein or be staved off with restrictive
monetary policies. Neither option bodes well for the economy.

We must also observe that competition for export markets among the free world countries will intensify under these circumstances. The competition will fray military alliances and, perhaps more important, make economic cooperation more difficult to achieve at the very time that it becomes more essential.

Gloomy though these projections are, we must stress that they do not represent a radically pessimistic assessment. Economists are almost universally agreed that prospects for stable, noninflationary growth around the world are uncertain in the next decade. There are too many structural weaknesses in the world economy for optimistic forecasts to be widely accepted — in contrast to the 1950s and 1960s, when economists as a group believed that the fundamental economic problems facing the world had been solved. The forces described in these projections are already at work, and counterforces are nowhere in sight.

The only prospect for avoiding this entire scenario seems to involve much more creative economic statesmanship than is now being exercised. Leaders of the advanced countries would have to agree first to coordinate their own policies more closely than they have done in the past and, second, to include the Third World countries in their planning. The necessary controls over the flow of international capital would be difficult to establish and probably impossible to enforce. From all points of view the chances of success, using current policies, seem remote.

Other forces already at work also permit us to make some observations about the future of American military strength. As the world economy bucks and slips, resistance to the American world order will stiffen in both the advanced and the developing countries. The advanced countries will feel greater pressure to reassert control over their own economic destinies; the Third World countries will be devastated by waves of economic catastrophe. The developing countries are more vulnerable to recession than the advanced ones. Developing countries depend more heavily on export markets, and their internal markets are too small to cushion them from the ups and downs of international trade. Their products are likely to be excluded by the advanced countries during any protectionist frenzy. The workers in these countries receive little in the way of social services like unemployment compensation or welfare; hundreds of millions, therefore, are exposed to the most terrifying privations by gyrations in the world economy that register in New York and London only as the rise and fall of a graph indicator. These people cannot all be expected to accept their fate with calm and resignation. Existing revolutionary movements will gain support and credibility; new ones will form.

Third World governments will have even fewer means to head off popular discontent than they do now. Non-oil-producing countries will face continuing foreign exchange problems, which hamper growth and keep the government permanently in hock to the banks. Unless the IMF changes its ways and attracts enormous sums of new capital, poor countries will have to cut back on social spending in times of economic trouble, a policy guaranteed to deepen social bitterness. Credit will be difficult for Third World governments to obtain under almost any circumstances; declining markets in the advanced countries mean declining receipts from the sale of raw materials and agricultural commodities. In the short run, the cheapest form of social control is repression, a point well understood in the Third World. The use of American advisers and American aid in the form of weapons will be among the growth industries of the next decade.

At the same time that Third World problems force the United States to extend military aid and perhaps introduce combat troops, economic developments at home will gravely weaken the U.S. military. Stab-in-the-back theorists of the Indochinese War forget that it was not just morale on the home front that fell during the war; morale in the army dropped to near catastrophic levels as the conflict dragged on. It was fortunate for American officials that the language and people of Vietnam were foreign to American GIs; a similar war in Europe or Latin America would have resulted in mass desertions. As it was, American troops were sometimes useless for combat. Motivation was low, drug use high; there were cases of "fragging" — throwing fragmentation grenades into the tents of officers who wanted to send their men on too many combat patrols. Desertion within the United States was high; the use of drugs spread from combat units into the American forces in Europe.

The situation was often blamed on the combination of a draft army and an unpopular war — a potent combination, to be sure, but not the only reason for American military weakness. The new volunteer army was to be a well-trained, professional fighting force, but today it contains many of the same old faces that were in the old draft army. Long-term unemployment among young people stands above 20 percent nationally and above 50 percent in some areas; this is as effective a draft as any devised by the Selective Service. But the "volunteers" are as much victims as the draftees ever were, and they feel it. Most Americans in the "political classes" have little or no contact with enlisted soldiers and so are unaware of the deep-rooted alienation and cynicism beneath the veneer of today's army. If our economic forecast is correct, society holds little for these men and women in the future. The American armed forces will remain vulnerable to disillusionment and cynicism, and will not reach a condition in which they are capable of defeating a disciplined, volunteer insurgency that, rightly or wrongly, believes itself to be fighting a just war in defense of its people.

The United States contains large numbers of underprivileged blacks and Hispanics. These groups are disproportionately represented in the combat units of the army. How reliable will these troops be in the case of prolonged counterinsurgency warfare in Latin or Caribbean countries? What quarrel will they have with black and Hispanic insurgents in this hemisphere?

The alternative to an army that is disproportionately nonwhite and even more disproportionately poor is a genuinely democratic draft army, one that puts the children of all classes on the firing line. Though the children of the middle and upper classes may have more stake in the defense of the empire, they are as unwilling to risk themselves in guerrilla war as anybody else — more so, because they have more to lose. And they, and their parents, have the means to voice their opposition. The practical result of this situation is to render incredible any threat of sustained military action by the United States. That can only weaken the American military and diplomatic position around the world.

This political limit on military power was an element in the settlement reached in Korea and was the cause of the American defeat in Indochina. Although American observers, unaccustomed to defeats and limits, look for scapegoats, neither of these experiences was new in history. The defeat of an insurgent army with broad popular support has always been one of the most difficult tasks in warfare. In the twentieth century, all of the European empires have been forced to retreat in the face of such movements. The French were not only forced out of faraway Indochina; they were also driven from French Algeria, legally a part of metropolitan France, with a population that included 800,000 determined settlers of French origin. The American people may lack what it takes to fight and win long imperialist wars, but in this they are no different from the Dutch, French, British, Portuguese, and Belgians, all of whom shrank from such wars in the last fifty years. American disillusionment and war weariness as the Indochina involvement dragged on were not the atypical consequences of a spineless intelligentsia and television coverage; on the contrary. America's Indochina experience ran along lines essentially similar to the experience of the other empires that have crumbled in the twentieth century.

Another consideration for the future is the cost of the empire, direct and indirect. For all the political groaning at the magnitude of the Reagan deficits, the United States had not yet reached its fiscal limits in the mid

1980s. Yet there was clearly more scrutiny of foreign aid and military budgets as the decade wore on; the resources of the United States are finite, and every military buildup has its limits. As the budget grows tighter, and social programs on which millions of taxpayers depend are squeezed, it will be more difficult to sell the American people on the necessity of spending billions of dollars to defend corrupt dictatorships in the Third World, underhanded trade rivals in the First World, and expansionist settler states in between.

American governments will find themselves increasingly harassed by those wanting to cut military spending even if it means cutting back on overseas commitments. This has happened before, notably to Britain, which was forced by economic reality to retreat from the eastern Mediterranean and the Middle East after 1945.

The American commitments to Europe and Japan, the cornerstones of the postwar order, have a compelling logic that is immediately apparent to policymakers. Public support for the alliances is spottier, and much of it is of the soft kind that can rapidly be eroded by events. America is not in Europe and Japan to prevent an invasion of the United States. The interests that bind the allies are economic, geopolitical, and ideological. Economically, the elements in the alliance need one another as sources of various products and as markets. Geopolitically, all share an interest in preventing the USSR from dominating the Eurasian land mass. Ideologically, the parties are linked by their anticommunism.

These interests were not enough to bring the American people into the Second World War. Only the attack on Pearl Harbor, and Hitler's subsequent declaration of war, could do that. After the war, popular sentiment once again favored isolation and disarmament, and the foreign policy Establishment had to work hard to gain a commitment to collective security. Anticommunism supplied the missing link in American commitment to its allies by spreading the idea that Moscow was behind a world plot that would, in the end, lead to an invasion of the United States. Vietnam was justified on those terms, too: "If we don't stop them here, we'll have to face them in Hawaii."

American support for its world alliances is unstable because the threat against which they are guarding is not the kind that galvanizes the average citizen. If every American soldier left Europe tomorrow, for example, the USSR is not likely to invade. Britain and France between them could destroy organized social life in the Soviet Union with nuclear weapons. A united Germany, even under a communist government, is not exactly the foreign policy goal toward which the Soviet Union is ceaselessly struggling.

In discussions about the future of the Western alliance, political leaders refer to a particular condition that American force is intended to avert. As Valéry Giscard d'Estaing, former president of France, told the influential Council on Foreign Relations, "What the Soviet Union would like to achieve is not a military invasion and occupation of Western Europe, but what is called, in an inappropriate term, and an inelegant term, 'Finlandization' of Western Europe."[1]

Finland is a country that lives under its own freely chosen economic and political system. Finns enjoy complete freedom of the press and of assembly, and they vote in regular, free elections. The country's economy has grown faster than that of the United States in the last twenty years. What the terrors of Finlandization are, that billions of dollars must be spent to avoid them, and that justify the threat of nuclear war, are difficult to explain to the person on the street. Finland has no gulags, no political prisoners, no heroic dissidents in psychiatric hospitals. The standard of living is comparable with that of many countries in NATO, and its economic relations with the USSR benefit its economy.

Yet the Finlandization of Europe would have consequences, many serious for the United States. Trade within the continent would increase, much to the benefit of the East. The Soviet bloc would have an easier time getting access to the latest technology. An eastward orientation in finance, planning, and commerce would adversely affect American companies. The balance of power in the Middle East would change; the United States would lose its bases in the Mediterranean.

But the Soviet slave masters would not haul trainloads of nuns to the gulags; Europeans would not stand, burlap-clad, in long lines to buy rutabagas; and the Red Army would not start to build landing craft in the Bay of Biscayne.

NATO is an essential instrument in the defense of the American Empire, but it is not an alliance to defend the territorial integrity of the United States. For this reason, it is always vulnerable to changes in American opinion, and declining American economic prowess, coupled with intensifying trade rivalries among the members of the alliance, will render this instrument increasingly controversial. At the least, pressure for troop withdrawals, always present, will grow stronger and may at some point become irresistible. To an empire in decline, no commitments are permanent.

17

THE POLITICS OF RECESSION

L OOKING AHEAD to a period characterized by stable or declining living standards for many people in the United States, we must mark the differences between the politics of a short-term, cyclical recession and the politics of structural economic decline. The American political system has managed to adapt itself rather well to the normal fluctuations of the business cycle. Since the decision makers in the federal government are well aware of the cyclical nature of economic activity, they are equipped with suitable policies that help alleviate suffering in the depths of a recession while paving the way for recovery. The population at large accepts the inevitability of recessions from time to time, and the most acute discontent is confined to the unemployed and the underemployed. Even those laid off in a typical recession remain confident that they will be rehired during the coming recovery. The permanently unemployed, or those so marginal that they never get steady work at a decent wage, have been effectively excluded from public life in any case. With discontent thus tempered or contained, a recession may pose problems for the party unlucky enough to be in power at its onset, but in no way does it raise unmanageable issues for society as a whole.

The period of long-term stagnation and decline now well into its second decade is another matter. Unlike recessions, it forces millions of people to make permanent adjustments in their expectations and life styles. The end of growth in employment in the highly paid heavy industries of the North and Northeast means that a generation of young people face a standard of living lower than that of their parents. The slow improvement in wages and benefits for those who still have jobs in the major industries can no longer be taken for granted. No projections of economic recovery suggest a return to rapid growth in either wages or total employment in the basic industries.

The numbers tell a grim story. The Bureau of Labor Statistics identifies seven major categories of nonsupervisory employment: manufacturing, mining, construction, wholesale trade, retail sales, the so-called FIRE sector (Finance, Insurance, and Real Estate), and services. Among the goods-producing jobs — manufacturing, mining, and construction — only mining (which includes oil and gas extraction) showed consistently rising wages and employment through the 1970s and early 1980s. In manufacturing, real wages fell a relatively modest 5 percent from 1973 to 1983, and employment edged slightly higher also. In construction, employment rose more vigorously, but real wages fell a striking 16 percent in that decade, below the levels of 1966.

Meanwhile, the service-producing jobs saw rising employment and falling real wages. Employment in retail sales rose by over three million jobs from 1973 to 1983, but the real wage fell 22 percent, to a level below that reached in 1955. The average gross weekly pay for retail sales personnel in 1983 was $104.64 in 1977 dollars. In wholesale trade, wages had fallen to the level of 1964; in the FIRE group to the level of 1962; and in services to the level of 1967.[1]

Thus, it was not only true that, as many observers noted, the service-producing jobs that characterized the emerging American economy paid less than the old goods-producing jobs. Wages in the service sector were falling, and falling rapidly. Overall, in spite of the increased number of women in the work force, and the rise in two-earner households, median family incomes in 1983 had fallen lower than the level reached in 1968.[2]

These falling wages did not, however, eliminate the differentials between compensation in the United States and key Third World countries. In 1975 (using current dollar figures), the cost of employing an American worker was $6.35 an hour. The same amount of labor time was $4.43 cheaper in Mexico, $5.52 cheaper in Singapore, $3.30 cheaper in Japan, and $5.99 cheaper in Korea.

By 1983, in absolute terms, the gap had grown. The current cost of an hour's labor time was $12.26 in the United States in current dollars. The hourly savings for using foreign labor that year amounted to $10.81 in Mexico, $10.09 in Singapore, $6.06 in Japan, and $10.97 in Korea.[3]

The immense political consequences of these changes can best be understood when compared with the modesty of the prevailing expectations of American workers. By and large, the American work force has not aspired to any fundamental change in the structure of society; workers are prepared to work hard for a modest living. American political journalism and economic literature is full of pronouncements from well-paid white-collar intellectuals about the alleged laziness and apathy of the American worker; one would think that the workers are the most coddled and pampered people in the country, with privileges and rewards that far outstrip those of, say, professors and management. Yet American blue-collar workers have been willing to work thirty and more years on dirty, dangerous, and difficult jobs, expecting security and a slowly rising standard of living in return. Those who believe that workers are overpaid and underworked should see how the children of many workers are urged by their parents to get advanced education so that they can have a better life. A decent existence within and a means to climb out of the industrial working class are the minimum demands that blue-collar workers have made of American society. From the Depression onward, that society has organized itself to meet these demands.

It seems that fewer and fewer workers will find these demands being met. Home ownership, access to college and graduate education, job security, rising real wages — these are available to decreasing percentages of American workers.

Assuming a continued decline, we can outline four areas in which the economic stress will result in bitter political conflict. We cannot predict the specific form such conflicts may assume; all we can do is note where conflicts will arise and try to gauge the intensity of the coming battles.

The first area of great controversy is the social wage — the package of benefits and services provided by the government to the general public. The last twenty years have witnessed steady and substantial cuts in the social wage, yet two decades of cheese paring have failed to put governments on a sounder financial footing. In the last analysis, the controversy over the social wage pits one class against another. The wealthy pay a disproportionate share of social costs, but they do not benefit proportionately from the expenditures. They educate their children in expensive private schools; high taxes for public school don't help them at all. Municipal hospitals, government aid for mass transit, police protection — the wealthy have little to gain from these. The rich can fend for themselves, better and less expensively. For middle- and lower-income people, on the other hand, the social wage is their only means of obtaining the basic requirements of life. Millions of people cannot get to work without mass transportation; millions of children receive only such education as is provided in the public schools; millions of elderly people have no medical care other than what is provided with government help. The average wage earner cannot live in a private security compound, nor can he or she afford private sanitation services or private pension plans.

When Social Security was introduced, wealthy people were angry because the program took their money and gave them little in return. As employers, they were taxed with contributions for their employees as well. Overall, the program was a net cost for them. For most people, of course, it was and is a godsend, the cornerstone of retirement planning for two hundred million people. The current controversies over the future of the system pit 80 percent of the population against 20 percent, yet the future projections for Social Security are anything but encouraging. A higher rate of structural unemployment reduces the fund's income; demographic trends indicate that large increases in payments lie ahead. Social Security benefits are indexed to the cost of living; many wage earners enjoy no such protection, with the result that, once again, the future liabilities and obligations of Social Security tend to grow faster than its assets. The political fireworks over Social Security will go off throughout the next decade; compromise will be harder to reach.

The cost of medical care will continue to rise, and access to it will grow as a political issue. Health care is a crucial element in the social wage; the American people already receive less help from government in meeting their basic health care needs than the citizens of other advanced countries. Politicians often cite Medicare as an entitlement program whose costs are "out of control"; having made the easy cuts, they must now face the question of whether the United States will continue to provide decent medical care to those most in need.

Furthermore, the decline of the smokestack industries means that millions of workers will no longer enjoy the stable employment and adequate medical coverage that once characterized these industries. With fluctuating incomes, and without the means to join medical plans comparable with those they had, these people and their families are now being asked to accept a reduction in care. Nor can state and local governments pick up the tab for decent public care. Cities with declining revenue bases have had to cut corners in their municipal hospitals.

The issue of health care and who pays for it is likely to return to center stage. The American people are unwilling to accept a decline in the quality of medical care, and as private alternatives to national health insurance become less successful in meeting their needs, the people will demand some form of universal health care, and they won't care who pays for it.

Rising tuitions and declining student aid limit young people's chance for a college education. Along with flat or declining disposable income, there has been a massive downward shift of educational expectations that will probably continue. Many who once would have attended private colleges are now at public four-year schools; others have switched from four-year university programs to two-year community college programs; others have abandoned altogether the idea of higher education and have joined the armed services or entered the work force.

This points to a more rigid stratification of society than we have lately experienced. As in the past, social class and wealth will affect the status of one's children. The wealthy will find it easier to get into the elite schools and in some cases will emerge better trained and better equipped for success. A larger number of people will be unable to get the training or the opportunities they want and were brought up to expect, and it is these undereducated, underemployed workers who will be the leaders and followers in populist protest movements.

One of the prominent features of liberal policies in the 1960s was the effort to educate and recruit minority group members for the managerial elite. The program infuriated many whites, who continued to suffer the pervasive economic- and class-based discrimination that makes the world of a secretary's child so different from that of her employer's country club offspring — but it did extend the size of the black middle class. It is difficult to see how these programs can be maintained at current levels without greater social conflict. Already black gains in college and professional school enrollments are beginning to erode. Any lowering of minority educational aspirations will accelerate the formation of the kind of bright and alienated minority leadership that the liberal social engineers of the 1960s hoped to prevent.

Another significant result of the declining social wage is the drop in white-collar professional openings for young workers. City planning authorities, schools, compensatory educational programs, social service professions, subsidized medical and legal help for the poor, jobs in cultural institutions — all these created job opportunities for thousands in the 1960s and early 1970s. Municipal layoffs do not only affect the careers of police, fire, and sanitation workers; they constrict the job market for those with college and graduate degrees as well. The right scorns the "new class" of social managers and considers them the enemies of productive workers and entrepreneurs. Yet the helping professions provided thousands of young idealists with opportunities to address social problems within the system, and their operations defused at least some social tension by meeting the needs of individuals and groups. Exacerbating simultaneously the discontent of the poor and the anger of society's educated idealists is a poor prescription for harmonious social development — yet that is precisely what this country has done and apparently must continue to do.

By the end of the 1960s, many of America's cities were in flames and its campuses in revolt. The social spending of that era was intended, in part, to convince angry ghetto residents as well as angry college students that they should work within the system. The state would respond to legitimate grievances and try to solve genuine problems. The strategy worked. By 1980 both the campuses and the cities were as quiet as they had ever been. But as the consequences of the shift in government policy made themselves felt, both the cities and the campuses revived. By 1984 Jesse Jackson's campaign had galvanized millions of black voters and become the focus of a new sense of militancy in the cities. The campuses too were stirring with a new generation of student activists bitterly opposed to U.S. policy in Central America and South Africa. Having chosen to present itself as tightfisted and uncaring, the state was beginning to reap the consequences of its own confrontational stance.

Yet the dilemma is real. The United States under current conditions can no longer afford the modern liberal response to social unrest. It can no longer employ black activists in federal antipoverty programs or conduct its foreign policy in a manner that will satisfy the scrutiny of its educated youth. The short-term consequence, already becoming evident, is the decay of social consensus and the return to more abrasive politics.

PROTECTION

Protectionism, another issue of the future, has returned from the graveyard of history to haunt the advanced liberal societies that thought it had vanished forever. Orthodox economists consider free trade the only route to prosperity, yet all the lectures by all the orthodox economists in the world, however eloquent, cut no ice with a steel worker who has just received a pink slip.

Free trade is a problem that cannot ultimately be resolved on the basis of unilateral action by any country. The issue of international trade in the coming years will be reformulated, and the shape it will assume will be an ominous one for those who uphold the existing world economic order.

We can see a labor movement that supports free trade on a free labor basis — that is, linking U.S. trade policies to the wages and conditions of workers in various countries. Duties on imported products might be levied not only to penalize state-supported production, as is now sometimes the case, but to penalize oppressive and exploitative labor practices.

Political demands along these lines have already forced some changes in American policy. The State Department must now include the rights of labor in its survey of human rights in the imperial satrapies; U.S. development aid and subsidies to American companies seeking to move production abroad have been somewhat restricted. The politics of free labor will grow, and the conflict over this issue will become bitter. It will reveal the extent to which "foreign" low-wage competition actually pits American investors against American wage earners — precisely the kind of issue that had been fading from U.S. politics since the Second World War.

American investors, corporate and individual, want and even need the freedom to invest wherever the return is greatest. Under current conditions, this means investment in low-wage production beyond the reach of American wage and safety laws. American workers, on the other hand, want and even need the kind of wages and benefits that can be retained only by limiting the freedom of investors to move their money around the world. In Pittsburgh, one of the first American cities to experience the full weight of the new conditions, angry workers have already identified the Mellon Bank as a target because of its investments overseas. The South Africa divestment campaign, which began among a few religious groups before swelling into a popular political movement, shows how a program to limit investment can gain ground and ultimately affect business conditions and international events. Yet South Africa is a "feel good" issue for the American people. Foreign low-wage competition is a bread-and-butter issue, and the political battle over this kind of investment has every potential to move to the forefront of American politics.

The idea of "democratic" control over corporate investment decisions is anathema to the American private sector. This idea has not been on the political agenda since the darkest days of the Depression; its presence there is a danger sign of the first magnitude for American private enterprise. All indicators suggest that this issue will play a large role in the politics of structural recession.

The problems of international banking raise these issues in another, but no less significant, way. Huge sums of money have been lent and, apparently, lost in the Third World since 1975. Repayment of these loans, or even payment of interest, requires that the debtor countries earn enough money from exports to service their debt. In effect, the health of the banks and the financial system depends on the continued loss of jobs in America and Europe to the Third World. And in order for their exports to remain high, these countries must keep their own domestic wages low enough to attract new investment and to compete successfully with First World manufacturers. Banks too can expect to become political targets in the coming years.

RED INK

The national debt, already a troublesome matter, can also be expected to loom large in the politics of the future. Interest payments on the spiraling debt of the Reagan budgets will soar; they will grow absolutely and relatively, soaking up a larger and larger share of federal revenues. As social services are strained and slashed, attention will turn toward the national debt and the interest on it — politically, a much more popular target for cuts than Social Security.

Once again this is an issue that pits owners against employees, the rich against the poor and the middle. We can expect years in which the total budget deficit is less than or equal to the interest on the existing national debt; suggestions for a moratorium will come from many quarters. Such a moratorium or even a repudiation would be ruinous for large investors and banks; it would have profound international consequences as well. It is an option that today seems unthinkable to any responsible person in American public life, but as time goes by it could seem far from unthinkable to millions of frantic citizens.

The politics of debt already dominate Latin America. There the conflict between honoring government debt and ensuring a rising standard of living for the populace has already become acute. What so far has held Latin America back from repudiation — aside from the dependence of the governing elites on their ties with the United States — has been a well-founded fear of the consequences. The Latin American nations are ill prepared to weather the consequences unless they can all stick together. The United States, now the world's largest debtor, is in a different position. As the debt burden grows, it will become easier to draw up plans to repudiate all or part of the debt that have consequences less onerous for ordinary people than the consequences of continuing to pay it.

Even the approach of public debate over these issues makes lenders jittery. As the United States debt approaches its credit limit — the amount lenders believe that the nation can sustain — interest rates will rise. Inflationary pressures, economic and political, will grow. The combination is a witch's brew of evils: political strife, economic difficulty, social division, and class conflict. All options turn sour; no solutions are adequate to the magnitude of the problems. These are the marks of an empire in decline.

In any case, the politics of debtor versus creditor, long banished from the American political scene, are staging an unwelcome return. As always, these issues poison public debate, erode consensus, and exacerbate the problems that gave them their birth.

THE ATTACK ON THE UNIONS

The pressure on wages and working conditions in the United States that results from the internationalization of the world economy has greatly weakened the American labor movement. Anti-union offensives have made significant gains since the late 1970s, notably after Reagan destroyed PATCO, the air traffic controllers' union, in 1981. Since that time, the newly deregulated industries and the smokestack industries have had bitter labor battles, and more often than not, labor has been on the losing side.

There is no reason to expect the pressures that push corporations into anti-union activities to diminish. They are rooted in the internationalization of the labor market and reflect the continuing tendency of American wages to fall toward world levels. What will change, has already begun to change, is the nature of the American labor movement and its leadership. Labor has enjoyed a long peace in the United States. Its leadership grew fat and complacent. Union leadership was not a particularly demanding career during the golden age of empire; management and labor were agreed that wages would slowly rise. Despite occasional quarrels over the rate of increase, union leaders were routinely able to bring satisfactory contracts to their workers.

In the initial battles with management during the new era of confrontation, union leaders were badly outclassed. They were unprepared for savage attacks by men who, until recently, they had regarded almost as colleagues. They forgot or lost the skills of hard bargaining and organizing effective strikes that had characterized labor during the more stressful periods in its history. Solidarity among unions waned; the idea that management and labor were engaged in a partnership spread beyond the circles of labor leaders to the rank and file.

Inevitably, the cutbacks and union busting of the 1980s created a reaction in the labor movement. There was a resurgence of labor militancy. In some cases, like the Minnesota meat packers' strike against Hormel, workers ignored the advice of a labor leadership they no longer trusted. In others, like the Phelps Dodge copper strike in Arizona, multiyear strikes that rivaled those of the 1930s divided communities and enjoyed the backing of a newly energized leadership. The AFL-CIO leaders endorsed Walter Mondale in the Democratic primary process in 1983–1984. Their assistance was unable to prevent Mondale from losing the election, but labor's backing was a key factor in his ability to turn back Gary Hart's challenge in the spring of 1984. Moreover, the move signaled a historic shift in labor's conception of its political role. Even the men most attuned to the old politics of compromise recognized the need for new tactics in the changing conditions of the era of imperial decline.

The attack on the unions is an attack on the stability of the American social order. That the attack is unavoidable is only a sign of the weakness and underlying instability of the social compromise between labor and capital that marked the postwar period. Organized labor loyally backed the bipartisan national defense policy through thick and thin; Nixon, in his efforts to escape with honor from Vietnam, found more support among labor leaders than in any other group of power brokers. To ask what the effect of heightened union militancy would be on this relationship is to answer it. The right-wing attack on labor has already begun to receive its just reward in the entrenched opposition to U.S. Central American policy in some of the country's most powerful unions.

A union-based opposition to war, backed by the muscle and voting power of a revitalized union movement, is something the United States has never yet seen. But the conditions that created this kind of conflict in other societies are in formation here.

No advanced capitalist country has ever failed to generate a union movement. In all the advanced countries the political leadership and big business recognized relatively early that trade unionists (like students and minorities) must be convinced that their basic goals can be reached by working through the system. To launch an attack on a moderate trade union movement, and to deprive its leadership of economic victories, is to drive both rank and file and leadership to assume radical positions. There will be gratifying victories for the anti-union forces along the way, but the harder labor is attacked, the harder it will fight back. The anti-union forces of the 1980s court trouble; they are waking a sleeping giant. The giant is stirring.

THE POLITICS OF CLASS

A population buffeted by economic ills on all sides and educated to look toward politicians for the management of the economy will be reluctant to believe the message that the Establishment will be forced to put across as time goes on: there are no quick economic fixes; sacrifice is the only road to recovery. There will be votes to be found by cultivating popular skepticism about Establishment spokesmen, and there will be politicians willing to build careers by catering to the hopes and inflaming the fears of the voters. The period since the Depression has been singularly free of crank economic theories like the single tax, bimetallism, and the multitude of homespun cures, but Laetrile economics flourishes in an era of fear and uncertainty, just as Laetrile treatment flourishes when science has no cure.

Voodoo economics was an early form of the Laetrile cures of the future. The collapse of American manufacturing was accelerated by Reagan's policies, but aside from the consequences for the newly unemployed, the ill effects of the voodoo program remained largely on paper — the $1 trillion of new national debt. As the consequences of economic failure mount, however, the price will be higher. When deficits doubled and tripled under Reagan, the economy shuddered, but it did not collapse. Another dose of Laetrile with a similar effect on the deficit would have more serious consequences.

The underlying strength of the American economy has permitted glib salesmen to govern by propaganda and deceit — to govern through what cartoonist Mark Stamaty calls the Office of Lip Service and the Bureau of Perception Management — but the chickens are coming home to roost. The margin of error for managers of the American economy becomes narrower, but the political system rewards campaigns based on fuzzy generalizations, misleading definitions of issues, and double talk. An economic situation already grave can only be worsened by politics as usual, but the difference between the interests of the managerial and financial elite in society and those of the middle and lower classes is so vast that the elite will soon find the political process inadequate for keeping the economy on an even keel.

These reflections lead to the conclusion that the continuing period of American economic decay will bring about a resurgence of the politics of class in the United States. Class polarization significantly increased through the 1970s and early 1980s; the long recession at the start of the 1980s saw workers and farmers blocking auctions and foreclosures with physical force, a truck strike that made shooting galleries of some stretches of highway, and the first mass labor demonstration, organized by the AFL-CIO, since the 1930s. These events took place under relatively benign conditions in a recession that, though severe by recent standards, was milder than the cyclical downturns of the pre–New Deal era.

Class politics are tricky and dangerous. They do not always take the expected forms or move in the expected channels. But given the explosive forces lying so near the surface in American life, one cannot discount the potential for a sweeping transformation of the political scene by a populist movement that is neither liberal nor conservative in traditional terms.

THE POLITICS OF WAR

MPIRE breeds resistance; all of history bears out this statement. The American Empire is no exception; political and military movements opposed to American power have sprung up on four continents since the Second World War. There is no reason to suppose that such developments will cease in the years to come. With the decline — real and perceived — in American power since Tet of 1968, such movements have grown in number, and they have enjoyed success in various parts of the world, from Iran to Nicaragua.

As the frontiers of empire contract, the remaining territories acquire new importance. The outlying portions go first, followed by regions that are more and more critical for the maintenance of imperial power. The war in Indochina was a war in an outlying province of the American Empire. The establishment of communist regimes there had a profound political significance but little military or economic meaning outside the region. Vietnam gave the Soviets a base in the South China Sea, but Vietnam does not control key shipping lanes or open up an avenue for further advances.

Vietnam was a limited war partly because American interests there were limited; its importance to the United States was only political. Similarly, the Marxist regimes in Angola and Mozambique threaten no vital American interest. They represent a weakening of the American position and they put new pressures on South Africa, but Americans have gone on very happily without integrating the territories of the former Portuguese Empire into their zone of control. The Iranian Revolution was a more serious matter; after the shah's fall, Carter announced to the world that no further erosion in the American position on the Persian Gulf would be permitted. Any radical revolution in Saudi Arabia would face a tougher response from the United States.

When the chips were down, America preferred retreat in Vietnam to the economic and political costs of the war. Withdrawal was an option, however distasteful, that in the last resort was more attractive than the domestic consequences of continuing the war. But one result of the American withdrawal from Indochina is that the option of withdrawal from the remaining portions of the empire has become less attractive. The current fighting in the Philippines, Central America, and South Africa illustrates the problem.

The United States is by no means the first empire to face this problem. The French, as we saw, faced the rebellion of Algeria after their defeat in Indochina. Indochina is thousands of miles from Paris; Algeria is a few hours by plane. Few Frenchmen lived in Indochina; for 125 years French citizens had settled in Algeria. Ultimately the same kinds of forces pushed France out of the Maghreb that had driven it from the Mekong; yet France fought harder to keep the more important territory, and its loss was far more disruptive.

In considering where future conflicts may arise, especially those that could require American involvement, we see three key trouble spots: Southwest Asia, East Asia, and Latin America. To a greater or lesser extent, conflicts in any of these areas would involve vital interests of the American Empire; the loss of wars in these regions would be attended by consequences vastly greater than those which followed the Indochina War.

Of all the regions of the earth, the one most likely to involve the United States in war is, of course, Latin America. Already American politics are convulsed by Central American events.

As North American attention shifts toward Latin America, the rationale for this interest is variously presented. Discounting the expressed desire of the American government to defend freedom south of the border, the motives that remain are the security of the Caribbean sea lanes, control of the Panama Canal, and the exclusion of refugees from communist rule. Also the domino theory has been resurrected from its grave in the South China Sea to explain that at stake is the future not only of El Salvador and Nicaragua, but of Costa Rica, Honduras, Belize, Guatemala, and even Mexico. Many skeptical of the latter rationale point to the economic interests of U.S. corporations in the banana republics, including the traditional agricultural interests (bananas, sugar, coffee, cotton) and the light industries that have appeared in more recent years. Fans of this theory cite studies showing that 92 percent of American underwear came from Central America in the late 1970s, and that American investment in Guatemala amounts to approximately one third of that country's gross national product.

Although this investment is large by Central American standards, the value is not great enough to justify American expenditures in the region. Total U.S. direct investment in Central America is estimated at $845 million as of 1979.[1] This is enough to create a Central America lobby seeking to influence the American political process, but by itself a sum of this magnitude would not draw the United States into war.

Control of the sea lanes and the Panama Canal are real motives and nearer the real U.S. interests in the region, interests that are political and military rather than economic. The United States has suffered immeasurable difficulty and humiliation because of Fidel Castro. His presence in Cuba after two decades of American sabotage, and what would be called terrorism if practiced by anyone other than ourselves, is a standing demonstration of the impotence of American power and of the incompetence of the CIA and other instruments of imperial rule. A perverse fate has seen to it that every illegal operation the United States carried out against Castro has humiliated American leaders — the exploding cigars of the Kennedy era, Nixon's swine fever caper, and the presence of CIA-trained Cubans at the Watergate break-in. A string of Castros from Panama City to Tegucigalpa sends shivers up the spines of more than a few American policymakers.

The domino theory in Central America has more to do with Latin America generally than it does with even Mexico or Panama. There is no country in Latin America where American influence is completely secure. U.S. support for Britain during the Falklands/Malvinas War, combined with the long-term irritation over the Latin debts, has excluded the United States from many of the circles that have traditionally supported it. Castro has overcome his United States–imposed diplomatic isolation and taken his place as a respected statesman throughout the continent. U.S. policy in Central America has deepened its isolation in the hemisphere; even regimes that do not like the Sandinistas like the prospect of Washington's interference even less.

Although Latin America as a whole is hardly on the verge of a communist revolution, Marxism is a vital force on the continent, influencing politicians and intellectuals from Tijuana to Tierra del Fuego. The failure of military regimes to overcome the region's economic problems has forced the armies back to the barracks but has done nothing to discredit the ideology of their left-wing opponents. Joined with the endemic anti-American sentiment in the region, Latin Marxism is a powerful and dynamic force that has the potential in the right circumstances to take power in more than one country.

Latin America as a whole is a vital interest of the empire. Direct investment, military considerations, bank loans, and trade relationships make South America absolutely crucial to the U.S. world position. When Reagan referred to Central America as the "front yard" of the United States, he enraged Latin American nationalists but spoke accurately. The willingness of the United States to use combat troops if necessary to prevent any more Cubas in Latin America preserves American credibility and influence throughout the region. If the United States cannot and will not defend its interests in Latin America, where will it defend them?

It happens that the American people are not ready and willing to fight a series of long, inconclusive actions to preserve the world position of the American Empire. The disinclination to fight is strongest among those who would be called on to do most of the dying. An unwillingness to kill or die in a cause of this kind is nothing to be ashamed of; if anything, the American people deserve congratulations for their reluctance to engage in more Vietnam-style adventures. It shows good strategic and moral sense. The situation, however, does not present itself in this light to those who have taken on the burden of defending the empire.

The result is a tactical problem for the United States that is both thorny and urgent. Those representing virtually the entire spectrum of allegedly responsible politics believe that the United States has a right to prevent the establishment of Marxist regimes in Latin America — in open and flagrant violation of the UN Charter and the Treaty of Rio. Most people in public life understand that the situation is one that could easily require U.S. combat troops, perhaps for a long time. In practical terms, the alternatives for U.S. policymakers are not intervention or isolation in Latin America, but forward defense or defense in depth.

Forward defense, the policy of the most aggressive factions of the Reagan administration, has as its goal the elimination of all Marxist influence in Latin America, especially in Cuba. Such a policy would lead to an invasion of Nicaragua, U.S. combat forces in El Salvador, and perhaps a blockade of Cuba. The realities of Latin American politics, the fears of the joint chiefs of staff, and the distaste of the American people have blocked this option and forced the administration to something more like a consensus policy: defense in depth.

This strategy depends on a concept that liberal critics of the administration find comfortable. It is more concerned with the defense of Latin America as a whole than it is with the defeat of any Marxist movement within it. Why win the battle that loses a war? A U.S. invasion of Central America, even if successful, would destroy the political position of the United States throughout the hemisphere. Any moves against Cuba run the risk of provoking the Soviet Union and alienating Latin America; in any case, the Cuban government is well entrenched and enjoys broad if not unanimous support.

The liberal concept that, *faute de mieux*, has been adopted by the Reagan administration depends on developing a "democratic center" — a body of opinion that is anticommunist but not identified with the traditionalist oligarchies. Christian Democrats, like José Napoléon Duarte, who favor reforms within the context of capitalist democracy, are the hope of the liberal policy. They can isolate the revolutionary left Latin countries while legitimating American support for democratic regimes.

In its pure form, the liberal solution has only one problem: it is unworkable. The search for the democratic center has hypnotized opponents of Bolshevism since the Allies backed the Mensheviks in 1917. Neither democratic centers nor revolutionary movements with broad popular support appear out of nowhere. Nor can they be created by the fiat of a foreign power, however well disposed. Each is created by historical forces, and generally speaking the forces that create one work against the other. There have been cases — Portugal is a good example — when judicious foreign support for moderate groups has blocked the ambitions of the revolutionary left, but in a region where American support is the kiss of death for almost any movement, such successes for a Menshevik policy will be harder to find. In Portugal, society had not disintegrated into bitter civil war; blood feuds played a relatively small role in the political contest. Even more important, the center held out solid hope for economic advance. The center has less to offer Latin America today. The countries most noted for their willingness to accept the edicts of the IMF — including Chile and Jamaica — have no more to show for their flexibility than do the countries that have taken a harder line.

"Fostering the development of a democratic center" in someone else's country is a delicate business, one that the U.S. government is not always well equipped to conduct. U.S. interests do not all speak with one voice; one man's courageous democratic reformer is another man's cryptocommunist. National security advisers squabble with secretaries of state; campaign contributors call up their senators; the senators call up ambassadors. The local ambassador warns the Latin military not to overthrow the democratic reformer; the ambassador to the UN hints that the American ambassador is out of touch with the real thinking of the administration. And so it goes. Authority is too diffuse in the American government for any administration to conduct a subtle, sophisticated, and consistent intervention under such pressures.

As an extreme example, the U.S. government regularly decries the cocaine trade — and has even contemplated using the army to interfere

with it. Yet the American people have made it clear that, regardless of
what their representatives say, a considerable number of them want the
trade to continue. The business interests that smuggle and distribute
cocaine represent an American influence in the grower countries that
undermines the official policy of the embassies. In the same way, legitimate companies that disagree with official U.S. policy are free to undercut it in their dealings with Latin governments. The corporations may
disagree that the best way to defend U.S. interests across the continent
is, say, to permit the nationalization of their local interests. These corporations are well entrenched in the countries concerned. They have
close and long-standing ties with elements in the military and economic
oligarchy, whose interests are also threatened by these "democratic reformers." They have connections, too, with the American government.
They have no intention of sitting on their hands while their interests are
undermined.

In any case, "democratic centers" that come to power with the help
of foreign money and foreign secret agents are less democratic than they
appear. Such movements would be fatally compromised if the extent of
their dependence on the United States became known or their ties with
the CIA were revealed. The local citizenry is likely to conclude that, far
from representing the interests of their own countrymen, these foreign-
backed politicians actually represent the United States. As of course they
do.

U.S. policy in Central America is reminiscent of Brer Rabbit's encounter with the Tar Baby. "Good morning, Tar Baby!" said Brer Rabbit — but he got no reply. The conservative solution is to punch the Tar
Baby right now to make it talk. Liberals want to tell it good morning
again, and more nicely. Perhaps it didn't hear properly the first time.
But if it remains silent, then liberals will hit it too. The consensus of
American politicians (but not of the American people) over Latin America
is broad and deep, despite disagreements over timing. The spread of
Marxist governments in that region poses an unacceptable threat to vital
American interests. Conservatives and hard-liners generally believe that
the time has come for quick, decisive action. Liberals cherish a probably
illusory hope that something will turn up. Both sides recognize that at
the present moment the United States cannot maintain a military presence
in the war zone; neither the civilian population nor the armed forces
support such a move. Conservatives believe that encouraging anticommunist sentiment and publicizing the current dangers in Latin America
will swing enough public sentiment behind government policy to make
intervention successful; liberals fear that the conservatives overestimate

the belligerence of the public and underestimate the political obstacles to successful American military action. The policy of each group will lead to war unless the progress of Marxism south of the border spontaneously stops. There are currently no signs of that happening.

THE CHARGE OF THE LIGHT BRIGADE

We have had occasion to survey more than one dreary prospect in the course of this study; the view we must now examine is the gloomiest yet: the consequences of a Latin American War for the American Empire. We can assume that such a war will be long and inconclusive, like a fire in a coal mine. It may appear variously as a civil war in which the United States intervenes directly or through proxies, and at other times it may take on the form of a war among states or groups of states. Clausewitz observed that war is the continuation of diplomacy; civil war is the continuation of politics. The colossal struggle between the United States and its oligarchical allies on one side and Marxism and related or associated movements on the other has been a constant feature of Latin American life since well before Castro; in recent years the struggle has moved toward the forefront of regional politics, and other, unrelated quarrels have been absorbed into it. It is useless to attempt specific predictions about the course of this struggle; all we can do is observe the pattern and suggest developments based on our observations. The region has been increasingly polarized between exponents of a Marxist-derived ideology of liberation and the friends of the existing order. Movements that seek a middle ground must constantly look over their shoulders at both extremes and are constantly vulnerable to attack from either side.

To the extent that trends can be discerned in the welter of Latin developments, there appears to be a weakening of the domestic, indigenous forces of social control. Discredited by economic failure and savage repression, the armed forces find their prestige and political strength fallen to new lows. Together with the long-term consequences of the continent's economic troubles, these factors justify our assumption that the future will see the United States more and more deeply involved in Latin American affairs, facing mounting pressures that will make it difficult in the end for the country to avoid sending its troops into combat.

Our concern here is to understand the domestic consequences of U.S. military intervention south of the border. The consequences for Latin

America — misery, slaughter, economic ruin, refugees in the millions, a legacy of hatred — are easier to predict than to contemplate.

Economically, U.S. involvement will be a disaster. A nation facing peacetime deficits of more than $200 billion simply cannot afford a war. Economists trace the inflation of the 1970s to the debt financing of the Indochinese War; there does not appear to be an alternative method for financing a Latin American War. War spending is inflationary by nature; the money produces no goods for the civilian market, so more dollars chase an unchanged number of consumer goods.

In the short run, employment in war-related industries and an expansion of the military may reduce unemployment, but at the cost of a long-term erosion of the American economy. The diversion of facilities and talent toward unproductive war industries introduces distortions into the economy and shifts investment from needed improvements in civilian industries. Cost-plus defense contracts favor inefficient producers and lure investment away from companies that operate in the far more competitive civilian market. We say nothing about the human cost to a nation whose resources and talent are consumed in the manufacture of the instruments of destruction.

On the political side, war will be no less disastrous. The effect of combat on the morale of American soldiers will be devastating. Many of the young people now in the army enlisted for lack of an economic alternative or because they were deceived by specious promises of technical training that would help them in civilian life. The veneer of patriotism inculcated by Rambo-like characters in popular entertainment will wear thin as the soldiers come to see the difference between combat and the movies. These soldiers are not likely to fight more aggressively than Salvadoran draftees to protect the Salvadoran oligarchy. In a protracted war, mutiny and mass desertions are distinct possibilities. An intelligent and resourceful enemy will receive deserting Americans with open arms and send them on to neutral countries in this hemisphere or in Europe.

Desertion in the field was impossible for most Americans in Vietnam; safety lay with one's unit. This will be much less the case in Latin America, where American soldiers can easily blend into the general population and where many speak the language and share a heritage. Armies traditionally shoot deserters when the problem becomes significant; such a policy cannot be guaranteed to improve morale either at the front or at home in the event of a long Latin American War.

The war will be fiercely unpopular. New England, the Middle West, and the Pacific Northwest will think it unnecessary. Their representatives and their officials will legitimate dissent; Hispanics will not be pressured into following the flag with the same force of public opinion that encouraged Japanese Americans and German Americans to support previous wars.

The Indochinese War created millions of American cynics, citizens predisposed to scoff at government justifications for war. The sight of ruined villages, bloody corpses, screaming casualties, and body bags being loaded onto cargo planes will rapidly revive nightmare memories of the last war — and spread panic among a generation of teenagers who have not been brought up in the martial virtues. The mothers and fathers of the 1988 class of eighteen-year-olds were the high school and college students of the late 1960s. Many of these parents would rather give their children bus tickets to Canada than send them to war. The teachers, coaches, and youth leaders of the 1980s and 1990s include former antiwar students and veterans, who will be quick to turn against new military adventures.

The horror of war will be more readily apparent to the American public in Latin America than it was in Vietnam. The Latin societies are more like our own than was Vietnam's, and millions of Americans have family ties in Latin America. Latin Americans are racially closer to most Americans; the necessary depersonalization of the enemy will be harder to achieve and to maintain. The principal religion of Latin America is that of the largest religious body in the United States. American missionaries will lead opposition to the war; the Catholic bishops will play an important role in the politics of any Latin American conflict. They will by no means be uncritical supporters of the Latin left, but the enthusiasm of active American priests and nuns will push the bishops to express their antiwar feeling.

Millions of Americans have visited Latin America and seen for themselves the contrast between rich and poor. Vietnam remained a social riddle to the American public up to and beyond the end of the war; the public never really understood the composition of South Vietnamese society or the social roots of the conflict. It will quickly understand that a war in Latin America, under whatever ideological guise, is fundamentally a war of the rich against the poor, with America backing the rich.

The experiences of the antiwar movement, the civil rights movement, and the nuclear freeze will enable those opposed to the war to organize rapidly and massively. By the mid 1980s anti-intervention networks were set up and working across the United States. Thousands of Americans had visited Nicaragua and returned to tell friends and colleagues about a reality at variance with government propaganda. Sanctuary activists in the churches had set up a national network to protect the victims of

United States–backed regimes in the zone of conflict. At a comparable period in the Indochinese conflict, few Americans had even heard of the region.

Public sentiment in another war will be heavily influenced by the weak economy. Vietnam came at the end of the long postwar boom; a Latin American War will come after fifteen years of declining real wages, falling expectations, and the politics of limits. Opposition to the war will more easily find common ground with a systematic opposition to the current American order. It will link up more closely with the union movement and the civil rights movement than the Indochinese War opposition was able to do.

The intermingling of the American societies and the ability of Latin Americans to blend into the American mainstream creates the possibility for the extension of the war into the United States. It is difficult to believe that Latin Americans would allow the United States to mount a massive campaign of intervention from privileged sanctuaries north of the border; we can foresee organized sabotage of defense plants, government offices, and key transit facilities. Any reliance on bombing of civilian targets by U.S. military forces — a key element in current military thinking about counterinsurgency warfare — would open the United States to retaliatory bombings, not by air forces but by individuals and small groups.

Under these circumstances it is not surprising that the joint chiefs of staff have advised strongly and publicly that United States combat forces not be sent to Latin America unless there is public backing for war. It should be apparent that this condition cannot be long maintained by normal constitutional means. Nixon's search for an honorable exit from Indochina caught him in the Watergate morass. Before it was over he had filled the White House with terrorists and lunatics, with safes stuffed with hundred-dollar bills, and had done more damage to the United States than any foreign foe could have dreamed of accomplishing. If burglary and espionage were required to manage the pace of American withdrawal from Indochina, what tools of statecraft will make it possible for the United States to enter an even more unpopular conflict?

There will be Deep Throats and Ellsbergs by the dozen in the next war; the tradition of resistance to war has been legitimated and hallowed, if not in every corner of the Republic, in enough places so that dissenters will feel themselves part of a noble heritage. If the stakes are high enough and the danger is real enough, will dissidents be free to carry on what some will consider treasonable activities? What are the limits of legitimate dissent when the army is restless and bitter?

We may well arrive at a situation where the Establishment in both parties and outside the government considers a deeply unpopular war to be a matter of vital national interest. The only way to make this case rationally and openly is to put the matter in terms of power and interest, not justice. Any attempt to link the war to the defense of human freedom in the land of what Reagan once called "tin-horn dictators" is bound eventually to fall flat with the American public. So will the concept of an invasion by the Red Army across the Rio Grande. The case can be made only by arguing on the basis of economic and political necessity — an argument that will alienate as many as it convinces and will ring hollow when the inevitable economic consequences of the war begin to appear.

The Latin American left is perfectly capable of reaching the conclusions we have outlined here and of drawing the appropriate strategic inferences. In this sense the domino theory has been vindicated. The triumph of revolution in one country encourages revolutionaries in others. But an image more useful than a line of dominoes is that of a pot of popcorn. When the oil reaches the right temperature, the kernels start to pop — first one, then another, then others.

No-win situations have been rare for the United States. We were history's golden boy; the world lay at our feet. Yet there is nothing new or even unusual about a historical situation that has no good solution. There was no way out for Russia in 1917 or for Britain in 1940. The Austrians saw onrushing doom at the time of Metternich, but they could not stop the dissolution of their empire. The British watched their industrial lead evaporate, saw their financial supremacy decay, and foresaw, without being able to arrest, the ultimate fall of their empire. Indochina was America's first recent experience with inevitable historical disaster. Once America's prestige had been engaged, and the enemy showed himself capable of withstanding the pressure that could be brought against him, defeat was only a matter of when and how. Like the French in Indochina and Algeria, like the British in Africa and the Middle East, like the Dutch in Indonesia and the Portuguese in Africa and the Belgians in the Congo, the Americans were unable to defeat an undersupplied and outnumbered enemy.

The American position in Latin America is irretrievably lost. It cannot be sustained without military involvement, but military involvement cannot succeed on any extended scale. The United States could not impose a regime of its choice on Mexico or Brazil in the face of sustained popular resistance.

"Losing" in Latin America brings a train of unwanted consequences, but winning is impossible. Realistic statesmen in this country would

eschew talk about will power *über alles* and make sober calculations about
the kind of arrangements that could be worked out with the emerging
forces in the hemisphere. Yet the American political system is unable to
embark on a course so starkly realistic. The tentative moves toward
accommodation ventured during the Carter administration caused a
backlash of chauvinistic insistence that no accommodation was necessary.

We shall see. But sad to say, the United States appears firmly committed to a policy that risks defeat for the empire and disaster for the
nation.

❧ 19 ❧

THE FUTURE
OF LIBERALISM

THE EVENTS of these years will put heavy strains on the political system, and the burden will fall most heavily on liberalism. We saw how in 1968 the liberal consensus bent and then broke under the strain of Vietnam, how four years after its triumph over Goldwater the Democratic Party was reduced to street fighting in Chicago. The 1970s brought a slow unraveling of the liberal center. A substantial minority went over to the right, calling themselves neoconservatives. In practice this term seems to mean only that they reserve the right to advocate conservative measures without giving up the moral authority they once enjoyed as liberal or socialist intellectuals.

Another group of ex-liberals attempted a radical critique of American society. This group began the rehabilitation of Marxism in American academic circles and achieved new prestige and currency for ideas that were developed in the United States but owed their ultimate inspiration to the old German philosopher.

But most liberals did not change their views much in the 1970s and 1980s. They acknowledged that some conservative criticisms of certain liberal programs were valid, and they recognized that they were not in a position to regain the initiative in national politics, but they felt that they needed new tactics and better organization, not a new view of the world.

Despite the two debacles of the Carter and Mondale candidacies of 1980 and 1984, liberalism retained great latent strength in the 1980s. Even in eclipse, liberalism set the limits on the changes Reagan has been able to make in the liberal state. The basic achievements of the New Deal and the civil rights movement could not be attacked. For six years Reagan accepted the SALT II Treaty on the same terms as Carter. He refrained from an invasion of Nicaragua. He abandoned Jean-Claude (Baby Doc) Duvalier and Marcos and swung the weight of the U.S. government toward the democratic opposition in those countries and in Chile.

Huge constituencies, popular and elite, continued to support the structure of the liberal state. Not only labor and minority organizations, but industries and financial interests looked to Reagan for, at most, midcourse corrections halfway through the American Century. Half a century of government intervention in the economy, as David Stockman discovered to his sorrow, had created an enormous network of institutions and people whose current lives would be impossible without the economic intervention of the state. The Democratic farm and labor coalition did not lose its appetite for food stamps; education remained a high priority with groups from all walks of life; cowboy diplomacy ran up against the real need of American industry for cooperative relations with the European allies and for a dollar whose price was not set in a free market. Reagan was elected to manage the liberal state, not to dismantle it.

On the other hand, the failure of liberalism under Carter could not have been more painfully evident. In the wake of its resounding defeats in 1980 and 1984, liberalism undertook a review of its basic tenets. New schools of liberals sprang up, dedicated to the proposition that the liberal tradition could be preserved and revitalized if a few basic changes were made.

The cornerstone of the New Liberalism is the understanding that government intervention in the economy is currently too haphazard to produce substantial results in the competitive world economic climate. While the United States has a vast array of programs designed to channel government support to various industries and other groups, it does not coordinate these programs well in an effort to reach selected national goals. Take the tax code as an example — the prime example — of the government's disarray: it encourages all kinds of economic behavior deemed helpful to the national interest. But most of its provisions were written in response to specific requests by specific interest groups, so the tax code as a whole ends up meeting many small needs but few large ones.

In the early years of the liberal state, it made sense to stimulate the economy by massaging each of its major constitutive elements. The national economy was not so well integrated in the 1930s as it is now, and the collapse was so general that virtually every industry needed all the help it could get. With all its inefficiencies and redundancies, the system worked well enough for a generation, because America did not yet need to be efficient to maintain its economic (and therefore its military and political) position in the world. Now, says the New Liberalism, times have changed.

America, the New Liberals say, must respond with intelligent planning to the age of limits and competition. America cannot permit its economy to operate spontaneously, guided only by the invisible hand. Instead, we must analyze our strengths and weaknesses as a nation, and concentrate tax breaks, credit help, and other forms of encouragement on the growth industries, where we can be competitive. The United States must emulate Japan and target industries for development. It follows logically that other industries must be considered terminal cases and should be allowed to die with dignity.

The New Liberals have put forward several interesting ideas along these lines, but they have not yet managed to build the kind of constituency that would propel them to power. Young professionals are drawn to these ideas, but for all their influence in the media, they form an insignificant portion of the electorate. The agenda of the New Liberals alienates vital elements in both the Republican and Democratic parties. Labor unions do not like to hear talk about dying industries; neither do the Chambers of Commerce in cities that depend on them. The family farm may be an antiquated economic unit headed for the junkyard of history, but the people of Iowa do not expect their elected representatives to accelerate the process. The realities of global competition may require a greater concentration of economic power in the hands of industrial and financial giants, but small businessmen aren't prepared to sit back and let it happen at their expense.

The task that confronts the New Liberals is to recast the New Deal, to design a "neo-deal" that offers enough benefits to enough of the electorate so that its essential legislation can pass through Congress. This will be difficult to do, barring a catastrophic turn in the economy; the original New Deal would not have been passed had it not been for the Depression. Such a program would involve brokering the claims of various regions and interest groups and would inevitably involve compromises of principle.

Woodrow Wilson's program included many features that became law under Roosevelt. FDR brought to fruition Wilson's ideas on bank regulation, on social programs, and on the proper American role in the world. Wilson left office a failure; he had correctly identified the needs of the emerging American order but was unable to build and maintain the political coalition that might have translated these perceptions into viable policies. Wilson wasn't wrong, but he was ahead of his time, and bad timing is the ultimate political sin.

Carter was the Wilson of the 1970s. His initiatives in energy policy, tax policy, domestic spending, and diplomacy indicated the path down which the nation was to travel, and they anticipated the policies of the

New Liberals. In 1920 as in 1980 the country concluded that it did not like the future and voted to return to the past. Conservative social issues (like Prohibition) triumphed; a resurgent fundamentalism sought to drive evolution from the public schools and to return the nation to its evangelical past; lynch law and Jim Crow reached the zenith of their power; the nation placed its faith in the invisible hand and pledged itself to battle Bolshevism and its allies. Through the 1920s Democrats and liberals groped toward an alternative to the Republicanism of Hoover and Coolidge, but only the crisis of 1929–1932 gave them their program and the power to implement it.

Beneath the surface of "normalcy" during the 1920s, the nation and the world were changing. The economic consequences of the First World War drew America's bankers — though not its politicians — into the affairs of Europe. The Catholic and Jewish immigrant communities in the northern cities learned to make themselves felt in state and national affairs; never again would the United States be a Protestant country. The children and grandchildren of the slaves made their way to the northern cities and began the cultural and political development that would transform the American scene. The automobile, and the mass-production techniques used to build it, had effects on American life more far-reaching than many political revolutions. The world's first consumer society appeared in a country that claimed to be living by its traditional values of thrift and sobriety. Having gotten the vote, women deepened their toehold in the professions, and even though the female vote was believed to have helped Warren Harding into the White House, the changing role of American women did more to undermine and transform American society than any group of revolutionaries.

By 1932 a social revolution in the United States was well under way. Large corporations were no longer confined to a few key industries; rural America was, economically and demographically, a shadow of itself; the economic life of the nation was more centralized than ever before. From one end of the country to the other, people ate and drank the same foods prepared by the same companies; they bought their goods in the same chain stores; they listened to the same radio programs and saw the same movies.

This society was ready for the centralization and concentration of political power that Roosevelt brought about. It made economic sense to subordinate state to federal authority and to extend federal power to major economic decisions. It was clearly necessary for the federal government to ensure the stability of the banking system and to insure its deposits. Only Washington could fund the public works and relief programs that the times required.

The United States must once again bring about a concentration of power. The nation's economy is much larger now than in 1932, and the country is much more of an economic unit. Furthermore, its links with the world economy are more important than ever. The great American corporations must now compete with Japanese and European institutions backed by the power of their own governments. The American government must be organized to act quickly and decisively; the federal government itself must become streamlined.

These are the realities that confront any political movement that seeks to exercise power in the United States today. The New Liberals believe they can put together a government that is competent, efficient, flexible, and responsive by forging a consensus among business interests, the labor movement, and the general public. It is, for example, obviously in the national interest to maintain the basic steel and automobile industries, regardless of their economic competitiveness. The Chrysler bailout, combining concessions from all parties, is a model for the New Liberal program.

We can make several comments about the New Liberal agenda. First, it is without a doubt the most promising strategy available for halting American economic decline. There are serious unintended consequences to be examined later, but we must first register our agreement with the advocates of national economic planning that it represents the most plausible course. Second, we can see that by systematizing the activity of government in the economy the New Liberalism essentially puts the capstone on the old liberal state.

The New Liberalism seeks to address social problems in a more systematic and organized fashion than the old liberalism of the New Deal. Liberals will attempt to integrate programs that assist the poor with overall economic planning. Education programs, training programs, public works employment, and so on will be designed to create a labor force and infrastructure suitable for the designated growth fields — bioengineering, computer technology, and so on.

Where social benefits are extended — probably in the field of health insurance — the New Liberalism will reject the piecemeal, add-on approach of existing programs. National health insurance under whatever form will be designed with a view to the finance and direction of health programs as a whole. Whatever form of national health insurance is adopted will be more carefully crafted than the hodgepodge of existing entitlements and subsidies. Already in Medicare we have seen the first efforts by the federal government to shape the fee and treatment structure of the programs it pays for. Health care was one of the last bastions of a decentralized profession in the American economy. Until recently doctors and hospitals were largely autonomous. With the spread of chain hospitals and health maintenance organizations, and with the gradual decline of the individual medical practice, it is both easier and more important for the federal government to intervene in the industry.

As at the time of the New Deal, a major factor shaping the liberal agenda is the need for an expanded government role in banking and finance. From the standpoint of other industries the recent explosion of financial service mergers and the steady circumvention by the banks of regulations intended to keep the giant banks from interstate activity have created a dangerous concentration of financial power. With hundreds of billions of dollars locked up in shaky loans overseas, with energy and agriculture banks strained to their limits, and with frenzied international competition in the money markets, small business in the United States has reason to be worried about its continued access to credit.

The bankers, on the other hand, also recognize a need for more government involvement in their industry. They rely on the government to keep the IMF in business and to back them up in international debt negotiations. Their need for government assistance and bailouts could become acute at any moment. They also need government policies that will either assist the farmers and oil companies who owe them billions or at least guarantee that banks will not be forced into insolvency by debtor defaults.

The natural outcome will be some kind of government-supported banking cartel with an integrated approach to the extension of credit. New banking legislation will be the centerpiece of the New Liberalism, as FDR's was the centerpiece of the New Deal and Wilson's of his reforms. If the government must underwrite the banks and in effect guarantee their loans as well as their deposits, it must involve itself at some point in formulating bank lending policy — not so much as a matter of fairness as of necessity. Government, bankers, labor, and management will have to work together on major economic decisions; each party must be willing to contribute to the success of the overall policy. For this type of partnership to work, collective bargaining in the traditional sense will have to give way to a new and more bureaucratic process in which wages will be determined as part of a credit allocation and planning process.

This is a program that at least potentially can restore the lost momentum of liberalism in American life — temporarily. It can regenerate the New Deal coalition with a promise to "get this country moving again." A typically liberal program, it will combine progressive features with the enthusiastic backing of some of the nation's most powerful corporations. But the New Liberalism will probably not repeat the success of FDR in achieving a generation of stability and progress. It may founder on the same shoals that wrecked Johnson's Great Society.

Foreign policy — specifically, American responses to the Third World resistance that is a permanent feature of any imperial order — will divide the liberal coalition, and national economic planning under actual conditions will always threaten to turn into a stampede to the national economic trough.

The New Liberalism cannot provide the secure and stable world environment that the economy requires. The advanced capitalist countries, including the United States, are neither willing nor able to transfer enough wealth to the Third World to meet the minimum demands of its peoples. The desire of hundreds of millions to eat every day, to clothe themselves, and to educate their children will continue to clash, often violently, with the need of the advanced economies for cheap labor, cheap resources, and secure markets. The paradox in which the advanced economies continue to rely on the low-wage labor abroad that undermines their security at home will weaken the international economic fabric. We have seen that the battle is likeliest to come to a head in Latin America; but wherever the next outbreak of resistance occurs, it will set the core constituencies of the liberal coalition at each other's throats.

Liberalism has two constituencies, and each secretly believes that it is using the other. On the one hand are the idealistic, sometimes naïve grassroots liberals who stand for progress, tolerance, democracy, and compassion. They believe that the present economic system can support all these values, and they believe that the United States can and should take the lead in easing the misery of the poor here and abroad. This popular liberalism in its dear fuzzy way hopes and believes that any advance in the welfare state and in central planning prepares the country for some form of social democracy, the peaceful transition to a mild form of socialism.

Corporate liberalism, the second constituency, believes that social programs are the grease that keep the wheels of industry turning. It would rather have the grassroots liberals administering social programs than scheming for social change; it favors government intervention in the economy because only such intervention can create the safe and predictable world in which large corporations can flourish.

Wars in the Third World expose the inner split in liberal ranks. They make clear who is using whom. Emerging social democracies do not intervene on behalf of blood-soaked oligarchies, but highly centralized corporate states do it all the time.

The other serious area of friction in the liberal coalition concerns the conflict over the domestic agenda. Corporate liberalism will be far more willing than popular liberalism to write off large sections of the work force. Corporate liberalism wants as large a dose as possible of disciplined, realistic planning; social benefits and high wages are a cost to be controlled, not a good to be sought. Corporate liberalism wants enough money in the ghettoes to keep them from exploding; popular liberals want to succor the needy urban poor.

The old liberalism of the last generation dealt with this conflict by maintaining that social spending stimulated demand for corporate production and thereby contributed to corporate profit. Bread cast upon the waters returned a hundredfold. This was all very well for the good old days, but wages and wage-related costs like social spending are now too high in the United States by world standards. The New Liberalism's idea of streamlining and redesigning social programs appeals to popular liberals because it opens the door to doing more for people who need it. The corporate liberals like it because it is a means to lower the overhead of social wages without causing so much political opposition. At some point in the near future, this difference in perspective will become acute.

Since 1984 the corporate liberals have had the upper hand in the liberal movement. The stagnation of the economy and electoral defeat have left the grassroots liberals weak and divided. They desperately need a program for economic growth and must jump on any bandwagon that will make room for them. This gives the upper hand to "designer liberals" like Gary Hart and to corporate liberals like Felix Rohatyn. The kind of liberal Republicanism that was defeated by Republican conservatives in 1980 may enjoy a second spring in the Democratic Party — without winning many friends for itself, however, in the labor movement or in black America.

THE PILGRIMS

Two groups of liberals, now ex-liberals, need to be considered. The neoconservatives and the radicals are the opposite sides of the same coin — the conviction that the grand liberal compromise will not work. The New Liberals think that the compromise can be resurrected, if in a somewhat different form; both radicals and neoconservatives are doubtful. Common to both groups is a belief that the world is involved in a struggle in which one side or the other must triumph. The neoconservatives believe they must defend Western civilization from Third World bar-

barians and Soviet commissars; the radicals believe that modern capitalism will engulf the planet in misery, war, and pollution.

Neoconservatism we can treat briefly. The fifteen-year decline in American power brought many former liberals to reflect on the causes and consequences of that decline. The myths of liberal illusions seemed to dissipate like fog on a winter morning; the golden haze vanished and they looked out over a bleak, Siberian landscape. Without further ado they signed on with the forces of freedom and did their best to make their peace with the fundamentalist Baptists, *arriviste* Sun Belters, and anti-Establishment populists who had held the true faith all along.

Calling themselves Scoop Jackson Democrats (after Senator Henry Jackson) and retaining some of their ties with the conservative wing of the labor movement, they organized themselves into groups with names like the Committee for the Free World and, in the midst of massive media coverage, were capable of asking why "no one" in America was talking about Pol Pot's genocide in Cambodia, or wondering why the American press ignored the plight of Soviet Jews. They claimed that opposition to Israel's interest as defined by the Israeli government was anti-Zionism and equated anti-Zionism with anti-Semitism.

For them the world had changed little since the 1930s. The Soviet Union was still the land of Stalinist terror. Anyone who disagreed was as blind or as duplicitous as the visitors of fifty years ago in the USSR. The clock of world diplomacy had stopped in September 1938; any compromise with an enemy was appeasement, and any appeasement was a prelude to enemy aggression.

The neoconservatives were blessed with articulate leaders, and they found a ready reception among the assorted funding sources that were looking for conservative intellectuals to support in the late 1970s and early 1980s. Yet for all their education and experience, the neoconservatives have not made a major contribution to American thought or politics. They have not made the late Scoop Jackson a figure of heroic intellectual or political stature; they have not suggested a genuinely new line of policy for the United States. They have not had new ideas or outlined a new perspective on history and politics; rather, they have simply changed their minds and joined Roy Cohn in the defense of Western moral values and Jerry Falwell in the defense of the European intellectual tradition.

The radical dissenters from the liberal consensus are on a more interesting trajectory. The Indochinese War and its aftermath had immense consequences for the American left. The national swing to the right since 1975 has obscured the important growth and change of the left — as opposed to the liberal — element in American life.

Although liberals and radicals are often found on the same side of an issue, and although radicals themselves support an enormous variety of beliefs, the two groups can be said to operate from basically opposed assumptions. The use of the terms *right* and *left* in politics can be misleading; they suggest a continuum in which liberalism fades into conservatism at one end and into radicalism at the other.

We can avoid some confusion by identifying liberalism not as a "left" movement but as part of the center in American politics. We then have three distinct movements — center, right, and left — each of which consists of various parts. The distinguishing mark of the American center is its belief that the existing order of society can be maintained, even improved, by the adroit management and compromising of political issues. Liberals believe that these adjustments should be in the direction of more "progressive" initiatives; conservatives believe that there should be few of these initiatives and that some of the ones already adopted should be curtailed. These liberals and conservatives agree that the present social order is workable and beneficial; their disagreements are over the tactics for preserving the beneficial qualities of the existing arrangements. It is a difference between liberal conservatism and conservative liberalism. All those in the liberal, centrist boat want to keep the boat on the river; they disagree on whether the best channel is along the river's right or left side.

The real left and right, by contrast, want to get out of the river completely. They disagree, though, about whether to land on the right or left bank. For most of the last fifty years there has been little sympathy in American politics for the extremists of either side. "Don't rock the boat" could have served as the motto for American politics. Only when the boat began to leak, so to speak, or, in Lyndon Johnson's metaphor, when the ship of state moved into troubled waters, did the extremes gain any support.

The American left is small, and it includes a large number of movements that have an extremely complex history. It comprises groups with a homespun radical philosophy and political parties organized on classic Marxist–Leninist lines. The impression it often creates among observers of hopeless factionalism and petty controversialism stems from this condition.

Small, complicated things are never grasped easily by large, general audiences, and the American left today is a mystery — a dull mystery — to most of those not involved in it. Even sympathetic and otherwise well-informed observers stumble over the left's reliance on Marxism, a subject not well understood in the United States. The consequences of the Cold War suppression of American Marxism are still with us today; only recently has a new generation of scholars begun to re-establish a significant Marxist presence in the universities. For the last thirty years Americans who wanted to learn about Marxism have taken their information from its opponents. This is a bad way to study any subject, especially one whose methods are as alien to contemporary academia as Marxism's. Few Americans have had the opportunity of understanding Marxism as it appears to Marxists, or indeed in any form but that of caricature, and the result is that even well-educated Americans find it nearly impossible to make sense of the theoretical and practical positions taken by communist countries or by American Marxists.

This is not a situation we can remedy here. Rather than give a misleadingly vague summary of the ideological evolution of the American left since the late 1960s, we will simply contrast the old New Left that emerged in opposition to the war in Vietnam with the new New Left (Neo–New Left? New Wave Left? Neocommunist?) that has emerged in opposition to U.S. policy in Central America. Our focus will be social and political, not ideological.

The New Left of the 1960s and 1970s was largely a campus-based movement. Its orientation was toward the "romantic" communists of its era — the Red Guard, the Red Brigades, and home-grown groups like the Black Panther Party. The New Left rejected the bureaucratic and cautious model of Soviet-brand communism; it preferred direct mass action and charismatic leadership. Because both the leaders and followers were very young, the New Left was a rapidly growing, easily energized, tactically innovative movement — but it was also vacillating, undisciplined, and without strong ties among its many parts. Left dogma blended uneasily with countercultural values.

Those who joined it were motivated not only by the war — and the draft; it was part of a larger generational rift that time still has not closed. The impact of hallucinogenic drugs on the young people of that era should not be underestimated; millions of students passed through the "doors of perception" into a type of experience for which their culture and its values had never prepared them.

The youth of the New Left may have been its determining feature. Because the liberal consensus in American society had been at its zenith in the years immediately preceding its decay, young people suddenly confronted with the war had few models and few sources of guidance. Politically inexperienced, still in their late adolescence, the members of the New Left were a generation confronting personal and political crises without adequate guidance from any adult quarter.

The young white radicals of that period were exposed to the new values of feminism, the mass availability of drugs, and the bloody consequences of what they believed to be an immoral war. Parental value judgments on race, politics, and culture were so totally discredited that adolescents were cut off from their own families and their parents' friends. It was not simply that young people felt traditional values to be old-fashioned or mistaken; they were so unsuited to the world of the young that they didn't apply.

How could an eighteen-year-old come home and say, "I took some acid and, well, I sort of understood, you know, for the first time that, uh, everything kind of, you know, fits together, you know, that we're all one only not really, because there's all this pollution and everything, and we have to, you know, stop it." The student barely understood himself; parents were aghast and horror-stricken, especially when the child went on to describe how he or she and a lover were dropping out of college and going to live off the land in a cabin in Vermont and raise goats.

The New Left's opposition to society tended to be both total and inexact. It was bound to oppose liberalism on a number of grounds. The cultural dissonance between the students and their liberal professors alone made it impossible for students to accept the liberal vision of a harmonious society marked by stability, reason, and compromise. That the society describing itself as enlightened and humane was at the same time dropping napalm on people and proposing to jail students who refused to participate in such activity added a terrible urgency to what might otherwise have remained a cultural battle, fought out in the arts.

This is precisely what happened as the war wound down. The youth culture remained vigorous and opposed to the Establishment. Young people were still conscious of living in a world that had undergone a complete transformation. Yet these changes were expressed in private life and in the cultural sphere in the years after the war. Even when the return of bad times compelled young people to think more carefully about earning a living, they did not revert to their parents' life styles. Students bound for M.B.A.s at elite universities took whatever drugs they found and slept with whomever they pleased. Gay corporate lawyers spent the day in pinstripe suits and their nights in black leather. Working-class young people similarly evinced an unprecedented disregard for traditional institutions and patterns of thought. Society eventually adjusted to the growing numbers of drug-ingesting, cohabiting young people. The generation gap closed as the older generation did what we all must — surrender to time and change. Though there was still a gap between contemporary society and its inherited values, society learned to live at its edge.

This amounted to a classic liberal solution to the problem of the New Left. The Indochinese War was an unmanageable problem and created unacceptable costs; liberal society liquidated the war. Once that was done, the remaining generational problems could be compromised. Drug laws remained on the books but were seldom invoked against private users. Dick and Jane stopped insulting their parents and denouncing the institutionalized hypocrisy of marriage; Mom and Dad learned to be nice to Dick and Jane's current "friends." Corporations stopped requiring Japanese-style social conformity among their employees; countercultural groups were able to create their own life spaces alongside the old, traditional world.

The growth of opposition to American involvement in Central America, and the strength of the anti-apartheid movement, has inspired some to hope and others to fear that another movement, similar to that of the Vietnam era will develop. Government spokesmen are heckled on college campuses; students are dragged from administration buildings by campus police; many a professorial veteran of the old New Left has observed the new protest with nostalgia and sympathy. But history never repeats itself exactly, and the emerging left already shows differences that distinguish it from the old movement.

To begin with, today's left is building on the experience of the Vietnam protests. We saw earlier that the memory of Vietnam gives the left an enormous advantage the second time around in building opposition. The massive deception and propaganda that accompanied the start of that war inoculated large sections of the population against unthinking credulity. Thousands of people acquired the organizational skills to mount demonstrations, teach-ins, and other forms of protest.

Much more important, the second time around the left starts with experienced leadership, a leadership that has formed a well-developed assessment of American involvement around the world. Vietnam stimulated the growth of a new generation of American Marxists, some active in grassroot and union politics, others in the universities. The self-defeating and naïve ideologies of the late 1960s will not easily reassert themselves against this experienced leadership. The left will seek to divert the energies of protest into less dramatic but more effective channels, and it will not be as prone to hysterical self-dramatization or outbursts of futile and nasty terrorism.

Opposition to the Indochinese War grew in a social vacuum. The prosperity of most Americans through much of that period made the war look like a horrible aberration in the operation of a basically beneficial system. The new opposition will link domestic economic problems with overseas military ones. There is a vast body of information on the ties of American corporations with Latin America, and left-oriented study groups are already pouring out plausible, well-researched studies to document U.S. involvement in torture and murder and to demonstrate the relation between Latin American debt, low Latin American wages, and the loss of jobs and fall in wages in this country.

If the United States is truly facing an era of stagnant or falling real wages combined with a succession of vicious little wars in the Third World, then Marxism is going to be a much more attractive ideology than it has been in the recent past. Millions of people rather than hundreds of thousands will begin to think in Marxist terms. This shift will not be limited to a youth culture or to minority groups; it will take place generally among those who have reason to fear for the future.

As time goes by, the dividing line between the Vietnam-era generation and the preceding one moves up. Vietnam veterans come largely from those born between 1945 and 1953; this cohort forms half of what is still known as the baby boom generation. Its members have experienced war or stagnation ever since childhood — and such experience inevitably colors their perception of the economic system under which they live. They have largely broken with such bearers of traditional values as the two parties and the churches; their allegiance to these institutions is conditional and tenuous even where it exists. These are people cut loose from their moorings, with a deep and abiding suspicion of the national Establishment and national policy. More ideological than their parents, they are accustomed to moving toward extremes. Raised in the hothouse patriotism of McCarthyism and the 1950s, they turned their backs utterly on traditional values during adolescence and early adulthood. When faced with the problems of adulthood and earning a living, they characteristically reacted by swinging back, hard, to a kind of doctrinaire conservatism or libertarianism. The link between their radicalism and their conservatism is their suspicion of the liberal Establishment.

All indications are that as time goes on this generation will suffer disappointment in their economic hopes. Not all the baby boomers can be yuppies; not all the yuppies can grow up to be CEOs. Unless real wages take a dramatic turn for the better, this generation will move through their late thirties and forties in a new mood of frustration and bitterness. External events, like another Vietnam-type conflict, can intensify their alienation from the liberal center and move them once again toward the left — not the uninformed, emotional left of their youth, but a more determined, more mature, and, from the standpoint of their opponents, a more dangerous principled opposition to the status quo.

In the meantime, the separate elements of a potentially powerful left movement are assembling just off the political stage. Jesse Jackson visited Cuba and Nicaragua during his 1984 campaign without alienating his core constituency. Since then he has attempted to broaden his base by reaching out to farmers and the newly unemployed. For the first time in fifty years white working-class youths are seriously angry. The troubadour of protest in the 1960s, Bob Dylan, appealed to a campus audience with lyrics that were literary and allusive — elusive, for many listeners. The 1980s troubadour, Bruce Springsteen, has a more direct approach and a more vital connection with his audience than Dylan ever had. He represents a much more serious and formidable social presence.

A consciously Marxist left alternative to liberalism is by no means on the verge of sweeping the nation. Even with "help" from war and recession, the left has a long way to go before it can present a serious alternative to the liberal vision — before it can be anything more than a movement of protest. Nevertheless, such a movement is a distinct possibility as America moves deeper into a period of uncertainty and crisis. This possibility will cast a shadow over American politics-as-usual as long as the basic economic and military situation remains locked into a slow decline.

THE FUTURE OF
THE RIGHT

L IBERALISM'S PROBLEMS are conservative opportunities, and never more so than when, as now, the liberal center is in disarray. The conservative movement that emerged to challenge liberal supremacy was, as we saw earlier, split between a populist and an elitist right on economic issues, and between tories and fundamentalists on social ones. The votes are among the social-issue populists and the pro–small business voters; the money is with the large agricultural, industrial, and financial interests who bankroll the right. Far from coinciding, the interests of these elements conflict all along the line. Their interests are similar only when they all confront a powerful liberal coalition; they splinter at the moment of triumph. For this reason the right is even less stable than the liberal coalition and even more dependent on the power of charismatic people — like Reagan — who can project an image that attracts mass support while they implement the policies of the bankrollers.

The right also depends on the widespread illusion that the free enterprise system is associated with and upholds traditional social and family values. The gap between illusion and reality here also must be covered by a charismatic personality, which can evoke traditional values even as they fade.

This right coalition is unstable and is a permanent minority in American life. Even in the best of times it governs only by deceiving the majority of its own constituents. Conservatives may argue that the liberal coalition also includes social elements with disparate goals, and if conservative corporatists and populists have their disagreements, so do their liberal counterparts. Yet there are differences.

Liberals as a group believe that the economic interests of the rich and poor in America are compatible. A refusal to believe in real, irreconcilable class conflict is close to the essence of liberalism. To believe that class struggle is the basis of social relations is to abandon the liberal center; liberals seeking compromise positions may be guilty of many things, but hypocrisy isn't one of them. Both corporate and populist liberal constituencies can and often do attempt to hornswoggle each other when it comes to political bargaining, but both parties agree that the political horsetrading takes place within recognized boundaries.

Conservative warfare is a more serious matter. The differences between the populist and corporate conservative movements surface more quickly than those among liberals, and they go deeper. Main Street and Wall Street have been at war through much of American history, and the partisans of both sides are easily reminded of their enmity. Modern American conservatives are more ideological than contemporary liberals; they are therefore quicker to spot heresy in their ranks and quicker to split over intellectual differences. Even more than the liberals, conservatives need charismatic leaders.

The conservative dilemma in the next period of American history will reflect this problem. Conservatives will believe that foreign policy conflicts are part of a life-and-death struggle that America must win at all costs. They will know — or think they know — what policies would enable the United States to win the coming battles, but they will not be able to follow these policies within the limits of constitutional government. We have already seen that the Constitution is a poor instrument for the conduct of foreign affairs, one that in practice is often ignored by American policymakers. The Constitution was not written to serve an imperial state with day-to-day responsibilities on every continent; the founders would have formed a different kind of government had they had such a state in mind.

The policies required to protect the American world position will call for some actions of which any nation could be proud, but as the empire declines they may involve the United States in a high proportion of shameful acts and link the country more closely to the destiny of unsavory regimes. Even the Carter administration understood that necessity places strict limits on any U.S. policy of human rights, yet the human rights policy may have helped weaken Anastasio Somoza Debayle and the shah of Iran.

The rationale of credibility advanced to defend American involvement in Indochina had a certain undeniable plausibility. Client governments around the world need to know — or to believe — that if they follow American instructions, they will be supported by American power. The sight of frantic South Vietnamese allies of the United States being pushed away at bayonet point from the evacuation helicopters had a profound effect on world politics. Every shah who dies in exile, every Somoza blown to bits, and every Baby Doc with his assets frozen transmits a message to the world's tyrants and thugs. Why should the government of Chile faithfully pay its interest on foreign debts, alienating its own people and warping its development, if the American ambassador will throw Pinochet to the wolves when his usefulness has ended? There is no reason on earth.

The human rights record of an ally may be good, bad, or indifferent, depending on the role of that country in the American Empire. A country whose role is to supply cheap labor and cheap raw materials will hate its role; many of its best citizens will oppose the government that wants to cooperate with the United States. Such a government will be driven to repression, and repression breeds opposition, creating the need for more oppression. In more fortunate provinces of the empire, the empire and therefore the local authorities have more to offer the populace. Living standards may rise; the economy may grow in such a way as to benefit more than a tiny elite. Such a government will need relatively little repression — yet which government has been the staunchest ally of the United States? Surely it is the less popular regime. The less popular regime is also the one that is more likely to face the kind of insurgent pressure that can force the United States to act. As a rule of thumb, the regimes with the worst human rights records are the ones that need the most foreign support.

The American people have neither the cynicism nor the martial will to back such a policy over the long haul. Yet the imperial interest requires it. This is the dilemma of the American right. This was the root cause of Watergate. It will produce immense difficulties in the future.

What we have called "extraconstitutional" government can range from the relatively benign to the tyrannic. No written document can cover every contingency. Thomas Jefferson violated his own understanding of the Constitution to make the Louisiana Purchase, but historians have not called him a dictator. The Constitution never contemplated a situation in which the unilateral, unchecked, and unbalanced decision of the chief executive could send ten thousand nuclear weapons to every quarter of the skies.

While current conditions make a mockery of the equality of the government's branches, there is no conceivable remedy for it. The nature of the case requires instant presidential decision in time of war, and with twenty minutes' warning time after an enemy launch, the president cannot even notify Congress, much less get a formal declaration of war.

Nuclear war is a clear case in which American defense policy requires a decisive extraconstitutional act under certain conditions. Conservatism can — and, in the end, must — argue that security in the Third World requires the same extraconstitutional freedom of action. Judged by international law, the CIA's history is a long chronicle of acts of war against other states. The abortive invasion of Cuba, the attempts to assassinate foreign leaders, and the round of bribery and espionage that makes up its quotidian tasks violate existing U.S. law, treaties, and the UN Charter. By Nuremberg standards, JFK should have been prosecuted on a charge of aggressive war. Yet these actions, illegal as they may have been, were in accordance with national policy and, it was thought, vital national interests. Certainly the only criticism that the Reagan administration might bring against the Bay of Pigs invasion would be its failure. The attempt to rescue the Iranian hostages was an act of war, or the phrase has no meaning — but it was undertaken with no declaration by Congress. Once again, it was condemned only because it failed.

Our point here is not to credit or blame the foreign policy of presidents going back to Jefferson, but to indicate that extraconstitutional government in foreign affairs has of necessity become standard operating procedure. Advocates of a hard line in contemporary international defense cannot be faulted if not all the measures they propose would bear the examination of a panel of Swedish secondary school civics teachers. We are constrained, however, to observe that the habitual reliance on such methods leaves both the government and individual officeholders dangerously exposed if public opinion turns against the policy in question.

The deceit required to carry out their policy in Indochina was beyond even the ample capacities of Nixon and Kissinger. The descent from secret plan to secret bombing to secret tapes was slippery and sure. Only success could have justified such activities — and the prospect of success would have made such secrecy unnecessary.

A hypothetical Nixon-Kissinger team of the future, confronted by an equally intractable war in a region of vital interest to the United States, would face many painful perplexities. The obvious American stake in the region — oil fields, the Panama Canal — might elicit initial support for the war. But anything less than a victory on the scale of the Grenada invasion would lead to a steady erosion in that support, both within and beyond the armed forces.

Assuming that a decisive military victory proved elusive — that the Nicaraguans or the Argentines or the Philippine communists or whoever else — resorted to prolonged and bloody guerrilla resistance, what then? Pressures to withdraw or to negotiate "from weakness" would mount; they would be felt throughout the political system. A public by turns uninformed, misinformed, and disinformed would weaken and waver. What then? Suspend civil liberties — officially and with fanfare or un-officially with goon squads? Lie about the progress of the war and the prospects for peace?

The national media might be persuaded to go soft on their coverage of national security and war information as long as they themselves were convinced that such action was in the national interest, but this would require the unanimous consent of a dozen major news organizations. If one broke ranks, the others would follow.

Doubts about the prospects of an uncertain war, and about the wisdom of fighting under such circumstances, have a way of spreading. They penetrate the citadels of power as well as the towers of academia. Elite opinion, or some of it, would turn against such a war; journalists would receive leaks and tips; publishers would be encouraged to tell what they know.

The hypothetical Bob Woodward and Carl Bernstein would sooner or later find their hypothetical Ben Bradlee; a hypothetical Daniel Ellsberg would find a hypothetical *Times, Post,* or *Globe* for his hypothetical papers. The Nixon of the future might not need to have his aides destroy incriminating papers; he might ask the head of the FBI to deep-six re-porters instead of documents. Once this happened, and bodies were flung into the Rubicon, there would be no going back to the old Republic.

There is more than one route to the Rubicon. The more circumstances force the government into lies and deceit, the more potent becomes the voice of dissent. Even if the American press could be cajoled or bludg-eoned into supporting the war with the necessary unanimity, the foreign press would supply ample information to arm American dissenters. No one is more isolated than a dissenter without institutional backing — unless the dissenter speaks for a popular cause that has developed its own networks and channels of information. Would campuses have to be closed, books censored, clergy arrested, others made to disappear? None of these steps is without political consequences, and the United States still lacks enough experience in the means of repression to carry them out smoothly and efficiently.

The onus of this kind of repression in all probability would fall on the right. A liberal government would have to declare war on its own con-stituency to carry out such a program; the right is more likely to include the hard-core supporters of unpopular wars and be more willing to tolerate certain excesses in order to win them.

It is beyond the scope of this book to discuss the possible forms and degrees of military or ultraright extraconstitutional government in the

United States. In general we can say that any open break with the forms of democratic government would signal a catastrophe of the first magnitude for the nation and for the right. Even after crossing the Rubicon, any sane figure would stay as close as the situation permitted to constitutional order and process.

The prognosis for such a regime would be gloomy indeed. Unable to win the war, the regime would labor under the double weight of having assaulted democracy in an unpopular cause. It would face immense difficulties administering the economy and would continually confront the choice between allowing the expression of dissent and resorting to additional repression. The end of such a course cannot be predicted, but the conclusion is unlikely to be favorable for the American Empire, for constitutional democracy, or for the regime itself.

This line of reasoning may strike the reader as being out of touch with reality, and we can only join the reader in hoping that events never take the course described here. Yet we must observe that, first, the U.S. government in the past has shown no reluctance to support military governments when it believed that U.S. interests benefited from their existence, even if such support meant direct American involvement in the subversion of existing democracies. Our question is not whether the United States is firmly committed to achieving its ends through democratic means only, but whether the strategies already in use around the world would, if needed, be used at home. Second, we must take note that events are conspiring to push the United States toward the slippery slope we have described. More, not fewer, potential Vietnams are springing up around the world.

It would be premature to accuse the Reagan administration of harboring any such intentions as we have described; the administration in all probability views the prospect of government by decree and martial law with the same horror we do — although perhaps for different reasons. Nevertheless, a substantial number of its policies have the effect of paving the way for massive, illegal repression. Unleashing the CIA, besides raising disturbing implications for foreign policy, causes concern on the home front as well. Restricting the Freedom of Information Act, rehabilitating the FBI, undertaking other, less-publicized programs, amount to a rearming of the state against all its enemies, including its peaceful political opponents. Neither the limited congressional oversight nor the views on civil liberties of key Reagan appointees indicate the administration's deep desire to avoid the abuses that characterized federal intelligence gathering in the past — abuses that did not stop short of murder. The eternal vigilance that is the price of liberty is not the intelligence gathering of the secret police, though the administration seems to have its doubts.

The sympathy of some sectors of the American right for embattled foreign oligarchies needs to be understood as a much more serious phenomenon than it is generally believed to be. Liberals, projecting their own sympathy for less than perfect movements of the left, assume that the right is "soft" on murderous dictatorships because it is blinded by anticommunist passion. In this view the right overlooks shortcomings out of an overriding concern with the common foe.

It is unfortunately accurate to say that some members of the American right support the tactics, as well as the stance, of the Latin American right. They tend to view death squads and states of siege as regrettable necessities — necessities that under some circumstances might be required inside the United States, too. To what lengths the right may be prepared to go to guarantee Viguerie's "rights" to be safe from communist subversion" cannot be predicted in advance. There is nothing in conservative theory that would stop its adherents from adopting Latin American–style police-state methods. That they have been spared the "necessity" of employing — or even thinking seriously about the need for — such draconian measures can be attributed to circumstance. And circumstance is changing.

The Outlook
for Democracy

The outlook for democracy in the United States is not good. Having outgrown its original Constitution, the government of the United States currently consists of an ad hoc collection of jerrybuilt institutions. Although some of them date back to the original Constitution, their powers and their relationships have changed substantially. For the most part, the state rests on the foundations laid between 1933 and 1952, when the Roosevelt and Truman eras saw the erection of the New Deal at home and the triumph of the empire beyond the borders. These foundations are crumbling visibly, and have been since 1968.

The Kennedy-Johnson years were the zenith of the liberal order created under Truman and Roosevelt. Liberal policies at home and abroad were implemented as fully as possible, but the results did not justify the expectations. Abroad, the doctrines of collective security and global free trade led to a disastrous war and to unexpected economic troubles; at home, the civil rights movement led to riots in hundreds of cities and a sullen white backlash. The institutions of the past weakened and threatened to dissolve in the face of the massive economic and social changes that accompanied the liberal era, and liberalism was unable to replace them.

The next three administrations (counting the Ford interregnum as part of the Nixon era) saw three different responses to the fact of liberal failure. Under Nixon, the United States attempted to recoup by diplomacy what had been lost on the battlefield while attempting to conserve the basic domestic achievements of the liberal state by retreating from its most advanced and exposed positions.

Carter strove to align the United States with the forces of change in the world, but to do so on the cheap. He was unable to find the political or the financial resources to accomplish this goal and, abandoning the attempt, anticipated many of the themes of the Reagan administration during his final year in office.

Reagan dreamed at first of restoring American primacy, but not with the tools of liberal statecraft. Attributing American decline to the effects of liberalism, he opened an attack on the liberal state at home and announced that he would chart an economic and foreign policy course with little regard for the nation's allies. This attempt to escape the realities of his era was gradually abandoned; the economic and geopolitical facts of life conspired to force Reagan back toward a Carter-like policy, coordinating economic decisions with the Western allies, and substituting rhetoric and spectacular but ultimately unimportant military gestures for the more vigorous program he and his followers had originally hoped for.

One by one, the United States has tried, then discarded, three distinct and coherent policies in the last generation. Despite the appearance of confusion and drift in American politics, the process has been relatively orderly, even logical in its way. At each point along the way, the United States opted for the most promising and least disruptive policy available. It swung more sharply toward the ideological right only after the successive failure of right-center and left-center experiments.

Each failed policy has left the United States in a more difficult position. Reagan's counteroffensive proved as useless as Nixon's scheming or Carter's compromises. As a society, the United States does not desire profound change. Many Americans want to tinker with the existing order; few want it dismantled. Reagan did well in 1980 only because the Democratic alternative was so clearly marked with failure; he did better in 1984 because people recognized that he had not subjected the country to the revolutionary enthusiasms of a David Stockman.

Nevertheless, the state of the world is unfavorable for moderate, centrist politics. Whatever the wishes of the American people, the nation's problems have no painless and simple solutions. Timid and unimaginative remedies for relieving or disguising the symptoms of national decline without addressing its causes will not succeed. Until and unless American political leaders become more creative and more courageous, we face an era when the policies of the American mainstream will continue to fail.

The slow drift toward ultra-right ideologies is one result of this situation. Pioneer ideology runs deep in the United States. The ghost of the frontier lives on in the American dream; it is not easy for Americans to realize that the world is both finite and round. We cannot perpetually reinvent ourselves and our society on new territory; we are stuck in the same world as five billion other people are — and not all of them like us very much.

The awareness that the years of American exceptionalism are over can be found at many levels in the United States today. Walker Percy expressed it in *Love in the Ruins,* his novel about life in an America where the center could no longer hold.

> Undoubtedly something is about to happen.
> Or is it that something has stopped happening?
> Is it that God has at last removed his blessing from the U.S.A. and what we feel now is just the clank of the old historical machinery, the sudden jerking ahead of the roller-coaster cars as the chain catches hold and carries us back into history with its ordinary catastrophes, carries us out and up toward the brink from that felicitous and privileged siding where even unbelievers admitted that if it was not God who blessed the U.S.A., then at least some great good luck had befallen us, and that now the blessing or the luck is over, the machinery clanks, the chain catches hold and the cars jerk forward?[1]

This sense of foreboding is not without foundation. Certainly if the founding fathers were to return to life and consider the state of the nation, they would not be optimistic about the future of republican institutions in the United States.

George Washington would see no reason to alter the warnings in his Farewell Address to the nation on leaving the presidency. His observations on foreign affairs were, for more than a century, considered a piece of wisdom on a par with the Constitution and the Declaration of Independence; the Farewell Address was read out on solemn occasions, and its principles were the axioms by which more than a few American statesmen guided their careers.

> The Nation, which indulges towards another an habitual hatred or an habitual fondness, is in some degree a slave to its animosity or to its affection, either of which is sufficient to lead it astray from its duty and its interest. . . .
> As avenues to foreign influences in innumerable ways, such attachments are particularly alarming to the truly enlightened and independent Patriot. How many opportunities do they afford to tamper with domestic factions, to practice the arts of seduction, to mislead public opinion, to influence or awe the public councils. . . .
> Against the insidious wiles of foreign influence, I conjure you to believe me, my fellow-citizens, the jealousy of a free people ought to be *constantly* awake; since history and experience prove that foreign influence is one of the most baneful foes of republican government. . . . Why, by interweaving our destiny with that of any part of Europe, entangle our peace and prosperity in the toils of European ambition, rivalship, interest, humor or caprice? Tis our true policy to steer clear of permanent alliances with any portion of the foreign world.[2]

Since the Second World War these sentiments have been derided and caricatured as isolationism. It is true that changes in the world over which we have no control make it impossible for us to remain indifferent to events at all points of the globe, but it does not follow that simply because we cannot take Washington's counsel we shall be protected from the consequences against which he warned.

When people recall Washington's warning not to engage in entangling alliances, they assume that his chief object was to keep the country out of war — a commendable goal, but only part of the first president's concern. Washington believed that foreign entanglements, even with democratic countries, even without the danger of war, were serious dangers to the Republic, and it is important to see why.

In the specific context of his remarks, Washington was warning against an ideological cast in foreign politics. It might seem that he was endorsing the kind of value-free *Realpolitik* that Nixon tried to practice, but nothing could be further from the truth. An ideological fondness for a foreign country (like the Jeffersonian admiration for republican France) or a fondness based on ethnic and sentimental attachment (like the closeness felt by the northern Federalists toward Britain) was to be feared because the agents of that foreign power, using its American admirers, could insinuate itself into the decision-making process of this country and ultimately corrupt the state.

Foreign countries are likely to consider money spent to purchase influence abroad a good investment. For its part, the United States does not pinch pennies with the CIA. British life in the seventeenth and eighteenth centuries gave many examples of the baneful influence of foreign money on public life; for many years the king of France sent a stipend to the king of Great Britain, much as the United States today might prime the pump of an important foreign ruler.

Washington believed that republics were particularly susceptible to foreign influences of this kind. This was not because aristocrats and monarchs were more virtuous than republicans, but because republican governments offered more opportunity to contending factions. A republic as the founding fathers understood it was a system of government in which no individuals were rich and powerful enough to oppress the rest. Kings and aristocrats might be rich enough to resist foreign bribes, but republican representatives not much richer than their constituents were more easily reached. The system of checks and balances also offered the agents of foreign power much latitude in shaping U.S. laws and policies.

Britain and France aided the Confederacy during the Civil War because they both expected to benefit from a divided America. This sort of activity, on a smaller scale, never ceases in peacetime, and it goes beyond the bounds of the political process.

Among a number of prominent examples of such tactics is one reported by Ronald Steel, the biographer of Walter Lippmann. Before the United States entered World War I, Lippmann's new magazine, *The New Republic,* took a strongly pro-Allied, pro-British position. As Steel writes,

> The British government, working through one of its publishing agents, offered to buy fifty thousand copies a week for the duration of the war if the *NR* continued to take a similar line.[3]

Steel reports that the editors of the magazine were shocked and indignantly turned down the proposal, but it passes belief that in the years since World War I every government has risen above the standards of Britain's conduct at that time, and that no journalist has sunk below the standards of Walter Lippmann.

Through most of modern history, the press has been notoriously corrupt. (Indeed, only in our own time, when the press has become more powerful than ever, do we hear on all sides that the press is honest.) The pay of journalists and editors is so low in comparison with the importance of their role in society that they have long been considered natural targets for bribery. As America became more involved in entangling alliances and foreign quarrels, it was only natural that foreign states and foreign factions would seek to further their interests by cultivating warm relations with underpaid reporters.

Perverting elected assemblies and corrupting the press strike at the life of republics. They block the essential processes of representation and informed public debate that give republican government its meaning. When constituents do not know the real reasons for their representatives' behavior, or are betrayed by their representatives, and when the press provides little or no meaningful information, then a republic rapidly degenerates.

Bribery of the press and politicians need not take crude forms. It does not even have to be illegal. Governments can establish high-level meetings where world statesmen and press figures are entertained lavishly, compensated handsomely, and required to do nothing in exchange. Public interest foundations can be set up, with generous salaries for directors and consultants, offering handsome grants and fellowships. Sovereign governments have many facilities for lavishing cash on those they wish to impress. Citizens can make "private" donations in cases where government sponsorship might look awkward. Journalistic careers can be advanced by a judicious policy of selected leaks. The intelligence services of dozens of countries are at work in this wicked world of ours, seeking to shape policy and opinion around the globe and, of course, above all in the United States.

There are many regimes, and even some countries, that depend absolutely on American support. It would be rash and foolish of these regimes to neglect any opportunity to help mold American opinion and American policy. We saw earlier that most of the real decisions in government are made far from public view — in sparsely attended subcommittee meetings, in executive deliberations, in closed meetings of powerful agencies. By its very nature, the American government lends itself well to bribery and influence peddling by foreign and by domestic lobbyists.

Foreign influence can be exerted in other ways, also perfectly legal. Thus, the chain of events that began with the admission of Iran's former shah to the United States almost led to war between the two countries. American officials were reluctant to let Pahlevi into the country, but Kissinger and David Rockefeller lobbied in his favor. Rockefeller was the chief operating officer of Chase Manhattan Bank, an institution that had enjoyed a long and profitable relationship with the shah. Kissinger had received a sizable Rockefeller retainer in the years before he joined the Nixon administration. There was nothing illegal in any of this, perhaps nothing improper — yet George Washington, hearing of such a state of affairs, might well have assumed that his worst fears for the Republic were being confirmed.

Besides having a horror of foreign affairs, the founders of the Republic were afraid of degeneracy, a concept more familiar in eighteenth-century political thought than in ours. Of course, as we opened the book by observing, the fish are always the last to learn that they are living in water.

If we think of degeneracy today, we generally mean sexual degeneracy, best defined as indulgence in sexual practices that do not much appeal to the speaker. The eighteenth century had something larger in mind — larger, more sweeping, and even more common.

It is a sorry truth that the great states of history have all died or decayed. Historians have traditionally been as interested in investigating the decay of great empires as in describing their rise, and in the eighteenth century, there was even a certain consensus as to why empires fell.

To the eighteenth-century observers, as to the ancients, it seemed that the simple life of farmers and hunters was the best school of virtue. Civilization sprang from the efforts of these hardy, primitive people, who in time developed the arts and the sciences and came to live in villages, towns, and at last cities. As their cities waxed large and their states waxed rich, the inhabitants lost the virtues that had made them great. The tendency of society to decline from a state of purity was what the eighteenth century understood by degeneracy, and it contrasts oddly with the modern love of progress.

Degeneration, like old age, could not be stopped, but wise legislation and prudent policy could slow its ravages. The ancients taught, and the moderns believed, that Sparta had preserved its freedom longer than its sister city-states because, in its faithfulness to the edicts of its lawgiver Lycurgus, it prohibited the importation of gold and silver and gave its young men a martial education.

Athens degenerated more quickly, not only because it allowed itself to be corrupted by riches, but because it diluted the blood of its original inhabitants with that of immigrants allowed to settle within its walls. The Greeks were not racists in the modern sense. They did not believe that the mixture of blood mongrelized their pure Aryan heritage. Instead, they held that immigrants, unaccustomed to the laws and the customs of their new country, weakened social cohesion and so undermined the institutions of their new home. Aristotle argued that the introduction of people not educated from childhood in the traditions of the state would loosen the hold of those traditions — the surest safeguard against degeneracy — on the state as a whole.

These arguments were once widely believed in the United States. They were invoked by those who opposed the mass immigration of Catholics and Jews in the nineteenth and early twentieth centuries. They were cited as justification for the 1920 immigration act that sought to freeze the ethnic composition of the American people by assigning immigration quotas in proportion to the number of American citizens who came from each foreign country. The belief that this immigration had destroyed the Protestant and Anglo-Saxon character of the North was expressed by William Faulkner in *Intruder in the Dust*:

> . . . the coastal spew of Europe which this country quarantined unrootable into the rootless ephemeral cities with factory and foundry and municipal paychecks as tight and close as any police could have done it. . . . Only a few of us know that from homogeneity comes anything of a people or for a people of durable and lasting value . . . most valuable of all a national character worth something in a crisis — that crisis we shall face some day when we meet an enemy with as many men as we have and as much material as we have and — who knows? — who can even brag and boast as we brag and boast.[4]

This view of mass immigration was also current in the time of the founding fathers; they would view our having forgotten it as a sign of how far our degeneracy has proceeded, rather than as a sign of our progress and enlightenment.

Rich people were another, and principal, cause of degeneracy in the state. Plato wished to keep such people out of his Republic; themselves corrupt, they corrupt others to do their bidding. The rich do not generally lead the virtuous, healthy lives of their thrifty, industrious ancestors. They pervert the state to serve their own economic interests (in the language of our times, they make campaign contributions), and they create a parasitic class of hangers-on. Unwilling to fight to defend the state, they use their wealth to defend themselves from its laws. Those who lack wealth but see it on every side are consumed with envy and consider life scarcely worth living unless it can be passed in enervating luxury.

In a state marked by great extremes of wealth, the dispossessed rabble would be stung to a frenzy of political activity. They would organize themselves into mass parties under the leadership of wealthy men who catered to the mob to advance their own ambitions. This was the course of Roman politics in the century before Christ; in contemporary American politics, with universal adult suffrage and billion-dollar election campaigns, the founding fathers would see the replay of the fall of the Roman Republic and would scan the political horizon anxiously for signs of a Catiline or a Caesar.

The rise and fall of the Roman Republic was much on the minds of the founding fathers. Successful foreign wars, climaxed by the conquest of Rome's great rival, Carthage, brought undreamed-of riches to the once-simple republic. Elections were openly bought and sold; corruption inserted itself into every cranny of the municipal government. Both rich and poor shook off the restraining bonds of custom, importing every luxury and dissipation — spiritual as well as sensual — from the conquered provinces. With the decline in civic virtue, the rich shook off their scruples and resorted to any means, however corrupt or ultimately however bloody, to seize and hold the offices of the state. The whole sordid process did not come to an end until a series of bloody civil wars, marked by attacks and reprisals, had laid waste the Roman world, exterminated the old Roman aristocracy, and replaced the old Roman Republic of laws and rights with an empire that worshiped its ruler as a god.

The founders feared, and attempted to prevent, the rise of a Catiline or a Caesar; they sought to pattern themselves after more virtuous figures from the earlier annals of Rome. In particular they admired Cincinnatus, the Roman farmer and general who, after defeating the enemies of his country, refused to take power in the city and returned to plow his ancestral acres. Revolutionary officers organized themselves into the Sons of Cincinnatus, and patriotic orators wishing to praise General Washington compared the careers of the American and the Roman.

If they looked at our era, the founding fathers would see signs that we have passed from the era of Cincinnatus to the era of Caesar. Our generals no longer retire to simple farms; they retire to executive positions with defense contractors. Our highest officials of state leave office to sell their knowledge and their connections to the highest bidder; former American secretaries of state and counselors to presidents sell themselves to private and even foreign interests. The founding fathers would tremble at the concentration of power in the Executive Branch, and they would shudder at the size of our growing urban underclass.

Much of what we consider politics-as-usual would strike them as the terminal practices of an empire in decay. Government by a class of professional politicians, who finance their careers with the contributions of those they are elected to regulate, would not impress the founders; they would doubt the strength of our institutions. And they would look with dismay on our huge standing army, our career bureaucracy, our secret police, and our network of spies. At their most optimistic they might echo the sentiments of Robinson Jeffers in the poem he wrote about the changes in the country during the twentieth century, "Shine, Perishing Republic."

> While this America settles in the mold of its
>   vulgarity, heavily thickening to empire,
> And protest, only a bubble in the molten mass,
>   pops and sighs out, and the mass hardens,
> I sadly smiling remember that the flower fades
>   to make fruit, the fruit rots to make earth.
> Out of the mother; and through the spring
>   exultances, ripeness and decadence; and home
>   to the mother.
>
> You making haste haste on decay: not blame-
>   worthy; life is good, be it stubbornly long
>   or suddenly
> A mortal splendor: meteors are not needed less
>   than mountains: shine, perishing republic.

> But for my children, I would have them keep
>   their distance from the thickening center;
>   corruption
> Never has been compulsory, when the cities lie
>   at the monster's feet there are left the
>   mountains. . . .[5]

This view has a certain horrible plausibility, and we cannot blithely ignore the manifold evidence that the political culture as well as the social fabric of the United States is far gone in decay. Still, the world has changed since the Battle of Actium. Not every change since Washington's term of office has been for the worse. We are not necessarily condemned to repeat the rake's progress of other societies.

Classical political theory never envisioned either the potential for mass education or the potential for mass affluence that has developed in modern times. The erosion of the middle classes on which American democracy originally rested — the small farmers and commercial proprietors plus the professional groups — has left the country divided essentially between a large group of wage earners and a small group of investors. According to both classical Marxist and classical Enlightenment political theory, this condition would normally lead to an end of liberal democracy. That it has not done so either here or in Western Europe seems the result of the high level of wages the system has afforded the majority of the workers and the social compromise that brought about the welfare state and the high-wage economy. If all employees do not have the same vested interests or attitudes of the old free proprietors, enough of them enjoy a high standard of living, and are firm in their belief that the system can provide good steady jobs for them and their children, to have a vested interest in the system.

Yet even if large numbers of people lose that vested interest as the system functions less effectively, the United States is not necessarily compelled to sink into Caesarism and slavery. An educated population, even if it is poor, is more than a rabble. The productive powers of the modern economy are such that, properly administered, they can guarantee a sufficiency — though not a limitless affluence — to the whole citizenry. This would be possible even without the exploitation of the inhabitants of the empire, people whose economic role resembles the slaves whose labor wiped out the independent Roman farmer and artisan.

POLITICAL AGENDA

Although the fate of Rome is not inevitably ours, that does not mean that the United States will have an easy adjustment. The strains brought on by the slow fall of the empire have already begun to expose the basic faults in society, and it is unreasonable to suppose that this process can continue without earthquakes. The politics of class, reintroduced by the New Right, are not going to fade. Union militancy, bread-and-butter fights in politics, and historic antagonisms will come to the fore — and not always in the ways and within the limits that the right has in mind. Fundamental questions about the survival of capitalism are likely to return, and not as exercises of ivory tower academics. When politics visibly revolve around class, then theories of politics that begin with class look plausible.

Rome preserved the façade of the republic long after it lost the substance. To some extent the same process has taken place in the United States. The document of 1789 does not fully describe the government of today. It may be that the coming years will simply widen the gap between the real and the official form of the American government, that a presidential Augustus will preserve a decent respect for the legislature even while he governs without it.

In any case, the United States has entered an era of high-stakes politics. The matters of ultimate concern that slept during the postwar era have awakened and returned to center stage. Elections are no longer contests between factions of the center; ideology came back to politics with the right, and a left is beginning to rise in response. In an era like this one, politics becomes the expression of apparently irreconcilable conflicts, and the process is more severely tested than usual.

If this period is to end with a renewed and invigorated democracy in the United States, both politicians and the leadership elite will have to raise their sights from politics-as-usual. In particular the question of popular power versus the power of wealth needs to be better understood. We have already observed that wealth in the late twentieth century has been largely emancipated from the ties that once bound it to local and regional interests. In a vast market for stocks, financial instruments, and commodity options, a market that is international in scale and almost perpetually active, money circles the earth at the speed of light, looking for the highest returns on a short-term basis. The market is dominated by large institutional investors subject to no constraints other than the need to report the highest possible earnings every quarter. It is not easy to see how the interests of this market can be reconciled with those of the American people — or of any people on the surface of the earth.

The decline of the empire will raise troubling questions. Since the Second World War, the advanced countries have been able to export much of their social conflict to less developed nations. As this system breaks down, as unemployment and low wages seep from the Third World into the First, social conflict will resume. It will be more bitter because it will involve a decline from standards once taken for granted. Promises have been broken, and someone will be expected to pay.

In order to resolve their social and political problems, the American people will need to show the revolutionary and political genius of the revolutionary and Federalist eras. Existing arrangements will have to be scrutinized critically, and new and constructive solutions will have to be found. This may seem a tall order for a nation that has fumbled and reeled for so long and shown such a capacity for resting in comfortable illusion, but the creativity and courage of the revolutionary period also emerged from an undistinguished culture.

The colonists of 1760 were as ill prepared for the coming storms as we are today. Independence from Great Britain, which became the linchpin of the struggle after 1776, was an unheard-of idea even ten years earlier. Although the colonists had a tradition of representative government, they had failed time and again to unite for collective action. There were no signs of the political genius that was so soon to emerge. Intellectually the North American colonies were a backwater, known more for theology than political science. The parents of Washington, Madison, Jefferson, Franklin, and Adams left no marks of any kind on the history of their country. The political genius of the colonists did not produce the turmoil of the revolutionary era; the revolutionary era called forth talents hitherto unsuspected among the colonists themselves.

These are reflections that can cheer us today as we contemplate the immense waves rolling toward the ship of state and the limited navigational skills of the officers and crew. There will be danger, and it will be aggravated by the follies, fantasies, panics, and blunders of a people accustomed only to the smoothest of seas. But the American people have resources and talents that have not yet been tapped. We shall have to look to these for help in the years to come, and I believe that, in the end, we shall not be disappointed.

PART SIX

Beyond
the Liberal Empire

FROM PERICLES TO CLEON

S O   F A R, this has not been a cheerful book; it has sounded the cry of
Chicken Little more often than the call of Chanticleer. Abroad, the
empire is falling, and at home democracy is endangered. We have
criticized flawed policies put forward by both political parties and argued
that neither party has so far advanced ideas capable of stabilizing either
the international or the domestic situation. Worse, the electorate has
demonstrated a preference for the politics of illusion at a time when the
country faces what could be its most critical period since the Civil War.
We have managed to paint this bleak picture without including the threat
of nuclear war, a menace that has vastly increased the penalties for mistakes in statecraft without adding proportionately to the store of human
wisdom.

Yet there are grounds for hope; the forces that are eroding the foundations of the American Empire are also creating an opportunity for a
postimperial world order that, in some respects, could be significantly
more prosperous and humane than the contemporary world. There is
also a real possibility of the revival of progressive and democratic politics
inside the United States. Although the magnitude of the problems facing
the country should not be minimized, there are serious reasons for optimism about the future of the American nation, if not of the empire.
We will now try to describe the challenge that the country must sur-
mount, and point out as clearly as we can the difficult but not impassable
road that lies ahead.

To begin such an enterprise we must return to the vision that guided
the statesmen who laid the foundations of the postwar American Empire.
Whenever American diplomats or politicians want to make a major proposal, they reach back to this time, suggesting that we set up a Marshall
Plan for Central America or for the Middle East or even for the American
ghettoes. We saw earlier that Carter used the Marshall Plan as an example
of a "disinterested" policy that served American interests best. Kissinger

and Nixon both looked back nostalgically to the Truman administration as a time when bipartisanship reigned (Nixon, as we saw, suffered from a convenient lapse of memory) and a strong and self-confident American Establishment conducted a firm, successful foreign policy.

From the perspective of the 1980s, the postwar era looks like an age of Pericles — a golden age when the foreign policy of the United States managed to meet its challenges with grace and style. American initiatives won the admiration of allies and the respect of adversaries with an approach that was at once flexible and firm. Since then, we seem to have progressed, or rather degenerated, into an age of Cleon, the Athenian leader who reminded his audience that

> to feel pity, to be carried away by the pleasure of hearing a clever argument, to listen to the claims of decency, are three things that are entirely against the interest of an imperial power.[1]

The United States no longer appears to stand for the rule of international law; in frustration it has partially withdrawn from the jurisdiction of the World Court as it openly undertakes activities that violate both the general law of nations and the specific treaty obligations of the United States. The American government sends warplanes to bomb a country with which we are at peace; the State Department expresses satisfaction about the outcome of an air raid whose casualties include the children of a foreign head of state; the United States drops all pretense of adhering to international law in its relations with Nicaragua.

Those who support the new orientation of the American government made no apologies for their taste in policy. We have seen how the prominent neoconservative writer Irving Kristol attacks the very idea of a community of nations living under the rule of law. Kristol and others believe we live in a jungle and must eat or be eaten. The liberal Hamlets with their pale countenances and their horrified sensibilities have lost their nerve; perhaps they have seen a ghost.

Yet if we go back to examine the beliefs of the men who constructed the framework of international relations that the present administration wishes to dismantle, we find that they did not think they were acting naïvely. The first thing we note about their approach was a balance between idealism and pragmatism that escapes simple categorization. Dean Acheson, who as Secretary of State George C. Marshall's deputy played an instrumental role in developing the Marshall Plan and who went on as President Truman's secretary of state to negotiate the NATO treaty, once wrote in a letter to his son that the important thing in thinking about international affairs is not to make moral judgments or apportion blame but to understand the nature of the forces which are at work as the foundation for thinking about what, if anything, can be done.[2]

He attacked those who called for a foreign policy based on morality, saying, "What they discuss seems more nearly moralism, the reduction of morals to maxims. These can easily be corrupted into slogans."[3]

Today's practitioners of what might be called *ersatz Realpolitik* believe that they are faithful followers of the maxims of the American statesmen who built the postwar order. They contrast the realism of Metternich and Talleyrand with the idealism of Wilson and argue that the United States must purge itself of Wilsonian illusions concerning the family of man, the rule of law, the rights of peoples to self-determination, and the remaining baggage of liberalism and enlightenment. They argue that the American leaders who created the postwar empire were practical statesmen who had no illusions about the morality of their actions, but that their Establishmentarian successors "lost their nerves" in Indochina, and ever since, paralyzed by the "Vietnam syndrome," have been too timid to formulate a policy for the real world.

This view confuses realism with nihilism, and its growing acceptance in the policymaking community is a sure sign that American foreign policy has passed from an age of Pericles to an age of Cleon. One is not surprised to find its advocates among those who bitterly opposed Truman's policies as cowardly and naïve in the late 1940s. It represents a flight from reality as extreme in its way as the stance of those who argue that if the United States were to act according to the principles of the Sermon on the Mount, the rest of the world would be inspired by its example to do likewise. The *nouveaux réalistes* of the 1980s have been unable to free themselves from the tendency to simplify and dogmatize that has always been the bane of American thinking about foreign affairs. While the hopeful liberals of this world comfort themselves by imagining past golden ages, when the United States was guided by altruism in its policies, the would-be realists embrace the diametrically opposed and equally misguided notion that — except as convenient window dressing to gull the public — liberal idealism has no part whatever in the formation of national policy. There is nothing more typically and depressingly American than a debate over foreign policy in which both sides assume that caricatured versions of Wilson and Machiavelli represent the only choices.

What both sides miss is the essence of statesmanship: the enlightened and rational self-interest that expresses itself in creative initiatives to advance one's own interest in harmony with those of other nations. Dean Acheson, perhaps the least Wilsonian member of the administration that created the Marshall Plan and NATO, was capable of writing prose that, except for its elegance, could have come from the pen of Richard Nixon. Dismissing the idea that international politics can or should reflect the values of a moral order, he observed that

> what we want of the world, and try to make of a sizeable part of it, is an environment in which what we call western civilization can exist and prosper. Do we really care whether this is moral? It is, to us, pretty essential. To do it we need enough force to protect our environment and coerce those who try to subvert it.[4]

Averell Harriman, discussing the war in Vietnam, went so far as to deny the possibility of applying moral standards of justice to international relations:

> I must say that I don't understand what a "just peace" means. Throughout history both sides have gone into war for a "just cause." But as we haven't got a referee, whose "justice" is going to be applied? That doesn't mean anything.[5]

These are hardly the sentiments of the Sunday school, but both men would have indignantly denied that their moral skepticism reduced them to the moral standards of a Cleon — or a Nixon. The same Harriman who scoffed at the idea of a just peace also quoted with approval from William Fulbright's famous observation that

> gradually but unmistakably America is showing signs of that arrogance of power which has afflicted, weakened, and in some cases destroyed great nations in the past. In so doing we are not living up to our capacity and promise as a civilized example for the world.

And, as Harriman went on to warn,

> small-minded people cloak themselves in American power and become arrogant. They talk about dropping bombs and forcing our will on others. These are things that appall me, and the influence in our political life of people with such attitudes has to be resisted.[6]

Enlightened self-interest, of course, is the bridge between the apparent cynicism and the apparent idealism of the men who established the post-war order. The connection between American self-interest and what some would call its moral responsibilities was made eloquently by Franklin Roosevelt in the series of speeches and declarations in which he expressed American war aims. The Four Freedoms, the Atlantic Charter, the declaration on Lend-Lease, and the various joint statements after meetings with other wartime leaders called for a postwar order in which the structural causes of war — poverty, tyranny, ignorance — would be removed or at least alleviated.

Even as the first flush of victory yielded to a sense that a long struggle with the former Soviet ally lay ahead, American policymakers continued to believe that the national interest was best advanced by constructive, creative statesmanship that sought to cure the causes, rather than to suppress the manifestations, of social unrest. In 1946 Ambassador George Kennan sent a long telegram from Moscow containing the themes that would mark the early years of what became the Cold War. This telegram, which played a critical role in the re-evaluation of U.S. policy toward the Soviet Union, was harsh and unsparing in its analysis of Soviet society and Stalin's aims in the aftermath of the war. Yet the telegram's predominant note was that of calm confidence, of a Periclean pride in the ability of the United States to overcome Stalin's challenge:

> Much depends on the health and vigor of our own society. World communism is like [a] malignant parasite which feeds only on diseased tissue. This is the point at which domestic and foreign policies meet. . . .
>
> We must formulate and put forward for other nations a much more positive and constructive picture of the sort of world we would like to see than we have put forward in the past. . . .
>
> Finally, we must have courage and self-confidence to cling to our own methods and conceptions of human society. After all, the greatest danger that can befall us in coping with this problem of Soviet communism is that we shall allow ourselves to become like those with whom we are coping.[7]

The proud confidence in American institutions and traditions that marked the Periclean age of the American Empire disappeared during the subsequent generation. Where Acheson, Harriman, Roosevelt, Marshall, and Kennan believed that Soviet communism was a dangerous, retrograde deviation from the course of world history, which would be undone by its own weaknesses and contradictions, the pessimistic oracles of the age of Cleon believed that the future of the United States hung by a thread. Writes Nixon:

> In the 1980's America for the first time in modern history will confront two cold realities. The first of these is that if war were to come, we might lose. The second is that we might be defeated without war.[8]

Nixon not only fears the military strength of the Soviet Union; he feels that the political organization of a Marxist-Leninist party gives it a decided advantage in any period of political turmoil:

> The professional revolutionaries move like hot knives through butter through societies that have come untracked. . . .
> Looking back, we must ask ourselves: What would have happened if the Soviet Union had been on the scene during the American Revolution?[9]

This comes close to conceding that Lenin understood the dynamics of revolution and colonialism better than Jefferson did; it also suggests a shocking ignorance of how Soviet theory views "wars of national liberation," like the American Revolution, in which a strong national bourgeoisie has a firm upper hand. A strong aversion to Soviet-style communism is one thing; a feverish combination of ignorance and fear is another. The first can give rise to creative, constructive policies; the second results in a blind, unthinking opposition that as often as not leads to disaster.

A generation ago Acheson and Keynes confessed that they found Marx too dull to read,[10] and in the 1980s Nixon wonders whether Marxism would have defeated Federalism in revolutionary America, Irving Kristol sees little evidence that the Leninists are wrong to believe that they shall inherit the earth, and Kevin Phillips, the Republican analyst, confesses that to analyze American society he finds himself driven to "neo-Marxian" categories. Liberals do not seem to be the only American intellectuals suffering from a certain weakness of nerves in the face of the challenge of Marxism.

The sad truth is that few liberals or conservatives today believe in the possibility of constructive statesmanship. Underneath the hoopla and the flag waving there is a bleak despair about the prospects for the American people and the peoples of the empire. Diplomats, politicians, and financial officials find their energy consumed by efforts to halt, or at least to slow, the erosion of the basic institutions of the American order. From international banking to farming to steel, the possibility of catastrophe hangs over the economy; the budget deficit casts its shadow over social programs that most Americans consider essential to their well-being; the crisis in the world economy threatens to turn into a political crisis of the gravest kind for an empire beleaguered and retreating on every continent.

This pessimism, almost universal, about the prospects for the United States is the real cause of the changing orientation of American foreign policy. The architects of empire believed that the future was theirs; history itself was cooperating in their labors. They felt free to erect a structure of international law and to press for economic cooperation because they believed that the interests of the United States and those of the rest of the world were fundamentally similar. What was good for the country was good for the world, and vice versa.

Both liberals and conservatives today seem to believe that the interests of the United States cannot be reconciled with those of the rest of the world — whether it is with our trade partners and rivals in the first tier of the empire or with the poorer countries lower down on the scale. In both national and international politics, many feel, we are condemned to play what the economist Lester Thurow has called a zero-sum game, in which the gains of one party must come at the expense of the others. Those who argue for a new era of growth — notably the supply siders and the "populist" wing of the New Right — support economic theories that are at best untested, and advance unrealistic, even naïve, ideas about markets, ideas that do not enhance the credibility of their approach.

The idea of the general interest, which was absolutely critical to the thinking of the empire's architects, has largely disappeared from contemporary discourse, displaced by various theories of irreducible, inevitable conflict. As in the 1930s, the last period of profound economic crisis, enemies on the left and the right denounce the "decadent" spirit of liberal democracy. For those who remain committed to democracy and to the politics of compromise that it implies, the recovery of a theory of the general interest is the primary task. Can the economic and political interests of the American people be reconciled with those of the other peoples of the world? Are we primarily competitors in an unending struggle for a place in the sun, or are we potential co-creators of a just and prosperous world? Much depends on the answers we give to these questions: the future of American democracy, the peace of the hemisphere, perhaps the fate of the earth itself.

23

THE DOG
THAT DID NOT BARK

THE AMERICAN POLITICAL LEADERSHIP of the Truman era believed that it understood the forces that shaped world history, and,
further, that history held no insurmountable challenges for the
United States. The Soviets were a dangerous and determined rival, but
the weaknesses of the Soviet system were so marked that, over the long
haul, the USSR could not compete with the United States for world
leadership.

Once the recovery of Western Europe and its progress toward economic integration appeared irreversible, the only force capable of de-
flecting the United States from its destined course was the blind obduracy
of a few ignorant congressional bigots, felt the diplomats. The red-
hunting Republicans — of whom Joseph McCarthy was the most egregious, but far from the only example — sought to force the United States
into a policy that was at once reckless and timid. The policy was reckless
because it favored bellicose statements and provocative acts at places and
times that risked war without offering hope of compensating advantage; the policy was timid because it lacked confidence in the strong strategic, economic, and moral — not moralistic — position of the United
States.

We have seen that American political leadership on both sides of the
aisle has lost its confidence since the Truman administration — and this
in the face of the remarkable success of the Truman-Marshall-Acheson
efforts to stabilize the West and to contain Stalin's ambitions. The serene,
even Olympian confidence with which the patricians of the foreign policy
Establishment viewed the world has disappeared, and no new basis for
constructive and imaginative American leadership has taken its place.

Conservatives argue that the cause of this erosion in national morale
is a wasting spiritual disease that makes the Western intellectual elites
too critical and moralistic in their evaluations of the United States and

too indulgent in their assessments of its enemies. In their view, we have too many liberal Hamlets. Liberals, the few that remain, have not been able to formulate a convincing reply to this charge, and as the Democratic Party edges toward the right, there is a certain silent tendency to concede that the conservatives have a point. They don't.

In reality, the statesmen of the Truman era, many of them veterans of the New Deal, had solid grounds for believing that the Roosevelt-Truman reforms in national and international relations were sufficient to clear up the remaining problems of liberal capitalism. They believed that they had made the world safe for industrial democracy, and that what remained was for societies based on it to continue their peaceful evolution toward the Swedish style of government, which safeguarded the democratic and the economic rights of the citizens. As Harriman wrote:

> Our social and economic system is working perhaps toward Swedish so-cialist concepts but not toward Soviet Communism. The government in Sweden has overcome poverty, achieved decent housing and medical ser-vices for all, but Sweden has in no way compromised the principle of representative government and concern for civil liberties.[1]

These liberal Democrats believed that they had already solved the first great problem of the twentieth century — that of social democracy — and, flushed with this achievement, they felt that they could, using es-sentially similar methods, solve the second great problem of the cen-tury — that of the development of the Third World. A generation of rapid change in the world has cast doubts on both of these beliefs, but as we examine the disappointments that have undermined the liberal promise, we shall find clues that point toward progressive initiatives for our time.

THE GREAT COMPROMISE

In the advanced countries, the twentieth century so far has been the century of the political and economic system known variously as the welfare state, social democracy, or liberal capitalism. Through all the terrible vicissitudes of a tumultuous century, this social system has be-come more deeply rooted and more widespread after every challenge. Countries as separated by geography and history as Sweden and Spain have embraced it; countries like Germany and Italy, which once affected to despise it, now warmly defend it. Its triumph has been so complete and, in the advanced noncommunist countries, so universal that we no longer consider its progress a remarkable event.

Yet the spread of this social system is that rarest of all historical phenomena, the unexpected piece of great good luck. A hundred years ago the industrial world was racked by torment. Conditions for factory workers were unimaginable by today's standards in the advanced countries: child labor, unsafe working conditions, low wages, long hours. For those injured in industrial accidents, too old to work, or laid off in one of the recurring panics and crashes of this "golden age of free market economics," there were only the meager and insufficient resources of private charity.

Industrialization unleashed a torrent of new social forces. The scale of its undertakings dwarfed all previous experience, and the suffering it brought in its wake overwhelmed the few provisions that the paternalism of the feudal past had made for the protection of the poor. The old laws and institutions that protected the wages and the rights of the poor were swept aside by the apostles of free competition and laissez-faire. Factory workers were considered expendable, and outside a few idealistic circles little thought was given to their needs or aspirations. Economists like Malthus wrote treatises to prove that the world's problem was that there were too many poor people, and that any attempt to improve their conditions of life would only encourage them to even greater excesses of breeding.

To any suggestion that child labor should be restricted, work houses upgraded, that workers should receive a living wage guaranteed by law, that the length of the work week should be regulated, or that factories and mines should be made safer places, the owners and the economists replied that meddling with free competition would destroy the economy. The costs of such changes would be prohibitive, and as a result many enterprises would be forced out of business. It was not likely, they asserted, that the condition of the working class would improve if well-meaning but muddle-headed humanitarians forced all the factories to close.

The "dismal science," as economics was commonly called in the days when free market theory reigned in all its moral grandeur, went on to observe that any reforms that forced manufacturers to raise wages would raise the costs of finished products. Thus, anything that the working class gained by earning higher wages would be lost as they paid the higher prices. Worse yet, the high costs that all this regulation would bring in its wake would stifle new investment and technological progress.

The manufacturers and the economists were able to demonstrate these conclusions with figures to their own entire satisfaction. Free market theory in its classical form was a Panglossian argument that whatever the present state of the people or the economy, however miserable, any purposeful measure to alleviate suffering would only make matters worse.

This bleak philosophy, supported by social Darwinism, held the hard-headed, practical men of affairs in its thrall during the nineteenth century, and no competing ideas were permitted to disturb the repose of academic departments of economics — but somehow the working class was not satisfied by the arguments that seemed so compelling in the classroom. It seemed to the millions of miserable toilers in the polluted and over-crowded cities that another sort of economic theory must be possible, one that would lead to lasting benefits for someone other than the owners of stocks and bonds.

At first the workers were too small a portion of society to make their views felt outside their immediate neighborhoods, but the success of industrialization increased the ranks of the working class without re-moving the causes of its anger. Eventually, it grew into a large and powerful mass able to make its weight felt by agitation and strikes. This new element in society developed its own culture, traditions, ideologies, and political parties, and by the twentieth century it was impossible for any country where industrialization was well established to exclude the new "proletarians" from public life.

The early socialists — Marx among them — hoped that the working class would replace the existing ruling classes and make a clean sweep of the institutions and property relations of the old societies of Europe and America. There were some close calls, but the twentieth century was emphatically the era when the socialist revolution did not happen — at least in the leading industrial countries.

Instead, the workers' movements took off in a direction that had not been fully anticipated by either their friends or their foes in the early years. Although the process began much earlier, it reached a milestone in 1914, when the socialists of France and Germany decided to follow their respective flags into the trenches. "I see no parties," said the jubilant kaiser, "only Germans."

Lenin and the internationalists thundered denunciations of these "op-portunists" and "renegades," but with disappointing results. The work-ing class did not turn on its opportunist and collaborationist leaders. To the socialist leaders of the West, and to most of their followers, there seemed more to be gained from a national alliance among different social classes than from an international, socialist, working-class movement.

The new reformist tendency in the working-class movement was welcomed by compromise-minded representatives of the factory owners and the other ruling classes. Whatever the dusty old economic textbooks said, it seemed more sensible to reform-minded capitalists to conciliate the working class with moderate measures than to drive it into open rebellion. Strikes are expensive, and civil wars are worse. From the point of view of both capital and labor, there was much to be said for social compromise in the advanced countries.

The keystone in the arch of the new, cooperative order was provided by the changing economic dynamics of the Western societies. To survive and compete, capitalist firms must grow; this much was always understood by capitalists — and those who failed to grasp the point were weeded out by a Darwinian competition. If enterprises are to grow, they must increase the scale of their production. Since production is useless without a market, the market must grow if production expands. There are many ways one can expand markets; the most efficient is to increase the buying power of the mass of the population. By the twentieth century this meant above all the buying power of the industrial working class. Keynes raised this intuition to the level of science, and with the practical discovery that Social Security and other social welfare programs helped to stabilize the economy and prevent a recurrence of the devastating crashes of earlier generations, the great compromise of social democracy and welfare capitalism won a lasting place as the centerpiece of Western politics.

The triumph of social democracy occurred within a brief period of time, even measured by the yardstick of a single human life. The political leaders of the Roosevelt-Truman era were born in a time of bitter social conflict. Many of them grew up in an atmosphere of privileged gloom among a ruling class that believed itself precariously seated on a smoldering volcano. In both Britain and America they had had to cope with violent social unrest amid scenes of economic collapse; they had witnessed the catastrophic revolutions of Russia and Germany, and they had successfully met some of the most dramatic challenges — military, political, and economic — that had been encountered by any generation of which history makes mention. Yet through it all, their dominant experience was not of chaos and war; they experienced life as a series of challenges met, of difficulties surmounted, and of compromises successfully reached to the benefit of all parties.

Theirs was a generation that saw impossible things: the two world wars, the Bolshevik and Nazi revolutions, radio, automobiles, airplanes, movies, the bomb. Yet the most remarkable thing about that time was the dog that did not bark — the class struggle that did not break out, the social peace that was strengthened, not overthrown, by the most revolutionary period in the history of mankind.

A modern industrial economy, under whatever type of political regime, requires the coordination of the activities of millions of people in thousands of enterprises. No police force, however intrusive, can adequately compel the peaceful, moment-by-moment cooperation without which the whole complex and vast structure of industry would crumble away. Modern society rests on the voluntary cooperation of its members — on the consent of the governed — in a much more immediate way than did pre-industrial regimes. Stalin, Hitler, and Roosevelt, who embodied the principal political alternatives known to the twentieth century, each met the challenge of obtaining the consent of the governed in a different way, but each was preoccupied with the need for his regime to establish and maintain an intimate link with even the humblest of the nation's citizens. The collectivized peasants may have been terrorized, browbeaten, and mystified into a reverence for Stalin and the Party, the Germans gulled into an atavistic dream of racial superiority and national community, but they felt themselves to be part of a national entity. In peace they worked to build it up, and in war they died by the millions for it.

Roosevelt accomplished the same feat of binding his country together for unprecedented efforts in peace and war, and he did it with a constructive program of social compromise and a series of radio talks. He showed that it was possible for a modern mass state to function effectively without the wasteful and disruptive means of repression employed by Hitler and Stalin. His associates can be pardoned if they supposed that the events of the 1930s and 1940s demonstrated the superiority of liberal capitalism not only in a moral and aesthetic sense, but in a practical sense as well. Liberal capitalism or social democracy was not only a preferable system of government; it was more efficient, capable of bringing about greater cooperative social action than its rivals, and destined to win the Darwinian competition for the leadership of the world. Fascism and communism would join feudalism, slavery, and absolute monarchy in the Chamber of Horrors in the Museum of World History while liberal capitalism sailed serenely on its destined voyage toward harmony and affluence achieved by a process of peaceful change.

That view seemed amply justified by postwar developments. The politics of liberal compromise moved beyond the narrow national limits of the prewar era. The United States abandoned its age-old isolationism, and the European democracies overcame their even more venerable mutual antagonisms. The German lion lay down with the French lamb. In

Japan the institutions of Western democracy and social compromise rapidly took hold, and the greatest threat to the security of the democratic alliances seemed, in a refreshing change, to come from German and Japanese pacifism.

There were, of course, thorns in this bed of roses. There was the Soviet Union, and there was the problem of what became the Third World, much of which was emerging from colonial status in the old European empires. But to a generation that had seen the triumph of nonviolent resistance in India, the reconciliation of Germany and France, and the abolition of racial segregation in the American South, the slow, relatively peaceful resolution of the world's remaining problems did not seem a hopeless aspiration.

CONVERGENCE AND CONTAINMENT

The Soviet Union of Stalin was a conspicuous exception to the worldwide shift toward the politics of moderation and compromise. Surly and suspicious, the Soviets proclaimed their undying devotion to the politics of class struggle, expressed a belief in the inevitability of war, and used every resource at their command to thwart American efforts to rebuild a shattered world in harmony with the principles of social compromise.

During the war Roosevelt had frequently expressed the hope that he and Stalin could come to an understanding that would permit continued cooperation after the war, but by the time of his death even Roosevelt was coming to the reluctant conclusion that Stalin could not be inveigled into a permanent partnership. Roosevelt, the most successful practitioner of the politics of compromise and accommodation in American history, had been the most optimistic of the leading foreign policy figures in the government, and after his death official American opinion rapidly crystallized into what became the received Establishment opinion about the Soviet Union and how to deal with it. While sharp divergences divided cautious figures like Acheson from the liberal wing of the Establishment, the general view of the Soviet Union covered a wide area of agreement.

The views of Averell Harriman, Roosevelt's wartime ambassador to the USSR, more or less summarize this consensus. First and fundamentally, the Soviet state was an unfortunate, regressive phenomenon. Harriman first visited Soviet Russia in 1922, when he operated a mining concession under the New Economic Policy, and he formed a basic opinion of that country that would not change for more than sixty years:

The Bolshevik Revolution was in fact a reactionary revolution and . . . it was not "the wave of the future." It denied the basic beliefs that we value so deeply — the rights and dignity of the individual, the idea that government should express the will of the people. . . . Nothing has happened since to alter my conviction that the Bolshevik Revolution, for all its manifest achievements, has been on balance a tragic step backward in human development.[2]

Nevertheless, Harriman rejected the crudest anti-Soviet view, almost as common now as then, that the system was so unworkable that it was threatened with imminent doom. Bad as it was, it was here to stay.

The third key point was that the Soviets were slowly changing, and if Soviet society was not becoming precisely democratic in the Western sense, it was "normalizing" itself after the death of Stalin.

Finally, this process was expected to continue until the Soviet Union — after a wait of decades or even generations — became something like the democratic and socialist society that Harriman believed the United States was becoming.

The Soviet Union, then, was a backward and repressive but stable society that was slowly evolving in the same general direction as the United States. This view led to the conclusion that, while it was necessary to contain the Soviet Union, there was no point in attempting to overthrow it or even in hoping for it to destroy itself. Although negotiations with the Soviet Union could be difficult, and though it was inappropriate to look for "good will" from a regime that considered our relationship one of irreducible antagonism, businesslike discussions could be held concerning areas of mutual interest.

The theory of convergence over the long term was an essential element in the argument for containment, the real basis of United States policy toward the Soviet Union ever since the Truman administration. Since revolutionary Bolshevism was not the "wave of the future," it was merely necessary to hold it in check while the processes of modernization and democratization swept through the rest of the world. Time was on our side. As both the USSR and the United States converged toward Swedish-style social democracy, the developing countries too would move in this direction. All roads led to Stockholm, although not all travelers moved at the same speed, and not all routes were equally direct. The central foreign policy challenge of the United States in this view was to maintain the stability of the noncommunist world while convergence gradually reduced the danger posed by the retrograde hostility of the Soviet Union and lessened the vulnerability of the developing world to Soviet subversion.

Implicit in convergence theory — at least in the form in which it was held by American policymakers — was the belief that the evolution of the West and the developing world into more complete social democracy would be smooth. There would be no repetitions of the Depression or of World War II. Under the enlightened leadership of the United States, the advanced Western countries would peacefully and steadily evolve as their economies grew, and the developing world would move along in their wake. Here and there a developing country might succumb to the blandishments, or the arms, of the communists, but such victories would be too few to change to any measurable degree the world balance of power. They would also be the result of Western mismanagement rather than of communist effectiveness.

Theories of convergence and containment depend on theories of reliable economic management. In the Periclean period of the American Empire, it was assumed that Keynesian economics provided a workable method for avoiding new economic crises. If it began to look as if the Western economies were still vulnerable to catastrophic economic collapses or hyperinflations, the policy of containment would lose much of its plausibility.

The generation of statesmen to which Harriman belonged understood, none better, that the political stability of the Western world depended on its economic prosperity. As Dean Acheson said in the opening salvo of the Truman administration's campaign for what became the Marshall Plan, "not only do human beings and nations exist in narrow economic margins, but also human dignity, human freedom, and democratic institutions."[3] Having witnessed the chaos in Europe following the two world wars, and seen at first hand the effects of the Depression on the United States, the men who were present at the creation of the postwar order knew all too well that prosperity was the sine qua non of the Great Compromise and the democratic development that went with it. "Communism breeds in the cesspools of capitalists," said Stalin to Harriman, and there were few ranking officials in 1946 who believed that communism could be blocked in Western Europe without economic recovery.

The economic stagnation of the 1980s, the mounting signs of crisis, and the continuing fall in living standards in so much of the capitalist world thus raise questions of the most alarming kind about the whole structure of convergence and containment. The road to Stockholm may be longer and more adventuresome than anyone supposed.

The founders of the postwar order faced a dangerous situation in Europe, but they had, or felt they had, the analytical and policy tools to overcome the problems confronting them. The difficulties of their successors have not yet become as imposing, but the lack of a conceptual framework for analyzing, much less overcoming, the contemporary crisis makes it potentially much more disturbing.

THE DANGERS OF DEVELOPMENT

There was always a fear that the developing world might upset the cherished plans of the West. The developing world was on the threshold of industrialization at the end of the Second World War, and as the Western nations had learned, industrialization is the most disruptive of all events in the life of a people. The original Bolshevik Revolution took place in the most primitive of the European states, one that occupied in many respects a position halfway between the advanced and the developing countries. Relations between the Western world and what is now the Third World had been poor for centuries; national resentment made Asia, Africa, and Latin America less sympathetic to the West and more receptive to the Soviets. Indigenous political leadership in many countries was weak and untested, and the distortions resulting from colonial rule meant that much of the Third World was without the economic or the human resources that would smooth the transition to independence.

In spite of these problems — to some extent because of them — the postwar leadership of the United States was determined to apply the principles of compromise and cooperation in the Third World that guided its relations with the Western countries, Japan, and with its own people. This was no more a symptom of disinterested benevolence than the Marshall Plan; it was evident that the poverty and underdevelopment of so much of the world posed a long-term threat to the advanced countries in much the same way that the misery of the working classes had threatened the stability of nineteenth-century capitalism.

The Americans elected to address these issues in three ways: the United States would further the breakup of the European empires, it would intervene directly — sometimes covertly — to create or to stabilize pro-Western regimes in the Third World, and it would support the economic development of the former colonies and of Latin America.

Like so much of American policy in the imperial age, Third World policy involved a combination of inspiring and sordid acts, and it was executed with varying degrees of competence and sensitivity. Our concern here is not that of a moral CPA trying to determine the moral "net worth" of American policy; we are after bigger game. An economic and political crisis in the developing world widened until it nearly engulfed the economies of the first-tier countries. By the 1980s it threatened to overturn the whole elaborate first-tier structure of social compromise so carefully created over the last hundred years. This crisis grew out of the development process itself, and it was accentuated by the success of a development strategy — export-led growth — that was urged on the developing world by the United States, among others.

To understand the dangers that flow from the process of development itself we can do no better than to look at South Africa, a country that, as we have already observed, contains within its relatively narrow boundaries the social variety of the larger empire — from white South Africa, so similar to the largely white countries at the pinnacle of the larger system, to the miserable, underdeveloped, and only nominally independent "homelands" festering in squalid poverty at the system's periphery.

Nixon and other conservative apologists, seeking to comfort Americans made nervous by the manifest horrors of the South African regime and by the growing resistance of the majority, have observed cheerfully that unjust systems can last for centuries. For most of the world's history tiny ruling elites have ridden comfortably if not always complacently on the backs of oppressed majorities. The conservatives attribute the restless stirrings among American liberals to the Western disease of self-doubt and finicky conscience and urge liberals to stifle their scruples and side with the Boers.

There was a time in South African history when the majority *was* very nearly helpless. Oppressed more thoroughly by the isolation and poverty of rural life than by any police force, and divided by language and tradition into rival tribes, the majority population boasted only a handful of political and intellectual leaders with a national consciousness, and both the leadership and the majority as a whole were incapable of a sustained fight against the powerful, organized minority.

But the system of privilege for the whites rested on the labor of blacks, and the economic needs of the whites pulled the blacks out of traditional life in the countryside. The mines and the factories, the retail stores, the restaurants, the post offices, and the banks all drew black labor into the townships, where a post-tribal society began, of necessity, to emerge. The townships, wretched as they were, necessarily created institutions to meet the needs of the urbanized blacks. White South Africa needed its black workers to be literate, which implied not only primary education for masses of laborers, but secondary and even university education for the teachers. The social and religious needs of the urban blacks could not be met without churches, newspapers, and civic associations; township life created niches for black entrepreneurs. The workplace, too, fostered relationships; the movement for black trade unions was as irresistible as the move for black churches, and all of these institutions served as the repositories of an emerging national awareness on the part of the majority and as bases that these newly self-aware people used in their struggle for their rights.

First thousands, then tens of thousands of educated blacks were literally conjured up by the unavoidable operation of the system of white privilege; even the concept of apartheid itself implied an educated elite group in each African tribal grouping. It was impossible that so many people could be educated, and so many institutions created by their labor, without the rise of an educated, experienced leadership determined to fight for majority rule.

The consequences of white privilege and black labor went farther than the training of a self-conscious black nationalist intelligentsia. They also created a national consciousness among the millions of ordinary working people who labored in the factories, mines, businesses, and homes of the white South Africans. The conservative social structures of tribal life began to dissolve under the stress of urban living; urban life created a melting pot in which millions of black South Africans began to exchange their tribal and regional identities for a national one. This black society — still struggling with its tribal heritage and still torn by divided allegiances — could not help being conscious of its own oppression and of its own growing strength.

The Americans who call for continued alliance or constructive engagement with the South African regime are correct in saying that injustice by itself has never doomed a social arrangement. What they fail to see is that white South Africa is doomed by the logic of its own development: it cannot live without the labor of the majority, and it cannot use that labor without continuing to strengthen a powerful antagonist. Its position visibly worsens from year to year; recently, from month to month. The hope of white South Africa rests on the tribalism of the majority and on a policy of divide and rule, but white South Africa's own economy is the force undermining tribalism and strengthening the base of a nationalist resistance. A classic revolutionary situation is taking shape at an indeterminate but accelerating pace in South Africa; the internal contradictions of the ruling regime are the secret ally and the prime source of strength for the revolutionary movement. The Boers have no one to blame but themselves; they were the ones who released the genie from the bottle and then refused to come to reasonable terms with it.

The racial composition of South African politics makes its social divisions unusually vivid, but we can see that development releases genies from their imprisonment all over the world and stirs long-dormant peoples from their slumber. The central political insight of both Marx and the reforming capitalists who attempted to come to terms with their industrial workers was this: a "proletarianized" industrial working class is a much more explosive and dynamic social force than the oppressed peasantry from which it usually springs.

Through most of history peasants have endured brutal oppression; only rarely have they been able to overthrow their oppressors. Wage workers in a modern industrial society have a much greater ability to deal with the conditions they dislike. As in South Africa, the conditions of their daily lives teach them to overcome the cultural and linguistic barriers of their past. The communal character of industrial work teaches the former peasants the value of cooperative action on a large scale, and the grievances they share about wages, hours, and working conditions encourage them to organize into trade unions. They soon learn that organization and solidarity are the keys to effective political and economic action, and unless their essential demands are met by their employers and the state, they are perfectly capable of moving from isolated industrial actions protesting particular grievances to sustained national political agitation.

Meanwhile the same forces of industrialization and development that created the working class now greatly increase society's vulnerability to economic disruption. Strikes and sabotage can wreak much more havoc in the delicate fabric of an advanced industrial economy than they can in a simple agricultural society.

The West faced an international problem similar to South Africa's domestic difficulty in the postwar generation. Development could not be stopped; the needs of the developed world irresistibly pulled the remaining underdeveloped portions of the globe into the vortex of industrialization. This further roused the gigantic, explosive social forces that were already clear during the Truman years in the political turmoil that shook India and China.

These were forces that could not be opposed; the architects of empire hoped to work constructively with them. The United States put its influence behind the movement for independence in the Third World; it offered trade and development assistance; it threw open its schools to the students of the emerging countries, and, through whatever means it had at its disposal, it sought to promote moderate democratic regimes that would work for the politics of social compromise in the emerging nations. No mushy-minded idealism here; the accommodation of the emerging nations by the existing powers was of vital importance for the peace of the world.

The prevailing view in liberal American circles about the process of development in the quarter century after the war was that industrialization was a stage of life in the growth of a nation comparable to adolescence in the life of an individual. Emerging nations were likely to experience growing pains during this difficult transition. The policy of the United States was to apply the appropriate mixture of firmness and tolerance. It was unwise to be angry with India when its ambassador to the United Nations attacked the West; this was merely an understandable adolescent response of a young nation in the throes of maturation. Like any good liberal parent, the United States tolerated the emotional excesses of youth, encouraged signs of maturity, and paid the bills. The greatest danger, against which the parent had to guard continuously, was that the natural impulsiveness and instability of youth would involve the young countries with the distinctly unsuitable USSR. If a young country showed a tendency to flirt with the Soviets, the wise parent refrained from excessive nagging or displays of anxiety, knowing well that parental hysteria had driven more than one youth into an unfortunate marriage.

Thus the guardians of the liberal empire were prepared for a stormy adolescence in the developing world. Nevertheless, they were confident that calm and rational parental behavior, combined with the self-evident maturity and reasonableness of the parental way of life, would eventually win over the restless young countries — just as most young Americans of good family in time give up their youthful rebellion and settle down to lives not all that different from those of their once-despised parents.

These hopes in some cases have been justified, but for the most part the developing world has not followed the path so hopefully and carefully laid out for it. The path to development has been more rocky than even the most disturbed adolescence. Worse, instead of the advanced countries exporting their social compromises to the developing world, the developing countries in the last twenty years have begun to export their conflicts to the First World, and, as we have seen, the social compromise of Western society, and the standard of living on which it rests, are more endangered today than at any time since the 1940s.

In earlier chapters we reviewed the progress of this disturbing development and saw that present policies promise no early end to the erosion of the society of the advanced countries. We also saw that the polarization of social life in the Third World is due to a state of arrested development — the inability of these societies to grow into mature social democracies.

The Soviets and the liberal paladins of the American postwar order had agreed that the world was on the path to some form of democratic socialism. The great difference between them was that the liberal capitalists believed that this development would go forward under conditions of peaceful reform, a belief that was supported by their own experience of the evolution of Western society in the first half of the twentieth century. The Soviets maintained that capitalism could not develop without causing economic crises of increasing severity, and that the process of capitalist development would create revolutionary situations in various parts of the world until, in the end, capitalism and capitalist democracy destroyed themselves as a result of their own "contradictions" — their unresolvable inner tensions.

All of this meant that the state of the world economy would not only affect the actual prospects of communism around the world; it would also have a profound effect on the way that American policymakers looked at the world situation. In particular, it would determine whether containment was a viable foreign policy. If we assume that the communists are right, and that capitalism will lurch through a series of deepening crises on a course of violent disintegration, then containment no longer works as an anticommunist theory. It is no longer a question of holding off the Soviet Union while the world proceeds on its "normal" course of modernization and democratic development; instead, it is a question of trying to protect democracy from destructive forces that may be invincible. The United States may be swimming against the current of history rather than riding with it, and the first activity requires more vigor and concentration than the second.

The establishment of communist regimes in Eastern Europe, followed by Mao's victory in China and Ho Chi Minh's successes in his wars against France, shook the confidence of the American people, although not of the liberal Democrats. These focused on the successful recovery of Western Europe and Japan and the creation of a stable alliance that comprised all of the world's most advanced countries, and they saw no reason to change their view that only blunders and irresolution by the United States could lose the Cold War.

But the Democrats lost the election of 1952, partly because of public reaction to communist advances. The early years of the Eisenhower administration were a period in which the United States attempted, without success, to roll back communism, as opposed to containing it, but gradually even the Republican administration regained its confidence about the course of history. The pace of communist advance slowed; in Korea and Indochina the communist forces were unable to gain complete success; in the rest of the world the long, unprecedented postwar prosperity was making the capitalist world more secure from internal subversion. The defection of Tito from the Stalinist camp, the continued political stirrings in Eastern Europe evinced by revolts in Poland, Hungary, and East Germany, and the ideological turmoil into which world communism began to fall after Khrushchev exposed Stalin's crimes in 1956 all created an impression that the communist ideology of Moscow lacked the political strength to wrap the world in its iron grip. The Sino-Soviet split of the early 1960s was further evidence that containment could work, that communism would ultimately break up. In the golden age of American liberalism before 1968, communism seemed the fading ideology of a bygone age.

Only in the 1970s, when a new period of communist advances — primarily in Indochina and in Portuguese Africa — coincided with the onset of a new era of economic instability in the capitalist world, did a spirit of pessimism begin to stir in the West. As the Western and capitalist Third World economies have lurched through the ensuing years, that spirit of pessimism has deepened.

Today there are few who share the realistic self-confidence of the postwar diplomats about the future of social compromise and democracy, even though life for the world's communist governments in the last generation has not been easy or smooth. If liberal capitalism must pass through periodic crises on the way to the future, communism too, it seems, must undergo a development that is anything but simple.

The question of whether liberal, progressive policies can once again come to the fore in American life is fundamentally a question of whether the politics of compromise that built the modern industrial democracies can address the world economic crisis of the 1980s. If the Western world could get back on track with steady economic growth and a rising standard of living, and if the Third World countries within the capitalist world were also moving forward, communism would no longer seem so menacing. The record so far has not been encouraging; economic developments have steadily undermined the politics of social compromise in all the countries of the capitalist world. Wages have been falling, social programs have been cut back, and in the Third World much of the population has endured catastrophic collapses of their standard of living. We have already seen where these trends lead if they cannot be reversed — to a progressive breakdown of order and even democracy itself, not only in the Third World, but also in the United States.

24

TOWARD THE
NEW SOCIAL CONTRACT

THE WORLD is in crisis today because of the speed of development, not because of its failure. The strategy of encouraging Third World growth by concentrating on exports for First World markets has succeeded beyond any expectation, and acquired a momentum that carries it forward beyond the conscious intention of any single agency or government.

The rapid spread of industrialism in the Third World has created many of the tensions that, in the advanced countries, led to the formation of the Great Compromise of industrial democracy, but the political evolution of the Third World has been blocked, and the dog that did not bark in the Western world is growling ominously in the developing countries. We saw in earlier chapters that foreign interests often exercise more influence than domestic forces, and that today's emerging industrial countries lack the opportunities to organize the wider world for their own benefit, the way the world's first industrial countries did.

As a result, the move toward democracy and toward a policy of consensus has been stunted in many of the Third World countries, particularly in those where the strategy of export-led growth has been most thoroughly adopted. Trade unions have been prevented from raising wages and improving working conditions, and political parties representing the working classes have been unable to make their weight felt in the councils of state.

The move toward industrial democracy in many of the advanced countries went hand in hand with a policy of national expansion and imperialism. In Britain, France, and Germany the improvement in conditions of the working class came as the rulers of each of those countries struggled to forge a strong national state that would be capable of exercising influence beyond its own boundaries. In Germany, France, and the United States industrialization went hand in hand with policies of extreme nationalism and protectionism, largely to defend their growing industries against British competition. Bismarck, Disraeli, and Teddy Roosevelt, pioneering figures in the politics of enlightened capitalism, were all convinced imperialists not widely noted for wishy-washy liberal idealism.

In the nineteenth century the politics of social compromise often made their first appearance in the form of a rabid national chauvinism. The centrifugal forces of class and regional differences were overcome by a new group consciousness of national identity, and a new society, on a much larger scale than any social organization previously known, pulled itself together. The European nation-state of the nineteenth century was not only a geographically extensive society; it was culturally intensive to a degree never before seen. The spread of primary education throughout Western Europe accompanied industrialization, and it brought about an unprecedented standardization of language and culture. The logic of economic development was creating larger, more cohesive societies that were increasingly hostile and suspicious of one another while simultaneously full of projects for self-improvement and brotherhood. Ultimately the needs of the European economies outgrew the confines of even the largest of the nation-states, and the stage was set for a new extension of the politics of compromise; but the politics of nation building played an indispensable role in the evolution of social compromise.

The leaders of the developed countries expected something along the same lines to take place in the Third World after World War II. This was the sober calculation behind the sometimes ludicrous expectation that the Third World countries would behave like troublesome adolescents. Yet the belief that these countries were developing into nation-states was paired with the belief that they would not, in the end, prove susceptible to communism. The same national elites that consolidated national political independence would have the kind of stake in private property that would make them resist communist subversion with a singlemindedness that no colonial administration could ever duplicate.

The country that has followed this script most closely and successfully is India. Despite continuing conflict among its hundreds of ethnic and religious minorities, India has emerged as a powerful country with a growing, modern economy. The leadership of the Congress Party often gave Western diplomats heartburn, especially in the 1950s, and India has never had anything but friendly relations with the Soviet Union. Yet India has been fierce to defend its independence from the East as well as the West, and forty years of independence have made it less likely to move toward communism, and more reliable and valuable as an international trading and diplomatic partner than many would have predicted in 1947.

The Indian model of development turned out to be conspicuous by its rarity among the industrializing countries after the war. The reasons are illuminating and help to clarify the nature of the economic and political crisis that began to make itself felt in the 1970s.

India relied heavily on the autonomous development of its own industries from its own capital. The Indians were — and to a great extent remain — extraordinarily suspicious of foreign firms and foreign investment. In part this was a reflection of an emotional nationalism and anticolonial feeling, but there was more to it than that. The process of national consolidation in Europe and the United States took place in a similar spirit. Every country that industrialized after Britain was concerned lest British technical superiority and British capital dominate the local economy, and virtually every country to industrialize after Britain did so behind a wall of protective tariffs. Most countries industrialized with the active participation of the state, which encouraged local entrepreneurs to set up the industries, like steel and railways, that were most important for national development. Usually the presence of investors (as opposed to lenders) from other countries in key industries was considered an actual or potential threat to national security. It was also a threat to the growth of local, national capital on which the long-term growth of the nation-state's economy depended.

The situation faced by the twentieth-century former colonies as they sought to build their industrial bases was even more difficult. Germany and France had faced the lower-cost, higher-technology competition of nineteenth-century Britain, but the developing countries of this century faced a whole host of industrialized countries. Improvements in transportation and communication since the nineteenth century were a very mixed blessing; they offered the new country more opportunities to sell in more markets, but they also made it much easier for the products of the advanced countries to flood the developing world and, with their technological and financial advantages, to overwhelm domestic competition.

The greater threat of foreign competition forced countries like India to erect even stiffer trade barriers than those put up in the nineteenth century; this threat was also one of several factors that increased the role of the state in the new industries of the developing world. While governments had played a major role in promoting industrial development during the nineteenth century, the increased scale of twentieth-century production and the capital shortages that plagued many postcolonial countries combined to give the state the central role in major industries. Only the governments could make the investments large enough to build steel industries, open mines, or form a transportation network. Naturally governments would be even more protective of their own enterprises than of their constituents'; naturally government enterprises would enjoy substantial advantages in the competition for scarce resources that helps shape every economy.

One result of government intervention was the unwelcome appearance in many Third World countries of the ineffective and corrupt bureaucracies that have stifled the development of several countries and hampered development where they have not blocked it altogether. Another result that proved awkward for the world economy was the imposition of high tariffs and other impediments to trade associated with import-substitution development; these run counter to the world's overall trend toward a more integrated economic structure. The advanced countries needed cheap and dependable supplies of raw materials in the Third World, and they needed easily convertible currencies and a minimum of red tape for their foreign ventures. There was therefore a built-in resistance on the part of the First World to a too-successful effort by the emerging countries to follow their development plans.

In another area of friction, many First World–based interests held extensive properties — usually mines, sometimes plantations — acquired during colonial times. The impact of these firms on the emerging local economies was severe, and newly independent governments seeking to protect their markets from foreign competitors found that there were numerous points at which their interests clashed with those of their corporate "guests." Nationalization of the foreign holdings was an attractive and obvious solution to the difficulty. It strengthened the local capitalists and eliminated a dangerous competitor. And since the nationalized holdings generally had readymade markets in the First World, these holdings could be valuable sources of badly needed foreign currencies.

The reaction of the First World countries to nationalization varied, depending on whose ox was being gored. When Iran tried to nationalize oil deposits in which the United States had an interest, the CIA was sent out to topple the offending government, and the French fumed about Anglo-Saxon imperialism. When President Gamal Abdel Nasser nationalized the Suez Canal, jointly owned by France and Britain, the French were utterly convinced that high principles were at stake, and the Americans were furious at the imperialist Franco-British intervention. In general, the advanced countries seemed to feel that a Third World leader who nationalized someone else's property was a reforming social democrat and an aspiring nation builder, but a tin-horn dictator who seized one's own property was a dangerous catspaw for the Kremlin. In any case, most of the Third World countries were too weak to assert the kind of control over their national resources that France, Britain, Germany, and the United States had wielded during their own industrialization.

Another limiting factor was the small size of the internal markets of most Third World countries. This meant that the nation-building, import-substitution development strategy worked only in relatively large countries. Mexico, Brazil, and India had opportunities that Gabon, Senegal, and Thailand lacked. The smaller Third World countries — numerically the large majority — were unable to take the nation building path.

The opposition of the First World, the bureaucratic inefficiency of many Third World governments, the limited size of internal markets, and the powerful forces working to integrate the world's economy all put limits on the success of the development strategy that was most favored in the years after the Second World War.[1] Even so, many countries of the Third World followed this strategy and saw the first signs of a politics of social compromise. Most of these countries were far too poor to institute the kind of welfare state that had become common in the advanced countries, but they were nevertheless able to establish a variety of subsidies and benefits.

There was, however, another model for economic development, and it proved to have a much wider applicability than the nation-building strategy. Export-led growth, pioneered by Japan and to a certain extent by other recovering First World economies after the war, proved to be a much more dynamic force on the world scene than anybody ever expected. In the classic Japanese model, the production of goods for export was accompanied by high protective tariffs to preserve the domestic market and strict capital controls to preserve domestic ownership of the national industrial plant. Export-led growth had the potential to disrupt world trade patterns if too many countries adopted the model or if one country followed the model too successfully, yet the potential for disruption was somewhat limited. Ownership of capital remained in the hands of national investors, and they had a strong interest in maintaining social stability. Japanese managers might get longer hours from their workers than American managers, and they might pay lower wages, but ultimately they were under the same constraints as the political elites in the rest of the advanced countries: they had to provide high enough wages and benefits to satisfy the demands of their population.

As the Japanese model was copied and was modified, these constraints ceased to apply. In the ultimate, purest form, export-led growth involves the establishment of export-processing zones, or EPZs. The host country builds an infrastructure capable of supplying power and water and handling basic transportation. Inside the EPZ, manufacturers, usually foreign, are free of all normal customs requirements as long as the goods they produce are exported. Wages may be lower than minimum wages in the surrounding countryside, strikes may be forbidden by law, and the workers in some cases live in barracks under the supervision of guards.

The arrangement has many defects, but it has never been surpassed as a means of producing large quantities of goods at low cost. EPZs have spread rapidly from their development in the late 1960s and play a large role in setting the prices for manufactured goods. Inside and outside the EPZs there has been an explosion of manufacturing capability in the Third World, ascending the same ladder from textiles and light plastics to electronic consumer goods, steel, automobiles, and ships first traversed by Japan.

While increasing industrial production, export-led growth has so far done little to stimulate the growth of social compromise in the countries where it flourishes. On the contrary, it seems to break down structures of compromise and social benefits where these already have been erected.[2]

The large number of developing countries, and the vast army of unemployed throughout the world, have created a buyer's market for firms looking to build new factories. Just as American cities and states compete with concessions and incentives to lure new investments, the world's developing countries and regions engage in a bidding war that is more desperate. With a labor glut, the lowest price tends to become the market price, so the wages of the cheapest labor exert a powerful influence on wages throughout the rest of the world.

Another effect of export-led growth has been an increase in the mobility of manufacturing. In past decades there were relatively few sites with the infrastructure and available work force for many types of industrial labor. In part because of the explosive growth of EPZs, and in part because of the gradual development of an industrial infrastructure in larger and larger areas of the Third World, facilities can be moved today with relative ease. The mobile manufacturer has less interest than the traditional, place-bound producer in the preservation of the environment, the provision of social services to the work force, and even the maintenance of good labor relations.

Export-led growth displaces the cohesive national elite class of capitalists and businessmen from the center of the economy. Foreign firms, no longer perceived as a danger, play a large role in the economy, and these firms have less interest in the maintenance of social peace.

The overall impact of export-led growth is the acceleration of industrial development and the retarding of political progress. This mixture of political and economic forces blocks the world's political development at a level that no longer suits its economic structure. It also causes the political backwardness of much of the world to work against the economic progress of the whole. The conditions that foster the progressive, compromise-oriented political structures which every industrial country requires cannot thrive in the Third World of today; as a result, semifeudal military dictatorships and kleptocracies anachronistically rule societies that need responsive, intelligent leadership.

Politically, these societies remain locked in the primitive type of class struggle that reigned in the earliest years of industrialism in Western Europe. The owning classes ruthlessly subject their industrial and rural workers to brutal working conditions at shockingly low rates of pay. The oppressed classes can see no way out of their difficulties other than by the extremist politics of resistance, which often take the form of communist insurgency.

What is ominous for the defenders of the established order is that these conditions resemble closely those which created the Russian and Chinese revolutions. We have already seen them breed in recent years a revolutionary army in the Philippines and destabilize some regimes in Latin America.

Yet this threat of revolution is hardly the only way in which conditions in these countries are adversely affecting life in the advanced countries. Political underdevelopment of the Third World has made itself felt in the economies of the advanced countries and threatens to turn the political crisis of the Third World into a generalized political and economic crisis of the First World as well.

The low wages in the Third World countries have led to an investment boom in them, throwing out of balance the equilibrium of supply and demand on which the economic stability of the capitalist world depends. When high-wage factories close and low-wage ones open, production (supply) stays constant or rises, but demand actually drops. The result is a constant pressure on prices, so many production facilities relocate in low-wage areas, thus accentuating the original problems.

In the case of commodity production, there is a similar effect. The advent of technology into the Third World has erased much of the advantage of the farming and mining sectors of the First World. Consequently, the low wages of the Third World are now pushing down commodity prices, too.

A move from high-wage manufacturing to low-wage manufacturing offers many opportunities for Keynesian disequilibriums to interrupt the smooth working of the world economy. When a $20-an-hour steel-worker in the United States loses his job to a $5-an-hour worker in Korea, $15 an hour disappears from the wage fund, the money available to would-be consumers. The missing $15 goes into the pockets of share-holders, and if they could be relied on to spend the money, supply and demand would still balance.

But rich people cannot be counted on to spend all their income. They have higher savings rates than the poor because they have more discre-tionary income. When income shifts from the poor or the middle class to the rich, aggregate economic demand falls. The cases of South Korea, Mexico, and Singapore show these forces at work.

In 1965, private consumption accounted for 72 percent of the GNP in Mexico, 83 percent in Korea, and 80 percent in Singapore. By 1984, consumption as a percentage of the GNP fell substantially in all three countries: to 61 percent in Mexico, 60 percent in Korea, and 43 percent in Singapore. The fall in consumption was matched by an increase in saving. The 1965 figures for savings in the three countries show savings at 21 percent of the GNP in Mexico, 8 percent in Korea, and 10 percent in Singapore. By 1985, savings represented 30 percent of the GNP in Mexico and Korea and 43 percent of the GNP in Singapore.[3]

A shift in investment from high-wage to low-wage countries interferes with the balance of supply and demand in another way. The low-wage scale in these countries translates into lower costs for construction and installation of new equipment. In some cases these may be partially offset by the higher costs of importing special equipment, but normally a dollar spent on new production capacity in, say, Korea will yield more capacity than that same dollar spent in Minneapolis. This means that investment in new production facilities sops up fewer dollars of savings, so there is a much higher potential for excess savings to push the economy into recession.

The result is a global instability, a chronic condition of overproduction in many basic commodities and industrial goods. Markets are not grow-ing as rapidly as output. If this process cannot be checked, the result will be a depression, perhaps on a scale similar to the worldwide collapse of the 1930s. Already there are signs of financial instability as grave as any seen in the years leading up to the Great Depression.

Meanwhile, the consequences for the advanced countries become daily more apparent. Unemployment is up even though real, inflation-adjusted wages are down. Governments everywhere suffer from the erosion of the tax base, and virtually every Western country is attempting to cut its social spending. Entire industries become uneconomical, usually the industries on which the advanced countries have traditionally founded their prosperity and where the best-organized workers are used to the highest and most secure standards of living. Besides the consequences to these workers themselves, the loss of these high-paying jobs creates a dangerous ripple effect as the amount of disposable income in their communities and regions precipitously declines.

The banking system, which must handle the flow of funds between the First World and the Third, grows measurably weaker from year to year and faces unparalleled political hostility in both worlds as the day of reckoning approaches. Given the conditions of domestic austerity that appear inevitable in the United States, it is hard to see the banks getting a hearing when they come to the Treasury for help with their Third World loans. It will also be evident to more and more people that the banks have no policy but to encourage Third World exports to pay the debts; in other words, the banks are actively helping to move American jobs to low-wage havens overseas.

All these strains have come upon the world economy at a time when the United States has lost much of its unilateral control over events. Problems involving currency values, banking stability, and trade must now be addressed by several countries simultaneously, and the process of conciliating their conflicting interests greatly complicates the formation of economic policy.

The growing economic impact of low-wage production on the advanced countries can be seen from the unexpected consequences of economic policies in the last decade. Keynesians, monetarists, and supply siders have been baffled by turns in an economy that simply does not act in accordance with the textbooks. Huge increases in the money supply, combined with the most stimulative fiscal policy ever devised, have failed to bring on a new bout of inflation. Prices have fallen when all the textbooks said they should rise. The unprecedented surge of imports into the United States refuses to obey the signals from currency markets that, historically, have been relied on to bring trade flows back into balance.

Essentially the new global economy, with its rigid division into high-wage and low-wage regions, has abolished the old relationship between government policy, economic demand, and economic activity that obtained during the postwar period in the United States. With so much productive capacity gone to the Third World, increases in demand in the United States do not necessarily lead to increased productive activity here. Instead, the demand is met by huge volumes of imports, so the rate of factory utilization and unemployment at the peak of the business cycle now stand at figures that once were reached only during the depths of recessions.

Measures taken to promote capital formation — tax cuts, subsidies, and such — do not stimulate the expansion of productive capacity in the United States in this brave new world. With excess capacity dogging almost every important productive industry in the country, new investment capital goes into anything other than new manufacturing capacity. Tax shelters, bonds, corporate takeovers within the United States; new factories and mines outside it — this is where the money goes.

Expansionary economic policy simply creates new capital that seeks a home overseas — or in dubious fiscal schemes on Wall Street. A restrictive policy also sends capital overseas. In a recession, when there is less demand in the United States for goods of every kind, there is more pressure on manufacturers to lower prices. The low-wage producers who can make their products for the least money are able to survive economic conditions that drive their high-cost competitors out of business.

There is a way out of this impasse, but like all answers to difficult situations, it is easier to describe than to implement. It can be stated simply: real wages in the Third World must rise. If the world has truly advanced to a condition in which wages seek a universal level, it is in the interests of everyone, and not just the workers, that those wages be high.

This of course was the understanding that lay at the root of the social compromises in what are now the advanced countries: on the one hand, badly paid workers cannot buy much, so their employers cannot sell much; on the other hand, well-paid workers do not conspire night and day to overthrow the established order. With a global economy more integrated today than many European economies at the turn of the century, it is past time for the same principles to be applied on a global scale that proved so successful in the history of the west.

The effects of a steady and substantial increase in the purchasing power of the Third World's wage workers — assuming, of course, such a thing to be possible — would be both rapid and gratifying. Let us not concentrate on the purely humanitarian gains of such an event. We are not the type of chuckle-headed liberal who dwells on such romantic and impractical concepts as decent housing and food, education for the world's youth, adequate medical treatment, care for the aged, and so forth. We would much rather look at benefits to our bank accounts and leave the contemplation of these social gains to sentimentalists.

Social tensions in the Third World would begin to diminish. To the extent that people can see and believe that their standard of living is rising and will continue to rise, and that their children can expect a wider life than they have had, they are deaf to the arguments of revolutionary violence. For some people considerations like this outweigh all the child-nutrition programs in the world; so be it. Progress is never a matter primarily of sentiment; it is the intersecting of desire and necessity.

The existing state of sullen polarization in much of the Third World would gradually yield to an atmosphere of compromise and accommodation — if real wages rise. The higher level of wages would increase the economic *Lebensraum* for the educated, professional groups that play such a large role in the advance of democracy. Workers with decent wages — and with a decent social wage as well — need and can support teachers, doctors, lawyers, poets, and politicians. An educated working class buys newspapers and reads books; it builds and furnishes houses; it agitates for and gets adequate mass transit and other social services. Most of all, it insists on a share in political power and, in proportion to its own stake in society, exercises that power reasonably and increasingly well.

The beneficial consequences of higher wages in the Third World would also be felt in the advanced countries. The adoption of something like a world minimum wage would put a floor under wages in the advanced countries in the same way that national minimum wages have done. No longer would every employee of an American — or German or French or British — firm live with the knowledge that there are millions of people ready to do the same job for one-tenth the pay. Nor would the local governments and businesses in the towns and regions where prosperity depends on industry live with the fear that at any moment the linchpin of the economy could be removed.

Moreover, Third World workers earning decent wages are much better customers than those working for coolie wages. Greater domestic demand would free the Third World countries from the one-sided emphasis on production for export that threatens to destabilize the whole world, and it would also increase their potential as export markets for the advanced countries. A better-paid work force eats higher on the food chain; the pigs, cows, and chickens those workers could afford would improve the balance sheets of meat and dairy farmers.

Healthy Third World economies based on high wages would help stabilize the Western banking system. Third World domestic expansion would create new and favorable investment opportunities, and the expansion of world trade would make present levels of debt easier to deal with. Furthermore, in the favorable political climate that would prevail as protectionist sentiment diminished, banks, governments, and multilateral agencies could put together durable arrangements freeing the major banks from their present difficulties.

Finally, the kind of substantial, sustained increase in wages of which we are speaking would lessen the dangers of war in the Third World. Besides the benefits to the thousands, perhaps millions, of people who would escape the direct horrors of war, there are the inestimable benefits to the United States of not having to face the dismal prospect outlined earlier. It was once suggested that the United States could have bought off the Viet Cong for $250,000 each and still saved money, not to mention lives. Although the payment of Danegeld has seldom preserved the peace for long, enlightened statesmanship that seeks to foster areas of common interest and to reduce outstanding points of conflict has often worked rather better. Against the cost of any program to raise wages in the Third World — and no program comes without a price — ought to be set the cost of refraining from such action, and in blood and gold such cost is far from insignificant.

It is beyond the scope of this book to delineate a detailed program by which wages in the Third World can be increased without massive disruptions or unacceptable costs. Yet we should not leave the subject without setting forth reasons for believing that such a program is well within the competence of the economic system and its leadership.

A large number of arguments can be marshaled against any policy that calls for increased wages and benefits in the Third World. One way or another, most of them boil down to the contention that such a change would be destructively inflationary. Either the higher wages would raise prices to astronomical levels, or the vast international bureaucracy set up to enforce the policy would so hamper trade and raise taxes that prices would rise in response.

The best refutation for such arguments comes from history. After all, they were first advanced, and vociferously so, in opposition to limiting the working day and regulating child labor in the advanced countries. Yet the century that saw great improvements in social programs, wages, and working conditions saw an increase in the purchasing power of every social class. Prices went up, but wages rose even faster. So did productivity. The cleaner, safer, more tightly regulated modern factory outproduces the steamy Victorian sweatshop, though the Victorian economist and manager would have believed this impossible.

Technology is one reason. A low-wage economy favors labor-intensive production. A high-wage economy favors technical innovation. Slave economies are always technologically backward. The United States gained a technical edge in the nineteenth century partly because the supply of inexpensive farmland gave workers an alternative to factory work, thereby forcing the factories to pay relatively high wages, and protective tariffs kept low-wage products out of the market. Ultimately technology yields products that can be made more cheaply than by the original labor-intensive processes, but unless there is the spur of high-wage costs, the initial investment in technological development comes more slowly, if at all.

There are other reasons that the advent of minimum wages, social benefits, and other forms of regulation did not, as predicted, destroy the Western economies. Higher wages mean larger markets; these favor large-scale production, meaning greater economies of scale. The larger markets also mean more opportunities for entrepreneurs; more people have the chance to exercise more choice in the marketplace; there are more economic niches for producers to fill. Social benefits like unemployment insurance and old age pensions help stabilize economic demand in times when recessions threaten to turn into depressions.

Depending on the amount of rainfall, a particular geographical area can support the relatively simple ecosystem of a desert or the richer and more varied system of a tropical rain forest. The historical experience of the West shows that the same societies can support vastly different economic ecosystems, that the transition from the low-wage environment to the high-wage system can be made with government help, and that the results of this change are almost uniformly beneficial. Societies that have not fostered rising wage levels often sink into decline. The social decay and ultimate political decadence of the Greek and Latin city-states were due in some part, historians say, to the effect of slave labor on the wages of free workers. With a large pool of slave labor to compete with, free workers could not push their own earnings above the meanest subsistence level. The antebellum history of the South also illustrates the dangerous impact on free workers of a large population that is forced to work under the conditions of slavery. Low-wage societies, like slave societies, generally experience the kind of decadence associated with great contrasts between wealth and poverty. High-wage societies tend to place a greater value on individual life and human dignity than do low-wage ones.

To bring about this kind of change in the Third World, governments and intergovernmental organizations in both the First and Third Worlds must combine incentives and disincentives. Countries and firms that work to implement agreed-on policies of minimum wages and benefits should be guaranteed free access to markets for their products and to funding sources for their borrowing needs. Countries and firms that choose not to participate in these efforts may face tariffs and quotas for trade and may have a more difficult time getting credit, particularly government-guaranteed credit.

Policies of this kind must be negotiated by all concerned parties, tailored to the very different conditions in different countries, and put into effect gradually to avoid unnecessary shocks and disruptions. For example, it would be unrealistic — and wrong — to seek a single minimum wage around the world under present conditions. In some countries — one thinks of those in East Asia — industrialization is well advanced; the work force is as competent and disciplined as any in the advanced countries. These countries are also the most important exporters in the Third World, and their minimum wages should be relatively high, close to if not equal to those in the advanced countries.

In other countries, industrialization is barely taking hold. There, productivity is low and start-up costs for production facilities are relatively high. These countries would benefit from policies designed to encourage the early stages of industrialization, and wages need not be as high as elsewhere.

The special relationships of some Third World countries with the First World would also make for different policy options. The United States–Mexico relationship is perhaps the most important example. The United States has such a strong, pressing interest in the political stability and the economic prosperity of Mexico that special bilateral arrangements concerning aid and trade could be of great mutual benefit. There are few goals more important to the well-being of the United States than the restoration of Mexico's prosperity; the extreme wage disparities on the two sides of the Rio Grande represent a clear and present danger to people in both nations.

The growing interdependence of the world's economy has already created many of the forums and agencies required to carry out policies of this kind. The multilateral financial institutions already serve as agencies where national economic policy and global development imperatives are jointly debated and policies formulated. Under the pressure of economic necessity, these agencies have even moved beyond their original narrow concern with Third World austerity and have recognized that without growth these countries can neither service their debts nor prevent political upheaval.

The specific policies by which global standards for wages, working conditions, and social benefits could be gradually established and strengthened cannot, of course, be predicted. Every aspect of these policies would be the subject of intense negotiation among many parties with vastly different points of view. However complex the execution of these programs, the underlying logic is simple and compelling, and that is our main point. To review this logic is to make the case that creative economic statesmanship is required to enable the world to move ahead on the path of peaceful development.

The inescapable logic of growth is converting the capitalist world into one giant, global market. As that market becomes more efficient and more unified, the price of every commodity — including human labor — moves toward one level. Under current conditions, this means that wages in the advanced countries tend to fall but that any countervailing tendencies of Third World wages to rise are blocked.

But the high wages of the advanced countries create the demand for goods and services that is essential to the world's economy. Any significant shift to low-wage production undercuts the world economy by destabilizing the relationship between supply and demand. New investment in productive capacity in the low-wage countries increases the world's supply of goods but does not increase the world's demand by an equal amount.

Unfortunately, this situation does not have a self-limiting feature that would restore equilibrium to the world economy. Instead, the problem feeds on itself. A shift of production to low-wage countries decreases demand while increasing, or keeping constant, the supply. The result is a fall in prices, which intensifies the cost pressure on suppliers, encourages more of them to move into low-wage environments, and applies downward pressure on both employment and wages in the high-wage countries. The snowballing of this effect has been responsible for an enormous increase in the productive capacity of the Third World, but at the cost of much instability in the world's political and economic systems.

The "classic" method for creating a stable social and economic order in the wake of massive industrialization is for capital and labor to negotiate a social contract, giving labor a stake in the economy without eliminating the role of private ownership of the means of production. Real wages rise, social benefits are extended, and the result proves beneficial to the economic and political stability of the advanced countries.

But the condition of blocked development in the Third World has so far prevented these societies from developing their own social compromises on a comparable scale. Foreign influence in business and government, the small size of many developing countries, and the dependence of the developing world on an international economic system dominated by firms based in the advanced countries have combined to frustrate the efforts of both local labor and management in much of the Third World to re-create the socialism in one country of the Western world.

Because much of the growth in industrialization is taking place in countries experiencing political deadlock, the world's political and economic institutions are approaching a point of crisis. Falling wages and rising unemployment are slowly eroding the social compromise in the advanced countries. Competition for export markets among these countries is limiting their ability to pursue coordinated economic policies in the face of common difficulties. At the same time, a powerful and oppressed social class is growing by leaps and bounds in the Third World, and the minimum aspirations of this class for political freedom and economic security cannot be achieved through the politics of peaceful protest and gradual evolution.

The escape from this impasse involves the enlightened action of the advanced countries. From these countries and especially from the United States must come the kind of leadership that can unblock the process of world development before the world's pent-up forces explode into costly and chaotic violence.

The liberal, progressive forces in the United States that constituted the New Deal coalition can reassemble for this mission and, by extending the politics of social compromise to a global scale, can win a new lease for social compromise within the United States and regain domestic political leadership for a program that is both pragmatic and progressive. As it did once before in this century, the Democratic Party has the opportunity — and the responsibility that comes with it — for creative statesmanship that advances the peace and prosperity of the world and safeguards the vital interests of the American people.

BEYOND THE LIBERAL EMPIRE

WHERE THERE is no vision the people perish, says the Bible, and the history of the Democratic Party justifies the warning. The aftermath of the last two presidential elections — the most lopsided defeats in living memory — saw the New Deal coalition reduced to the level of panic-stricken sleigh riders, trying to decide whom to throw to the wolves so that the rest might escape. In 1981 the party regulars decided that the ideological and social fringe had ruined the party in 1972 and 1980, and that they had alienated the core Democratic constituencies, particularly the labor movement. Lesbians and gays to the wolves! Peaceniks to the wolves! Econuts to the wolves!

The party rules were rewritten to ensure that only "responsible" candidates could survive, and the labor unions played a key role in selecting the nominee and in writing the platform. The result, in 1984, was a worse defeat than the McGovern debacle, and a new cry went up: Labor to the wolves! Blacks to the wolves! Tip O'Neill to the wolves! There weren't many people left in the sleigh.

If things had kept up that way, white Southern Democrats might have succeeded in re-creating the conservative Democratic Party of days gone by. This party met all the specifications of the new era Democrats: it was populist, profamily, and strong in the South. The last Democratic candidate who fully met these qualifications was William Jennings Bryan, the darling of the party for a full generation. No apple pie was ever more American than Bryan; no one ever loved his mother more sincerely or looked on the flag with greater devotion. No one was more popular in the South, and no one got the farm vote like Bryan. Of course, he was defeated in three presidential elections, but then the modern Democrats had won only one of the five elections since 1968.

Judging by the numbers, there was not much hope for the Democrats. There have been thirty-two presidential elections since the first Republican was elected in 1860; the Republicans have won twenty of them and the Democrats twelve — and just three candidates (Roosevelt, Wilson, and Cleveland) account for two thirds of the Democratic victory total. Except for Franklin Roosevelt, no Democrat has served two full terms in office since Woodrow Wilson, and since Andrew Jackson left office in 1837, Wilson and Roosevelt were the only two Democrats to win two presidential elections in a row.

From 1860 to 1896 the Democrats won two presidential elections and lost eight; they averaged 136 electoral votes to the Republicans' 212. From 1900 to 1928 the Democrats won two of eight contests and averaged 190 electoral votes to the Republicans' 305. From 1932 to 1948 the Democrats won all five elections and averaged 436 electoral votes to the Republicans' 87. From 1952 to 1984, however, the parties reverted to their historical form. The Democrats won three of the nine elections, a record slightly better than average, but their electoral vote average, 169, was below their pre-Roosevelt level.

In other words, at the level of presidential politics, the Democrats have been in the minority ever since the Civil War, with the single exception of the Roosevelt-Truman era. Most of the Democratic victories can be attributed to unusual circumstances: the Bull Moose split in 1912, the threat of war four years later, the Depression and war during Roosevelt's four races, reaction to the Kennedy assassination in 1964, and the aftermath of Watergate in 1976. Only the narrow victories of Truman in 1948 and Kennedy in 1960 show Democrats winning in "normal" peacetime elections under no especially favorable circumstances.

Some political scientists speak of periodic party realignments, with the two parties alternating between majority and minority status. At the presidential level, it is more meaningful to speak of a normal condition of Republican dominance punctuated by occasional Democratic victories. Only with Roosevelt at the top of the ticket did the Democrats enjoy an extended period of control in the White House; otherwise, there has been no alternation of majority and minority parties since the Civil War.

Although the two parties have swapped positions on almost every issue since 1860, the coalitions that make them up have remained relatively stable. The Republicans have represented corporate America, and the Democrats have taken the rest. An incautious Republican once characterized the Democrats as the party of the three *r*'s — rum, Romanism, and rebellion; the ensuing squabble cost the Republicans New York State and the presidential election, but the description was not without merit. When Spiro Agnew referred to George McGovern as the Triple A candidate — acid, amnesty, and abortion — he was expressing the same feeling: that, at least in presidential politics, the Democratic Party is the party of dissent, what Evelyn Waugh might have called "the odds and sods" of politics.

The dissent that the Democrats embodied in the eighty years after the Civil War was the resistance of agricultural and laboring interests to the industrialists, who were the big winners in the war. Midwestern farmers in revolt against tight money, low commodity prices, and the power of the railroads joined forces with southern whites and eastern working people. All of these elements wanted to see the economic power of the corporations curtailed, but their political aspirations were thwarted by a hand that at times, as in the Rutherford B. Hayes–Samuel Tilden contest of 1876, lost all claim to invisibility.

During their years in the wilderness, the Democrats always had a program. "Thou shalt not crucify mankind upon a cross of gold," said Bryan, although not even he was quite sure what he meant. They had a vision, too, of a sort, but it was a nostalgic vision of an America that was being swept away by the progress of industrialization. The solid South looked back with nostalgia on the antebellum era, when it dueled for national dominance on even terms with the North; the West looked back to the age of the prosperous family farm. The Democratic Party stood for the sectors of American life that were being hurt by the natural tendencies of economic development. This situation gave the party a stable and loyal electoral base, and from every defeat it returned to the fray with new vigor; but the same circumstances limited the party's ability to win elections or, having won, to govern. Grover Cleveland, once elected, proceeded to carry out a tight-money, probusiness policy that caused Woodrow Wilson to label his administration a conservative Republican affair. Wilson himself, elected on a platform of peace, found himself dragged into World War I at the behest of the great Republican interests of the country.

Only during the Roosevelt years was the Democratic Party able to carry out policies that were recognizably organized for the benefit of its loyal constituents. The South, scorned and exploited for two generations, began to receive federal assistance for the first time since Fort Sumter. TVA, rural electrification, commodity price supports, and other programs laid the foundation for the South's emergence from conditions of life more like those of the Third World than of the First. The trade union movement received the equivalent of its bill of rights, and the basic elements of the liberal welfare state gave working people their first real taste of economic security. Farmers achieved levels of economic assistance and easy credit Bryan never dreamed of; even blacks, who abandoned the party of Lincoln for the party of Roosevelt, received federal help for the first time since Reconstruction.

The reason that the Democrats under Roosevelt were suddenly able to get elected and then to reward their constituents on a colossal scale was that, under Roosevelt, the Democratic Party for the first time in a century stood for a program that was progressive in the fullest sense of the word. Previously their programs had been sympathetic, decent, and humane (always excepting the Southern Democratic love of Jim Crow), but they were the proposals of the defeated.

The New Deal vision first linked these yearnings to the actual needs of the developing economy, although, as we saw earlier, many of the New Deal themes briefly surfaced during the Wilson administration. The New Deal Democrats stood for a modernization of American life. They were no longer the party of states' rights, small business, and backwoods idealism; they were the party that put forward a rational, practical program to get the nation as a whole back on its feet.

We are still too close to Franklin Roosevelt to appreciate the magnitude of his accomplishments. We can say of him what Milton said of God: "Dark with excessive bright thy skirts appear." But of all his accomplishments this was not the least: to take the battered and backward old Democratic Party and forge it into a political instrument that could reorganize first the American Republic and then the whole Western world.

What made this possible was the realization to which we have referred: that a modern industrial economy can function only when the masses are prosperous. The stone that the builders had rejected became the cornerstone for the political and economic edifice of American life; for the first time since Emancipation the Democratic Party had found a line of policy that was progressive in both economic and humanitarian terms.

Modern Democratic strength has always found its source in this union of the good and the useful. When the party can synthesize the moral and the economic yearnings of the masses of the people into a line of pragmatic policy, then it is invincible. When it fails, it loses.

The current debate over the future of the party reflects the difficulties inherent in re-creating Roosevelt's political achievement. The core constituencies of the party naturally see it as an instrument for defending their economic interests against all comers and for advancing them where possible. Naturally labor and the other core constituencies would rather win than lose elections, but they are not playing politics for their amusement.

Although the Democrats lost most of the presidential elections between 1860 and 1932, they maintained strong local party bases. Their congressional power enabled them to frustrate Republican programs even when they were powerless to implement their own. Their grip on state governments gave them limited power to control events and, critically, enabled them to refresh the party faithful with frequent libations from the public fountain.

The core Democratic power centers would, if forced to make the choice, rather lose elections and keep their power in the party than win national elections at the cost of losing their hold on the party. This is an eminently sensible position for them to take; administrations come and go, but parties last forever. The party that loses a presidential election can still have a measurable effect on national policy, but an interest group not reliably represented by a party is out in the cold. In 1984 it was better for labor to lose with Mondale than to win with Hart, even had that alternative been possible.

The result of these cross-currents is to make the Democrats an irresistible force when they are united around a progressive, practical vision, and an immovable object when they are not. The key to understanding the party, so often neglected by hopeful reformers, is that its progressive, dynamic layer is the more recent stratum, dating back to the New Deal. Beneath this lies the ancient determination of the South not to be ruled from Wall Street, the grim determination of the trade unions to hold on to the wages they have, and the resolution of the family farmers to hold on to the land.

The goals of the farmer-labor coalition that makes up the core of the old Democratic Party involve blocking new developments that it dislikes, not in forming new policy initiatives. The old coalition does not want corporate agribusiness to complete the elimination of the family farm, and it does not want U.S. industry to move — lock, stock, and barrel — to the Third World. It favors a dogged defense of New Deal subsidy programs and new subsidies in the form of protection for domestic industries.

Although this program would, for a while, protect the income of some farmers and workers, it is a negative program and would end in economic stagnation and decline for the country. If the Democratic Party allows its emotions to rule, it will adopt a policy along these lines and sink once again into the condition of permanent and futile opposition in which it has vegetated for most of the last 130 years.

This would be bad for the party and worse for the country, and it is this course from which the neoliberals are laboring to turn the party. Yet the neoliberal program has never been able to avoid the suspicion that it will be directed in practice against the core Democratic constituencies — that neoliberalism is a threat to the trade union movement and the family farm. Though neoliberals talk about building new industries that are competitive on the world's markets, they never address the question of how to maintain employment and wages at current levels while making this transition.

Neoliberalism seems to offer labor hope for the future and cuts in the present, and to hold out the same prospect for other Democratic groups, like minorities and farmers. This is not a program calculated to win the support of an increasingly bitter and suspicious union movement.

The suspicions are not unwarranted. Too often the neoliberals have referred to obsolete labor practices and work rules as hampering the ability of American factories to compete on world markets. No doubt, labor observes dourly, if American wages were cut to the levels that prevail in Taiwan and American workers were forbidden to strike and compelled to work sixty-hour weeks, American goods would be more price-competitive, but this hardly strikes labor as a solution to its problems.

The New Liberals have yet to understand the seriousness of low-wage competition from the Third World. Like Carter seeking cheap grace for the "sins" of American foreign policy, the neoliberals want easy solutions for the nation's economic problems. But the search for easy solutions is sparked by political expediency. More thorough approaches — less "easy" solutions — might alienate potential supporters, the reasoning goes, and so the New Liberals limit themselves to analyses that do not depart much beyond existing opinion and to policies that represent only incremental and marginal change. While such an approach may minimize opposition, it also minimizes support, and, as Carter was not alone in discovering, it minimizes the chances of success. The built-in compromises and the timidity of such approaches ensure that policies based on them will fall short of even the modest expectations they have aroused.

An eagerness to embrace superficially promising solutions that avoid the essence of the problem has already embarrassed the neoliberals. In the youth of their movement they were known as Atari Democrats, after the video-game manufacturer who seemed to combine the promise of technology with the creation of new industries to replace the ones being undermined from abroad. The name was hastily dropped when Atari moved its production facilities to Singapore, but the former Atari Democrats did not fully comprehend the lesson. A chorus of hymns went up to the other high-tech industries that were going to transform the economy and replace the basic manufacturing industries. Too quickly for comfort, American microchip and personal computer manufacturing went into a slump, and semiconductor makers joined the line at the Department of Commerce, begging for protection from "unfair" competition.

Almost any production technique can be exported today; gone are the days when a technological edge could give a country a generation of superiority. The Third World today is full of computer technicians, software writers, and engineers, all of them available for lower wages and longer hours than their Western counterparts. The industries that are the most difficult to export are the heavy industries, intensive in both capital and labor. A computer plant, or even a research facility, is easier to build and to staff than a steel mill. Light, skill-intensive industry travels easily in today's world.

The neoliberal premise that technological superiority — itself a wasting asset — can guarantee superior productivity and wages for the mass of the population clearly cannot stand scrutiny; neither can the claim that the United States will remain prosperous as the world's financial center. Already four of the five largest banks in the world are Japanese; Japanese banks hold more financial assets overall than American banks, and their lead is increasing with every passing year. The last nation to argue that its financial primacy would compensate for relative industrial decay was the Britain of the 1920s and 1930s.

There is in fact only one U.S. industry that is relatively safe from foreign competition. Because of the national security implications of their work and because of their close ties with the Pentagon, defense contractors enjoy the greatest protection in the domestic market and the easiest access to export markets of any American industry. In practice the "new wave" boom in high-tech industry owed more to the military buildup than neoliberals cared to admit; in effect, the defense industry runs on the old principles of government subsidy and import protection — not exactly the brave new computer utopia of neoliberal fantasy.

The New Liberals are correct to believe that the core Democratic constituencies, committed to the politics of protectionism and stagnation, cannot permanently regain the political initiative, but they have not come forward with a realistic alternative. As long as the Atari Democrats insist that domestic industrial policy by itself can solve the economic problems of the nation, our labor leaders will correctly view the New Liberals as so many Greeks bearing gifts.

The New Liberals will be able to make their fullest contribution to the nation and the party only if they can bring themselves to embrace wholeheartedly a "no cuts" philosophy. When they begin to join those who maintain that U.S. wages are "too high," they need to stop and think much more carefully about what this means. How much money is too much for a blue-collar worker? For a secretary? A policeman? A senior executive in a major corporation? A teacher in a ghetto school?

What will replace the purchasing power of the American consumer as the force that drives the American economy if wages keep falling? Just how far do American wages have to fall before the New Liberals would say, "Enough, no more"? What forces do they think will halt the decline in wages and make good the losses of the last ten years?

In a sense, the Democrats have come full circle from the New Deal. Programs that once were progressive have been left behind by the changing economy. Once again the Democrats have formed a coalition of economic losers, attempting to defend the heritage of the past from the heartless demands of a more cruel present. Events constantly threaten to split the Democrats into isolated groups that do not like each other very much: urban blue- and pink-collar workers, southern whites, midwestern farmers, and blacks. In the Democratic politics of today, the only thing these groups have in common is discomfort in the face of economic change.

The current malaise in Democratic ranks has its roots in the different problems that beset the most important elements in the coalition. These problems have made the Democrats slow to understand the nature of their current weakness and have hindered their efforts to come to terms with changing conditions. A look at these problems reveals a changing balance of power within the New Deal coalition and suggests that a new leadership will emerge, and that the party will adopt a more promising approach to its responsibilities than retreating into the sterile defense of policies that can no longer serve their goals.

THE GALBRAITH EFFECT

Like the American right, which we anatomized in an earlier chapter, the American liberal coalition consists of populist and elitist and economic and social sectors. The various interests and attitudes of these groups bring them into kaleidoscopically changing relations of mutual support and hostility as they respond to changing conditions. "Limousine liberals" and "lunch bucket liberals" are sometimes at one another's throats and sometimes on the best of terms. "Peace and justice" movements have complex relationships with the labor movement and with the old Establishment; the feminist movement and the civil rights movement have changing points of view regarding each other; and the relationship of both of these movements to all the others in the liberal coalition has been in a state of flux for generations.

For the purposes of understanding the transformation of contemporary liberalism, we should draw that most important distinction, the one between the popular and elite wings of American liberalism. The crisis of liberalism has affected each in a different way, and the orientation of the emerging movement will, in reflecting the consequences of these changes, differ significantly from the liberalism we have grown used to in the last generation.

It was John Kenneth Galbraith who provided the key to understanding the crisis of the popular wing of the liberal coalition. In *The New Industrial State,* first published in 1967, when the labor movement still regarded its future with cheerful confidence, Galbraith looked at the record of falling membership and drew what seemed a startling, even a perverse, conclusion: American unions were working toward their own destruction.

The program of the American labor movement had been essentially fixed for a generation: government policies to reduce unemployment and relieve its associated suffering, a national minimum wage, and rising wages with job security in the most intensively unionized industry. In reviewing this record Galbraith made the succinct observation that this program

> was the thing most designed to make the unions less needed. . . . Power passes to the technostructure and this lessens the conflict of interest between employer and employee which gave the union much of its reason for existence. . . . The regulation of aggregate demand, the resulting high level of employment together with the general increase in well-being all, on balance, make the union less necessary or less powerful or both.[1]

In other words, the society that emerged from the Depression and the war was one in which the class conflict that gave the unions meaning and strength was replaced by a social compromise that made unions less important even to their own members. Paradoxically, it was the success of the unions in advancing the interests of their members that rendered them redundant in the new age.

And there was more. The general improvement in the labor relations, standards of living, and conditions of work that accompanied the social compromise all undercut the attempts of unions to organize new industries and new regions. The changed conditions also subtly altered the character of the labor movement's leadership. In the days of sit-down strikes and company goons, labor leaders had to be courageous and magnetic personalities. They had to be able to mobilize their members for dangerous industrial actions; the ties that bound the leaders and the members of the labor unions had to be strong, and without constant involvement and passionate commitment on the part of the membership, the unions would not long have survived.

These things all changed in the long, drowsy era of the great social compromise. Union bureaucracies grew up, and the day-to-day involvement of the members atrophied. The charismatic outsider was at a disadvantage in the new politics of unionism; the office-politics infighter and the bureaucrat with the cast-iron rear tended to do better in this world.

Although the leaders of some unions were exceptions to the trend, overall the union leadership became less inspired, more bureaucratic, and less intimately acquainted with the aspirations and the values of the rank and file. These leaders usually lacked the experience or the imagination to understand the growing threat to the status quo that began to appear in the 1970s. They did not think of the New Deal–era social compromise as a temporary arrangement reflecting a convergence of certain interests and a balance of forces. For them, the assumptions of social compromise and of labor relations in the United States of the 1960s and early 1970s were laws of nature. The rules of the game were givens; if they changed at all, they changed slowly. Labor believed that its strength was its political clout in Congress, its allies in the bureaucracy, and its ability to deliver money and other resources to its chosen candidates.

At their worst, the labor bureaucracies were like tourists in a coastal community. The radio says something about a hurricane watch, but the tourists look outside and see the bright sun shining in a cloudless sky. A refreshing breeze skips along the beachfront, and they cannot believe in the menace a few hundred miles away. And anyway, how bad can a hurricane be? A few tree limbs torn down, perhaps a power line or two. They slap on more suntan lotion and sit on the beach, where they cannot see the locals boarding up their windows and heading for the hills.

In any case, the long social peace weakened the institutional base of the labor movement and assisted the mediocre and the unimaginative in their efforts to rise through the ranks of union leadership.

The labor movement was not the only victim of its own success during the liberal era. The civil rights and feminist movements similarly passed through a stormy age of heroic struggle before settling in, they hoped, to enjoy the fruits of their victories in peace. Both of these movements were undercut as well by their own successes. Every victory for black rights lessened the need for civil rights organizations, and every victory for feminism made feminist organizations and feminist ideas less necessary for the daily lives of women who just wanted to live in peace.

The most dangerous symptom of the decay of these popular progressive causes was the extent to which their victories took on the character of transactions with the bureaucratic and judicial branches of the government. *Roe* v. *Wade* lulled many feminists into believing that the battle for abortion rights had been won, though in fact it was only beginning. Busing and affirmative action decisions by courts and commissions were victories for the civil rights organizations, but recourse to administrative action insidiously weakened the movement's hold on public opinion and made room for a resurgence of racism. Once minority and feminist rights found stronger support from the bureaucracy and the courts than from the elected legislatures and public opinion, a danger point had been reached. If the representatives of "popular" causes and the "people's will" must rely on the least populist, least democratic elements of the state for relief from the actions of elected assemblies, they have little to hope for and much to fear from the future.

It was one thing for the civil rights movement to call on every branch of the federal government to enforce the Constitution against the patently illegal actions of the states. In the great series of battles from *Brown* v. *the Topeka Board of Education* to the showdown in Selma, the civil rights movement used every forum open to it, but it understood that its primary mission was political, not administrative; its primary battleground was the streets, not the corridors — hearts and minds, not rules and regulations.

There is nothing wrong, of course, in citizens going to court to defend their rights, or in working to receive the most favorable treatment possible at the hands of the federal bureaucracies; but even as the shift to the courts and the federal agencies brought victories in its wake, it created new dangers. The civil rights movement and the feminist movement found themselves in a position similar to that of the labor movement: each had a leadership increasingly composed of lawyers, accountants, and bureaucratic infighters; their members were less involved and less committed to the movement; and they were facing a dangerous backlash with which they were ill equipped to deal.

The success of the social compromise, then, created new problems for the popular elements in the liberal coalition; the limousine liberals, too, had their problems, and to these we now turn.

THE POISONED CUP

The popular segment of the liberal coalition fell into a kind of decadence during the liberal empire; the Establishment was sinking toward its dotage. Although the Establishment had always been a numerically insignificant part of the liberal coalition, it had played the central role in the formation of the foreign and domestic policies of the liberal era. In a real sense, it was the Establishment that had given shape to the formless dissatisfaction of the American people at the time of the Depression, and it was the Establishment that impressed its stamp on the foreign policy of the 1940s.

That Establishment was a unique growth in American history. The rich have always played an important role in American life, but the periods in which they dominated the public as well as the private life of the country have been the exception. The log cabin, not the silver spoon, has traditionally been the childhood companion of American presidents. The Virginia Establishment and the Adams family controlled the presidency for the first forty years of the Republic, but Andrew Jackson and universal male suffrage drove the old elite from the citadels of power. Henry Adams, descended from two presidents and son of an ambassador to Britain, lamented that men of good family and education were barred from national politics in his lifetime.

The Establishment of the twentieth century had its origins in the rule of the robber barons of the late nineteenth century rather than to a colonial aristocracy that had maintained its political power since the days of George III. Theodore Roosevelt was its first member to hold high office; to a surprising extent the modern Establishment owed its cohesion to the inspiration of TR and the life's work of Endicott Peabody, an Episcopalian Socrates who set himself the task of concentrating the attention of the sons of the Morgans and the Harrimans on *ho kalos kai ho agathos,* the Good and the Beautiful. They also studied the Useful.

From Peabody's elm-girded school poured forth two generations of statesmen, the builders and the guardians of empire; from the first pressing of a crop including Auchinclosses, Biddles, Morgans, and du Ponts came Franklin D. Roosevelt, '00; W. Averell Harriman, '09; Sumner Welles, '10; and Dean Acheson, '11. These young men passed their adolescence in the atmosphere of Anglo-American Empire; Peabody himself had been schooled in Britain and was well connected with the British Establishment. Teddy Roosevelt was a frequent visitor and speaker; the boys debated the leading issues of the day and were schooled in such topics as Admiral Alfred Mahan's views on the importance of sea power.

The young Franklin Roosevelt wrote a letter to his mother in which he expressed some sympathetic feeling for the Boers, then fighting for their freedom against a British presence that included the young Winston Churchill. Mother was alarmed: Was Franklin yielding to sentimentality? He returned a reassuring answer:

> I think you misunderstand my position in regard to the Boers. I cannot help feeling convinced that for the past ten years they have been *forced* into this war. I am sure you will feel this if you only read up on the Boer case. *However,* undoubtedly, now that the war is actually on, it will be best from the humanitarian standpoint for the British to win speedily and civilization will be hurried on, but I feel that the same result would have been surely obtained without war.[2]

Here from a boy in his teens are all the careful balances, the mixed firmness and fairness, the desire for progress and the sense of the practical — with not a small dose of smug self-satisfaction — that will be found in the policies of his administration and its successor.

We have already referred to the remarkable historical experience of this generation; it is worth examining further. Their lives were perfectly — one might almost say providentially — timed so that they could witness in extreme youth the zenith of Britain, observe its decline during most of their lives, and, at the time of their maturity, assist in the transfer of power from the British Empire to the nation over the water. What Bishop Berkeley had prophesied, they saw:

> Westward the course of empire takes its way;
> The four first acts already past,
> A fifth shall close the drama with the day:
> Time's noblest offspring is the last.

Franklin Roosevelt was a boy in school when Victoria celebrated her Diamond Jubilee and Kipling wrote "Recessional."

During the first half of this century it was still possible to speak of an Anglo-Saxon ruling class, dominant in both Britain and America and united by sentiment, culture, education, and marriage. Mrs. Simpson's marriage to Edward VIII was notable as one of the few Anglo-American marriages that were social failures; Churchill's mother was an American, and his daughter-in-law would marry Averell Harriman. The intimacy of the connection, and the common bonds of education and acquaintance, made Britain's decline extraordinarily vivid to the American cousins. Since the decline of Britain's Empire accompanied the decline of its former ruling class, the American Establishment was better situated than almost any class in history to appreciate and even anticipate the dynamics of its own decline.

We have already seen that Averell Harriman looked forward with apparent calm to a socialist future for the United States. Roosevelt clearly believed during most of the war that he and Stalin could reach an understanding, and he made no secret of his impatience with Churchill's attempts to turn the war to the advantage of Britain's imperial position. Even Acheson, by far the most conservative of the great Establishment figures, viewed the left wing of the British Labour Party with a complacent fondness rare in this eminent specimen of the Anglo-Saxon iceberg.

It was almost instinctive for these men to look at Britain to understand the American future. At the height of American success, they saw Britain's decline; with their class at the pinnacle of its influence, they saw a more egalitarian future. They understood that their task in life was to rule the empire that had fallen into their laps, and they knew that the fate that gives gifts of this kind also takes them back.

They were not frightened by this prospect. They did not, themselves, expect to see either the fall of the American Empire or any advanced signs of the triumph of American socialism. We love our grandchildren, but we do not lose much sleep over the political problems they will face in their maturity.

The experience that the Establishment had with British socialists, particularly after the Labour Party defeated Churchill in 1945, was reassuring. Acheson deeply admired Ernest Bevin, the illegitimate son of a British housemaid who left school at eleven and educated himself while working at odd jobs before ultimately being named to the Foreign Office by Clement Attlee. This son of the working class, a hard-bitten union organizer, was not, Acheson found, a bad fellow at all:

> It was like him, too, to study not only current international problems, but the history of his office and the history of his predecessors. He read their papers; he talked of them as of slightly older people whom he knew with affectionate respect. . . . One got the sense that, sitting at the familiar desk, under the portrait of George III, he felt himself surrounded by their benign shades, sympathizing with him in his worries. . . . I could believe that a Tudor monarch could well have seen in the short, powerful figure . . . an instrument well fashioned to safeguard English interests.[3]

Well, how bad could socialism be? Good Queen Bess and Bad King George combine to bless it from the grave. The British socialists were, in any case, reliable allies against the Soviets. Perhaps, in the fullness of time, a descendant of Acheson's would serve in a government with the son of a housemaid.

The sense of peaceful decline into a comfortable old age hung over the Anglo-Saxon Establishment in the 1950s. On the seventy-fifth anniversary of the founding of Groton, Peabody's school, the trustees published a book of essays by graduates and friends that sounded the note of change. Christopher Rand, an alumnus and parent of three Groton boys, and a distinguished contributor to, among other publications, *The New Yorker,* noted signs of change:

> As for the social change, I would say that the best index is bedmaking. I never learned to make a bed, and I never intend to, but I believe that my sons have made over a thousand apiece at Groton.[4]

But there were other, more far-reaching changes. Groton boys now had to compete for places at Harvard and Yale. The sons of immigrants, even of housemaids, even of Catholics and Jews, were competing for the same places in college and the world. The non–Anglo-Saxon elements of the American population were beginning to exert a more important and, felt the old stock, generally baneful influence on American policy. Isolationism before the war, wrote Rand, and McCarthyism after were both largely products of the German and Irish populations in the Midwest, aided in the second case by the "violent anti-Russianism [of] our Central European minorities." Although the "Anglican or Anglophile element" in the population was not without biases of its own,

> I believe that the Anglophile element, which looks seaward and is cosmopolitan, should keep free to lead the country, as needed, into new stages of foreign policy.

Yet the Anglo-Saxon cosmopolitans lacked the numbers and were losing their monopoly on places in the leading colleges and professions. How then would the Anglophile element lead?

> The trick is to bloom together with the other flowers in our "plural society" — with the Catholics, Navajos, Lutherans, etc. — but to bloom so well in our own style that the whole scene will be enlivened by it. The Brahmin caste led India centuries ago, and is leading India today, not by force, but by moral and intellectual superiority, which is maintained by dedication and by rigorous schooling of the Brahmin boys.[5]

The Brahmins of India had more success with such measures than the Boston variety. Rand's essay was published in 1960, just as the "best and the brightest" of the Brahmin boys were preparing to bloom in the gardens of Camelot. That flowering proved to be an Indian summer for the Establishment, not a second spring. Worse, the inheritors, so far, of the Establishment's mantle have been those the Establishment viewed as the most retrograde and unfortunate characters on the American scene — the Nixon and Reagan elements in the Republican Party. Acheson would have certainly preferred turning over the State Department to his housemaid's son than seeing Richard Nixon in charge of foreign policy, but that's what he saw.

One can say of the Establishment what Acheson once said of Britain: it has lost an empire and not yet found a role. The attempt to guide society from the foundations, the think tanks, and the major universities — to exert influence through the rigorous education and training of the Brahmin boys — soon turned into a caricature of the old liberal arrangement. In the vital days of American liberalism, the masses seethed, and the elites devised policies to contain that discontent and alleviate grievances. In the days of liberal decadence, the masses lost interest in social reform, but the mandarins of the Establishment continued to put out blueprints for new reforms, new accommodations to an upsurge of the masses. Meanwhile, the masses were listening to Spiro Agnew read speeches by William Safire.

The successes of the unions, the feminists, and the civil rights movement undercut the movements that made those successes possible; the success of the liberal Establishment in domesticating popular unrest obviated the need for a liberal Establishment. Franklin Roosevelt had never been particularly popular with most of the rich. At best he was considered a necessary evil; at worst, a traitor to his class. Once the New Deal and the associated programs of liberal reforms had been enacted and social peace restored, the rich — new and old — showed a marked tendency to return to the less enlightened views they had held before the Great Crash disturbed their peace.

Other forces weakened the Establishment in the postwar period. The long economic expansion after 1945 created new fortunes, often based in the Sun Belt. This new money saw no reason to make common cause with the "decadent" old rich of the East. From the point of view of the new entrepreneurs, old-fashioned capitalism was as healthy as ever. They were not interested in the British Empire and its troubles; no premonitions of inevitable decline haunted them; they saw no reason to suppose that the future held anything but more power and wealth for the United States.

The new fortunes were only one economic challenge to the Establishment during these years. The days when a handful of bankers and financiers controlled the American economy were coming to an end. Driven by market forces, high-level finance became more like a business and less like a gentlemen's club. More and more talented outsiders reached important positions in the business world, and the Darwinian logic of capitalism favored the companies that made room for the new breed of aggressive, sometimes unscrupulous managers. Famous investment banks went public; the Old Boy network was a less potent factor on Wall Street.

The success of liberal policies in promoting the economic growth of the United States was making the country less and less manageable. Instead of a small, tightly knit Establishment, the nation's "power elite" had become a diffuse cluster of rival groups.

Even as the Establishment lost its monopoly over the business and intellectual life of the nation, it was being sapped from within, losing its faith in the liberal policies of the last generation. The catastrophic consequences of American intervention in Indochina diminished the Establishment's confidence in foreign affairs; the urban riots shook its faith in the liberal approach to national social problems; and the great inflation of the 1970s undermined its faith in Keynesian economic policies.

The "failure" of Keynesianism was the most important of these factors. Unlike the Indochinese War and the urban riots, which could be written off as the consequences of tactical blunders in carrying out policies that remained essentially sound, the Establishment's disenchantment with Keynesianism reflected a real limit of the old liberal synthesis.

Keynesian economics had been presented in the United States as a value-free, socially neutral tool for managing the economy. Textbooks on economics presented Keynes's theories as a series of equations, deriving the multiplier from the marginal propensity to consume, and demonstrating the relationship between fiscal policy, interest rates, and the GNP. Keynes's social thought was generally ignored, and most of those who professed undying adherence or bitter opposition to "Keynesianism" had only a limited idea about what they were debating.[6]

Keynes himself believed that his economic theories, if adopted, would lead to a social revolution within a relatively short time.[7] For Keynes, modern society was composed of three classes: the workers, the entrepreneurs, and the rentiers. Workers received their income from wages, and entrepreneurs from the profits on business activity. As for the rentiers, they were like the lilies of the field: they toiled not, neither did they spin, but they lived very well, all the same. The rentier derived his or her income as a return on capital lent to the entrepreneur. While communists considered the entrepreneur and the rentier both to be members of the capitalist class, with interests directly opposed to those of the workers, Keynes held that the entrepreneur and the worker had significant interests in common, and that the great chasm in society lay between the rentiers and the other two classes.

The class conflict as conceived of by Keynes becomes clear as we look at his idea of the affluent society, the goal of economic policy. For Keynes, the affluent society was one in which human ingenuity, not capital, was the limiting resource in economic development. An affluent society is one that possesses a relative abundance of capital. The entrepreneur has no difficulty in finding capital to back his ideas, and since capital is not a scarce resource, interest rates on borrowed capital are so low as to be practically nonexistent. In such a society wages would be high, because there would be an abundance of enterprises; entrepreneurial profits would be moderate, but sufficient; the rentier alone would suffer. Indeed, in the near future the rentier would disappear as a class; Keynes spoke cheerfully of the consequence of his program as "the euthanasia of the rentier."

These consequences of Keynesianism would become apparent only over time, he believed. Like Marx, although he had different reasons, Keynes believed that the rate of profit or, more precisely, the marginal efficiency of capital tended to fall. The most profitable investments, Keynes argued, would be made first, leaving the less attractive investments for later. New investment in real productive capacity would only be forthcoming as long as the rate of return on such investment was greater than the interest rate. Interest rates therefore had to fall in step with the marginal efficiency of capital so that new investments would continue to be made.

Keynesianism was, at least from the point of view of the rentiers, a poisoned cup. It promised to save them from a depression, only to kill them later at leisure. What was perceived as a failure of Keynesian economic management in the 1970s — an inflation that eroded the value of capital assets and favored the producers of commodities over the holders of financial assets — was in part simply the poison taking effect at long last.

The difficulties this posed for the Establishment were far reaching. After all, the Establishment was something like the organized voice of the American rentier. Harvard, Yale, the great foundations — from an economic standpoint, they are all rentiers, and they suffered severely as inflation eroded the value of their endowments. Liberal professors saw their real incomes decline as financially strapped private universities cut costs; liberal foundation and church bureaucrats had less grant-making power.

These developments could not fail to sap the confidence of Establishment liberals. Liberalism looked more like a utopian aspiration than a pragmatic policy, and the old Establishment lost its appetite for even the watered-down Keynesianism of the last generation.

In the Keynesian script this was the moment at which an alliance of vigorous, democratic socialists and progressive entrepreneurs would take over from the enfeebled Establishment and complete the euthanasia of the rentier class by smothering it in its sleep. But the Galbraith Effect had paralyzed American liberals and social democrats at the critical moment. Power passed, temporarily, into the hands of a conservative counter-Establishment that owed everything to an alliance of the new, not particularly enlightened, rich and those of the old rentier class who were resolved not to go gently into that good night; together, these groups would rage, rage against the dying of the light.

THE FOURTH REPUBLIC

The first American republic was an oligarchy. A limited franchise ensured that the wealthy, educated minority would control the government. The second republic was more democratic; the Jacksonians extended the franchise and, by introducing to the civil service the principle of rotation in office, crushed a nascent bureaucracy. The third republic, in whose dying decades we live, is once again bureaucratic and oligarchical. The liberalism of the Establishment made the bureaucratic republic work; the decay of the liberal Establishment signals the end of the third republic.

The decline of the social compromise that marked the heyday of the third republic stirred the popular and the Establishmentarian factions of the old liberal coalition back into action, but the resurgent liberalism of the 1980s and 1990s will not be a simple revival of the old liberalism of the third republic. The consequences of the Galbraith Effect on the popular wing of the coalition are transitory, but the decline of the Establishment is more lasting.

The Establishment will not be in the same position to supply the leadership for the next liberal wave. The popular wing of the liberal movement now has a much greater potential to provide its own leaders. Any newly resurgent liberal movement will have a more populist orientation than the New Deal. The next wave will have a more socialist and less liberal coloration than the first one; in this sense the intuition of the Establishment will be fulfilled; it will hand over power to the children — not only the sons — of its housemaids. The old liberal firm will be back in business at the old stand, but the positions of the partners will change, and the populist wing will ultimately emerge as the new senior partner.

This is a shift that will have great implications for the future, and these cannot be fully discussed here. One of them, however, deserves to be mentioned: the primary instrument for social change in the old liberal coalition was the appointed government of experts — the bureaucratic state. This was one of the threads that tied together the whole program of Establishment reform from the age of Theodore Roosevelt to the age of Robert McNamara. The purely political process was suspect; the administrative solution was the channel through which enlightened self-interest could flow. If liberalism and bureaucracy are almost synonyms in today's political lexicon, this is the consequence of a century of commissions and authorities. Franklin liked them as much as Theodore; they are still not without charm for Establishmentarian reformers. The only serious political misstep Franklin Roosevelt ever made was to threaten to pack the Supreme Court, the branch of government that most nearly corresponds to the ancient dream of benevolent aristrocrats: government by philosopher-kings. The court-packing scheme brought out all the "moderates" against him; to lay hands on a "nonpolitical" board for the sake of a "political" goal is the Establishment liberal's sin against the Holy Ghost.

With the ascendancy of the populist wing of liberalism, the throne of bureaucracy will tremble. The administrative structures that were the glory of yesterday's reformers are the objects of today's populist wrath. Antibureaucratic feeling and anti-Establishment passion are marks of the populist revolt that so far has embraced "conservative" issues. As the bread-and-butter issues move to the forefront, and the answers given by official conservative leadership begin to sound as inadequate as they did from 1929 to 1932, that populist movement will examine its economic interests more closely. Kevin Phillips has described the situation with his customary brilliance:

Many Southern fundamentalist and Northern right-to-life voters have been historically associated with a politics whose economics is more populist and activist than doctrinally conservative . . . . The voting blocs represented have often cheered such opponents of the prevailing power elite as Andrew Jackson, William Jennings Bryan, Franklin D. Roosevelt, and George C. Wallace . . . . In one form or another American populism has gathered force and helped to give ideological direction to the nation when it confronted various historical crossroads.[8]

The old social democratic coalition that made the New Deal has a long way to go before it can assume a new, coherent political shape. Yet this motley crew, this disorderly party, carries the future of American democracy, and perhaps much more than that, in its midst. If the Democrats can raise their sights high enough, history today may offer them another chance like the one they grasped in 1932. The Democratic Party is the natural and traditional home of American populism; that populism was shaped and guided in the Roosevelt years to sustain the vast growth of the American state and the extension of American power to every corner of the earth. Now, once again, populism — always primarily a movement of protest — must provide the basis for a sustained period of economic and political reform.

The reforms must go far beyond those of the Roosevelt period. The changes in international life will require a postimperial America to assume the more complex responsibilities of the *primus inter pares* in a kind of global commonwealth. The classic liberal response to this situation would be to increase the administrative element in government and to diminish the role of elected officials, but the altered balance of power within the liberal coalition makes it less likely that such a vast abdication of the power of democracy will be acceptable. Until and unless the present period of tension and crisis yields to another long, prosperous boom, an aroused public will want a government that is more, not less, responsive to the will of the people and even to their changing moods.

The old Establishment was, typically, the first section of the liberal coalition to perceive the importance of changing economic conditions, particularly as these affected the relationships among the leading countries of the Western alliance. One response among several was to organize the Trilateral Commission, whose mandate was to bring together key figures from Europe, America, and Japan in order to build bridges among those who were to find their destinies interwoven.

Anyone who follows economic news is aware that the economic policies of the major Western allies and the Japanese cannot be undertaken in isolation. What one does affects all, and given the potential instabilities in the economic system, it is foolish to rely on the chance that the allies will pursue policies that complement each other unless there is some kind of coordination.

This much is true regardless of who makes foreign policy. But if the process of international coordination goes on as envisioned by the elite —

central bankers huddling in secret meetings, unelected officials making policy choices binding each of their governments — then those parts of the government over which the public exercises its tenuous control will be effectively excluded from even a nominal role in setting economic policy.

The Establishment has always felt, with some justification, that this was the only way to carry out both foreign and economic policy. The American people have not distinguished themselves by the depth of their knowledge of international affairs. *Procul, o procul este, profani* was the old cry to the uninitiated to absent themselves from the site of secret rites, and in the realms of finance and foreign policy, the Establishment is as jealous of its mysteries as any ancient priest.

Such an attitude offends the democratic sensibility, but it has a more important flaw today: both foreign and international policies cannot long be carried out without the consent of the governed. The world's central bankers can meet all they want, but the American people will not be impressed by proposals that U.S. taxpayers pay $50 billion to bail out commercial banks with bad foreign loans. Boards of experts and non-political commissioners can negotiate all the trade treaties they want, but if protectionist feeling rises much higher in the United States, those treaties will become unenforceable.

Bureaucracy — government by a permanent class of unelected civil servants with considerable freedom to define policy — re-creates on a small scale the liberal coalition in which the Establishment is the senior partner. A small and powerful executive board of trustees exercises power in the interests of society; to a large extent this is how the liberal Establishment viewed itself in its heyday.

To find alternatives to bureaucracy for running the business of a large modern state will be a critical task of the new populist movement. Just as Nixon and Kissinger could not carry out a foreign military policy that the American people did not fully support, so diplomats and bankers will find their options limited — unless more effective means can be found to make the state so responsive to the popular will that the banking and foreign policy "communities" would never dream of setting policies that go beyond the limit of public tolerance.

This is not a matter simply of foreign policy. The growing interdependence of modern life requires an expansion of the role of government in almost every field. Urban planning has imposed itself as a responsibility on the most laissez-faire of Sun Belt cities; environmental necessities, resource planning, and regional development programs all stand to grow in future years, and they all require substantially greater government presence. There are signs that the bureaucratic model of government has reached its limits in coping with the complexity of society's needs. Fiascos like the ten-year New York City battle over Westway and the years of court and agency battles over such projects as nuclear power plants strongly suggest that the bureaucratic agency is an inappropriate institution for making many of the decisions needed by the United States. These agencies are less and less capable of doing what they were, supposedly, created to do: act in the general interest and rescue important decisions from the delays and chicanery of politics.

It may be that some variant of the jury system can be found to supplement bureaucratic government: boards of citizens either elected or selected by lot to hear cases made by adversarial experts and make findings of fact under the guidance of a "judge" trained in proper procedure. It may also be that greater use will be made of the referendum to decide specific major issues. In any case, bureaucracy is becoming an intolerably inefficient as well as a damnably unrepresentative governing tool, and major overhauls will soon be demanded by a frustrated public.

One consequence of this shift will be that our present politics of spectacle will slowly yield to a politics of education; the balance of power in electoral campaigns will shift from rich white politicians who project meaningless images in advertising blitzes. Politicians who rely on this kind of publicity will start to look glib and superficial as the public grows more concerned about the future. Those who can command the loyalty of active voluntary grassroots organizations and who can speak meaningfully to the issues facing the country will find that plain speaking brings political rewards.

To represent this antibureaucratic but progressive movement a new style of leadership will be required, one that emerges from popular movements instead of imposing itself on them. This may be frustrating to the Democratic elite, which feels itself trained and prepared to lead the masses better than they can lead themselves, but the needs of the country require that its leaders come from the grassroots, not from the ivory towers. When a new generation of leadership has emerged from the beleaguered farm, labor, feminist, black, and other populist movements, the disillusioned Reaganites not irrevocably wedded to reactionary chauvinism will find that this leadership is infinitely more capable of advancing the interests of the general population than are most current conventional leaders on either the right or the left.

TOWARD A NEW DEMOCRATIC AGENDA

We have already seen that the crux of the contemporary economic crisis lies in the blocked political development of the Third World countries; that the democratic and working-class forces are unable to forge the kind of social compromise there that brought stability to the developing West. Only the active support of the powerful democratic forces in the advanced countries can resolve the impasse in the Third World; only a resolution of the Third World's political problems can protect the social compromise in the advanced countries.

Once again, interest and morality coincide, and enlightened American statesmanship has the opportunity to advance the interests of the American people by making the world a safer and more humane place for all its peoples. The weight of the American government and of the allied industrial countries must be thrown into the scales on the side of social compromise in the developing world — minimum wage, health care, education, pollution control, and other programs that increase consumption in the Third World countries. The world has grown too small to contain the extremes of wealth and poverty now found in it, just as the United States once grew too small for slavery and free labor to coexist any longer.

The mid 1980s witnessed a quantum leap forward in the concern of the American public with international trade and political issues. A movement against apartheid spread through the country and led many municipal and state governments and churches to disinvest, to take economic measures to affect an international political issue. The Filipino Revolution of 1985 was made possible in part because of widespread popular American support for the democratic forces in the Philippines; they created a situation in which the American government had no choice but to work for the restoration of democracy. At the same time, various "Buy American" campaigns were gaining strength — often, but not always, among an entirely different portion of the citizenry.

To merge these movements should be the goal of the Democratic Party. The moral indignation and warm sympathy that Third World injustice has begun to evoke among the American public can complement the public's fear of low-wage foreign labor. Democrats — and people of good will of whatever party — should campaign for free trade for fair pay and work to tie American trade and tax concessions, foreign aid, and commercial loan guarantees to wage scales. Within limits, access to American markets and government assistance should be restricted to products made under decent conditions. Countries, firms, and industries that do not meet the appropriate standards for wages and benefits should find their products subject to sanctions that range from consumer boycotts to punitive tariffs to total embargoes. An anti-exploitation movement should unite labor, anti-intervention, peace and justice, and civil rights movements in a campaign that serves the general national interest.

Without a unifying vision of this kind, the New Deal coalition threatens to dissolve even more. Labor could sink into a sullen and purely negative campaign for protection, the rest of the world be damned. To fight for a Balkanization of the world economy would be disastrous, win or lose, and it would betray both the interests and the ideals of American working people.

As in the time of the first New Deal, a revitalized Democratic Party would have to take on the full fury of corporate America, but as in the age of Roosevelt, the Democrats would find not a few allies among the more intelligent business circles. The majority of multinational corporations unfortunately can be counted on to respond with all the sensitivity of a Victorian coal-mine operator to any suggestions that wages and working conditions be improved in foreign parts. Public relations firms will earn millions for campaigns to demonstrate that everything is as it should be in this best of all possible worlds.

But there will be allies. The Catholic Church has sought this kind of social compromise between labor and capital since the reign of Leo XIII. Domestic manufacturers will recognize that this policy orientation represents a long-term survival strategy for them. The more flexible and intelligent bankers and multinational corporate managers will understand that, however distasteful initially, action along these lines is overdue and represents in the long run their best hope for continued profitability.

The populist movements now loosely grouped in the New Right will find this program surprisingly attractive, particularly as its supporters shed the bureaucratic bias of old liberal politics. The free market is never so unpopular as when it has operated for a few years. More people observe that the market's race goes less often to the swift than to the large; whole regions as well as whole industries learn that the market has no pity for the unlucky.

The unfortunate tendencies toward racism and superpatriotism among the contemporary populists of the right are not as deeply rooted as some hope. They rest on the unfounded and ultimately unsustainable belief that the living standard of the American people can be defended by a politics of confrontation with the rest of the world. The populism of the Jackson era similarly began on a distinctly bigoted note, but within a generation it had matured into a populism that was antislavery, pro–trade union, and, by the standards of its time, staunchly feminist. Those who believe that the revival of evangelical religion presages an era of conservative populism should also look carefully at the historical record. The previous great awakenings in American history have ushered in periods of intense political struggle for progressive goals — the Revolution itself in the eighteenth century and the antislavery and agrarian movements in the nineteenth.

The deafening silence from the baby-boom generation and the apparent acquiescence of youth to the ideological climate of the Reagan years do not mean that the postwar generations have given their permanent allegiance to the right. The career of David Stockman, the first member of the baby-boom generation to reach the inner circles of national power, is instructive in this regard. According to Stockman's own account of his life, before he left his thirties he had lost faith in three different political philosophies: the traditional conservatism in which he was raised, the fashionable radicalism he adopted in his youth, and the supply-side Reaganism that made him famous. The constants in Stockman's life have been a sense that the nation faces a crisis of major proportions, and that the formulas of conventional wisdom do not adequately deal with it. At the time he wrote *The Triumph of Politics,* Stockman had not yet found a political philosophy to which he could make a lasting commitment; a career that had already carried him to the political and financial summit left him still unformed in his views, still skeptical of the conventional wisdom, and still convinced that the nation was in crisis.

One cannot predict the evolution of David Stockman beyond speculating that he may not find satisfactory answers to the great questions of life among the bond analysts at Salomon Brothers; for our purposes it is important to note that only his great success sets him off from his contemporaries. Like them, his life has been spent in a search for a working system of belief; like them, he has brought to each of his commitments, however temporary, an intensity of energy that has changed the American landscape.

In the 1960s, at a time when the intellectual and political potentates of the liberal tradition were glorying in their triumph and prophesying new victories for their ideas, the younger generation took note that this complacency expressed a failure to comprehend the drift of the times, not a mastery of the tides of history. While the shepherds of the liberal flock made afterdinner speeches to memorialize their exciting new discoveries in husbandry, the lambs slipped out of the sheepfold. Some wandered into the mountains and fell from the cliffs; others were eagerly met by wolves and other bad characters only too happy to introduce the young innocents to the doctrines of Ayn Rand and Milton Friedman.

The postwar generation grew up in a society without a working political and philosophical world view. Thrown on their own resources, they embraced and discarded a succession of religious and political ideas, working by trial and error toward a world view of their own. In youth, their attempts were not particularly successful. A generation that took Jerry Rubin and Bobby Seale for serious political thinkers in its teens can be forgiven a similar mistake with Arthur Laffer and George Gilder in its twenties. The baby boom generation was no more fortunate with its religious gurus; its pilgrimage from the Maharishi to the 700 Club has been motivated by discontent with the old American consensus, but it has not yet found something that can replace it.

The postwar generation is still restless, still searching. One does not know how many of the lost sheep of liberalism can be reclaimed for the flock, but we can hope that a regenerate liberalism can say, with a much greater shepherd, "My sheep know my voice." The values that made the old American liberalism — for all its shortcomings — a powerful force for progress remain the most deeply felt values of the American people. Cooperation, tolerance, and human solidarity are values for which contemporary conservatism has little room, yet these values exercise a compelling attraction to the American mind. The generation of Americans now moving toward maturity is more responsive than most to these values; its impact on American life will not be complete until it recasts the liberal, democratic American vision in terms suited to the world in which it lives, and then reshapes the American scene in harmony with this vision.

The liberal vision — we could just as well say the American vision — at heart is a vision of gradual democratization. It holds that in spite of the crimes and horrors that illustrate the annals of humanity, we *are* making progress. The slaves are free, women have the vote, children go to school and not to the mines, and old people get checks from the government. The French, the Germans, and the British have stopped their endless warfare; Catholics sit in the House of Commons; the Inquisition has put away the thumbscrews.

While examples of new horrors could be adduced to offset any catalogue of crimes put behind us, the experience that keeps alive faith in progress is the experience we have of the free cooperation on a wide scale that makes daily life possible in the intricately interdependent society in which we live. No system that rests on naked force could operate a modern economy, and the history of the last century in the Western democracies has been the gradual replacement of force and oppression by cooperation and compromise. It seems inevitable that, as life continues to grow more complicated, cooperation will become ever more widespread.

That cooperation once seemed to stop at national boundaries, but no longer. The Western industrial democracies together have achieved a degree of political and economic integration that compares favorably with that of any individual European state before the Industrial Revolution. The fierce nationalism that once served the emerging industrial countries as a social bond to mitigate class conflict has largely disappeared. Two devastating wars in this century did not produce a new legacy of hatred; rather, they convinced all the peoples most directly involved of the utter futility of war.

The logic of liberalism holds that the world will continue to become a more cooperative place. The spread of industrialization will, one way or another, raise living standards in the Third World and usher in more democracy. This process may take longer than the optimistic American diplomats projected in the euphoria of 1945, when the world seemed to be ours; there may be more twists and turns than anyone anticipated on that road to Stockholm on which Harriman thought we were all traveling. Even so, we seem to have made some headway.

Americans were not wrong to build the politics of compromise in the twentieth century. Liberal capitalism, the welfare state, social democracy, whatever name we give to this system, it brought us many benefits and spared us many sorrows. The architects of that order had too simple a view, we now know, of the course of world development. They felt that, once achieved, the social compromise of social democracy would put an end to economic crises and to the kinds of political upheaval that have so scarred the planet in the twentieth century.

To our sorrow, we know that this was not true. There is nothing eternal about the great liberal compromise. Society continues to evolve; its political and cultural forms must change with it.

We cannot even say that the present crisis is the last. We can extend the social compromise into the Third World, and we can reform the political system in our own country, but there is no assurance that the next decade or the next generation won't bring on some new challenge. One seems to be brewing already: the progress of technology promises (or threatens, depending on one's point of view) to replace human labor in most industrial applications. It is one thing to contemplate a wonderful world where no one has to work for more than ten hours a week; it is quite another to develop programs that could win the necessary political support for moving from here to there.

It seems to be our fate, as far as the eye can see, to live in a world in which titanic forces are precariously balanced. There is nothing about the political or economic facts of contemporary life that automatically brings order out of chaos.

Nothing, that is, except the unconquerable will of human beings to build a decent world for themselves and their children, and their ability to organize themselves for whatever challenges they are given by history and fate.

Notes
Selected Bibliography
Index

NOTES

Chapter 1

1. Thucydides, *The Peloponnesian War*, Rex Warner, trans. (New York: Penguin, 1952), p. 105.
2. Winston Churchill, *The Second World War*, vol. 1, *The Gathering Storm* (Boston: Houghton Mifflin, 1950), p. 33.

Chapter 2

1. Bishop George Berkeley, *The Works of George Berkeley, Bishop of Cloyne*, vol. 7, A. A. Luce and T. E. Jessup, eds. (London: Nelson, 1955), "On the Prospect of Planting Arts and Learning in America," p. 373.
2. For an estimate on Native American population in 1500, see Samuel E. Morison, Henry Steele Commager, and William E. Leuchtenburg, *The Growth of the American Republic*, seventh edition (Oxford: Oxford University Press, 1980), vol. 1, p. 13. For the nadir of the Native American population, see U.S. Bureau of the Census, *Historical Statistics of the United States: Colonial Times to 1970* (Washington, D.C.: 1975), tables on p. 14 and note on p. 3.
3. Churchill, *Second World War*, vol. 2, *Their Finest Hour*, p. 566.
4. A. J. P. Taylor, *English History, 1914–1945* (Oxford: Oxford University Press, 1965), p. 599.
5. Churchill, *Their Finest Hour*, p. 568.
6. For Soviet casualties in the siege of Leningrad, see Harrison E. Salisbury, *The 900 Days: The Siege of Leningrad* (New York: Harper and Row, 1969), pp. 514–517. For U.S. casualties in previous wars, see *The World Almanac and Book of Facts: 1986* (New York: Newspaper Enterprise Association, 1985), p. 333.

Chapter 4

1. Thucydides, *The Peloponnesian War*, p. 145.
2. For a detailed description of the involvement of American, European, and Japanese firms in selected Far Eastern low-wage countries, see Business International Asia/Pacific Ltd., *World Sourcing Sites in Asia*. See also individual country reports in the series *Investment Climate in Foreign Countries*, U.S.

Department of Commerce, International Trade Administration (Washington, D.C.: 1983).

Chapter 5

1. Bureau of Labor Statistics, *Earnings and Employment* (Washington, D.C.: 1986), June 1986.
2. B. R. Mitchell, *European Historical Statistics,* second revised edition (New York: Facts on File, 1980), pp. 378–379.
3. Richard Nixon, *The Real War* (New York: Warner Books, 1980), p. 238.
4. Ibid., p. 23.
5. Ibid., p. 25.
6. Ibid., pp. 4, 43, 83, 166.
7. Ibid., pp. 3, 12.
8. Ibid., pp. 244–245.

Chapter 6

1. Kissinger, *White House Years,* pp. 513–514.
2. Ibid., p. 298.
3. Speech, delivered on October 16, 1952.
4. Henry A. Kissinger, *Years of Upheaval* (Boston: Little, Brown, 1982), p. 308.
5. Richard Nixon, *RN: The Memoirs of Richard Nixon* (New York: Warner Books, 1979), vol. 2, p. 249.
6. John Dryden, "Absalom and Achitophel," *Poems and Fables of John Dryden,* James Kinsley, ed. (Oxford: Oxford University Press, 1970), p. 205.
7. Kissinger, *White House Years,* p. 37.
8. Ibid., p. 59.
9. Ibid., p. 1357.

Chapter 8

1. *Economic Report of the President: 1985,* table B-109, p. 356, shows the Soviet GNP growing at a faster rate than that of the United States from 1960 to 1976 and again after 1980.
2. U.S. Bureau of the Census, *Statistical Abstract of the United States: 1986,* 106th edition (Washington, D.C.: 1985), pp. 417, 390, 438, and 445.
3. U.S. Bureau of the Census, *Statistical Abstract of the United States: 1984,* 104th edition (Washington, D.C.: 1983), p. 403.
4. Richard S. Hofstadter, *The American Political Tradition and the Men Who Made It* (New York: Vintage, 1974), p. 317.
5. Jimmy Carter, *Keeping Faith: Memoirs of a President* (New York: Bantam, 1982), p. 142.
6. Douglas Botting, *From the Ruins of the Reich: Germany, 1945–49* (New York: Crown, 1985). See especially pp. 141–143.

7. Richard J. Barnet, *The Alliance: Europe, America, Japan: Makers of the Postwar World* (New York: Simon and Schuster, 1983), p. 102.
8. Alfred Grosser, *The Western Alliance: European-American Relations Since 1945* (New York: Vintage, 1980), p. 92.
9. Carter, *Memoirs,* p. 141.
10. Ibid., p. 80.

Chapter 9

1. Alexis de Tocqueville, *Democracy in America* (New York: Anchor, 1969), p. 722.
2. A. J. P. Taylor, *English History,* p. 94.
3. Article IV, *The Articles of Confederation.* See *American Historical Documents 1000–1904,* Harvard Classics, vol. 43, Charles W. Eliot, ed. (New York: Collier, 1910), pp. 158–168.
4. de Tocqueville, *Democracy,* p. 722.

Chapter 11

1. Gilder, *Wealth and Poverty* (New York: Basic Books, 1980), p. 21.
2. Richard A. Viguerie, *The New Right: We're Ready to Lead* (Falls Church, Virginia: Viguerie Company, 1980), pp. 58–59.
3. Gilder, *Wealth and Poverty,* p. 21.

Chapter 12

1. Viguerie, *The New Right.*
2. Kristol, *Confessions of a Neoconservative: Looking Back, Looking Ahead* (New York: Basic Books, 1983), p. 227.
3. Psalm 37:2,10, Revised Standard Version.
4. Churchill, *The Gathering Storm,* p. 320.
5. Kristol, *Confessions,* pp. 241–242.
6. From Falwell's Introduction to Viguerie, *The New Right* (no page number in text).
7. See Viguerie, *The New Right,* Chapter VII "Our Goal, Military Superiority," pp. 133–154.
8. These facts were widely reported during and after the invasion of Grenada. For one day's harvest, see the following articles from the October 27, 1983, issue of the *New York Times:*
   "Reagan Aide Says U.S. Invasion Forestalled Cuban Arms Buildup" by Hedrick Smith, p. A-1.
   "U.S. Bars Coverage of Grenada Action; News Groups Protest" by Phil Gaily, p. A-1.
   "First Evacuees in U.S. From Grenada" by Fay S. Joyce, p. A-1.
9. Kristol, *Confessions,* p. 273.

Chapter 13

1. Kevin Phillips, *Post-Conservative America: People, Politics and Ideology in a Time of Crisis* (New York: Vintage, 1983). See especially Chapter 3, "To the Nashville Station: The (Partial) Transformation of U.S. Conservatism."
2. See Hal Lindsey with C. C. Carlson, *The Late Great Planet Earth* (Grand Rapids, Michigan: Zondervan, 1970), and Hal Lindsey, *The 1980's: Countdown to Armageddon* (New York: Bantam, 1980). Lindsey was reputedly the best-selling American writer in the 1970s.
3. John Kenneth Galbraith, *The New Industrial State* (Boston: Houghton Mifflin, 1967), Chapter Two, "Imperatives of Technology."
4. Richard Olney to C. E. Perkins, quoted in Matthew Josephson, *The Politicos* (New York: Harcourt, Brace, 1938), p. 394.

Chapter 14

1. Richard A. Viguerie, *The Establishment vs. The People: Is a New Populist Revolt on the Way?* (Chicago: Regnery Gateway, 1983). See Chapter 3, "Big Business."
2. From "The Voice of the Lobster," by Lewis Carroll. Gavin Ewart, ed., *The Penguin Book of Light Verse* (Harmondsworth, England: Penguin, 1980), p. 338.
3. Aleksandr Solzhenitsyn, *The Gulag Archipelago: An Experiment in Literary Investigation V–VII* (New York: Harper and Row, 1978), pp. 475–476.
4. Gilder, *Wealth,* p. 140.
5. Ibid., p. 12.
6. Ibid., p. 66.
7. Ibid., pp. 114–115.
8. Ibid., pp. 149–152.
9. Ibid., p. 21.
10. Ibid., p. 124.
11. Nixon, *The Real War,* p. 35.

Chapter 15

1. Inter-American Development Bank, *Economic and Social Progress in Latin America: 1986 Report* (Washington, D.C.: Inter-American Development Bank, 1986), p. 58, Table IV-5.
2. *Economic Report of the President: 1986,* p. 301, Table B-42.
3. Ibid., p. 378, Table B-110.
4. Tamar Jacoby, "Reagan's Turnaround on Human Rights," *Foreign Affairs* 64 (Summer 1986), p. 1067.
5. John Wilmot, Earl of Rochester, "Impromptu on Charles II." Gavin Ewart, ed., *Light Verse,* p. 130.
6. *Economic Report of the President: 1986,* p. 378, Table B-110.

7. David Gordon, "The New Class War," *Washington Post* (October 26, 1986), p. B-1.
8. Ibid.
9. Institute for Labor Economics and Research, *What's Wrong with the U.S. Economy? A Popular Guide for the Rest of Us* (Boston: South End Press, 1982), p. 355. See Figures 20.5a and 20.5b.
10. Rudyard Kipling, *Rudyard Kipling's Verse: Definitive Edition* (Garden City, New York: Doubleday, 1940), p. 327.

Chapter 16

1. Valéry Giscard d'Estaing, *Foreign Affairs* 62 (Fall 1983), p. 186.

Chapter 17

1. Bureau of Labor Statistics, *Handbook,* pp. 204–205, Table 81 and *Economic Report of the President: 1986,* pp. 298–299, Table B-40.
2. *Economic Report of the President,* p. 264, Table B-27.
3. Bureau of Labor Statistics, *Handbook,* p. 435, Table 132.

Chapter 18

1. For a discussion of historical and contemporary United States interests in Central America, see Jenny Pearce, *Under the Eagle: U.S. Intervention in Central America and the Caribbean* (Boston: South End Press, 1979).

Chapter 21

1. Walker Percy, *Love in the Ruins: The Adventures of a Bad Catholic Near the End of the World* (New York: Farrar, Straus and Giroux, 1971), p. 3.
2. *American Historical Documents,* p. 233.
3. Ronald Steele, *Walter Lippmann and the American Century* (Boston: Little, Brown, 1980), p. 89.
4. William Faulkner, *Intruder in the Dust,* p. 153.
5. Robinson Jeffers, *The Selected Poetry of Robinson Jeffers* (New York: Random House, 1931), p. 168.

Chapter 22

1. Thucydides, *Peloponnesian War,* p. 216.
2. David S. McClellan and David C. Acheson, eds., *Among Friends: Personal Letters of Dean Acheson* (New York: Dodd, Mead, 1980), p. 28.

3. Dean Acheson, *Grapes from Thorns* (New York: W. W. Norton, 1972), p. 126.
4. McClellan and Acheson, *Among Friends*, p. 190.
5. W. Averell Harriman, *America and Russia in a Changing World: A Half Century of Personal Observation* (Garden City, New York: Doubleday, 1971), p. 150.
6. Harriman, *America and Russia*, pp. 169–170.
7. George F. Kennan, *Memoirs: 1925–50* (Boston: Little, Brown, 1967), p. 599.
8. Nixon, *The Real War*, p. 2.
9. Ibid., pp. 41, 42.
10. McClellan and Acheson, *Among Friends*, p. 169.

Chapter 23

1. Harriman, *America and Russia*, pp. 166–167.
2. Ibid., p. 7.
3. Dean Acheson, *Present at the Creation: My Years in the State Department* (New York: W. W. Norton, 1969), p. 229.

Chapter 24

1. For a critical analysis of the inefficiencies of import-substitution development strategies, see Anne O. Krueger, *Trade and Employment in Developing Countries*, volume 3, *Synthesis and Conclusions* (Chicago: University of Chicago Press, 1983), especially pp. 40–54.
2. For a discussion of the scope and consequences of export-led growth policies, see Folker Frobel, Jürgen Heinricks, and Otto Krege, *The New International Division of Labour*, Pete Burgess, trans. (Cambridge: Cambridge University Press, 1980), part 3.
3. Source: The World Bank, *World Development Report: 1986* (Oxford: Oxford University Press, 1986).

Chapter 25

1. John Kenneth Galbraith, *The New Industrial State* (Boston: Houghton Mifflin, 1967), p. 276.
2. Elliott Roosevelt, ed., *F.D.R. His Personal Letters: Early Years* (New York: Duell, Sloan and Pearce, 1947), p. 378.
3. Dean Acheson, *Sketches from Life of Men I Have Known* (New York: Harper and Brothers, 1961), p. 16.
4. Christopher T. E. Rand, "The School in Time and Space," in *Views from the Circle: Seventy-Five Years of Groton School* (Groton, Massachusetts: Trustees of Groton School, 1960), p. 219.
5. Ibid., p. 225.

6. For a discussion of resistance to "left-Keynesianism" and the transformation between the Keynesianism of Keynes and that of American policymakers, see Alan Wolfe, *America's Impasse: The Rise and Fall of the Politics of Growth* (Boston: South End Press, 1981), Chapter 3, "Counter-Keynesianism."
7. For these aspects of Keynes's theory, see John Maynard Keynes, *The General Theory of Employment, Interest and Money* (New York: Harcourt, Brace and World, 1936), Chapter 24, "Concluding Notes."
8. Kevin Phillips, *Post-Conservative America,* p. xxii.

Selected Bibliography

It would be neither possible nor desirable to list all the works consulted in the preparation of *Mortal Splendor*. The books and articles listed here include those (except newspaper articles cited in the notes) quoted in the text, those most likely to be helpful to the curious reader, and those to whom the author's debt is so great that they cannot be omitted.

Acheson, Dean. *Sketches from Life of Men I Have Known*. New York: Harper and Brothers, 1960.

———. *Present at the Creation: My Years in the State Department*. New York: W. W. Norton, 1969.

———. *Fragments of My Fleece*. New York: W. W. Norton, 1971.

———. *Grapes from Thorns*. New York: W. W. Norton, 1972.

Agee, Philip. *Inside the Company: CIA Diary*. New York: Stonehill Publishing, 1975.

Ahlstrom, Sydney. *A Religious History of the American People*. New Haven: Yale University Press, 1972.

Ambrose, Stephen E. *Rise to Globalism: American Foreign Policy, 1938–1980*. Pelican History of the United States. Vol. 8. Second revised edition. New York: Penguin Books, 1980.

American Historical Documents, 1000–1904. Harvard Classics. Vol. 43. Charles W. Eliot, ed. New York: P. F. Collier, 1910.

Anderson, Perry. *Passages from Antiquity to Feudalism*. London: Verso, 1978.

———. *Considerations on Western Marxism*. London: Verso, 1979.

———. *Lineages of the Absolutist State*. London: Verso, 1979.

Arendt, Hannah. *On Revolution*. New York: Viking Compass, 1965.

Aristotle. *Politics*. Modern Library. 1943.

Aronowitz, Stanley. "The Decline of American Liberalism." *New Politics* I (Summer 1986).

Ashburn, Frank Davis. *Fifty Years On: Groton School 1884–1934*. New York, privately printed, Gosden Head, 1934.

Bahro, Rudolf. *The Alternative in Eastern Europe*. London: Verso, 1981.

Banfield, Edward C. *The Unheavenly City Revisited*. Boston: Little, Brown, 1974.

Barnet, Richard J. *The Alliance: America, Europe, Japan: Makers of the Modern World.* New York: Simon and Schuster, 1983.

Barnet, Richard J., and Ronald E. Muller. *Global Reach: The Power of the Multinational Corporations.* New York: Simon and Schuster, 1974.

Barraclough, Geoffrey. *An Introduction to Contemporary History.* Baltimore: Pelican, 1970.

Barrone, Michael, and Grant Ujifusa. *The Almanac of American Politics, 1984: The President, the Senators, the Representatives, the Governors: Their Records and Election Results, Their States and Districts.* Washington, D.C.: National Journal, 1983.

Barry, Colman J. *Readings in Church History: The Modern Era: 1789 to the Present.* New York: Newman Press, 1965.

Beard, Charles Austin, and Mary R. Beard. *New Basic History of the United States.* Revised by William Beard. Garden City, New York: Doubleday, 1968.

Bello, Walden, and David Kinley. *Development Debacle: The World Bank and the Philippines.* Washington, D.C.: Institute for Food and Development Policy, 1982.

Benson, Mary. *Nelson Mandela: The Man and the Movement.* New York: W. W. Norton, 1986.

Berger, Peter L., and Michael Novak. *Speaking to the Third World: Essays on Democracy and Development.* Washington, D.C.: American Enterprise Institute for Public Policy Research, 1985.

Berger, Peter L. "Democracy for Everyone?" *Commentary* 76 (September 1983).

Berkeley, Bishop George. *The Works of George Berkeley, Bishop of Cloyne.* A. A. Luce and T. E. Jessup, eds. Vol. 7. London: Nelson, 1955.

Biko, B. Stephen. *Steve Biko: Black Consciousness in South Africa.* Millard Arnold, ed. New York: Random House, 1978.

Blumberg, Paul. *Inequality in an Age of Decline.* Oxford: Oxford University Press, 1980.

Botting, Douglas. *From the Ruins of the Reich: Germany, 1945–49.* New York: Crown, 1985.

Bottomore, Tom. *A Dictionary of Marxist Thought.* Cambridge, Massachusetts: Harvard University Press, 1983.

Bowles, Samuel, and Herbert Gintis. *Democracy and Capitalism: Property, Community and the Contradictions of Modern Social Thought.* New York: Basic Books, 1986.

Brandt, Willy, and Anthony Sampson. *North-South: A Program for Survival.* Cambridge, Massachusetts: MIT Press, 1980.

Bressard, Albert. "Mastering the 'Worldeconomy.' " *Foreign Affairs* 61 (Spring 1983).

Buckley, William F., Jr. *A Hymnal: The Controversial Arts.* New York: Putnam, 1978.

———. *Up from Liberalism.* New York: Stein and Day, 1984.

Bullock, Alan Louis Charles. *Hitler, A Study in Tyranny.* Revised edition. London: Hamlyn, 1973.

Bureau of Labor Statistics. *Handbook of Labor Statistics: 1985*. Washington, D.C.: 1985.

Business International Asia/Pacific, Ltd. *World Sourcing Sites in Asia: Manufacturing Costs and Conditions in Hong Kong, Korea, Singapore and Taiwan*. Hong Kong: Business International Asia/Pacific, Ltd., 1979.

Brzezinski, Zbigniew. *Power and Principle: Memoirs of the National Security Advisor, 1977–1981*. Revised edition. New York: Farrar, Straus, and Giroux, 1985.

Burbach, Roger. "Revolution and Reaction: U.S. Policy in Central America." *Monthly Review* 36 (June 1984).

Burnham, James. *The Coming Defeat of Communism*. New York: John Day, 1950.

Caro, Robert A. *The Years of Lyndon Johnson: The Rise to Power*. New York: Alfred A. Knopf, 1982.

Carr, Edward Hallet. *The Bolshevik Revolution*. Three vols. New York: W. W. Norton, 1985.

Carter, Jimmy. *Keeping Faith: Memoirs of a President*. New York: Bantam, 1983.

Castro, Fidel. *The World Economic and Social Crisis: Report to the Seventh Summit Conference of the Non-Aligned Countries*. Havana: Publishing Office of the Council of State, 1983.

Chaikin, Sol C. "Trade, Investment and Deindustrialization: 'Myth and Reality.' " *Foreign Affairs* 60 (Spring 1982).

Chomsky, Noam. *Towards a New Cold War: Essays on the Current Crisis and How We Got There*. New York: Pantheon, 1982.

Chomsky, Noam, and Edward S. Herman. *The Political Economy of Human Rights*. Montreal: Black Rose, 1979.

———. *The Washington Connection and Third World Fascism*. Boston: South End Press, 1979.

Churchill, Winston S. *The Second World War*. Six vols. Boston: Houghton Mifflin, 1948–1953.

Clarke, Roger A., and J. I. Matkow Dubravoko. *Soviet Economic Facts, 1917–1981*. Second edition. London: Macmillan, 1983.

Cline, William R. "Mexico's Crisis, The World's Peril," *Foreign Policy* 49 (Winter 1982–1983).

The Commonwealth Group of Eminent Persons. *Mission to South Africa: The Commonwealth Report*. Harmondsworth, England: Penguin, 1986.

The Complete Anti-Federalist. Herber J. Storing with Murray Day, eds. Chicago: University of Chicago Press, 1981.

Corbo, Vittorio, Anne O. Krueger, and Fernando Ossa, eds. *Export-Oriented Development Strategies: The Success of Five Newly Industrializing Countries*. Boulder, Colorado: Westview Press, 1985.

Deutscher, Isaac. *Stalin, A Political Biography*. Second edition. London: Oxford University Press, 1966.

Diebold, William, Jr. "The United States in the World Economy: A Fifty-Year Perspective." *Foreign Affairs* 62 (Fall 1983).

Dobb, Maurice. *Theories of Value and Distribution Since Adam Smith: Ideology and Economic Theory*. Cambridge: Cambridge University Press, 1973.

Drew, Elizabeth. *Politics and Money: The New Road to Corruption.* New York: Macmillan, 1983.

Drucker, Peter F. "The Changed World Economy." *Foreign Affairs* 64 (Spring 1986).

Dryden, John. *The Poems and Fables of John Dryden.* James Kinsley, ed. Oxford: Oxford University Press, 1970.

Eagleson, John, and Philip Scharper, eds. *Puebla and Beyond: Documentation and Commentary.* John Drury, trans. Maryknoll, New York: Orbis Books, 1979.

Economic Report of the President: 1985. Washington, D.C.: 1985.

Economic Report of the President: 1986. Washington, D.C.: 1986.

Ewart, Gavin, ed. *The Penguin Book of Light Verse.* Harmondsworth, England: Penguin, 1980.

Fallows, James. *National Defense.* New York: Random House, 1981.

Faulkner, William. *Intruder in the Dust.* New York: Random House, 1948.

Frank, André Gunder. *Capitalism and Underdevelopment in Latin America: Historical Studies of Chile and Brazil.* New York: Monthly Review Press, 1969.

Friedman, John S., ed. *First Harvest: The Institute for Policy Studies, 1963–1983.* New York: Grove Press, 1983.

Frobel, Folker, Jürgen Heinricks, and Otto Krege. *The New International Division of Labour.* Pete Burgess, trans. Cambridge: Cambridge University Press, 1980.

Galbraith, John Kenneth. *The Affluent Society.* Boston: Houghton Mifflin, 1958.

———. *The Liberal Hour.* Boston: Houghton Mifflin, 1960.

———. *The New Industrial Society.* Boston: Houghton Mifflin, 1967.

———. *A Life in Our Times: Memoirs.* Boston: Houghton Mifflin, 1981.

Garwood, Darrell. *Under Cover: Thirty-Five Years of CIA Deception.* Black Cat Edition. New York: Grove Press, 1985.

Gettleman, Marvin E., Patrick Lacefield, Louis Menaske, David Mermelstein, and Ronald Radosh. *El Salvador: Central America in the New Cold War.* New York: Grove Press, 1981.

Gibbon, Edward. *The Decline and Fall of the Roman Empire.* Three volumes. Modern Library Edition.

Gilder, George. *Wealth and Poverty.* New York: Basic Books, 1981.

Giscard d'Estaing, Valéry, "New Opportunities and New Challenges." *Foreign Affairs* 62 (Fall 1983).

Goodman, Paul. *Growing Up Absurd: Problems of Youth in the Organizational System.* New York: Random House, 1960.

Gramsci, Antonio. *Selections from the Prison Notebooks of Antonio Gramsci.* Quentin Hoare and Geoffrey Nowell Smith, translators and eds. New York: International Publishers, 1971.

———. *Selections from Political Writings (1921–1926), with Additional Texts by Other Italian Communist Leaders.* Quentin Hoare, trans. and ed. New York: International Publishers, 1978.

Gross, Bertram. *Friendly Fascism: The New Face of Power in America.* New York: M. Evans, 1980.

Grosser, Alfred. *The Western Alliance: European-American Relations Since 1945*. Michael Shaw, trans. New York: Vintage Books, 1982.

Hacker, Andrew, with Lorrie Millman. *U/S: A Statistical Portrait of the American People*. New York: Viking, 1983.

Haig, Alexander Meigs. *Caveat: Realism, Reagan and Foreign Policy*. New York: Macmillan, 1984.

Halberstam, David. *The Best and the Brightest*. New York: Random House, 1972.

———. *The Reckoning*. New York: Morrow, 1986.

Hammond, Bray. *Banks and Politics in America from the Revolution to the Civil War*. Princeton: Princeton University Press, 1957.

Harriman, W. Averell. *America and Russia in a Changing World: A Half Century of Personal Observation*. Garden City, New York: Doubleday, 1971.

Harrington, Michael. *Decade of Decision*. New York: Simon and Schuster, 1980.

Harrop, David. *World Paychecks: Who Makes What, Where and Why*. New York: Facts on File, 1982.

Hart, Gary. *A New Democracy*. New York: Morrow, 1983.

Hayek, Friedrich A. *The Road to Serfdom*. Chicago: University of Chicago Press, 1944.

Heilbroner, Robert L. *Marxism For and Against*. New York: W. W. Norton, 1980.

———. *The Worldly Philosophers: The Lives, Times and Ideas of the Great Economic Thinkers*. Fifth edition. New York: Simon and Schuster, 1980.

Herman, Edward S. *Corporate Control, Corporate Power*. A Twentieth Century Fund Study. Cambridge: Cambridge University Press, 1981.

———. *The Real Terror Network: Terrorism in Fact and Propaganda*. Boston: South End Press, 1982.

Herman, Edward S., and Frank Brodhead. *Demonstration Elections: U.S.–Staged Elections in the Dominican Republic, Vietnam, and El Salvador*. Boston: South End Press, 1984.

Hersh, Seymour M. *The Price of Power: Kissinger in the Nixon White House*. New York: Summit Books, 1983.

Hession, Charles H. *John Maynard Keynes: A Personal Biography of the Man Who Revolutionized Capitalism*. New York: Macmillan, 1984.

Hill, Christopher. *The Century of Revolution, 1603–1714*. Norton Library History of England. General eds., Christopher Brooke and Denis Mack Smith. New York: W. W. Norton, 1982.

Hobsbawm, E. J. *The Age of Revolution, 1789–1848*. New York: New American Library, 1962.

———. *Industry and Empire from 1750 to the Present Day*. London: Weidenfeld and Nicolson, 1968.

Hofstadter, Richard. *The American Political Tradition and the Men Who Made It*. New York: Alfred A. Knopf, 1948.

Johnson, Paul. *Modern Times: The World from the Twenties to the Eighties*. New York: Harper Colophon, 1985.

Inter-American Development Bank. *Economic and Social Progress in Latin America:*

1986 Report. Washington, D.C.: Inter-American Development Bank, 1986.
International Labour Office. *Yearbook of Labour Statistics.* Forty-fifth edition. Geneva: International Labour Organization, 1985.
Institute for Labor Education and Research. *What's Wrong with the U.S. Economy? A Guide for the Rest of Us.* Boston: South End Press, 1982.
Jacoby, Tamar. "Reagan's Turnaround on Human Rights." *Foreign Affairs* 64 (Summer 1986).
Jeffers, Robinson. *The Selected Poetry of Robinson Jeffers.* New York: Random House, 1931.
Josephson, Matthew. *The Robber Barons: The Great American Capitalists, 1861–1901.* New York: Harcourt, Brace, 1934.
———. *The Politicos: 1865–1896.* New York: Harcourt, Brace, 1938.
Karnow, Stanley. *Vietnam, A History.* New York: Viking, 1983.
Kaufman, Henry. *Interest Rates, the Markets and the New Financial World.* New York: Times Books, 1986.
Kennan, George F. *Memoirs: 1925–1950.* Boston: Atlantic Monthly Press, 1967.
Keynes, John Maynard. *The General Theory of Employment, Interest and Money.* New York: Harcourt, Brace and World, 1936.
———. *The Economic Consequences of the Peace.* The Collected Writings of John Maynard Keynes. Vol. 2. Royal Economic Society Edition. London: Macmillan, 1971.
Kimball, Penn. "A New Direction for the Democrats?" *Commentary* 74 (October 1982).
King, Martin Luther, Jr. *Why We Can't Wait.* New York: Harper and Row, 1963.
Kipling, Rudyard. *Rudyard Kipling's Verse: Definitive Edition.* Garden City, New York: Doubleday, 1940.
Kirkpatrick, Jeane J. "Dictatorships and Double Standards," *Commentary* 68 (November 1979).
Kissinger, Henry. *White House Years.* Boston: Little, Brown, 1979.
———. *Years of Upheaval.* Boston, Little, Brown, 1982.
Kozlov, G. A., general ed. *Political Economy: Capitalism.* Jane Sayer, trans. Moscow: Progress Publishers, 1977.
Kristol, Irving. *Two Cheers for Capitalism.* New York: Basic Books, 1978.
———. *Reflections of a Neoconservative: Looking Back, Looking Ahead.* New York, Basic Books, 1983.
———. "The Political Dilemma of American Jews." *Commentary* 78 (July 1984).
Krueger, Anne O., et al., eds. *Trade and Employment in Developing Countries.* 3 vols. Chicago: University of Chicago Press, 1983.
Kwitney, Jonathan. *Endless Enemies: The Making of an Unfriendly World.* New York: Congdon and Weed, 1984.
Lasch, Christopher. *The Culture of Narcissism: American Life in an Age of Diminishing Expectations.* New York: W. W. Norton, 1979.
Lekachman, Robert. *Greed Is Not Enough: Reaganomics.* New York: Pantheon, 1982.

Lelyveld, Joseph. *Move Your Shadow: South Africa, Black and White*. New York: Times Books, 1985.

Lenin, Vladimir Ilich. *Selected Works in Three Volumes*. Revised edition. Moscow: Progress Publishers, 1975.

Leonard, Wolfgang. *Three Faces of Marxism: The Political Concepts of Soviet Ideology, Maoism, and Humanist Marxism*. Ewald Osers, trans. New York: Holt, Rinehart and Winston, 1974.

Lernoux, Penny. *Cry of the People: The Struggle for Human Rights in Latin America — The Catholic Church in Conflict with U.S. Policy*. New York: Penguin Books, 1982.

Leuchtenburg, William E. *The Perils of Prosperity, 1914–32*. Chicago History of American Civilization. Daniel J. Boorstin, ed. Chicago: University of Chicago Press, 1958.

Lindsey, Hal. *The 1980's: Countdown to Armageddon*. New York: Bantam Books, 1980.

Lindsey, Hal, with C. C. Carlson. *The Late, Great Planet Earth*. Grand Rapids, Michigan: Zondervan, 1970.

Lippmann, Walter. *Drift and Mastery*. Classics in History. William E. Leuchtenburg and Bernard Wishy, eds. Englewood Cliffs, New Jersey: Prentice-Hall, 1961.

Lissakers, Karin. "Dateline Wall Street: Faustian Finance," *Foreign Policy* 51 (Summer 1983).

Luttwak, Edward N. *The Grand Strategy of the Soviet Union*. New York: St. Martin's Press, 1983.

Marx, Karl. *Capital: A Critique of Political Economy*. New York: International Publishers, 1967.

———. *A Contribution to the Critique of Political Economy*. Maurice Dobb, ed. S. W. Ryazanskaya, trans. New York: International Publishers, 1981.

Marx, Karl, and Friedrich Engels. *Selected Works in One Volume*. New York: International Publishers, 1968.

———. *Selected Correspondence*. S. W. Ryazanskaya, ed. I. Lasker, trans. Third revised edition. Moscow: Progress Publishers, 1975.

Maurois, André. *Disraeli: A Picture of the Victorian Age*. Hamish Miles, trans. New York: Modern Library, 1942.

Mayer, Martin. *The Bankers*. New York: Weybright and Talley, 1974.

———. *The Money Bazaars: Understanding the Banking Revolution Around Us*. New York: Dutton, 1984.

McClellan, David S., and David C. Acheson, eds. *Among Friends: Personal Letters of Dean Acheson*. New York: Dodd, Mead, 1980.

Medvedev, Roy A. *Let History Judge: The Origins and Consequences of Stalinism*. David Joravsky and Georges Haupt, eds. Colleen Taylor, trans. New York: Vintage Books, 1973.

———. *On Socialist Democracy*. Elled de Kadt, ed. and trans. New York: Alfred A. Knopf, 1975.

———. *Khrushchev*. Brian Pearce, trans. New York: Anchor Press, 1983.

Mendelievich, Elias, ed. *Children at Work*. Geneva: International Labour Office, 1979.

Mitchell, B. R. *European Historical Statistics*. Second revised edition. New York: Facts on File, 1980.

Morison, Samuel Eliot, Henry Steele Commager, and William E. Leuchtenburg. *Growth of the American Republic*. Two vols. Seventh edition. Oxford: Oxford University Press, 1980.

Morris, Edmund. *The Rise of Theodore Roosevelt*. New York: Coward, McCann and Geoghegan, 1979.

Naisbitt, John. *Megatrends: Ten New Directions Transforming Our Lives*. New York: Warner Books, 1982.

Naude, Beyers. "Where Is South Africa Going?" *Monthly Review* 37 (July–August 1985).

Neuhouse, Richard John. *The Naked Public Square: Religion and Democracy in America*. Grand Rapids, Michigan: Eerdmans, 1984.

Nixon, Richard. *Six Crises*. Garden City, New York: Doubleday, 1962.

——. *RN: The Memoirs of Richard Nixon*. New York: Grossett and Dunlap, 1979.

——. *The Real War*. New York: Warner Books, 1980.

——. *Leaders*. New York: Warner Books, 1982.

Novak, Michael. *The Rise of the Unmeltable Ethnics: Politics and Culture in the Seventies*. New York: Macmillan, 1972.

——. *The Spirit of Democratic Capitalism*. New York: American Enterprise Institute/Simon and Schuster, 1982.

——. "In Memoriam: Henry M. Jackson." *Commentary* 77 (January 1984).

Novak, Michael, and Michael Jackson, eds. *Latin America: Dependency or Interdependence*. Washington, D.C.: American Enterprise Institute for Public Policy Research, 1985.

O'Brien, David J., and Thomas Shannon, eds. *Renewing the Earth: Catholic Documents on Peace, Justice and Liberation*. Garden City, New York: Image Books, 1977.

Oxford Analytica. *America in Perspective: Major Trends in the United States Through the 1990s*. David R. Young, managing director. Boston: Houghton Mifflin, 1986.

Oye, Kenneth A., Robert J. Lieber, and Donald Rothschild. *The Eagle Defiant: United States Foreign Policy in the 1980's*. Boston: Little, Brown, 1983.

Payer, Cheryl. *The Debt Trap: The IMF and the Third World*. New York: Monthly Review Press, 1974.

Pearce, Jenny. *Under the Eagle: U.S. Intervention in Central America and the Caribbean*. Boston: South End Press, 1982.

Peet, Richard. "Class Struggle, the Relocation of Employment and Economic Crisis," *Science and Society* 48 (Spring 1984).

Percy, Walker. *Love in the Ruins: The Adventures of a Bad Catholic Near the End of the World*. New York: Farrar, Straus and Giroux, 1971.

Phillips, Kevin P. *Post-Conservative America: People, Politics and Ideology in a Time of Crisis*. New York: Vintage Books, 1983.
——. *Staying on Top: The Business Case for a National Industrial Strategy*. New York: Random House, 1984.
Plato. *The Collected Dialogues*. Bollingen Series LXXI.
Plutarch. *The Lives of the Noble Grecians and Romans, Translated by John Dryden*. Revised by Arthur Hugh Clough. Modern Library Edition, 1932.
Podhoretz, Norman. "Appeasement by Any Other Name." *Commentary* 76 (July 1983).
Polybius. *The Histories*. W. R. Payton, trans. Six vols. Loeb Classical Library edition.
Reich, Robert B. "Making Industrial Policy." *Foreign Affairs* 60 (Spring 1982).
——. "Beyond Free Trade." *Foreign Affairs* 61 (Spring 1983).
——. *The Next American Frontier*. New York: Times Books, 1983.
Ribeiro, Darcy. *The Americas and Civilization*. Linton Lomas Barret and Marie McDavid Barret, translators. New York: Dutton, 1972.
Ricardo, David. *The Works and Correspondence of David Ricardo*. Vol. 1. Piero Sraffa, ed. Cambridge: Cambridge University Press, 1981.
Rodney, Walter. *How Europe Underdeveloped Africa*. Washington: Howard University Press, 1974.
Rohatyn, Felix. *The Twenty-Year Century: Essays on Economics and Public Finance*. New York: Random House, 1983.
——. "The Debtor Economy: A Proposal." *New York Review of Books* 31 (March 29, 1984).
——. "The New Chance for the Economy." *New York Review of Books* 33 (April 24, 1986).
Roosevelt, Elliot. *F.D.R.: His Personal Letters: Early Years*. New York: Duell, Sloan and Pearce, 1947.
Said, Edward W. *The Question of Palestine*. New York: Times Books, 1979.
Salisbury, Harrison E. *The 900 Days: The Siege of Leningrad*. New York: Harper and Row, 1969.
Schapiro, Leonard. *The Communist Party of the Soviet Union*. Second edition. New York: Vintage Books, 1971.
Scherer, John L., ed. *U.S.S.R. Facts and Figures Annual: Vol. 10, 1986*. Gulf Breeze, Florida: Academic International Press, 1986.
Schlesinger, Arthur M., Jr. *The Age of Jackson*. Boston: Little, Brown, 1945.
——. *The Age of Roosevelt*. Boston: Houghton Mifflin, 1957–1960.
——. *The Imperial Presidency*. Boston: Houghton Mifflin, 1973.
——. *The Cycles of American History*. Boston: Houghton Mifflin, 1986.
Slovo, Joe. "New Phase of Struggle in South Africa," *Political Affairs* 44 (November 1985).
Smith, Adam. *An Inquiry into the Nature and Causes of the Wealth of Nations*. Modern Library Edition.
Solomon, Robert. "The Elephant in the Boat? The United States in the World Economy," *Foreign Affairs* 60 (America and the World, 1981).

Solzhenitsyn, Aleksandr I. *The Gulag Archipelago 1918–1956: An Experiment in Literary Investigation, V–VII.* Harry Willets, trans. New York: Harper and Row, 1978.

Somoza, Anastasio, as told to Jack Cox. *Nicaragua Betrayed.* Belmont, Massachusetts: Western Islands Publishers, 1980.

Steel, Ronald. *Walter Lippmann and the American Century.* Boston: Little, Brown, 1980.

Stockman, David A. *The Triumph of Politics: How the Reagan Revolution Failed.* New York: Harper and Row, 1986.

Taylor, A. J. P. *The Struggle for Mastery in Europe, 1848–1918.* Oxford: Clarendon Press, 1954.

——. *English History, 1914–1945.* Vol. 15 in the Oxford History of England. Sir George Clark, ed. Corrected edition. Oxford: Oxford University Press, 1970.

Thompson, Edward P. *The Making of the English Working Class.* New York: Pantheon, 1964.

Thucydides. *The Peloponnesian War.* Rex Warner, trans. Revised edition. New York: Penguin, 1974.

Thurow, Lester C. *The Zero-Sum Economy: Distribution and the Possibilities for Economic Change.* New York: Basic Books, 1980.

——. *Dangerous Currents: The State of Economics.* New York: Random House, 1983.

de Tocqueville, Alexis. *Democracy in America.* J. P. Mayor, ed. George Lawrence, trans. Revised edition. New York: Anchor Books, 1969.

Trilateral Commission, The. *Task Force Reports 1–7.* New York: Trilateral Commission, 1977.

——. *Task Force Reports 9–14.* New York: Trilateral Commission, 1978.

——. *Task Force Reports 15–19.* New York: Trilateral Commission, 1981.

Trustees of Groton School. *Views from the Circle: Seventy-Five Years of Groton School.* Groton, Massachusetts: Trustees of Groton School, 1960.

Tsagolov, Georgi. *War Is Their Business: The U.S. Military Industrial Complex.* Dmitry Belyavsky, trans. Moscow: Progress Publishers, 1985.

Tsongas, Paul. *The Road from Here: Liberalism and Realities in the 1980's.* New York: Alfred A. Knopf, 1981.

Tutu, Desmond M. *Crying in the Wilderness: Struggle for Justice in South Africa.* John Webster, ed. American edition. Grand Rapids, Michigan: Eerdmans, 1982.

——. *Hope and Suffering: Sermons and Speeches.* Muthobi Mutloatse, compiler. John Webster, ed. Grand Rapids, Michigan: Eerdmans, 1984.

Ulmer, Melville J. "Economics in Decline," *Commentary* 78 (November 1984).

U.S. Bureau of the Census. *Historical Statistics of the United States: Colonial Times to 1970.* Two vols. Washington, D.C.: 1975.

——. *Statistical Abstract of the United States: 1985.* 105th edition. Washington, D.C.: 1984.

———. *Statistical Abstract of the United States: 1986.* 106th edition. Washington, D.C.: 1985.

U.S. Department of Commerce, International Trade Administration. *Investment Climate in Foreign Countries.* Washington, D.C.: 1983.

U.S. Department of State. *A Decade of American Foreign Policy: Basic Documents, 1941–49.* Washington, D.C.: 1950.

Vance, Cyrus Robert. *Hard Choices: Critical Years in America's Foreign Policy.* New York: Simon and Schuster, 1983.

Vidal, Gore. *Matters of Fact and of Fiction: Essays, 1973–1976.* Random House: New York, 1976.

Viguerie, Richard A. *The New Right: We're Ready to Lead.* Falls Church, Virginia: Viguerie Company, 1980.

———. *The Establishment vs. The People: Is a New Populist Revolt on the Way?* Chicago: Regnery Gateway, 1983.

Wanniski, Jude. *The Way the World Works.* Revised and updated edition. New York: Simon and Schuster, 1983.

Wattenberg, Ben J. *The Good News Is The Bad News Is Wrong.* New York: Simon and Schuster, 1984.

Weinberger, Caspar W. "U.S. Defense Strategy," *Foreign Affairs* 64 (Spring 1986).

Will, George F. *The Pursuit of Virtue and Other Tory Notions.* New York: Touchstone, 1983.

Wills, Gary. *Nixon Agonistes: The Crisis of the Self-Made Man.* Boston: Houghton Mifflin, 1969.

Wilson, Edmund. *To the Finland Station: A Study in the Writing and Acting of History.* New York: Doubleday, 1940.

Wolfe, Alan. *America's Impasse: The Rise and Fall of the Politics of Growth.* Boston: South End Press, 1981.

The World Almanac and Book of Facts. New York: Newspaper Enterprise Association, 1985.

The World Bank. *World Development Report 1986.* Oxford: Oxford University Press, 1986.

"World Top 500." *The Banker* 136 (July 1986).

Wright, Gordon, and Arthur Mejia, Jr. *An Age of Controversy.* New York: Dodd, Mead, 1963.

Wriston, Walter. *Risk and Other Four Letter Words.* New York: Harper and Row, 1986.

Yakolev, A. N., S. I. Beglov, N. B. Bikkenin, K. N. Brutents, V. J. Kelle, A. Z. Okorokov, F. F. Petrenko, A. I. Volkov, and V. V. Zagladin. *Fundamentals of Political Science: Textbook for Primary Political Education.* David Fidlow, trans. Revised edition. Moscow: Progress Publishers, 1979.

Zinn, Howard. *A People's History of the United States.* New York: Harper and Row, 1980.

INDEX